SO YOU WANT TO SING ROCK

So You Want to Sing

Guides for Performers and Professionals

A Project of the National Association of Teachers of Singing

So You Want to Sing: Guides for Performers and Professionals is a series of works devoted to providing a complete survey of what it means to sing within a particular genre. Each contribution functions as a touchstone work not only for professional singers but also for students and teachers of singing. Titles in the series offer a common set of topics so readers can navigate easily the various genres addressed in each volume. This series is produced under the direction of the National Association of Teachers of Singing, the leading professional organization devoted to the science and art of singing.

So You Want to Sing Music Theater: A Guide for Professionals, by Karen S. Hall, 2013
So You Want to Sing Rock 'n' Roll: A Guide for Professionals, by Matthew Edwards, 2014
So You Want to Sing Jazz: A Guide for Professionals, by Jan Shapiro, 2015
So You Want to Sing Country: A Guide for Performers, by Kelly K. Garner, 2016
So You Want to Sing Gospel: A Guide for Performers, by Trineice Robinson-Martin, 2016
So You Want to Sing Sacred Music: A Guide for Performers, edited by Matthew Hoch, 2017
So You Want to Sing Folk Music: A Guide for Performers, by Valerie Mindel, 2017
So You Want to Sing Barbershop: A Guide for Performers, by Diane M. Clarke & Billy J. Biffle, 2017
So You Want to Sing A Cappella: A Guide for Performers, by Deke Sharon, 2017
So You Want to Sing Light Opera: A Guide for Performers, by Linda Lister, 2018
So You Want to Sing CCM (Contemporary Commercial Music): A Guide for Performers, edited by Matthew Hoch, 2018
So You Want to Sing for a Lifetime: A Guide for Performers, by Brenda Smith, 2018
So You Want to Sing the Blues: A Guide for Performers, by Eli Yamin, 2018
So You Want to Sing Chamber Music: A Guide for Performers, by Susan Hochmiller, 2019
So You Want to Sing Early Music: A Guide for Performers, by Martha Elliot, 2019
So You Want to Sing Music by Women: A Guide for Performers, by Matthew Hoch and Linda Lister, 2019
So You Want to Sing World Music: A Guide for Performers, edited by Matthew Hoch and Linda Lister, 2019
So You Want to Sing Spirituals: A Guide for Performers, by Randye Jones, 2019
So You Want to Sing with Awareness: A Guide for Performers, edited by Matthew Hoch, 2020
So You Want to Sing Cabaret: A Guide for Performers, by David Sabella and Sue Matsuki, 2020

SO YOU WANT TO SING ROCK

A Guide for Performers
Updated and Expanded Edition

Matt Edwards

ROWMAN & LITTLEFIELD
Lanham • Boulder • New York • London

Published by Rowman & Littlefield
An imprint of The Rowman & Littlefield Publishing Group, Inc.
4501 Forbes Boulevard, Suite 200, Lanham, Maryland 20706
www.rowman.com

86-90 Paul Street, London EC2A 4NE

Copyright © 2024 by The Rowman & Littlefield Publishing Group, Inc.

All rights reserved. No part of this book may be reproduced in any form or by any electronic or mechanical means, including information storage and retrieval systems, without written permission from the publisher, except by a reviewer who may quote passages in a review.

British Library Cataloguing in Publication Information Available

Library of Congress Cataloging-in-Publication Data Available

ISBN 978-1-5381-8570-4 (cloth)
ISBN 978-1-5381-8571-1 (pbk.)
ISBN 978-1-5381-8572-8 (electronic)

SO YOU WANT TO SING ROCK

A Guide for Performers
Updated and Expanded Edition

Matt Edwards

ROWMAN & LITTLEFIELD
Lanham • Boulder • New York • London

Published by Rowman & Littlefield
An imprint of The Rowman & Littlefield Publishing Group, Inc.
4501 Forbes Boulevard, Suite 200, Lanham, Maryland 20706
www.rowman.com

86-90 Paul Street, London EC2A 4NE

Copyright © 2024 by The Rowman & Littlefield Publishing Group, Inc.

All rights reserved. No part of this book may be reproduced in any form or by any electronic or mechanical means, including information storage and retrieval systems, without written permission from the publisher, except by a reviewer who may quote passages in a review.

British Library Cataloguing in Publication Information Available

Library of Congress Cataloging-in-Publication Data Available

ISBN 978-1-5381-8570-4 (cloth)
ISBN 978-1-5381-8571-1 (pbk.)
ISBN 978-1-5381-8572-8 (electronic)

To Jackie, Everett, and Gavin
for their never-ending love and support.

CONTENTS

List of Figures		ix
Series Editor's Foreword		xiii
Acknowledgments		xv
Online Supplement Note		xvii
1	Introduction: Getting Started	1
2	Singing and Voice Science *Scott McCoy*	13
3	How Learning Works: An Introduction to Motor Learning Theory *Lynn Helding*	31
4	A Listening Journey through the History of Rock 'n' Roll *Jacqlyn Zito-Edwards*	61
5	The Basics of Singing Rock 'n' Roll	111
6	Tips for Beginners	159
7	Tips for Those Already Singing Rock 'n' Roll	179
8	Crossing Over from Classical or Musical Theater	199
9	Developing Your Style	217

10	Using Audio Enhancement Technology	239
11	Vocal Health for Singers *Wendy LeBorgne*	261
12	Navigating through an Ever-Evolving Musical Landscape *Rod Vester*	279
13	Improving Your Skills after Reading This Book	307
14	Final Thoughts	325

Appendix A: Vocal Exercise Patterns	327
Appendix B: Phonetic Symbols	329
Glossary	331
Index	337
About the Authors	341

LIST OF FIGURES

Figure 2.1.	Location of the diaphragm.	15
Figure 2.2.	Intercostal and abdominal muscles.	16
Figure 2.3.	External oblique and rectus abdominus muscles.	18
Figure 2.4.	Layered structure of the vocal fold.	20
Figure 2.5.	Cartilages of the larynx, viewed at an angle from the back.	21
Figure 2.6.	Primary modes of vocal fold vibration.	22
Figure 2.7.	Natural harmonic series, beginning at G2.	23
Figure 2.8.	Typical range of first and second formants for primary vowels.	26
Figure 5.1.	A linear system.	114
Figure 5.2.	A nonlinear system.	114
Figure 5.3.	The six points of balance.	116
Figure 5.4.	Singing without respiratory management.	126
Figure 5.5.	Singing with respiratory management.	127
Figure 5.6.	Full chest (left) and full head (right). The middle section is called mix, but that can be broken down further into chest-dominant mix and head-dominant mix. Within each zone, a multitude of vocal qualities can be produced.	135

Figure 5.7.	The front-room/back-room metaphor posited by Ken Bozeman.	143
Figure 5.8.	Place your fingers gently on your larynx to monitor its movement.	144
Figure 5.9.	Monitoring pharyngeal narrowing.	147
Figure 5.10.	Massaging the masseter muscle.	151
Figure 5.11.	Massaging the temporalis muscle.	152
Figure 7.1.	Nine-tone stamina drills.	184
Figure 7.2.	Straw phonation.	196
Figure 9.1.	Common rhythmic patterns.	219
Figure 10.1.	Compression and rarefaction.	240
Figure 10.2.	Two instruments playing the same pitch.	241
Figure 10.3.	Basic design of a dynamic microphone.	243
Figure 10.4.	Basic design of a condenser microphone.	244
Figure 10.5.	Example frequency response graphs for the Oktava 319 and the Shure SM58.	245
Figure 10.6.	Example of a microphone polar pattern diagram.	247
Figure 10.7.	If the amplitude response curve intersected with point A, there would be a −10-dB reduction in the amplitude of frequencies received by the microphone's diaphragm at that angle.	248
Figure 10.8.	Diagram 1 represents a bidirectional pattern; diagram 2 represents a cardioid pattern.	249
Figure 10.9.	Diagram 3 represents a supercardioid pattern; diagram 4 represents a hypercardioid pattern.	249
Figure 10.10.	Diagram 5 represents a shotgun pattern; diagram 6 represents an omnidirectional pattern.	249
Figure 10.11.	Frequency amplitude curves showing the effect of applying shelf EQ to an audio signal.	250
Figure 10.12.	Frequency amplitude curves displaying two parametric EQ settings.	251
Figure 10.13.	Example of a parametric EQ interface.	251
Figure 10.14.	Example of a graphic equalizer interface.	252
Figure 10.15.	This graph represents the effects of various compression ratios applied to a signal.	253
Figure 10.16.	This diagram illustrates the multiple lines of reflection that create reverb.	255
Figure 10.17.	This diagram illustrates how a direct line of sound followed by a reflected line of sound creates delay.	255

LIST OF FIGURES

Figure A.1.	1-2-3-2-1 pattern.	327
Figure A.2.	1-2-3-4-5-4-3-2-1 pattern.	327
Figure A.3.	5-4-3-2-1 pattern.	327
Figure A.4.	1-3-5-3-1 pattern.	327
Figure A.5.	1-3-5-8-5-3-1 pattern.	328
Figure A.6.	Octave scale.	328
Figure A.7.	Nine-tone pattern.	328
Figure A.8.	1-5-1 glide.	328
Figure A.9.	1-8-1 glide.	328

SERIES EDITOR'S FOREWORD

After *So You Want to Sing Cabaret*, the twentieth book in the So You Want to Sing series, was published in 2020, we made the decision to turn our attention toward second editions of selected titles. I was particularly interested in prioritizing revisions of the first three volumes, all of which preceded my editorship of the series. Our endeavor was set into motion in 2022 with the publication of *So You Want to Sing Musical Theatre* by Amanda Flynn. This title was simultaneously a revision of the first So You Want to Sing book—*So You Want to Sing Music Theater* by Karen Hall, originally published in 2014—and also the twenty-first volume in the series.

We are now pleased to bring you the revised and expanded second edition of Matt Edwards's book, *So You Want to Sing Rock*. This book was originally published in 2014, and from the moment I assumed editorship of the series, I have desired another publication written by Matt. Not only has this been one of the best-selling books of the entire So You Want to Sing series, but Matt's career has also exploded over the past decade; he has rapidly become one of our profession's most important and influential commercial music voice pedagogues with a reputation that precedes him both nationally and internationally. As director of the annual CCM Vocal Pedagogy Institute at Shenandoah University for the past decade, he had mentored hundreds of singing teachers via this summer seminar in Winchester, Virginia. His scholarship and leadership in our field has been recognized through his peer-reviewed publications and presentation of workshops at national conferences and numerous universities. Matt is the recipient of the 2017 Van L. Lawrence Fellowship; awarded jointly by the Voice Foundation and the National Association of Teachers of Singing (NATS), this is perhaps the most prestigious national award in the field of voice pedagogy. In 2018, he was invited to be a master teacher for the NATS Intern Program at the University of Colorado Boulder—one of the youngest master teachers in the program's three-decade history.

The content present in this new edition of *So You Want to Sing Rock* reflects and embodies a new decade of wisdom that has been earned by this accomplished pedagogue. Every chapter has been carefully rewritten to reflect both recent scholarship and practical knowledge. Matt's rich experiences are evident in his down-to-earth writing style, which unceasingly offers advice to a younger generation of pedagogues as well as more seasoned teachers of singing who may be interested in continued professional development and a fresh perspective on approaches to commercial singing. Additional chapters by Jacqlyn Zito-Edwards, Rod Vester, and Lynn Helding represent an expansion of the original content of *So You Want to Sing Rock*, and revised versions of core chapters by Scott McCoy and Wendy LeBorgne offer essential content and help to round out the revised volume.

The collected volumes of the So You Want to Sing series offer a valuable opportunity for performers and teachers of singing to explore new styles and important pedagogies. I am confident that voice specialists, both amateur and professional, will benefit from this long-desired expansion and revision of Matt Edwards's important book, now the twenty-second volume in the ever-expanding So You Want to Sing series. It has been a privilege to work with him on this project.

Matthew Hoch
Series Editor

ACKNOWLEDGMENTS

Welcome to the second edition of *So You Want to Sing Rock*! The first edition hit the shelves in 2014, and since then, I have had the privilege of collaborating with hundreds of singers and teachers in both one-on-one lessons and workshop settings for universities and professional organizations all over the world. These experiences have been instrumental in refining my approach, prompting a significant update to the majority of this book. I am grateful for how those experiences have helped me become a better teacher.

I have been teaching voice for more than twenty years, and the one constant has been having my wife Jackie by my side. We started teaching when we were dating, took our first voice pedagogy class together in graduate school, and ever since then, we have spent countless hours brainstorming ideas to develop an approach that caters to students of all genres and backgrounds. While I am the one drawn to writing and presenting, not a presentation, article, book chapter, or book has materialized without Jackie's invaluable input. I am particularly thankful that she joined me on this project to write the chapter on rock history.

There is a saying in academia that we stand on the shoulders of giants. This means that none of us who research and write today would be able to do so were it not for those who came before us in this profession or those who we work alongside today. I extend my gratitude to my colleagues in the National Association of Teachers of Singing, the Pan American Vocology Association, and the Voice Foundation for their ceaseless dedication to the voice. Their research, presentations, and discussions constantly inspire my work. I am especially thankful for Allen Henderson, who asked me to write the first edition; Karen Hall, who helped edit it; and Matthew Hoch, who has helped me bring this edition to press along with Michael Tan and the rest of the team at Rowman & Littlefield.

I am thankful for my colleagues in the voice, theater, and commercial music divisions at Shenandoah Conservatory. It takes a village to train an artist, and I am fortunate to work in an amazing village. The work within this book has been most directly influenced by my colleagues at the CCM Vocal Pedagogy Institute, listed alphabetically: Jess Baldwin, Alison Crockett, Julie Dean, Melissa Foster, Marcelle Gauvin, Kathryn Green, Wendy LeBorgne, Edrie Means-Weekly, David Meyer, Ed Reisert, Marci Rosenberg, and Jacqlyn Zito-Edwards. The perspectives they bring to the institute each summer inform and enrich my work, making me a better teacher. This book would not be what it is without them.

I want to give a heartfelt thanks to my parents for unwaveringly supporting my musical pursuits, shuttling me to voice lessons as a teenager, enduring hours of Metallica guitar riffs echoing through the house, and tolerating endless band practices in the basement. They put up with a lot but never gave up on me.

Finally, I am grateful for Everett and Gavin, my two amazing boys. They have endured thousands of hours of singing, listening to singers, and hearing pedagogical discussions all around the house. I'm grateful for the times they have reminded me that playing together and exploring the world is indeed just as important as going down a pedagogical rabbit hole. Every day is an adventure with them that challenges me to become a better person in ways I never knew possible.

Thank you for giving this book a chance. I hope it helps you expand your knowledge about your voice and artistry so that you can take your singing to the next level.

ONLINE SUPPLEMENT NOTE

So You Want to Sing Rock features an online supplement courtesy of the National Association of Teachers of Singing. Visit the link below to discover additional exercises and examples as well as links to recordings of the songs referenced in this book.

http://www.nats.org/So_You_Want_To_Sing_Book_Series.html

A musical note symbol ♪ in this book will mark every instance of corresponding online supplement material.

INTRODUCTION

Getting Started

It has been more than seventy years since the term "rock 'n' roll" was first used to describe an emerging style of music that was an outgrowth of the blues. With the passage of time, new technologies and subgenres have emerged, and hundreds of thousands of unique artists have been labeled "rock" artists. However, it is impossible to codify the exact qualities that qualify one as a "rock singer," as the spectrum of rock music is wide and always evolving.

When record labels controlled the music industry, there was a codified rock sound. The labels were in the business of making money from music, so when they discovered a sound that audiences liked, they sought out other artists with a similar sound to capitalize on the marketplace. This created a barrier to entry to the mass market. However, in 1999, a company called Napster democratized music distribution through its online platform, and everything changed.

Before the advent of digital music distribution, artists had to get signed to a label or self-publish. If they were signed to a label, there was a chance that they could become an international sensation. There was also the chance that their recordings could be shelved and that nothing would happen with their career. If they chose to self-publish, they had to tour endlessly and sell their music at their shows or travel from record store to record store to sell their music on consignment. When the record labels held power over the artists, they also held power over the music.

Digital distribution made it possible for anyone to publish their music online alongside the major labels, eliminating the need for corporate support to build an audience base. Platforms like YouTube made it possible to distribute videos of live performances and self-produced music videos. Myspace, X (formerly Twitter), and Facebook made it possible to connect with fans from all over the world. This further helped independent bands find and develop their audience base. Because of this, artists were empowered to have more control over their music and artistry than ever before.

In today's music landscape, artists have the freedom to define their own sound without having to conform to corporate expectations or stereotypes. That's why in this book, I will not be defining exactly what you have to do to have a rock sound. Instead, I will be guiding you through the process of learning from others with an eye on developing your own unique voice through range-of-motion exercises that coordinate your instrument, giving you endless options for vocal production. Then you will need to deepen your understanding of the genre to develop your own style.

To deepen your understanding, you need to study rock history and absorb the influences that have been part of its evolution. As you will learn in chapter 4, artists have been doing this for years. Many of the artists you admire have combined traits from other artists to form their own signature sound. This process is written about extensively in Austin Kleon's book *Steal Like an Artist*. Kleon provides dozens of quotes from famous artists talking about building their creative process on the work of others. He quotes Francis Ford Coppola as saying, "We want you to take from us. We want you, at first, to steal from us, because you can't steal. You will take what we give you and put it in your own voice, and that's how you will find your voice. And that's how you begin. And then one day someone will steal from you."[1]

FORMAL TRAINING

One thing that has always amazed me is that while instrumentalists know a lot about how their instrument works, singers often know very little. From the beginning of their training, guitarists learn how to position their body and hold their instrument so they do not get shoulder or back problems.

They learn how to position their fretting hand without putting undue stress on their wrist, and they coordinate their left and right hands to do different actions, which is akin to rubbing your stomach while patting your head. Intermediate to advanced guitarists know how to string their guitar, adjust the truss rod, make bridge adjustments, and tweak their amplifier settings to dial in their signature sound. Keyboardists know how to program new tones, and drummers know how to tune their heads, adjust their pedals, and choose different sticks for different sounds.

Singers, on the other hand, often assume that it should all just come together, that they should be able to sing the way they want to sing by willing it so. That's understandable; after all, many of us have been singing in some form since childhood. Some people continue to experiment with their voices, singing throughout their lives, and appear to have "natural talent." Others do not sing in their youth for one reason or another and decide to sing later in life but are discouraged that they do not seem to have "natural talent." The reality has very little to do with talent and a lot more to do with lived experience and time spent coordinating the voice.

Singing is an athletic event. In order to sing, you must coordinate your body to perform specific actions in a manner that is repeatable and sustainable. There is no singular form of singing that is inherently better than another form; instead, there is a wide spectrum of possibilities. Classical singers live on the left side of the spectrum, where there are specific standards for language, vibrato, resonance, and tone. Singer-songwriters live on the right side of the spectrum, where there are no standards or expectations for how one is supposed to sound. Rock singing lives in shades of the middle to the right side of the spectrum. If you are in a cover band performing top 40 hits originally performed by rock bands in the 1980s, there are expectations for what you should sound like. That's because you are following the model of bands that came before you. However, if your band performs original songs, you will live in a more open-ended world of expectations where you can develop your own signature sound without conforming to any set standards.

Regardless of where you lie on the spectrum, you will need to develop the coordination required to produce the vocal qualities you want to use in performance. The process of doing this work is called skill acquisition. The process of skill acquisition requires you to know what you are trying to do (how you want to sound) and how to do it (the coordination necessary to execute an action).[2] In my experience, many singers lack the knowledge of what to do, so they struggle to do it. In this book, I am going to help you gain a better understanding of your instrument, giving you the same insight about your voice as a guitarist or drummer has about their instrument when they practice and perform. That knowledge will help you choose exercises that target specific skills that will help you master your instrument so that you can sing with greater freedom.

WORKING PROFESSIONALS NEED HELP TOO

It is also important to point out that many of the artists you admire have had some help along the way, even if they do not acknowledge it publicly. A few simple internet searches reveal that Ozzy Osborne, Axl Rose,[3] Tina Turner, Paul Stanley (Kiss), Chester Bennington (Linkin Park),[4] Alissa White-Gluz (Arch Enemy), Courtney Love, and Daughtry[5] have all worked with a vocal coach at some point in their career. There are countless others who study privately with teachers who do not list the names of their clientele in their marketing. The reality is that everyone needs a little help from time to time.

Football players have personal trainers, and there is no reason that singers shouldn't have them as well. Our bodies change as we age, and unless you personally keep up with all the research, you probably do not know how aging has impacted your respiratory system or phonatory system. You may not understand how neglecting your head voice can lead you to lose your high notes. You may be warming up in ways that are detrimental to what you actually need for the kind of music you sing. Professional teachers and coaches can help you learn about your instrument, which can help you do more with your voice while making it easier to get through your performances. Do not let stories of "self-taught" performers stop you from seeking help if you are not getting results you are looking for on your own. There are a lot more success stories of people who got at least a little help along the way than there are self-taught success stories.

THESE EXERCISES MIGHT SOUND WEIRD TO YOU

Most of the exercises in this book are designed to coordinate your vocal tract; they are not designed to sound good by themselves. For example, sticking your tongue out and vocalizing on /ae/ produces a harsh tone that will rarely if ever be used in a song. However, it trains your body to stop retracting the tongue when singing. Once you have trained your body to stop retracting the tongue when singing, it will be easier to navigate the upper range of your songs. However, you have to work through the "ugly duckling" phase of the exercises to get the payoff in your performances. As you work through the exercises, keep your focus on the task you are working toward (i.e., adding more chest to your mix) instead of pursuing a final sound. The final product will come when your voice is coordinated to a level where you can focus on connecting with the lyrics and your audience instead of on technique.

STAGES OF LEARNING

"Skill acquisition" is a term we use to describe the process of learning a new movement pattern in your body, such as coordinating your head register, improving forward tongue articulation, or removing nasality. The process of skill acquisition can be divided into three stages: cognitive, motor learning, and automatic.

The cognitive stage is the first stage of skill acquisition, where individuals are introduced to the skill and begin to learn the basics. During this stage, individuals rely on conscious thought and deliberate practice to develop their understanding of the skill. They may struggle to execute the new movement pattern they are working on and will likely make many mistakes along the way. In this stage of learning, repetition, or "blocked practice," is important. This means that you will attempt to execute the task over and over again until you get it right. You will make a lot of mistakes, and many times you will not be sure if you are executing the task correctly, which is why external feedback is a critical part of learning at this stage. External feedback is usually best delivered by a guide who has experience in your genre. However, if you do not have someone to work with, you can use an audio or video recording device to record yourself and act as your own guide.

The motor learning stage is the second stage of skill acquisition. This is the stage where you will begin to develop your muscle memory and refine the movements you are practicing. During this stage, you will notice that you are able to perform the skill more smoothly and accurately, and your performance will become more consistent. Skill acquisition will be improved by switching from blocked practice to "random practice," which is the process of alternating between vocal qualities to help your brain distinguish the difference. External feedback is also important during this stage, but slowly, you will begin relying more on intrinsic feedback. That means that you will begin to have the self-awareness to know when you have executed the task correctly and when you need to try again. A guide can still be helpful at this stage, but you should be moving toward a place where you are no longer dependent on external feedback.

The automatic stage is the final stage of skill acquisition. This is the stage where you have reached a high level of proficiency in the skill and are able to perform it with little conscious thought. You will know that you are in this stage when you can perform the skill effortlessly and with great accuracy and the ability to adapt to changing circumstances without much effort. This stage is characterized by automaticity, where the skill becomes almost second nature and you are able to perform it without much conscious attention.

As you work through the exercises in this book, take note of where you are in the learning process. If you are in the cognitive stage, you should expect that you are going to struggle a bit. Be patient with yourself and keep drilling the task at hand. Eventually, your body will understand what you are trying to do, and you will notice improvement. If you are in the motor learning stage, enjoy the discoveries you make along the way, but remember that you have to keep practicing. One good day of getting the task right does not mean that you are in the automatic phase; it just means you are on your way to that phase. Keep practicing, and when you are consistently hitting the target every day for a week, you will know that skill has shifted toward automaticity, and you can move on to the next skill. So, for example, if you are learning to coordinate your head register, you will want to repeat head register exercises every day for several weeks until you can vocalize in your head register with little thought. Once you have mastered that skill, you can begin training your voice to intensify toward a head-dominant mix. By allowing yourself the time to build your instrument piece by piece, you will get faster results than trying to do it all at once.

BEWARE OF COGNITIVE DISTORTIONS

The process of developing the singing voice can be frustrating for some people. When we encounter a problem that is difficult to solve, our brain tends to go toward fighting, fleeing, or freezing. For our purposes, the fight response usually leads to doing the work. Singers who respond by fighting go into a practice room, work through the frustrations they are feeling, and pursue vocal development with a strategic practice routine. Those who find new concepts overwhelming often feel the urge to flee. They try to avoid confronting what is difficult and look for other explanations for their difficulties instead of taking on the work necessary to make a change. Others find the work so overwhelming that they freeze. Analysis paralysis leads them to give up on developing their voice, and they miss out on the possibilities for growth that come from strategic practice.

The desire to flee or freeze is often heavily influenced by cognitive distortions. These are the little lies that we tell ourselves. When we start to believe them, we can manifest them into reality. There are dozens of these distortions that people struggle with in their training. The most common ones I see among singers are magnifying, catastrophizing, mind reading, negative focus, and polarized thinking. When you learn to recognize these distortions, you can reframe the situation and get into a mental space that is more conducive to making vocal progress.

When people magnify, they make a small problem a big one. So, for example, while reading this book, you may discover that you have no access to your head voice. You understand that developing your head voice is critical to accessing your upper range, but it seems so elusive that your brain begins to magnify the problem. Your inner voice starts telling you that you have so much work to do in this part of your voice that you will never figure it out, and you feel a strong desire to give up. In such cases, it is easy to become overly critical and focus solely on negative outcomes, which only exacerbates the problem.

Catastrophizing is a common tendency where we tend to perceive situations to be far worse than they are in reality. For example, if you experience a slight tightening in your voice and notice a slight loss of power while singing, your brain may automatically jump to the worst-case scenario, leading you to scour the internet for self-diagnosis of vocal injuries. This kind of thinking can be counterproductive and often leads to unnecessary stress and anxiety. Instead, it is better to approach the situation with a more rational and objective mindset, seeking professional advice if necessary and taking practical steps to address the issue. By reframing the situation in a more positive light, you can avoid needless worry and keep moving forward with your vocal development.

Mind reading refers to the tendency to try to infer the thoughts and opinions of others without any direct communication from them. This phenomenon is common among singers who often try to read their audience's reaction before, during, and after their performance. This can manifest as worrying about whether the audience likes your voice and becoming overly self-critical, assuming that the audience is judging you negatively. However, it is essential to remember that such assumptions are often misguided and based on false beliefs. In reality, the audience may be enjoying the performance, but their expressions or body language may not convey that message for reasons that have nothing to do with you. It is vital for singers to avoid mind reading and to focus on their performance without overthinking the audience's reactions.

Negative focus is a cognitive bias where you are drawn primarily toward negative feedback while positive feedback is ignored or discounted. For example, if you hear a negative comment about your performance, you may become fixated on that comment, disregarding any positive feedback you receive. This pattern of thought is also known as filtering, meaning that you filter out positive feedback, focusing solely on the negative. Such thinking can be detrimental, as it amplifies negative thoughts and can lead to a lack of self-confidence. To overcome negative focus, it is essential to develop a more balanced perspective, giving equal weight to positive feedback and not allowing a single negative comment to overshadow everything else. By focusing on both positive and negative feedback, you can use constructive criticism to improve your performance and move forward with confidence.

Polarized thinking is a cognitive bias where you become fixated on viewing things as either right or wrong with no middle ground in between. This kind of thinking can be limiting, as it often leads to a narrow and inflexible mindset, preventing you from exploring new ideas and possibilities. By overly focusing on polarities, you can miss out on the valuable insights and opportunities that lie in the middle ground. When you acknowledge and explore the middle ground, you gain a more balanced perspective with a broader range of ideas and solutions.

As you read through this book, you will likely be confronted by cognitive distortions. If that happens, I want you to think of alternative points of view. For example, if you find that you struggle with a tongue articulation exercise and your thoughts drift toward magnifying, it is important to label that thought as a distortion. Then seek alternative perspectives that can help you reframe the situation positively. Instead of assuming that you'll never get the exercise, recognize that you are likely in the cognitive stage of learning and that with practice and patience, you will see improvement. By reframing your thoughts in this way, you can shift from a fixed mindset to a growth mindset, empowering you to tackle challenges with greater resilience and determination.

FIXED VERSUS GROWTH MINDSET

Psychologist Carol Dweck's theory of fixed and growth mindsets explains how individuals' beliefs about their abilities can impact their approach to challenges and setbacks. Those with a fixed mindset tend to believe that their abilities and intelligence are predetermined traits that cannot be developed. This mindset can lead to a lack of motivation and a reluctance to take on new challenges due to fear of failure and the potential for negative feedback or judgment. Conversely, those with a growth mindset believe that their abilities can be cultivated through hard work, dedication, and perseverance. People with a growth mindset tend to embrace challenges, viewing them as opportunities for learning and development.

Singers with a growth mindset tend to have better outcomes than those with a fixed mindset. This is because a growth mindset fosters a belief in one's ability to improve and succeed, leading to increased effort and persistence in the face of challenges. In contrast, a fixed mindset can lead to a fear of failure and a reluctance to take on new challenges, which can limit personal and professional growth. Cognitive distortions attempt to push you toward a fixed mindset. When you make the effort to look for alternative points of view, you can guide yourself to adopt a growth mindset instead, which will provide better outcomes as you develop your voice.

KNOW YOUR DESTINATION

Understanding the end goal is crucial in any athletic pursuit. Simply aspiring to "be able to run" lacks the specificity needed for effective training. While sprinting falls under the umbrella of running, so do hurdling and marathon running. Focusing solely on sprinting will not prepare you for a marathon. To excel as a marathon runner, a precise training regimen is vital. It involves honing body coordination to optimize stride, gradually building strength to cover longer distances, and progressively increasing endurance from one mile to two and so on until reaching the ultimate goal of 26.2 miles.

This principle of strategic training also applies to singing. Knowing your desired outcome is key to charting an effective course of action. Each exercise you choose should align with the skill set you are trying to develop. While adjusting your destination is acceptable during the journey, maintaining a clear direction in your training is paramount.

DEFINE YOUR GOALS AND SET AN INTENTION

Establishing clear intentions before diving into this work will enhance your journey through this book. By solidifying your purpose, you will attract the resources and knowledge you need to improve your singing. When you are focused on a specific purpose, you will be less distracted by cognitive distortions and information that does not apply to your needs.

To begin, find a notebook that you can dedicate to your singing and define what you want to achieve by reading this book. Are you seeking to refine your high notes? Do you want to develop a richer palette of vocal colors? Have you realized that it is time to transition from mimicry to cultivating your own distinct voice? Whatever your goals are, jot them down while leaving space to take notes as you read. As you encounter content in this book (or other resources) that addresses your specific needs, make a note, including the page number. Through this process, you will compile a customized reading list. This curated reading list will serve as a reference point to help guide your progress as you work on applying the concepts.

VOCAL RANGE

It is important to consider pitch range when working on vocal exercises. Many instruments, including the voice, are classified by the terms "soprano," "alto," "tenor," "baritone," and "bass." These terms identify pitch ranges where instruments usually play or where voices usually sing. While we do not find many sopranos in rock styles, you can point to bands like Nightwish and artists like Madison Cunnigham, who do occasionally sing into the soprano range. Soprano ranges usually start around the A below middle C (C4) and extend to somewhere around the C two octaves above that note (C6). Alto voices usually extend lower, many times reaching the F (F3) or E (E3) below middle C. Their upper range usually extends to somewhere around the A two octaves above (A5). Both sopranos and altos can belt, with many being able to carry that quality as high as F#5.

For tenors, the low range extends slightly lower than an alto, usually down to at least D3. Their upper range will usually extend to somewhere around B♭4. Baritones will often vocalize to a low A2 and up to around a G4. Basses hold the lowest part of the voice's range, extending from F2 to around F4. Most tenors, baritones, and basses can belt throughout their range, whereas sopranos and altos will have upper notes that go into a more "classical" vocal quality that is different than their belt voice. Tenors, baritones, and basses usually have a falsetto range that extends up to D5 or higher. Some singers use the term "falsetto" to describe not only the upper extension of tenors, baritones, and basses but also the breathy head register quality of soprano and alto voice types.

In this book, we will use the abbreviation SA to denote soprano and alto voices. We will use TBB to denote tenor, baritone, and bass voices. There is no universal agreement on what terms are best for any singers let alone rock singers. The author acknowledges that some readers may not identify with these terms. Therefore, readers are encouraged to use the terms that they identify with in their own work. However, these terms will at least enable us to talk about the best ranges for certain exercises introduced in this book.

WORK AT YOUR OWN PACE

This book consists of thirteen chapters. Chapter 2 introduces you to voice science. For some readers, this chapter may feel a bit tedious. However, knowing how your voice works is the key to making it work for you. Chapter 3 introduces you to how learning works. Again, this chapter may feel overwhelming at first, but understanding the learning process will help you accelerate your progress. Chapter 4 takes you on a listening journey of rock from its history to the present day. Unlike other books, this book will teach you about history through listening. To develop yourself as an artist, you will want to take in as many influences as possible. By working through the listening examples, you will absorb new ideas that you can draw from when creating your own interpretations of songs. This chapter will also help you build a vocabulary to identify the types of vocal qualities that are found within rock music. In chapter 5, you will learn about the basics of rock singing. These are the core concepts you will use throughout the rest of the book as you coordinate your instrument. Chapters 6 through 8 address the specific needs of beginners, those already singing rock music, and those crossing over from classical and/or musical theater. Chapter 9 shows you how to bring songs to life by focusing on stylistic traits, and chapter 10 shows how audio technology impacts our perception of the singing voice. The content in chapter 11 is focused on vocal health and is critical to maintaining your instrument. This information can be read at any time but should not be ignored. The tissues that make up the larynx are irreplaceable. So understanding how to keep that part of your instrument healthy is critical for your long-term success. Chapter 12 gives business advice for developing your career, and chapter 13 gives you advice on where to go with your training after finishing the book.

CONCLUSION

There is a lot of information to work through in these pages, so take your time and progress at your own pace. You may be able to read this book in a week, but the concepts will take months to work into your voice. That may seem like a long time, but think about how long guitarists work to perfect their playing, how long basketball players work to perfect their shots, and how long visual artists work to hone their craft. Learning to sing is a journey, so enjoy the process and take your time. Keep your notebook close by, make lots of notes, and remember that experimentation often leads to the best discoveries. The more you explore, the more you will discover about your voice and the more options you will have available to bring your songs to life. Enjoy the journey.

NOTES

1. Austin Kleon, *Steal Like an Artist* (New York: Workman Publishing, 2012), 37.
2. Lynn Helding, *The Musician's Mind: Teaching Learning and Performance in the Age of Brain Science* (Lanham, MD: Rowman & Littlefield, 2020), 72.
3. Ron Anderson, "About Ron Anderson Vocal Coach of Stars," https://ronandersonvocals.com/about-ron-anderson-vocal-coach-of-stars, accessed October 27, 2023.
4. Seth Riggs, "Clients," http://www.sethriggs.com, accessed October 27, 2023.
5. Melissa Cross, "Client List," http://www.melissacross.com, accessed October 27, 2023.

2

SINGING AND VOICE SCIENCE

Scott McCoy

This chapter presents a concise overview of how the voice functions as a biomechanical, acoustic instrument. We will be dealing with elements of anatomy, physiology, acoustics, and resonance. But don't panic: the things you need to know are easily accessible even if it has been many years since you last set foot in a science or math class!

All musical instruments, including the human voice, have at least four things in common, consisting of a power source, a sound source (vibrator), a resonator, and a system for articulation. In most cases, the person who plays the instrument provides power by pressing a key, plucking a string, or blowing into a horn. This power is used to set the sound source in motion, which creates vibrations in the air that we perceive as sound. Musical vibrators come in many forms, including strings, reeds, and human lips. The sound produced by the vibrator, however, needs a lot of help before it becomes beautiful music—we might think of it as raw material, like a lump of clay that a potter turns into a vase. Musical instruments use resonance to enhance and strengthen the sound of the vibrator, transforming it into sounds we identify as a piano, trumpet, or guitar. Finally, instruments must have a means of articulation to create the nuanced sounds of music. Let's see how these four elements are used to create the sounds of singing.

PULMONARY SYSTEM: THE POWER SOURCE OF YOUR VOICE

The human voice has a lot in common with a trumpet: both use flaps of tissue as a sound source, both use hollow tubes as resonators, and both rely on the respiratory (pulmonary) system for power. If you stop to think about it, you quickly realize why breathing is so important for singing. First and foremost, it keeps us alive through the exchange of blood gases—oxygen in, carbon dioxide out. But it also serves as the storage depot for the air we use to produce sound. Most singers rarely encounter situations in which these two functions are in conflict, but if you are required to sustain an extremely long phrase, you could find yourself in need of fresh oxygen before your lungs are totally empty.

Misconceptions about breathing for singing are rampant. Fortunately, most are easily dispelled. We must start with a brief foray into the world of physics in the guise of Boyle's law. Some of you no doubt remember this principle: the pressure of a gas within a container changes inversely with changes of volume. If the quantity of a gas is constant and its container is made smaller, pressure rises. But if we make the container get bigger, pressure goes down. Boyle's law explains everything that happens when we breathe, especially when we combine it with another physical law: nature abhors a vacuum. If one location has reduced pressure, air flows from an area of higher pressure to equalize the two and vice versa. So if we can create a zone of reduced air pressure by expanding our lungs, air automatically flows in to restore balance. When air pressure in the lungs is increased, it has no choice but to flow outward.

As we all know, the air we breathe goes in and out of our lungs. Each lung contains millions and millions of tiny air sacs called alveoli, where gases are exchanged. The alveoli also function like ultraminiature versions of the bladder for a bagpipe, storing the air that will be used to set the vocal folds into vibration. To get the air in and out of them, all we need to do is make the lungs larger for inhalation and smaller for exhalation. Always remember this relationship between cause and effect during breathing: we inhale because we make ourselves large, and we exhale because we make ourselves smaller. Unfortunately, the lungs are organs, not muscles, and have no ability on their own to accomplish this feat. For this reason, your bodies came from the factory with special muscles designed to enlarge and compress your entire thorax (rib cage) while simultaneously moving your lungs. We can classify these muscles in two main categories: any muscle that has the ability to increase the volume capacity of the thorax serves an inspiratory function, and any muscle that has the ability to decrease the volume capacity of the thorax serves an expiratory function.

Your largest muscle of inspiration is called the diaphragm (figure 2.1). This dome-shaped muscle originates from the bottom of your sternum (breastbone) and completely fills the area from that point around your ribs to your spine. It's the second-largest muscle in your body, but you probably have no conscious awareness of it or ability to directly control it. When we take a deep breath, the diaphragm contracts, and the central portion flattens out and drops downward a couple inches into your abdomen, pressing against all of your internal organs. If you release tension from your abdominal muscles as you inhale, you will feel a gentle bulge in your upper or lower belly (or perhaps in your back), resulting from the displacement

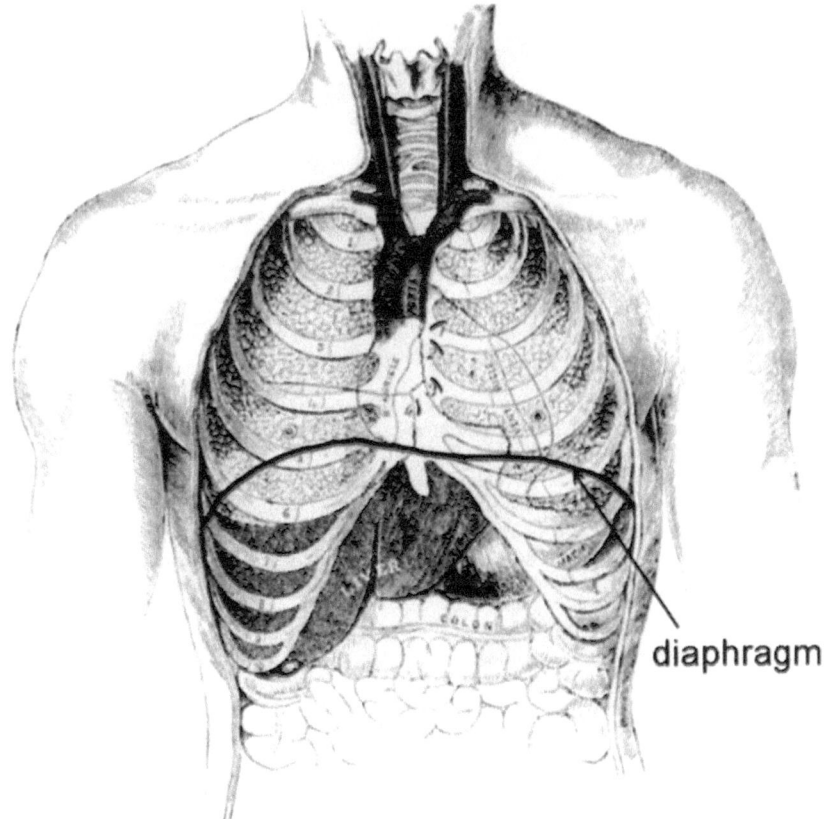

Figure 2.1. Location of the diaphragm. *Courtesy of Scott McCoy*

of your innards by the diaphragm. This is a good thing and can be used to let you know you have taken a good inhalation.

The diaphragm is important, but we must remember that it cannot function in isolation. After you inhale, it relaxes and gently returns to its resting position through an action called elastic recoil. This movement, however, is entirely passive and makes no significant contribution to generating the pressure required to sustain phonation. Therefore, it makes no sense at all to try to "sing from your diaphragm"—unless you intend to sing while you inhale, not exhale!

Eleven pairs of muscles assist the diaphragm in its inhalatory efforts, which are called the external intercostal muscles (figure 2.2). These mus-

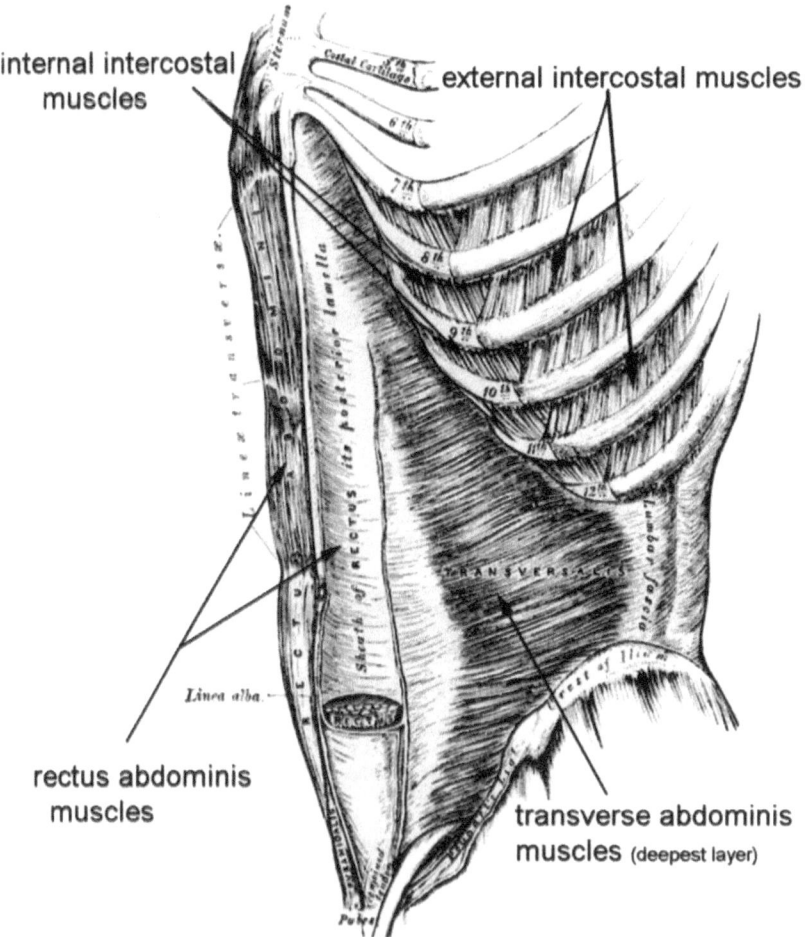

Figure 2.2. Intercostal and abdominal muscles. *Courtesy of Scott McCoy*

cles start from ribs 1 through 11 and connect at a slight angle downward to ribs 2 through 12. When they contract, the entire thorax moves up and out, somewhat like moving a bucket handle. With the diaphragm and intercostals working together, you are able to increase the capacity of your lungs by about three to six liters, depending on your gender and overall physical stature; thus, we have quite a lot of air available to power our voices.

Eleven additional pairs of muscles are located directly under the external intercostals, which, not surprisingly, are called the internal intercostals (figure 2.2). These muscles start from ribs 2 through 12 and connect upward to ribs 1 through 11. When they contract, they induce the opposite action of their external partners: the thorax is made smaller, inducing exhalation. Four additional pairs of expiratory muscles are located in the abdomen, beginning with the rectus (figure 2.2). The two rectus abdominis muscles run from your pubic bone to your sternum and are divided into four separate portions, called bellies of the muscle (lots of muscles have multiple bellies; it is coincidental that the bellies of the rectus are found in the location we colloquially refer to as our belly). Definition of these bellies results in the so-called ripped abdomen or six-pack of body builders and others who are especially fit.

The largest muscles of the abdomen are called the external obliques (figure 2.3), which run at a downward angle from the sides of the rectus, covering the lower portion of the thorax, and extend all the way to the spine. The internal obliques lie immediately below, oriented at an angle that crisscrosses the external muscles. They are slightly smaller, beginning at the bottom of the thorax rather than extending over it. The deepest muscle layer is the transverse abdominis (figure 2.3), which is oriented with fibers that run horizontally. These four muscle pairs completely encase the abdominal region, holding your organs and digestive system in place while simultaneously helping you breathe.

Your expiratory muscles are quite large and can produce a great deal of pulmonary or air pressure. In fact, they easily can overpower the larynx. Healthy adults generally can generate more than twice the pressure that is required to produce even the loudest sounds; therefore, singers must develop a system for moderating and controlling airflow and breath pressure. This practice goes by many names, including breath support, breath control, and breath management, all of which rely on the principle of muscular antagonism. Muscles are said to have an antagonistic relationship when they work in opposing directions, usually pulling on a common

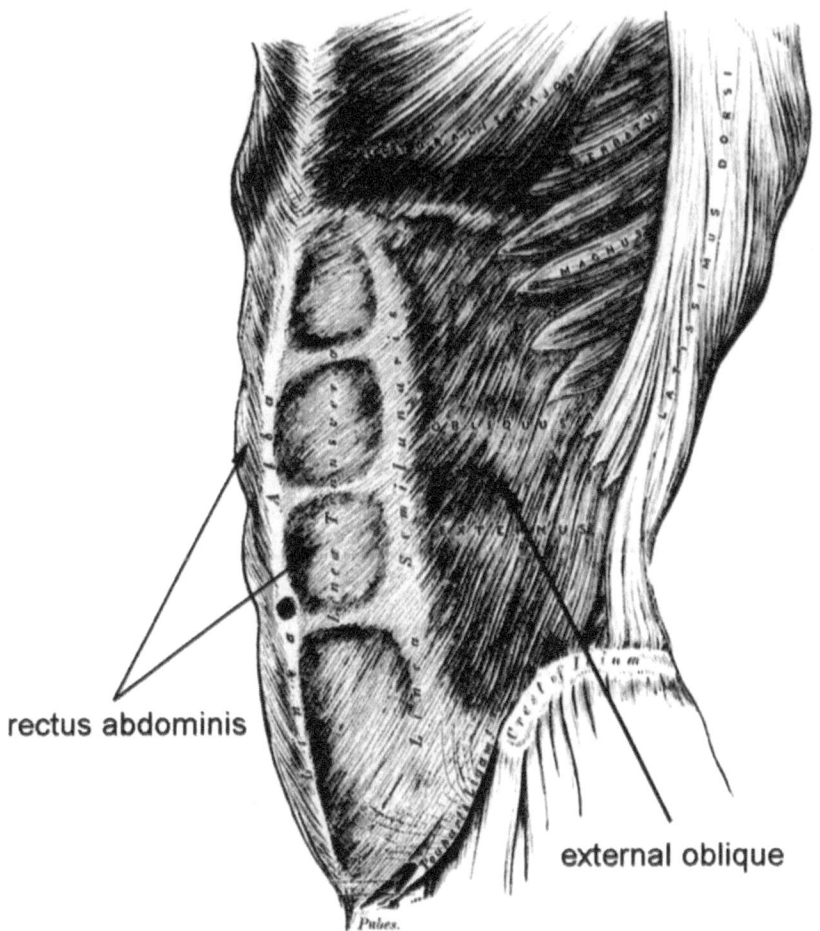

Figure 2.3. External oblique and rectus abdominus muscles. *Courtesy of Scott McCoy*

point of attachment, for the sake of increasing stability or motor control. You can see a clear example of muscular antagonism in the relationship between your biceps (flexors) and triceps (extensors) when you hold out your arm. In breathing for singing, we activate inspiratory muscles (e.g., diaphragm and external intercostals) during exhalation to help control respiratory pressure and the rate at which air is expelled from the lungs.

One of the things you will notice when watching a variety of singers is that they tend to breathe in many different ways. You might think that voice teachers and scientists, who have been teaching and studying singing for hundreds if not thousands of years, would have come to agreement on the best possible breathing technique. But for many reasons, this is not the case. For one, different musical and vocal styles place varying demands on breathing. For another, humans have a huge variety of body types, sizes, and morphologies. A breathing strategy that is successful for a tall, slender woman might be completely ineffective in a short, robust man. Our bodies actually contain a large number of muscles beyond those we've already discussed that are capable of assisting with respiration. For an example, consider your latissimi dorsi muscles. These large muscles of the arm enable us to do pull-ups (or pull-downs, depending on which exercise you perform) at the fitness center. But because they wrap around a large portion of the thorax, they also exert an expiratory force. We have at least two dozen such muscles that have secondary respiratory functions, some for exhalation and some for inhalation. When we consider all these possibilities, it is no surprise at all that there are many ways to breathe that can produce beautiful singing. Just remember to practice some muscular antagonism—maintaining a degree of inhalation posture during exhalation—and you should do well.

LARYNX: THE VIBRATOR OF YOUR VOICE

The larynx, sometimes known as the voice box or Adam's apple, is a complex physiologic structure made of cartilage, muscle, and tissue. Biologically, it serves as a sphincter valve, closing off the airway to prevent foreign objects from entering the lungs. When firmly closed, it also is used to increase abdominal pressure to assist with lifting heavy objects, childbirth, and defecation. But if we gently close this valve while we exhale, tissue in the larynx begins to vibrate and produce the sounds that become speech and singing.

The human larynx is a remarkably small instrument, typically ranging from the size of a pecan to a walnut for women and men, respectively. Sound is produced at a location called the glottis, which is formed by two flaps of tissue called the vocal folds (aka vocal cords). In women, the glottis is about the size of a dime; in men, it can approach the diameter of a quarter. The two folds are always attached together at their front point but open in the shape of the letter V during normal breathing, an action called abduction. To phonate, we must close the V while we exhale, an action called adduction (just like the machines you use at the fitness center to exercise your thigh and chest muscles).

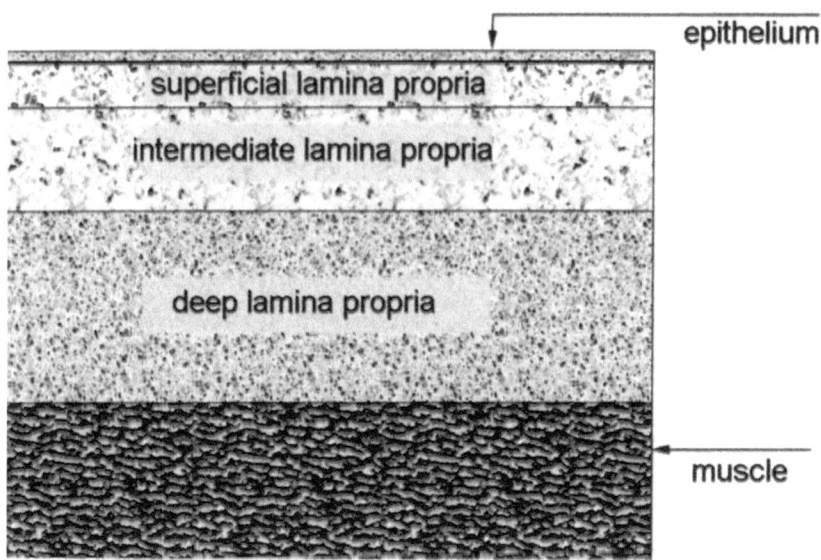

Figure 2.4. Layered structure of the vocal fold. *Courtesy of Scott McCoy*

Phonation is possible only because of the unique multilayer structure of the vocal folds (figure 2.4). The core of each fold is formed by muscle, which is surrounded by a layer of gelatinous material called the lamina propria. The vocal ligament also runs through the lamina propria, which helps to prevent injury by limiting how far the folds can be stretched for high pitches. A thin, hairless epithelial layer that is constantly kept moist with mucus secreted by the throat, larynx, and trachea surrounds all of this. During phonation, the outer layer of the fold glides independently over the inner layer in a wavelike motion, without which phonation is impossible.

We can use a simple demonstration to better understand the independence of the inner and outer portions of the folds. Explore the palm of your hand with your other index finger. Note that the skin is attached quite firmly to the flesh beneath it. If you poke at your palm, that flesh acts as padding, protecting the underlying bone. Now explore the back of your hand. You will observe that the skin is attached quite loosely—you easily can move it around with your finger. And if you poke at the back of your hand, it is likely to hurt; there is very little padding between the skin and your bones. Your vocal folds combine the best attributes of both sides of your hand. They provide sufficient padding to help reduce impact stress while permitting the outer layer to slip like the skin on the back of your hand, enabling phonation to occur. When you are sick with laryngitis and lose your voice (a condition called aphonia), inflammation in the vocal folds couples the layers of the folds tightly together. The outer layer no longer can move independently over the inner, and phonation becomes difficult or impossible.

The vocal folds are located within the five cartilaginous structures of the larynx (figure 2.5). The largest is called the thyroid cartilage, which is shaped like a small shield. The thyroid connects to the cricoid cartilage below it, which is shaped like a signet ring—broad in the back and narrow in the front. Two cartilages that are shaped like squashed pyramids sit atop the cricoid, called the arytenoids. Each vocal fold runs from the thyroid cartilage in front to one of the arytenoids at the back. Finally, the

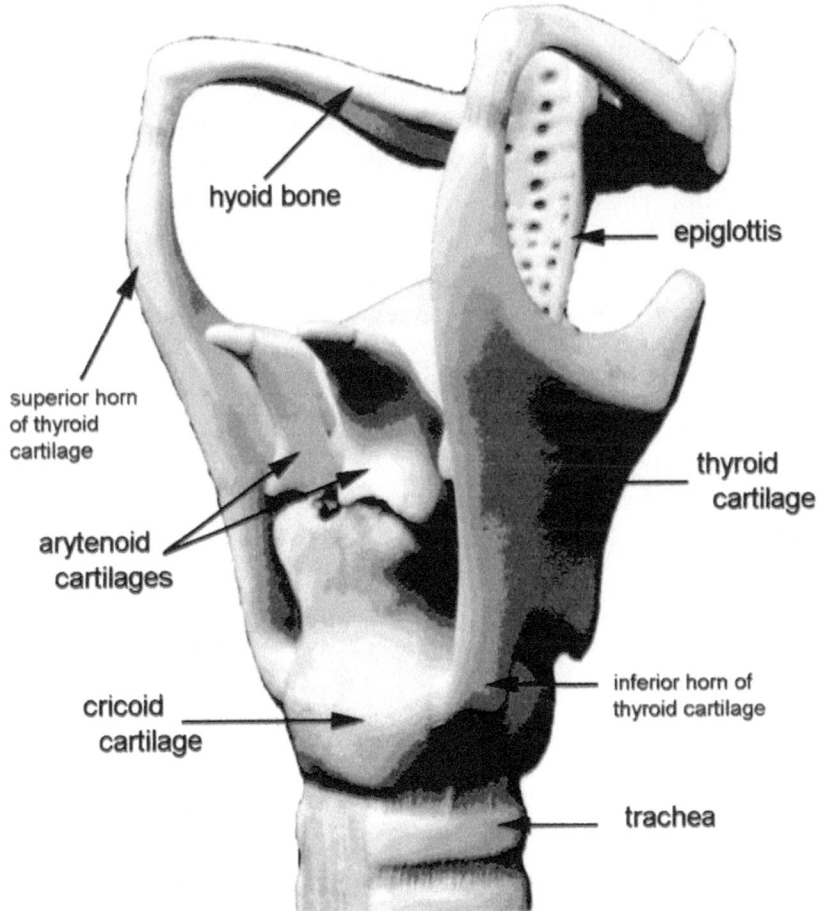

Figure 2.5. Cartilages of the larynx, viewed at an angle from the back.
Courtesy of Scott McCoy

epiglottis is located at the top of the larynx, flipping backward each time we swallow to prevent food and liquid from entering our lungs. Muscles connect between the various cartilages to open and close the glottis and to lengthen and shorten the vocal folds for ascending and descending pitch, respectively. Because they sometimes are used to identify vocal function, it is a good idea to know the names of the muscles that control the length of the folds. We've already mentioned that a muscle forms the core of each fold. Because it runs between the thyroid cartilage and an arytenoid, it is named the thyroarytenoid muscle (formerly known as the vocalis muscle). When the thyroarytenoid, or TA muscle, contracts, the fold is shortened, and pitch goes down. The folds are elongated through the action of the cricothyroid, or CT muscles, which run from the thyroid cartilage to the cricoid cartilage.

Vocal color (timbre) is created by the combined effects of the sound produced by the vocal folds and the resonance provided by the vocal tract. While these elements can never be completely separated, it is useful to consider the two primary modes of vocal fold vibration and their resulting sound qualities. The main differences are related to the relative thickness of the folds and their cross-sectional shape (figure 2.6). The first option depends on short, thick folds that come together with nearly square-shaped edges. Vibration in this configuration is given a variety of names, including mode 1, thyroarytenoid (TA) dominant, chest mode, or modal voice. The alternate configuration uses longer, thinner folds that make contact only at their upper margins. Common names include mode 2, cricothyroid (CT) dominant, falsetto mode, or loft voice. Singers vary the vibrational mode of the folds according to the quality of sound they wish to produce.

Before we move on to a discussion of resonance, we must consider the quality of the sound that is produced by the larynx. At the level of the glot-

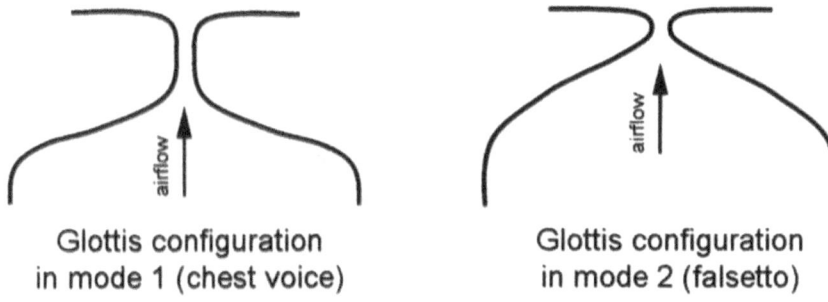

Glottis configuration in mode 1 (chest voice)

Glottis configuration in mode 2 (falsetto)

Figure 2.6. Primary modes of vocal fold vibration. *Courtesy of Scott McCoy*

SINGING AND VOICE SCIENCE

tis, we create a sound not unlike the annoying buzz of a duck call. That buzz, however, contains all the raw material we need to create speech and singing. Vocal or glottal sound is considered to be complex, meaning that it consists of many simultaneously sounding frequencies (pitches). The lowest frequency within any tone is called the fundamental, which corresponds to its named pitch in the musical scale. Orchestras tune to a pitch called A-440, which means that it has a frequency of 440 vibrations per second, or 440 Hertz (abbreviated Hz). Additional frequencies are included above the fundamental, which are called overtones. Overtones in the glottal sound are quieter than the fundamental. In voices, the overtones usually are whole number multiples of the fundamental, creating a pattern called the harmonic series (e.g., 100, 200, 300, 400, and 500 Hz, or G2, G3, D4, G4, and B4—note that pitches are named by the international system in which the lowest C of the piano keyboard is C1; middle C therefore becomes C4, the fourth C of the keyboard) (figure 2.7).

Singers who choose to make coarse or rough sounds as might be appropriate for rock or blues often add overtones that are inharmonic, or not part of the standard numerical sequence. Inharmonic overtones also are common in singers with damaged or pathological voices.

Under most circumstances, we are completely unaware of the presence of overtones—they simply contribute to the overall timbre of a voice. In some vocal styles, however, harmonics become a dominant feature. This is especially true in throat singing or overtone singing, as is found in places like Tuva. Throat singers tune their vocal tracts so precisely that single harmonics are highlighted within the harmonic spectrum as a separate, whistle-like tone. These singers sustain a low-pitched drone and then create a melody by moving from tone to tone within the natural harmonic series. You can learn to do this too. Sustain a comfortable pitch in your range and slowly morph between the vowels /i/ and /u/. If you listen carefully, you will hear individual harmonics pop out of your sound.

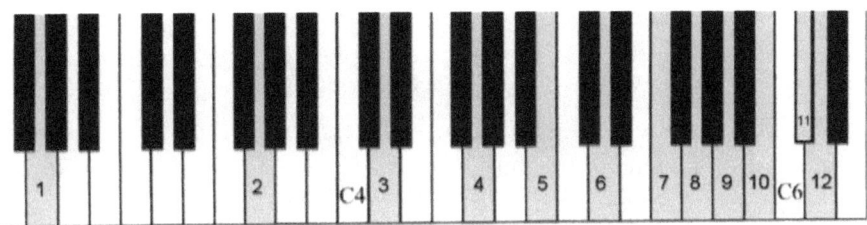

Figure 2.7. Natural harmonic series, beginning at G2. *Courtesy of Scott McCoy*

The mode of vocal fold vibration has a strong impact on the overtones that are produced. In mode 1, high-frequency harmonics are relatively strong; in mode 2, they are much weaker. As a result, mode 1 tends to yield a much brighter, brassier sound.

VOCAL TRACT: YOUR SOURCE OF RESONANCE

Resonance typically is defined as the amplification and enhancement (or enrichment) of musical sound through supplemental vibration. What does this really mean? In lay terms, we could say that resonance makes instruments louder and more beautiful by reinforcing the original vibrations of the sound source. This enhancement occurs in two primary ways, which are known as forced and free resonance (there is nothing pejorative in these terms: free resonance is not superior to forced resonance). Any object that is physically connected to a vibrator can serve as a forced resonator. For a piano, the resonator is the soundboard (on the underside of a grand or on the back of an upright); the vibrations of the strings are transmitted directly to the soundboard through a structure known as the bridge, which also is found on violins and guitars. Forced resonance also plays a role in voice production. Place your hand on your chest and say /a/ at a low pitch. You almost certainly felt the vibrations of forced resonance. In singing, this might best be considered your private resonance; you can feel it, and it might impact your self-perception of sound, but nobody else can hear it. To understand why this is true, imagine what a violin would sound like if it were encased in a thick layer of foam rubber. The vibrations of the string would be damped out, muting the instrument. Your skin, muscles, and other tissues do the same thing to the vibrations of your vocal folds.

By contrast, free resonance occurs when sound travels through a hollow space, such as the inside of a trumpet, an organ pipe, or your vocal tract, which consists of the pharynx (throat), oral cavity (mouth), and nasal cavity (nose). As sound travels through these regions, a complex pattern of echoes is created; every time sound encounters a change in the shape of the vocal tract, some of its energy is reflected backward, much like an echo in a canyon. If these echoes arrive back at the glottis at the precise moment a new pulse of sound is created, the two elements synchronize, resulting in a significant increase in intensity. All of this happens very quickly—remember that sound is traveling through your vocal tract at more than seven hundred miles per hour.

Whenever this synchronization of the vocal tract and sound source occurs, we say that the system is in resonance. The phenomenon occurs at specific frequencies (pitches), which can be varied by changing the position of the tongue, lips, jaw, palate, and larynx. These resonant frequencies, or areas in which strong amplification occurs, are called formants. Formants provide the specific amplification that changes the raw, buzzing sound produced by your vocal folds into speech and singing. The vocal tract is capable of producing many formants, which are labeled sequentially by ascending pitch. The first two, F1 and F2, are used to create vowels; higher formants contribute to the overall timbre and individual characteristics of a voice. In some singers, especially those who train to sing in opera, formants 3 through 5 are clustered together to form a super formant, eponymously called the singer's formant, which creates a ringing sound and enables a voice to be heard in a large theater without electronic amplification.

Formants are vitally important in singing, but they can be a bit intimidating to understand. An analogy that works really well for me is to think of formants like the wind. You cannot see the wind, but you know that it is present when you see leaves rustling in a tree or feel a breeze on your face. Formants work in the same manner. They are completely invisible and directly inaudible. But just as we see the rustling leaf, we can hear (and perhaps even feel) the action of formants through how they change our sound. Try a little experiment. Sing an ascending scale beginning at B♭3, sustaining the vowel /i/. As you approach the D♮ or E♭ of the scale, you likely will feel (and hear) that your sound becomes a bit stronger and easier to produce. This occurs because the scale tone and formant are on the same pitch, providing additional amplification. If you change to an /u/ vowel, you will feel the same thing at about the same place in the scale. If you sing to an /o/ or /e/ and continue up the scale, you'll feel a bloom in the sound somewhere around C5 (an octave above middle C); /a/ is likely to come into its best focus at about G5.

To remember the approximate pitches of the first formants for the main vowels, /i–e–a–o–u/, just think of a C-major triad in first inversion, open position, starting at E4: /i/ = E4, /e/ = C5, /a/ = G5, /o/ = C5, and /u/ = E4 (figure 2.8). If your music theory isn't strong, you could use the mnemonic "every child gets candy eagerly." These pitches might vary by as much as

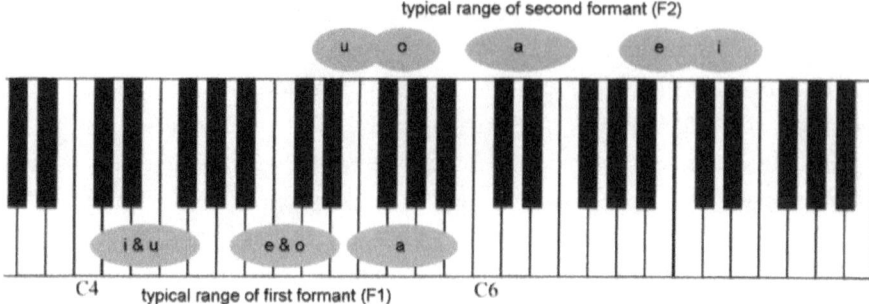

Figure 2.8. Typical range of first and second formants for primary vowels.
Courtesy of Scott McCoy

a minor third higher and lower but no farther: once a formant changes by more than that interval, the vowel that is produced must change.

Formants have absolutely no preference for what they amplify—they are indiscriminate lovers, just as happy to bond with the first harmonic as the fifth. When men or women sing low pitches, there almost always will be at least one harmonic that comes close enough to a formant to produce a clear vowel sound. The same is not true for women with high voices, especially sopranos, who routinely must sing pitches that have a fundamental frequency higher than the first formant of many vowels. Imagine what happens if she must sing the phrase "and I'll leave you forever," with the word "leave" set on a very high, climactic note. The audience won't be able to tell if she is singing "leave" or "love"; the two will sound identical. This happens because the formant that is required to identify the vowel /i/ is too far below the pitch being sung. Even if she tries to sing "leave," the sound that comes out of her mouth will be heard as some variation of /a/.

Fortunately, this kind of mismatch between formants and musical pitches rarely causes problems for anyone but opera singers, choir sopranos, and perhaps ingenues in classic music theater shows. Almost everyone else generally sings low enough in their respective voice ranges to produce easily identifiable vowels.

Second formants also can be important but more so for opera singers than everyone else. They are much higher in pitch, tracking the pattern /u/ = E5, /o/ = G5, /a/ = D6, /e/ = B6, /i/ = D7 (you can use the mnemonic "every good dad buys diapers" to remember these pitches) (figure 2.8). Because they can extend so high, into the top octave of the piano keyboard for /i/, they interact primarily with higher tones in the natural harmonic series. Unless you are striving to produce the loudest unamplified sound possible, you probably never need to worry about the second formant; it will steadfastly do its job of helping to produce vowel sounds without any conscious thought or manipulation on your part.

If you are interested in discovering more about resonance and how it impacts your voice, you might want to install a spectrum analyzer on your computer. Free (or inexpensive) programs are readily available for download over the internet that will work with either a PC or a Mac computer. You don't need any specialized hardware—if you can use Skype or FaceTime, you already have everything you need. Once you've installed something, simply start playing with it. Experiment with your voice to see exactly how the analysis signal changes when you change the way your voice sounds. You'll be able to see how harmonics change in intensity as they interact with your formants. If you sing with vibrato, you'll see how consistently you produce your variations in pitch and amplitude. You'll even be able to see if your tone is excessively nasal for the kind of singing you want to do. Other programs are available that will help you improve your intonation (how well you sing in tune) or enhance your basic musicianship skills. Technology truly has advanced sufficiently to help us sing more beautifully.

MOUTH, LIPS, AND TONGUE: YOUR ARTICULATORS

The articulatory life of a singer is not easy, especially when compared to the demands placed on other musicians. Like a pianist or brass player, we must be able to produce the entire spectrum of musical articulation, including dynamic levels from hushed pianissimos to thunderous fortes, short notes, long notes, accents, crescendos, diminuendos, and so on. We produce most of these articulations the same way instrumentalists do, which is by varying our power supply. But singers have another layer of articulation that makes everything much more complicated: we must produce these musical gestures while simultaneously singing words.

As we learned in our brief examination of formants, altering the resonance characteristics of the vocal tract creates the vowel sounds of language. We do this by changing the position of our tongue, jaw, lips, and sometimes palate. Slowly say the vowel pattern /i–e–a–o–u/. Can you feel how your tongue moves in your mouth? For /i/, it is high in the front and low in the back, but it takes the opposite position for /u/. Now slowly say the word "Tuesday," noting all the places that your tongue comes into contact with your teeth and palate and how it changes shape as you produce the vowels and diphthongs. There is a lot going on in there—no wonder it takes so long for babies to learn to speak!

Our articulatory anatomy is extraordinarily complex, in large part because our bodies use the same passageway for food, water, air, and sound. As a result, our tongue, larynx, throat, jaw, and palate are all interconnected with common physical and neurologic points of attachment. Our anatomical Union Station in this regard is a small structure called the hyoid bone. The hyoid is one of only three bones in your entire body that do not connect to other bones via a joint (the other two are your patellae, or kneecaps). This little bone is suspended below your jaw, freely floating up and down every time your swallow. It is a busy place, serving as the upper suspension point for the larynx, the connection for the root of the tongue, and the primary location of the muscles that open your mouth by dropping your jaw.

Good singing—in any genre—requires a high degree of independence in all these articulatory structures. Unfortunately, nature conspires against us to make this difficult to accomplish. From the time we were born, our bodies have relied on a reflex reaction to elevate the palate and raise the larynx each time we swallow. This action becomes habitual: palate goes up, larynx also lifts. But depending on the style of music we are singing, we might need to keep the larynx down while the palate goes up (opera and classical) or palate down with the larynx up (country and bluegrass). As we all know, habits can be very hard to change, which is one of the reasons that it can take a lot of study and practice to become an excellent singer. Understanding your body's natural reflexive habits can make some of this work a bit easier.

There is one more significant pitfall to the close proximity of all these articulators: tension in one area is easily passed along to another. If your jaw muscles are too tight while you sing, that hyperactivity will likely be transferred to the larynx and tongue—remember, they all are interconnected through the hyoid bone. It can be tricky to determine the primary offender in this kind of chain reaction of tension. A tight tongue could just as easily be making your jaw stiff, or an elevated, rigid larynx could make both tongue and jaw suffer.

Neurology complicates matters even further. You have sixteen muscles in your tongue, fourteen in your larynx, twenty-two in your throat and palate, and another sixteen that control your jaw. Many of these are very small and lie directly adjacent to each other, and you often are required to contract one quite strongly while its next-door neighbor must remain totally relaxed. Our brains need to develop laser-like control, sending signals at the right moment with the right intensity to the precise spot where they are needed. When we first start singing, these brain signals come more like a blast from a shotgun, spreading the neurologic impulse over a broad area to multiple muscles, not all of which are the intended target. Again, with practice and training, we learn to refine our control, enabling us to use only those muscles that will help while disengaging those that would get in the way of our best singing.

FINAL THOUGHTS

This brief chapter has only scratched the surface of the huge field of voice science. To learn more, you might visit the websites of the National Association of Teachers of Singing (NATS), the Voice Foundation (TVF), or the National Center for Voice and Speech (NCVS). You can easily locate the appropriate addresses through any internet search engine. Remember that knowledge is power. Occasionally, people are afraid that if they know more about the science of how they sing, they will become so analytical that all spontaneity will be lost or they will become paralyzed by too much information and thought. In my forty-plus years as a singer and teacher, I've never encountered somebody who actually suffered this fate. To the contrary, the more we know, the easier—and more joyful—singing becomes. ♪

3

HOW LEARNING WORKS

An Introduction to Motor Learning Theory

Lynn Helding

Voice science has influenced voice pedagogy since the famous Spanish voice teacher Manuel García II (1805–1906) procured two dental mirrors, slid one into his mouth, and aimed the other at just the right angle to catch a ray of sunlight, revealing the marvel of the human vocal folds.[1] Thus, voice *physiology* (the way in which body parts function) was established as the first pillar of voice science. This view held sway until the 1970s, when Swedish voice scientist Johan Sundberg (b. 1936) published research on the acoustics of the singing voice that revealed a special resonance cluster that male opera singers exhibit that allows them to be heard over an orchestra.[2] Dubbed the "singer's formant," Sundberg's discovery firmly established voice acoustics as the second pillar of voice science, creating a firm foundation for the field of voice *pedagogy*, defined as the art and science of teaching. This fact, that pedagogy is about teaching—or, more pointedly, as professor of education Deborah Loewenberg Ball (b. 1954) once commented, "Teaching depends on what other people think"— makes it all the more ironic that what has been missing from voice pedagogy until very recently is both the delivery system and the receptacle for voice science information: the human mind.

The fund of voice science knowledge that has accumulated since García's time is rich with insight about the human voice. This bounty inspired pedagogue Richard Miller (1926–2009) to admonish singers to take advantage not only of everything that was known two hundred years ago but also of everything that is known today. The most urgent questions for those who rise to this challenge are "How might I gain this knowledge?" and—more important—"How might I apply it to singing?" Answering these questions requires an understanding of how humans learn.

Learning is the vital question of *cognitive science*, an interdisciplinary science that arose when the cognitive revolution of the 1950s swept aside *behaviorism* as the dominant field in psychology. Learning itself is not a single entity but a complex activity comprised of many interrelated processes. Cognitive science, built on the foundation of psychology, reflects this complexity by including neuroscience, artificial intelligence, linguistics, anthropology, sociology, and philosophy to study human perception, thinking, and learning. We may now turn to cognitive science as the third pillar in the field of voice pedagogy.

TWO BASIC MODES OF LEARNING

The ancient Greek philosophers identified two primary sources of human knowledge: knowledge that is gained by exercising the human attribute of reason, or *rationalism*, and knowledge gained through sensory experience, known as *empiricism*. This dichotomy is still reflected in standard modern learning theories despite the terms used to describe them. Two of the most accepted are *declarative learning* and *procedural learning*; in philosophy, these two modes are identified as "know-that" and "know-how." Declarative learning ("know-that") is information about which one can speak, or "declare." The construction "know-that" refers to knowledge of facts, as in "I know that a formant is a resonance of the vocal tract." This kind of knowledge is not innate; it has to be "declared" to the learner and is best elucidated by an expert teacher as a guide. Declarative learning typically takes place over a time period of days, weeks, or months. Memory for words and life episodes also fall under declarative learning.

Procedural learning ("know-how") refers to learning physical skills (procedures) by doing and is inclusive of both those innate movements with which we are born, like crawling, as well as advanced skills, such as learning to ride a bicycle or learning to play a musical instrument.[3] The field of study dedicated to research in procedural learning is called *motor learning*, wherein "motor" refers both to motion and to the *motor neurons* (brain cells) that create movement.

Procedural learning in humans begins almost from birth. We are, one might say, preprogrammed to learn to grasp and crawl and to walk all on our own as toddlers, which we do by trying, falling, and trying again—no teacher is necessary. Acquisition of the physical movements needed for survival advances relatively quickly, usually in a matter of hours. Thus, a crucial difference between declarative learning and procedural learning is the speed with which each adheres.

However, advanced skills—also called *higher-order* skills, such as those on display in a concert pianist—do not come preinstalled in humans. These skills must be learned via a combination of declarative and procedural learning. Singing displays this dual nature: we explore the range and extent of our own voices by wailing, giggling, and cooing as babies. As we mature, we can easily find our own singing voice, particularly if our surrounding culture provides for it and supports it; family sing-alongs and community singing in religious services provide these opportunities. Many singers of popular styles report these experiences as formative and rightfully claim to be self-taught.

However, those wishing to learn the Western, classical tradition of singing—which is distinguished by a large pitch range, sustained breathing, natural amplification, seamless register shifts, and agile execution of rapid scale passages—must first be led by a master teacher as their guide and then must practice with regularity and discipline. Similarly, singers of contemporary commercial music (CCM) who wish to extend their vocal range, stamina, and control should consult a voice teacher if they wish to excel.

These kinds of singing styles are considered to be higher-order tasks, more complex and refined than generic voicing. Higher-order and complex muscular tasks all have one attribute in common: they all require practice over time. The amount of practice time required to become an expert is estimated to be about ten thousand hours. This number was arrived at by combining more than a century's worth of studies by multiple researchers. K. Anders Ericsson (b. 1947), a founder of the field of expertise studies, further identified that the quality of practice required to become an expert is even more crucial than simply logging practice hours. He dubbed this high-quality type of practice *deliberate practice*, defined as "an effortful activity designed to improve individual target performance."[4] Higher-order muscular tasks are situated at the nexus of declarative and procedural learning: we must first "know that" in order to "know how." Table 3.1 illustrates the standard synonyms in use for declarative and procedural learning as well as their attributes.

Table 3.1. The Two Basic Modes of Human Information Processing and Their Attributes

DECLARATIVE LEARNING or MEMORY	PROCEDURAL LEARNING or MEMORY
Propositional	Tacit
Explicit	Implicit
Controlled	Automatic
Learned	Inherent
Slow	Fast
Demands attention	Can multitask
Avoidable	Unavoidable
Volitional	Not volitional
Know-that	Know-how
Top-down (refers to the *executive control center* of the brain)	Bottom-up (the intuitive responses of our *autonomic nervous system*)

LEARNING DEFINED

Learning has been the most assiduously studied topic in psychology, from its inception as a field in the early nineteenth century throughout the twentieth. Schools of thought and their resultant vocabularies sprang up around the world, yet in the face of the subject's enormity and without the connective power of the internet, the creation of a commonly accepted definition of learning was nearly impossible. In the twenty-first century, the ability to view the brain's inner workings in real time via *functional magnetic resonance imaging* and the rapid dissemination of digital information have generated only more information, not more clarity toward a definition of learning.

Nevertheless, we will need a working definition if we are to understand some fundamental properties of learning. Therefore, two simple definitions for each of the modes of learning are offered here based on the most common elements found in accepted learning theories.

- Declarative learning: A process that results in a permanent change in behavior as a result of *experience*
- Procedural learning: A process that results in a permanent change in behavior as a result of *practice*

Notice that both definitions are exactly the same except for the crucial factor that causes each type of learning to adhere, or "cause a permanent change in behavior." In the case of *declarative learning*, if the information presented is easily understood, it is enough to simply be introduced to a topic to be able to claim it as learned. For example, in chapter 2 of this book, it may have surprised you that the diaphragm muscle is attached to the bottom of the sternum and is therefore more highly situated in the body than many people imagine. If that information held particular meaning for you, you would likely not forget it. However, other types of declarative information contained in this book, such as the names, locations, and functions of all the other respiratory muscles, must be studied in order to be truly learned. And as any student knows, studying facts to the extent that they can be successfully recalled for an exam requires motivation and diligence. Thus, a key attribute of declarative learning that distinguishes it from procedural learning is volition—the learner must want to learn.

Conversely, procedural learning requires doing. No substitutions are viable. Procedural learning of basic human skills occurs concurrently with the development of *proprioception*, the body's own sense of its movements, positions, balance, and *spatial orientation* (where it is in relation to other people and objects). Learning these most fundamental human physical skills is largely non-volitional; we learn them by experiencing the world, and thus the learning will occur whether we wish it to or not as a matter of survival. Procedural learning and declarative learning exhibit significant differences regarding speed of acquisition and volition. But both types of learning share certain commonalities. We will now consider these commonalities before returning to focus on their differences.

HOW LEARNING WORKS: THE TRIUMVIRATE OF ATTENTION, LEARNING, AND MEMORY

The human brain is perhaps the most complex system in the known universe. Exactly how humans learn is still not completely understood, but at present, it is accepted that learning is not one discrete entity but rather a three-step process of *attention, learning itself*, and *memory*. These three phases display their own attributes while attending to both declarative and procedural learning. The box below offers a very simplified scheme of these phases for reference as we consider both the psychological and the neurobiological processes that underpin our most fundamental and complex activity: learning.

ATTENTION, LEARNING ITSELF, AND LONG-TERM MEMORY

- Step 1: Attention. This is the prerequisite condition for learning. Learning cannot happen until and unless one first pays attention. Note that attention has a limited capacity in the human brain.
  - Brain activity: Biochemical changes, specifically the release of the chemical messengers called *neurotransmitters*. In the early stages of learning, the *synapses* (the gaps between brain cells where chemical messages are exchanged) are temporarily destabilized.
- Step 2: Learning itself. The dynamic process whereby new information is first absorbed (called *short-term memory*) and then sorted (called *working memory*) and manipulated, which features the act of *constructive memory*.
  - Brain activity: More release of neurotransmitters. With repetition, the number of synaptic connections in the brain begins to stabilize. This process is called *memory consolidation*.
- Step 3: Long-term memory. Once a thing is learned (past tense), it has exited the realm of learning (*short-term* and *working memory*) and exists in the realm of *long-term memory*. Long-term memory is like a treasure chest where things of value are stored and from which they can be retrieved. The evidence that a thing is learned is its repeatability; in the motor realm, this is called *automaticity*.
  - Brain activity: Anatomical changes in brain tissue are observed. The brain has reorganized itself.

Step 1: Attention

Attention is the prerequisite condition for learning, but what is it exactly? Attention is a complex neurological system distributed throughout the brain via a connected neural network as opposed to a single entity. The attention network is best understood as an attentional filtering system, called the *autonomic nervous system* (ANS), which incessantly sifts the information that bombards our senses every second, parsing the important from the trivial. The ANS is essentially distributed between two systems: the *sympathetic nervous system* (SNS) and the *parasympathetic nervous system* (PNS).

The SNS, borne from the "bottom up" or *intuitive response*, is primed to alert in the presence of danger or excitement, such as sexual arousal. This alerting operates rapidly and largely outside our awareness and control. Some typical body signs that the SNS is fired up are increased heart rate, shortness of breath, weak knees, loss of appetite, and sweaty palms. The SNS is linked to the *fight-or-flight* response, which is the impulse to either stand one's ground in the presence of danger or flee.

Unfortunately, the SNS is also operational in times of purely psychological stress, such as the disorienting experience of *music performance anxiety* (MPA). Apparently, the SNS does not always differentiate between a hungry animal bearing down on you in the wilderness and a full house in a concert hall. A vexing question regarding MPA is whether it is a condition unique to music performance per se or rather a manifestation of a broader psychopathology. At present, MPA remains vastly understudied (especially in comparison to anxiety in sport performance), as does the efficacy of certain treatment methods.

The PNS operates from the "top down" or *executive control center* of the brain and works to calm the body—after fear, flight, or arousal—and restore it to a resting state. Executive attention governs conscious control of attention (also called *selective attention*), which is what allows us to filter out the most important bits from the wealth of stimuli that assaults our senses from moment to moment. We can choose attention by exerting the human parameter of free will but only when desire and motivation inspire us do so. Thus, a subgenre of attention research is a condition called *preattentive processing*, which is a particularly significant component of voluntary attention. Committed learners will want to know how they might prime their attention for success before they enter a learning situation.

Desire and Motivation Learners must first want to pay attention before they truly can. Desire and its twin, motivation, are both the simplest and yet the most elusive of conditions for learning, as anyone who has tried to commit to a study schedule, exercise routine, or diet can attest. Before we consider what does work to ignite motivation, let us quickly dispense with a popular yet ultimately counterproductive method: the use of rewards, such as candy, praise, or money. Research has shown that such rewards are not the primary forces that stimulate human endeavor and creativity. Rather, so-called intrinsic rewards are the best motivation—for example, the joy found in pursuing the endeavor itself, the excitement of discovery, and the freedom of charting one's own course.

One of the best techniques shown to ignite motivation is *goal setting*, the conscious act of listing one or several goals one wishes to reach. Goal setting stimulates motivation and, when applied consistently, can actually increase achievement. Goal setting concretizes vague notions of achievement and also promotes focus, cultivates self-regulation by aiding impulse control, and helps calibrate efficient use of time and financial resources. These various benefits accrue to promote positive feelings, which in turn feed more motivation.

Four of the most important parameters to consider if using this technique are *specificity, format, difficulty*, and *process*. In order, goals must (1) be very specific rather than general; (2) be written down, not merely kept in mind; (3) be challenging, not easy—note that this factor echoes Ericsson's definition of deliberate practice; and (4) answer the question "How?"

Students who answer this last question by listing exactly how they intend to achieve their goals are more likely to succeed.

Emotion We have considered desire and motivation as the twin ignition systems of attention. But once attention is fired up, how does it keep going? One simple answer is "emotion." But as with everything else having to do with the human condition, emotion is far from simple. It is a vast and complex topic as well as an age-old conundrum. Emotion has bedeviled human beings for as long as we have been sentient.

Pathé is a term for emotion developed by Aristotle (384 BCE–322 BCE). *Pathé* is variously translated as "desires" or "appetites." During the seventeenth century, René Descartes (1596–1650) recognized the physiological upheavals generated by these appetites as "passions of the soul" and attributed this agitation to the pineal gland in the brain, which he believed to be home base for the human soul. Eighteenth-century beliefs about emotion were particularly influenced by romantic thought, which regarded emotion as a natural and raw human attribute that was enchained by propriety and longed to escape its fetters. This take on emotion persisted throughout the nineteenth and early twentieth centuries and is still present in popular culture today.

In the early twentieth century, emotion experienced a kind of banishment at the hands of behaviorist psychologists, who eschewed emotion as far too frivolous for serious scientific study. The cognitive revolution chipped away at behaviorism and eventually displaced it by ushering in the current era of brain science, but the pioneers of cognitivism in the 1950s had as much interest in emotion as their predecessors, which is to say almost none.

Throughout most of the twentieth century, rational thought was exalted as the pinnacle of human wisdom, while emotion was not only deemed worthless as a serious research topic but also branded as downright seditious: emotion bewitched and muddled rational thought. Emotion is still commonly viewed as an element that one must tame, silence, or outgrow.

The very newest research on emotion from the field of neuroscience reveals that emotion—rather than being rationality's polar, frivolous opposite—is actually fundamentally entwined with human reason. Neuroscientists like Jaak Panksepp (1942–2017), Antonio Damasio (b. 1944), and Joseph LeDoux (b. 1949) have worked to repair the mind–body split that Descartes proposed by plucking emotion from the ephemeral realm of the spirit and grounding it within the physical functions of the body. LeDoux defines emotions as "biological functions of the nervous system."[5] Damasio, through his now famous *somatic marker hypothesis*, has advanced emotion as a critical component of human decision making and thus an assistant to reason—a far cry from its centuries-old characterization as a fickle temptress.[6] "Emotion," Damasio notes, "is not a luxury."[7]

Emotion plays a critical role in sustaining attention during learning, for emotion necessarily attends motivation and desire. Unless people care enough to expend some effort, they will not learn because they will not have "attended." Emotion also assists encoding our experiences into long-term memory—a process called *memory consolidation*—particularly if the emotions were strong ones. Joyful life episodes, such as one's wedding day or elation at the birth of a child, become permanently fixed in our memory. It is perhaps for this reason that extreme technical breakthroughs in a voice lesson or superlative achievements reached in performance are deeply remembered.

On the other end of the emotion spectrum, extremely frightening or humiliating events can become so encoded in memory that certain stimuli, especially smells and sounds, can activate the "alerting network" of the ANS. Harmless sounds like fireworks can recall a returning war veteran's memory of enemy fire with devastating consequences for mental health, as is seen in posttraumatic stress disorder (PTSD). Even the scent of a certain aftershave or a personal ringtone on a cell phone, if they are entangled with memories of particularly brutal or humiliating events, can engender symptoms of PTSD. Note, however, that emotion's role in attention, learning, and memory has been qualified as necessarily "strong" in order to assist. Tripping during a stage entrance or enduring the tirade of a nasty conductor, as unpleasant or unwarranted as such events might be, is not encoded in the long-term memories of most people or to such a degree as to cause long-term damage.

Sleep Along with desire, motivation, and emotion, a final parameter to consider in regard to attention is sleep. Sleep is understood by researchers as a complex set of brain processes, not a single state of being. It is well established in science research that lack of sleep impairs brain function, damages learning, weakens performance in cognitive tests, and slows reaction time for physical tasks that require alertness, such as driving and operating heavy machinery. Yet the underlying, biological reasons that sleep deprivation is so damaging—and conversely why abundant sleep is so restorative—are still something of a mystery. Several studies offer some clues.

An important sleep study in 2013 revealed that sleep may be critical for what amounts to brain cleaning. According to these researchers, the brain lacks the conventional version of the *lymphatic system*, which clears cellular debris out of the body. Therefore, it evolved its own metabolic system, the *glymphatic system*, which operates during sleep to flush away waste products accumulated during wakefulness that are toxic to brain cells. According to this theory, the uncluttered and detoxified brain should rise from sleep refreshed and more able to pay attention.

Another theory concerns *synaptic pruning*, the processes by which *synapses* that are weak (due to lack of attention and practice) wither away with no trace in the brain, leaving only the strongest synaptic connections behind. It is believed that sleep is the state most conducive to this pruning process because the brain is least subject to interference from incoming stimuli. A related theory is that the purpose of sleeping and dreaming is to replay short-term memories gathered throughout the previous day and, in so doing, strengthen the neural pathways of those memories and send them along their journey to long-term memory consolidation, which we will revisit below in depth in "Step 2: Learning Itself." But before we leave the topic of attention, we must consider a relatively recent cultural phenomenon known to be toxic to attention: *multitasking*.

Attention and Multitasking   The term "multitask" first appeared in the nascent computer technology of the 1960s, but since the advent of the World Wide Web in the 1990s, the word was absorbed into the popular lexicon. While multitasking per se has been a part of human activity for millennia, the current manifestation of the term "multitasking" refers to the mingling of one or more technology-based tasks: reading e-mail while listening to music, texting while watching television, or driving a car while following a GPS. Research on human multitasking in the digital environment has zeroed in on the following parameters listed in the box below.

PARAMETERS OF MULTITASKING

- Attentional filtering: The ability to successfully filter relevant from irrelevant information
- Task switching: Shifting from task to task and/or returning to an important task after distraction by a task of lesser importance
- Organization of thoughts: Keeping cognitive results organized for later retrieval (Note: This is a hallmark of learning; a thing is not truly learned if it cannot be retrieved and repeated.)

Multiple studies have shown that the vast majority of people manage all these parameters extremely poorly when faced with digital distractions. This is due to our limited attentional capacity. Stated simply, it is very difficult for people to pay deep attention to more than one thing at a time.

Because multitasking is toxic to attention, it also degrades learning itself. Multitaskers demonstrate decrements in their ability to engage in higher levels of thinking, such as analytical reasoning. And even if a learner is able to muster some attention while still multitasking, the learned thing acquired in this fraught state has been shown to be less flexible, making later retrieval more difficult. As we shall see, retrieval is proof that a thing is learned.

Worse, habitual multitasking makes our attentional abilities degrade over time. An influential series of studies conducted at Stanford University showed that the more chronic a person's multitasking habit, the less possible it was for them to ignore irrelevant distractions. The terms "acquired attention deficit disorder" and "attention deficit trait" have been introduced by two psychiatrists—John Ratey (b. 1948) and Edward Hallowell (b. 1949), respectively—who posit that heavy technology use may be actually creating attention deficit disorders in people not otherwise disposed toward them. It appears that we can remodel our brains both for good and for ill.

Step 2: Learning Itself

As the ancient Greek philosopher Aristotle wrote in his treatise *Metaphysics*, "If you are learning, you have not at the same time learned." This simple statement perfectly captures two important facets of learning. First is its essence, or its dynamic nature. That is, learning is marked by change, even instability. Learning is messy. If approached with a no-holds-barred spirit of adventure, learning can be fun. But learning can also be challenging to the point of joylessness, distress, or even humiliation. Nevertheless, learning is a fundamental—some say *the* fundamental—activity of life.

Yet given learning's dynamic nature, we cannot always be in a state of upheaval and transition. Learned items must be stowed in order to make way for new experiences and ideas and also for later retrieval. Thus, once learning has progressed from the transitive to the past tense (as in "I have learned"), one is no longer actively learning. The second facet of Aristotle's astute observation is realized: the learned thing is a fait accompli, stored in *long-term memory*. This process—from "learning" to "have learned"—is called *memory consolidation*.

Much research is devoted to this storage process, from the moment new information is absorbed and held in mind for a period of seconds, called *short-term memory*, to how this information is then sorted and manipulated while actively learning, called *working memory*. Some researchers refer to this process as *maintenance* and maintenance plus *manipulation*, respectively. For our purposes, let us think of short-term memory as a "brain pad" of "sticky notes"—a place to temporarily jot down impressions or facts. And just like a collection of those small bits of paper, they may be easily misplaced if we are not attentive to them.

Working memory may be thought of as learning itself: that process whereby we are able to hold several bits of information in mind (and that includes sensory information in motor learning) as we toss those bits about, consider or try them from different angles, and recombine them with facts we already know—and experiences we have already had—in order to make sense of them. Here is this last sentence restated in more compressed fashion to allow in one new piece of information:

> **DEFINITION OF WORKING MEMORY**
>
> *Learning itself* is that *process*
> whereby we hold about seven *bits*, or four *chunks*, of information in mind,
> *manipulate* those bits or chunks,
> and *recombine* them with facts or experiences we already know.

Working memory, or *learning*, is a process that starts as we consider a few *bits* of information—"seven (plus or minus two)," the compound number that George Miller (1920–2012), a founder of cognitive psychology, famously posited in 1956—and more recently understood as *chunks* of information, of which we seem to be able to manage around four. Let us consider how this works.

Working memory is what is allowing you to read this chapter and hopefully learn from it. As your reading progresses, your success is partially dependent on the ability to maintain the information from the previous paragraphs in your mind; each successive paragraph can build on the next only by your understanding of the former. For example, if you have been reading with attention, you know that we are now considering step 2 of the learning process, learning itself. Step 1 was the topic of attention with side trips featuring bits of information that were all related to the main topic. Therefore, we may call the topic of attention a *chunk*, made up of minicomponents. Researchers have invented a new verb—"chunking"—to describe this process. Chunking itself is the subject of much research and seems to be a key talent that people with superior memories possess. However, all of us can learn to use chunking to improve learning and develop superior memory techniques.

One final component of learning from the last line of our definition in the box above deserves mention: the notion of *recombination*. As we have already seen, learning begins with attention, followed by absorbing new bits of information into our short-term memory, then using working attention to manipulate those bits, and finally storing those bits in long-term memory. But no learner is a blank slate, and our individual slates become more populated with ideas and experiences as we navigate our lives. We call these ideas and experiences *memories*.

Any process of absorbing new information will necessarily collide with our previous memories. Therefore, in order to calm the collision and make sense of it all, we recombine the new information with the memories we already own. This dynamic moment in the learning process is called *constructive memory*. The main benefit of constructive memory is its cumulative quality: we use past experiences to change our actions in the present and also to imagine the future. We learn from our mistakes. But detriments due to constructive memory abound, chief among them being memory's fallibility. It is now known that human memory is enormously prone to distortion and outright error. Since what we encode in memory is always mixed up with what we already know (or think we know), our memories are never completely pure. As our memories pile up, our minds create frameworks to keep them organized. These frameworks are called *schemas*. A schema may be defined as a cognitive structure for representing, organizing, and retrieving related information. Schemas (also called *schemata*) are particularly important in motor learning.

STEP 3: LONG-TERM MEMORY

The complex neurobiological process of learning itself is encoded in the well-known maxim called Hebb's rule: "Neurons [nerve cells] that fire together, wire together."[8] Recall that learning begins when a thought or a sensation excites the synapses (the gap between neurons). With the addition of attention, emotion, and desire, short-term memory rapidly progresses to working memory—otherwise known as learning. As this nascent memory is manipulated, the already excited neural pathways are reactivated. Repeated reactivation of the same neurons (through repetition or practice) is what creates a neural pathway—a memory. The process of encoding working memory to long-term memory is called memory consolidation; thus, memory may be considered synonymous with the term "learned."

Neuroscientist Eric Kandel (b. 1929) was awarded a Nobel Prize in 2000 for his groundbreaking discoveries about the biological bases of this process. Kandel realized that short-term memory is not a diminutive version of long-term memory, as was previously believed, but is altogether biologically distinct. Short-term memories cause biochemical changes in the brain, indeed, by the release of neurotransmitters. Long-term memories, however, cause anatomical changes in brain tissue by increasing the number of synaptic connections. Kandel's discoveries, which occurred in tandem with other significant brain research at the very end of the previous century, led to the astounding realization that the brain continually remodels itself. Before the 1990s, it was believed that the adult brain could not change much past childhood and was, by all accounts, fixed. But it is now accepted wisdom that brain cells (neurons) can regenerate (*neurogenesis*) and that the brain changes continually in response to experience. This process is called *neuroplasticity*.

We have now considered what declarative and procedural learning share in common. To understand their differences—and specifically what cognitive processes undergird the attributes needed for mastering performance art—we can now turn to research in the field of motor performance and learning.

MOTOR LEARNING AND PERFORMANCE

As noted in the simple definitions in the second box, the crucial factor that distinguishes declarative from procedural learning is practice. More motor learning occurs with more practice. Two leaders in motor learning research, Richard Schmidt (1941–2017) and Tim Lee (b. 1955), dubbed this concept the "Power Law of Practice" while also conceding that this law is so obvious that it should not have to be mentioned.[9] This is true until one considers an astounding finding from motor learning research: performance improvements generally accelerate rapidly for novices and generally decelerate the more experienced one becomes. In other words, the rate of growth slows as motor performance improves. To make sense of this and other key findings from the field of motor learning research, let us start by considering a more complex definition of motor learning:

DEFINITION OF MOTOR LEARNING

Motor learning is a *process*,
which is *inferred* rather than directly observed,
which leads to *permanent changes* in *habit*
as the result of *experience* or *practice*.

There are many variations of this definition, but the most prominent ones accepted by researchers contain the six italicized components. The term "process" underscores the dimension of time. The acquisition and retention of physical skills occur along a continuum. Temporary breakthroughs notwithstanding, progress happens not all at once but over a period of time.

That this process is *inferred* refers to learning's dynamism, for learning itself can never be directly observed; we can only assume it is happening and wait for proof that the learned thing has adhered. This proof shows up in two guises, the first being the relatively *permanent changes* that distinguish procedural from declarative learning; the second is that these changes are stable enough to be called physical *habits*, even under variable conditions. Finally, these conclusions are all based on the supposition that students will continue to *experience* sensations that they will then repeatedly *practice*.

Now that we have made one pass through the complex definition of motor learning, the following components from this definition are worth even deeper inspection: *permanent changes*, *practice*, and *habit*, respectively. As we do so, it is important to note the essential difference between learning and performance.

Learning is the process by which one acquires skill or knowledge. Remember that learning is dynamic, unstable, and messy. *Performance* refers to the manner or quality with which someone functions. Performance is like the freeze-frame button on a video projector—it captures where the learner stands at that point in time along the learning continuum. Because of this frozen quality, most of us want our performances to be as polished as we can manage, which is the opposite of unstable and messy. In other words, the goals of learning and performance are—and should be—not just different but diametrically opposed to one another. When these goals are conflated, both learning and performance may suffer.

PERFORMANCE SHIFTS: MASTER CLASS SYNDROME

The evidence that a motor skill is truly learned is its repeatability, especially under many different conditions. These two parameters are called *retention* and *transfer*, respectively. Without proof that the learning has been retained, we can only say that the learner was merely exposed to the information. What about changes observed during training that are not permanent? Motor learning researchers call these changes *performance shifts*, and they can be both positive and negative. Motor learners can absorb powerful lessons from both. Let us begin with positive performance shifts.

Most singers are familiar with the phenomenon of instant success on a first or second trial, which may occur in the midst of a voice lesson or solo practice session but then vaporize moments or hours later. This phenomenon may occur in weekly singing lessons, especially if the students feel they never sing as well in their own practice or performance as they do in their lessons. This phenomenon is particularly common in a one-time master class setting, in which a guest master teacher is able to evoke a positive vocal response from the singer on display but only in that moment. The student is at a loss to recapture that magical moment later in his or her own practice. These are prime examples of positive performance shifts. While these positive experiences may have been significant moments for the student, real learning has not occurred due to the lack of proof that there were retrievable and permanent changes. I have dubbed this phenomenon "master class syndrome" and counsel students to run, not walk, to the practice room immediately following a successful experience. There is some evidence that by doing so, it is possible to re-create the experience for oneself.

What is revelatory—and perhaps even shocking—is that habitual manipulations by coaches or teachers that improve performance in the moment may actually stifle long-term learning. Why is this? Part of the answer lies with one factor we have already considered in tandem with practice: *effort*. Research into the biochemistry of the brain reveals that the more difficult a task is, the more "neuronal firing" from our brains is required; in essence, we must dig deeper for more complicated tasks. Repeated firing of the neurons from this deeper place creates a neural pathway that becomes stronger each time it is activated during learning. As we have seen, this is the explanation of what happens during working memory and the neuroscientific definition of practice. With enough practice, difficult tasks become easier and eventually, if mastered, are stored in long-term memory.

Cognitive psychologist Robert A. Bjork (b. 1939) labeled such tasks "desirable difficulties" because obstacles must form the foundation of any viable teaching method, especially if the goal is true learning and not simply improved performance in the short term. Researchers have concluded that the solutions that learners discover for themselves, through effort, are truly learned and are thus retained and retrievable. This conclusion explains why withholding "desirable difficulties" may actually damage learning.

Performance shifts can also be negative, brought on by illness, depression, or injury. But negative performance shifts may also signal the phenomenon of *unlearning*. This theory holds that when someone is attempting to learn a new motor skill, there may be a simultaneous destabilization of the previous, habitual motor pattern. This is both good news and bad news. The bad news is that unlearning can cause psychological distress. In addition, musicians should note that multitasking and task-switch cost may be particularly toxic to motor learning due to unlearning. If distractions are allowed to poison attention during this crucial phase of learning, the learner may wind up in a lose-lose situation: the new task attempted is certainly not gained, but the old, comfortable habit may become damaged as well. For example, a baritone who transitions to tenor may wager he has nothing to lose in the attempt; he assumes that the familiar voice will always be there, just like an old pair of jeans—or Colline's old coat in *La bohème*! Such singers may be distressed to find that, after a time, the old habit no longer "fits"; however, the new technique does not fit either, for it has not yet stabilized. Therefore, this particular juncture in motor skill learning appears to be particularly vulnerable. Musicians would do well to ban distraction from the practice room and pay total and complete attention to the task before them.

On the whole, though, negative performance shifts can be seen as positive signs that a new, learned skill is actively destabilizing an old, ingrained habit. Exactly how the destabilized habit becomes a stable new skill occurs via the last component of our complex definition of motor learning: practice.

THE PATH TO CARNEGIE HALL

"How do I get to Carnegie Hall?" the hapless New York City tourist asks. "Practice!" goes the punch line. This maxim is Schmidt and Lee's "Power

Law of Practice," which was introduced above. We must add to this power law that quantity and quality matter: specifically, ten thousand hours of high-quality, deliberate practice—marked by effortful engagement with desirable difficulties—are required to become an expert. Motor learning researchers study many discrete parameters of practice, and while the results are numerous, the following three essential rules of effective practice for motor learning can be gleaned from them.

Distributed Practice Is More Effective Than Massed Practice

People whose regular practice sessions alternate with periods of rest retain more than piling information on all at once in long mega-practice sessions. Even more compelling is the finding that the longer the rest session is between practice sessions, the better the learning, as evidenced by both retention and transfer in later performance. This phenomenon could be at least partly due to the cognitive benefits of sleep, as previously noted. What this means for musicians is this: practicing every day for one hour proves to be much more beneficial than practicing twice a week for three and a half hours per session even though the total number of hours per week are the same.

An added benefit of *distributed practice*—or *spaced practice*—is protection from injury. Athletes studied in motor learning research are more at risk for injury during massed practice. Why is this? The answer is quite simple: massed practice without rest leads to muscle fatigue, and tired muscles are more vulnerable to injury.

A side note here is that too little practice also makes musicians and athletes vulnerable to injury due to lack of fitness. Musician guilt over lack of preparation may feed prerehearsal panic that in turn fuels the desire to mass practice. Therefore, distributed practice is not only cognitively beneficial for learning but also a sensible strategy for developing a safe and healthy vocal training regimen and has the added potential for keeping anxiety levels in check.

Varied Practice Is More Effective Than Constant Practice

This rule of practice is about conditions of practice and is somewhat dependent on whether the skill one is practicing already displays an inherent amount of variability (an *open-skill task*) versus one that does not (a *closed-skill task*). Examples are downhill skiing (an open-skill task), in which conditions are constantly varied, versus bowling (a closed-skill task), in which the setting is fairly predictable.

Learning to sing is an inherently open-skill task; variability is "built in" to the endeavor. Consider the trajectory involved with learning a singing role from beginning to opening night: there are vocal technique lessons with a teacher, coachings with a pianist for style and diction, staging rehearsals with a director, and dress rehearsals with a conductor and an orchestra. All of these carefully rehearsed parameters may yet be varied again by costumes, makeup, and jitters in front of a live audience. Clearly, honing one's craft as a performer involves doing so under a lot of variable conditions.

How does this relate to the second rule of effective practice? Recall that the evidence that a thing is learned is its repeatability and that a goal of motor learning is that the task remains repeatable even under variable conditions. Therefore, the second rule of practice means that variation in practice, while potentially unnerving, is actually quite good for learning—so good, in fact, that it not only strengthens the task at hand but also has been shown to positively boost other related skills. This latter effect is called *generalizability* in motor learning research. The next time you feel thrown off by a change in venue—or you encounter new timbres when hearing orchestral rather than piano accompaniment—embrace these variations as vitamin packs for learning that boost both the target skill itself and the many related skills needed for performance. This type of multitasking is anything but toxic to learning!

Randomly Ordered Practice Is More Effective Than Blocked Practice

Blocked practice focuses on training one movement over and over again until mastery is gained. The use of blocked practice is a popular method for inculcating discrete skills that make up complex activities, particularly when training beginners. For example, singers may be required to practice vocal onset exercises over and over again in middle voice range until glottal onsets disappear. While this method may seem to make common sense, *randomly ordered practice* has been shown over decades of motor learning research to be more effective for long-term learning than blocked practice. That is, singers will ultimately be more successful at clean onsets if they practice vowel onsets interspersed with onsets featuring voiced and unvoiced consonants—and onsets at variable pitch levels—than if they were to practice each of these components in repetitive isolation.

Note the use of the phrase "long-term learning," which highlights an interesting twist regarding this rule of practice: blocked practice actually boosts performance in the short term, that is, during the skill-acquisition phase. This explains the one condition in which blocked practice is preferable, and that is for rank beginners. But if testing the viability of such boosts in real-world performance venues is delayed or avoided altogether, blocked practice can eventually lead to a false sense of accomplishment for both student and trainer. Such musicians make excellent "practicers," but they tend to fall apart in performance. The salient point here is that while both *randomly ordered practice* and *varied practice* may degrade immediate performance, they boost long-term learning as evidenced by superior retention (memory) and transfer because they hold up in many different situations.

CONTROLLED VERSUS AUTOMATIC PROCESSES

An ancient distinction has existed between things we do with conscious attention and those things we do automatically. In motor learning, these modes are called controlled versus automatic processing, respectively, and these modes have received quite a lot of attention over the past two decades. The resulting research has painted a mixed picture, with strongly held views on both sides. A similarly mixed picture, with equally strongly held opinions, can be seen in the field of voice pedagogy between those who promote a technical, or science-based, approach and those who prefer more intuitive methods.

Teaching methods that employ specific, frank instructions, such as "lift your soft palate as you ascend in pitch" or "engage your abdominal muscles as you crescendo," are examples of directives that evoke controlled processing. In contrast, automatic processing does not call attention to these mechanics. Teachers who use a combination of emotion (e.g., a "stifled sob"), imagery ("imagine an inflatable swimming ring around your middle"), or allusion to common physical gestures ("inhale through a yawn") are evoking automatic processing.

Many voice teachers use a combination of controlled and automatic directives. Regardless of which directives are used, in a typical voice lesson, singers are being showered with feedback, simply defined as any and all information available to the learner. Feedback is therefore an essential part of motor learning. There are two main types of feedback: inherent feedback—what the learners themselves perceive or feel—and augmented feedback—which is information delivered from an external source (like a coach or teacher). Augmented feedback also includes auditory and visual information delivered through a device such as a mirror, a video camera, an audio recording, or computer voice analysis. Augmented feedback in the form of verbal instruction given from teacher to student exerts such a powerful influence on motor learning that it is second only to practice itself. Due to this power, augmented feedback has received a lot of scrutiny in motor learning research. We shall consider a few facets of feedback before we return to the controlled versus automatic processing controversy.

Feedback frequency (how often a voice coach should provide augmented feedback) is one of several parameters studied by scientists. A commonsense approach, backed up by scientific research, is for teachers to provide frequent feedback in the early stages of vocal study, and as mastery increases, this feedback should decrease, especially in light of what we now know about how immediate performance gains depress long-term learning.

Another consideration is timing. Is augmented feedback best used by the student terminally—after the lesson—or concurrently—while the singer is engaged in singing? This question is especially important when considering computer-aided display devices, such as VoceVista, which operates in real time; in fact, it is this feature that its proponents tout as an advantage for use in the voice studio. Results from studies in motor learning have yielded varied results on the question of timing, but the following seem to be the most effective forms of feedback, in ranked order.

Immediate augmented feedback—verbal commentary from teacher to student provided during the lesson—appears to be the most effective feedback timing but after a short time delay (short meaning a few seconds). Terminal feedback is also effective; this is feedback given after a period of time has elapsed, for example, several days. Also, learners can provide their own terminal feedback, for example, by self-evaluation through journaling. This kind of feedback can receive a boost if paired with goal setting.

Concurrent augmented feedback—a stream of verbal coaching while the student is singing or an overdependence on spectrographic feedback—should be used sparingly. Besides distracting learners from the ability to receive their own sensory information (biofeedback), concurrent augmented feedback also displays the troublesome characteristic of potentially boosting short-term performance but depressing real learning. Note that spectrographic feedback used for research or to target specific vocal phenomena do not bear this caution.

A cautious note is in order regarding the physical feedback known as manipulation. This is literally the "hands-on" teaching approach in which the teacher touches a student's body in order to elicit a physical or tonal response. Ethical and legal considerations aside for the moment, the evidence suggests that manipulative correction sometimes follows the same outcome as controlled processing and concurrent augmented feedback: such solutions may temporarily benefit performance but ultimately may not take root in the singer's long-term memory. Nevertheless, anecdotal evidence does suggest that the immediate benefit from manipulation techniques may be retained if learners can encode the desired sensations in their own memory banks.

Regarding the ethical and legal considerations of teacher-to-student touching: the potential for misunderstanding, misuse, or outright abuse among both parties is high, particularly if there are no witnesses present. This is often the case in one-on-one studio teaching, where student and teacher are alone, behind closed doors. Teachers should be aware that simply asking permission to touch a student may not be enough due to the asymmetrical power dynamic inherent in the teacher–student relationship; students may not feel free to say no. For their part, students should know that they have the fundamental human right to forbid touching—even if doing so creates awkwardness or anxiety. Yet despite these significant concerns, physical guidance or manipulation remains a very useful tool for motor learning. Therefore, a simple and sensible solution to these dilemmas is for the teacher to demonstrate on his or her own body, never directly touching the student but instead guiding the student acting in mirror imitation on his or her own body. Another solution is for the teacher to give written instructions for what to do as homework—literally "put your hands here"—followed by what the learner should seek: "Notice when the spine is aligned that the jaw tends to relax."

THE THEORY OF ATTENTIONAL FOCUS

Expert athletes, dancers, instrumentalists, and singers all share the central objective of muscular efficiency, the ability to enact fine movement with the least amount of energy necessary for the task. Other common motor learning goals are accuracy, speed, consistency, and especially automaticity. The mark of the expert is said to be that their performances are achieved automatically, outside of their conscious awareness, and this view has gone unchallenged until very recently.

How to achieve automaticity revolves around the question of where the performer should place his attention: on the target or on the mechanics of achieving that target? In motor learning research, the theory of attentional focus holds that motor skills are best accomplished when the performer focuses on an external goal rather than on internal mental processes. For example, in a dart task, people are much more likely to achieve success if they focus on landing the dart in the center of the bull's-eye than if they turn their attention inward to the mechanics of their movements, such as the best angle to hold the arm or the degree of flexion to rotate their wrist. An external focus of attention for motor tasks (the target), rather than an internal focus of attention (the mechanics), has shown strong positive results in lab studies, particularly athletic pursuits that feature balance and those that feature manipulation of objects, such as balls, clubs, darts, and rackets.

As further evidence for the superiority of an external focus of attention, many studies have revealed that an internal focus of attention has been shown to actually harm motor learning and performance. When this occurs as a performance gaffe in front of an audience (like missing a putt in golf), it is known in both scientific and popular sports literature as choking. To explain the choking phenomenon, motor learning researcher Gabriele Wulf (b. ca. 1960) developed the constrained action hypothesis, which holds that an internal focus of attention interferes with automatic control processes. Her hypothesis is based on the observation that automatic responses are accomplished much more rapidly than consciously controlled ones.[10] Since processing speed has been positively correlated with all of the goals of motor learning, the constrained action hypothesis holds that all of these parameters are harmed when performers slow down their own motor system by, in popular parlance, "thinking too much." Antidotes for choking are reflected in such popular sayings as "don't overthink," "stay out of your own head," and "go with the flow."

The constrained action hypothesis has been expanded to include the observation that when performers are induced to think of their bodies during performance, this triggers an internal focus of attention that begets a rapid spiral of self-evaluation, self-consciousness, negative emotion, and paradoxical attempts to stop all such thinking. Wulf has dubbed these spirals "micro-choking."[11]

It is important to note that choking of any type is directly proportional to ability: the more expert the performer, the more spectacular the mistake. In popular parlance, the higher you climb, the harder you fall. Experts choke, but beginners simply fail. Why is this? The answer lies in the performer's abilities at the time of performance. Researcher Sian Beilock (b. 1975), an expert in motor learning research and the choking phenomenon, notes that beginners have no fund of procedural knowledge; we might say that they have no flow with which to go. Because of this, Beilock notes that the early stages of learning may actually require an internal focus of attention, with a step-by-step approach to the mechanics of movement until learners have established the necessary motor patterns that allow them to put those learned skills on "automatic pilot," thus freeing up the brain for other cognitive tasks.[12]

Yet questions remain concerning attentional focus. At what stage in the learner's journey might he or she abandon an internal focus for an external one? Do all advanced performers use an external focus of attention and under all conditions? Have all motor pursuits been put to the test to determine whether an external focus of attention applies to all motor skills?

On this last question, prominent researchers like Wulf are so confident of the superior effectiveness of an external focus of attention that they claim that this principle is generalizable to virtually every skilled motor pursuit, including music. This confidence is so ubiquitous that the dancer and philosopher Barbara Gail Montero (b. ca. 1971) dubbed it "the Maxim":

> Both in the ivory tower and on the football field, it is widely thought that focusing on highly skilled movements while performing them hinders their execution. Once you have developed the ability to tee off in golf, play an arpeggio on the piano, or perform a pirouette in ballet, attention to your bodily movement is thought to lead to inaccuracies, blunders, and sometimes even utter paralysis. At the pinnacle of achievement, such skills, it is urged, should proceed without conscious interference. . . . Let me call the view that bodily awareness tends to hinder highly accomplished bodily skills "the Maxim."[13]

Recently, Wulf conducted a review of the extant research and concluded that in her overview of eighty different studies, "in no case was an internal focus advantageous."[14] In addition to Wulf's constrained action hypothesis, several more hypotheses were offered in support of the superiority of an external focus of attention.

One suggests that directing attention to mechanical movement actually causes existing muscular patterns to stabilize, thus working in opposition to the positive benefits of unlearning. A related theory involves the degree of freedom with which the body operates most efficiently and observes that an internal focus of attention seems to exert a "freezing" effect on the joints. Another theory holds that analytical thinking, the province of the brain's executive control center, processes information more slowly than the intuitive responses of our ANS, and this slow pace impedes motor learning and performance.

Finally, the limitations of language have been noted as a barrier to motor learning because of the difficulty in describing physical sensations in words. It is reasoned that poorly described sensations are, in essence, tracked into the nonmotor regions of the brain, where they are essentially "lost in translation."

CHALLENGES TO "THE MAXIM"

Recent challengers to "the Maxim" question whether all performers use an external focus in all situations, whether automaticity always attends higher-order motor tasks, and whether automaticity is even a goal valued by all expert performers in all domains.[15] Their research is based in part on firsthand accounts of what expert instrumentalists, dancers, and athletes actually think about in real performance situations. This is in stark contrast to previous research that has been carried out largely with nonexperts using simple motor tasks and conducted under laboratory, not real-world, conditions.

New research is finding that many experts do exert executive control by issuing mechanical directives to themselves when engaged in high-skill activity. This is quite the opposite from operating automatically. Thus, challenges to "the Maxim" are based on three key criticisms: (1) that research subjects are generally not experts or even very high-skilled performers, (2) that lab studies do not (and cannot) study complex motor skills, and (3) that studies conducted in a lab rather than on a court, on a mountainside, or in a theater are not "ecologically valid."

An additional note is that very little motor learning research has been carried out on performance artists. This makes the automaticity account especially troubling for the fundamental reason that automaticity may be desired in athletics but absolutely not in performance art. In other words, taking risks in athletic performance may have dire consequences, from losing a championship match to broken bones. However, a goal for many artists is anything but automaticity; this is a particularly salient point for expert musicians, most of whom strive to keep their performances fresh and exciting and may even introduce an element of risk or improvisation to prevent well-worn repertoire from becoming stale. Yet a reasonable argument in favor of automaticity in performance art persists: firsthand accounts by successful performers indeed describe an automatic response to the nimble fingering required for executing rapid scale passages, and decrements are ascribed to overthinking in this scenario.

A second challenge to automaticity as a valued goal involves performers' reactions to changed or changing conditions. For example, downhill skiers report the necessity and benefits of issuing technical commands to themselves (using an internal focus) during performance when changed snow conditions force them to be more strategic and less automatic. No one could argue that performance artists like singers, actors, and dancers do not also face constantly changing performance conditions, ranging from daily internal fluctuations like muscle fatigue and hoarse voice to external changes such as humidity levels and performance space acoustics.

A third challenge to automaticity is the observation that the mark of an expert is the continual quest for improvement; the only way to improve is to counteract automaticity through deliberate practice. If we match this observation with the powerful finding from motor learning research mentioned at the beginning of this section (that the rate of growth slows as motor performance improves), then we must conclude that the only way to improve after one has achieved an excellent level of ability is to design deliberate practice regimens featuring tasks of greater and more varied difficulty; until learned, these tasks would seem to require an attentional focus on mechanics. Critics of "the Maxim" cite this last reason when noting that an internal focus of attention is required when experts decide to radically alter ingrained habits in order to learn new techniques.

Current research on attentional focus in high-level performers is offering powerful evidence that attention itself is trainable. A recent theory is the "AIR" approach—Applying Intelligence to Reflexes—defined as training that aims to develop "dynamic repertoires of potential action sequences which can be accessed, redeployed, and transformed" in response to changing performance conditions.[16] Exactly how this might be accomplished is also being scrutinized. Among the various techniques proposed are (1) contrast drills, in which the learner in training toggles back and forth between correct and incorrect movement, and (2) developing a repertoire of cue words that operate as linguistic nudges intended to evoke desired action—the latter is related to chunking. This process builds and accesses flexible links between knowing and doing, thus building bridges between declarative and procedural learning. Motor learning research on musicians is still in its infancy; practically none to date have used singers. Therefore, singers are encouraged to experiment with both internal and external foci.

FINAL THOUGHTS

Voice pedagogy is a dance between science and art. Since García first opened the possibility of using voice science to advance vocal art, voice science has influenced and even defined voice pedagogy. In doing so, García unwittingly unleashed a historic schism between science and art in cultivated singing—between those who feel that science drains the mystery out of artistic singing and those who believe that science can inform quality teaching methods based on physiological and acoustic facts. For singers and teachers who seek to practice a flexible and balanced approach between the two, the multidisciplinary field of cognitive science is proposed as the best arena for performing this dynamic dance between voice science and vocal art.

NOTES

1. This chapter was adapted from the my chapter "Brain" in Scott McCoy's *Your Voice: An Inside View*, 3rd ed. (Gahanna, OH: Inside View Press, 2019). Portions of this chapter also appear in my book *The Musician's Mind: Teaching, Learning, and Performance in the Age of Brain Science* (Lanham, MD: Rowman & Littlefield, 2020).

2. Johan Sundberg, *The Science of the Singing Voice* (DeKalb: Northern Illinois University Press, 1987).

3. Although the average age at which babies typically begin to crawl is nine months, no one teaches them how do it; absent any frank physical disorders, all that is necessary is the opportunity to do so. Babies know how to crawl on their own because this knowledge is encoded in their DNA. In other words, they are born with this knowledge "preinstalled."

4. K. Anders Ericsson, Ralf T. Krampe, and Clemens Tesch-Römer, "The Role of Deliberate Practice in the Acquisition of Expert Performance," *Psychological Review* 100, no. 3 (1993): 363–406.

5. Joseph LeDoux, *The Emotional Brain: The Mysterious Underpinnings of Emotional Life* (New York: Simon & Schuster, 1996), preface.

6. The somatic marker hypothesis proposes that emotional processes guide (or bias) behavior, particularly decision making. Somatic markers are feelings in the body that are associated with emotions, such as the association of rapid heartbeat with anxiety or of nausea with disgust. According to the hypothesis, somatic markers strongly influence subsequent decision making. Within the brain, somatic markers are thought to be processed in the ventromedial prefrontal cortex and the amygdala.

7. Antonio Damasio, *Descartes' Error: Emotion, Reason and the Human Brain* (New York: G. P. Putnam's Sons, 1994), 130.

8. Hebb's rule—also called Hebb's postulate, Hebbian theory, or cell assembly theory—was developed by the Canadian psychologist Donald O. Hebb (1904–1985), who introduced the concept in his book *The Organization of Behavior: A Neuropsychological Theory* (New York: Wiley, 1949).

9. Richard A. Schmidt and Timothy A. Lee, *Motor Control and Learning: A Behavioral Emphasis*, 4th ed. (Champaign, IL: Human Kinetics, 2005), 322.

10. Refer back to the first box and note that declarative learning is generally slow, while procedural learning is relatively fast.

11. Gabriele Wulf, "Attentional Focus and Motor Learning: A Review of Fifteen Years," *International Review of Sport and Exercise Psychology* 6, no. 1 (2013): 77–104.

12. Sian Beilock, Thomas Carr, Clare MacMahon, and Janet Starkes, "When Paying Attention Becomes Counter-Productive: Impact of Divided versus Skill-Focused Attention on Novice and Experienced Performance of Sensorimotor Skills," *Journal of Experimental Psychology: Applied* 8, no. 1 (March 2002): 6–16; Sian Beilock, Bennett Bertenthal, Annette McCoy, and Thomas Carr, "Haste Does Not Always Make Waste: Expertise, Direction of Attention, and Speed versus Accuracy in Performing Sensorimotor Skills," *Psychonomic Bulletin and Review* 11, no. 2 (April 2004): 373–79.

13. Barbara Gail Montero, "Does Bodily Awareness Interfere with Highly Skilled Movement?," *Inquiry: An Interdisciplinary Journal of Philosophy* 53, no. 2 (March 2010): 105–6.

14. Wulf, "Attentional Focus and Motor Learning," 77.

15. Barbara Gail Montero, *Thought in Action: Expertise and the Conscious Mind* (New York: Oxford University Press, 2017); John Toner, Barbara Gail Montero, and Aidan Moran, "Considering the Role of Cognitive Control in Expert Performance," *Phenomenology and the Cognitive Sciences* 14, no. 4 (December 2014): 1127–44; John Sutton, Doris McIlwain, Wayne Christensen, and Andrew Geeves, "Applying Intelligence to the Reflexes: Embodied Skills and Habits between Dreyfus and Descartes," *Journal of the British Society for Phenomenology* 42, no. 1 (January 2011): 78–103.

16. Sutton et al., "Applying Intelligence to the Reflexes."

4

A LISTENING JOURNEY THROUGH THE HISTORY OF ROCK 'N' ROLL

Jacqlyn Zito-Edwards

To learn the history of any musical style, you have to do more than read a book. The best way to learn is by listening and experimenting. However, many of the singers I work with do not know what to listen for or why they should listen to artists of the past. In this chapter, I am going to introduce you to a way of thinking about rock history that can help you learn to be a better singer. We will not be able to take a deep dive into any part of the history, but my hope is that these brief introductions will spark your interest to learn more by showing you how to think analytically. If you want to read more about the history, I recommend the books in the bibliography at the end of this chapter as well as the podcast *A History of Rock Music in 500 Songs*.

ROCK MUSIC IS ROOTED IN BLACK AMERICAN MUSIC

The first edition of *So You Want to Sing Rock* highlighted the African roots of rock music. Those roots are increasingly being referred to as Black American Music, and if you really want to understand American popular music, you need to spend time learning about Black American Music. There is no doubt that the earliest rock music was created by black artists.

It was record companies eager for profits from a nationwide audience in a segregated country who brought in white artists to cover songs written by black creators to transform the look of rock 'n' roll. This had an extremely negative impact on the lives and careers of the original artists. It is important history that is not as well known as it should be. The true story behind the birth of American popular music deserves more attention than a few paragraphs in this book. Therefore, readers are referred to *African American Music: An Introduction*, edited by Mellonee V. Burnim and Portia K. Maultsby, to gain a comprehensive understanding. There is also helpful information in *So You Want to Sing Gospel*, *So You Want to Sing the Blues*, and the works cited at the end of this chapter.

ONLINE RESOURCES

The digital resources for this book feature a playlist of the songs discussed in this chapter. To derive the most benefit from this exploration, I encourage you to engage in active listening as you read. Also take notes in your notebook if you find information that aligns with your goals. ♪

1950s

In the decades leading up to the 1950s, various musical influences were converging in the United States. Rhythm and blues (R&B), blues, gospel, swing, and country artists had increasing exposure to each other through recordings. Before the advent of commercial recordings, different regions of the country were known for specific types of music and sounds. Outside of those regions, the music was often unknown. When artists were able to hear styles and genres they had never been exposed to before, they began to experiment with music in new ways. This cross-pollination accelerated the development of popular music.

In 1949, record companies started releasing 45-rpm vinyls, which revolutionized commercial music production.[1] One of the popular styles of music around this time was called the "jump blues." When you listen to this music, you can hear the roots of what we now know as rock 'n' roll. In fact, some of these songs even used the word "rock," like "Good Rockin' Tonight" (1947), "Rock the Joint" (1949), and "We're Gonna Rock" (1948), which also included the lyrics "we're gonna roll." But before 1948, these songs were known not as rock 'n' roll but as "Race Records" because they were the creation of black artists. In 1948, RCA Victor started marketing these records under the umbrella of "rhythm and blues" in order to move away from race.[2] However, it was well known at the time that the jump blues was Black American Music, so even this label indicated the race of the performer, just less explicitly.

In 1951, a Cleveland record store owner named Leo Mintz told a disc jockey named Alan Freed that white kids in his store were buying "rhythm and blues" records. At Mintz's insistence, Freed started playing some of those records on the air, and it was a huge success. However, Freed knew that playing music of black artists on air could be divisive. So in 1951, he started calling songs by those artists "rock 'n' roll."[3] By removing the race of the creator, Freed was able to share the music with a wider audience, forever changing the future of commercial music. By 1954, he had moved to New York City, where he started *Moondog's Rock'n'Roll Party*, and from that point forward, the popularity of rock 'n' roll snowballed.[4]

In this section, we are going to examine a few songs from the first decade of rock music by Big Mama Thorton, Little Richard, Wanda Jackson, Ritchie Valens, and Chuck Berry. These songs are emblematic of the style and influenced generations to come. We will briefly discuss a few of the key moments that influenced the development of their artistry and then take a listen to the vocal qualities and traits that make them memorable. For more detailed information about their careers, consult the books listed in the bibliography.

"Hound Dog" (1952)

Big Mama Thornton

Big Mama Thornton was born Willie Mae Thornton in Ariton, Alabama, on December 11, 1926. Her family had a strong connection to music through the church with her father serving as a minister and her mother singing in the church choir. Growing up in a household of seven siblings, Thornton was immersed in a rich musical environment that had an impact on the rest of her career.[5]

Thornton's unique musical talents extended beyond her singing. She was a gifted harmonica player and drummer, traversing genres from country to urban blues. She also performed as a comedienne.[6] It was her diverse range of abilities that set her apart and helped her develop her signature sound.

The name "Big Mama" was given to Thornton by Frank Schiffman, the manager of Harlem's Apollo, who was captivated by her commanding presence. She was an impressive six feet tall and had a spirited personality and a commanding voice. She once boldly stated that her voice was louder than any microphone and that she had no desire for any microphone to outshine her. She shared, "My singing comes from my experience. . . . My own experience. I never had no one teach me nothin'. I never went to school for music or nothin'. I taught myself to sing and to blow harmonica and even to play drums by watchin' other people! I can't read music, but I know what I'm singing! I don't sing like nobody but myself."[7]

Notably, Thornton holds the distinction of being the first to record and perform two songs that later gained iconic status: "Hound Dog," famously covered by Elvis Presley, and her original creation "Ball and Chain," which was made famous by Janis Joplin.[8] The song "Hound Dog," penned in 1952 by white songwriters Jerry Leiber and Mike Stoller, is a twelve-bar hokum blues song. A hokum blues song is one that jokes about adult relationships but centers on sexual relations. Another song that has a hokum blues feel is "Tutti Frutti," which is discussed later in this chapter. Leiber and Stoller wrote "Hound Dog" for Big Mama, which portrays a woman ejecting a male gigolo from her life. In slang at the time, the term "hound dog" was a synonym for gigolo and referred to a man seeking a woman to support him. Reflecting on the inspiration behind the song, Stoller stated in a 1990 interview with *Rolling Stone*, "She was a wonderful blues singer, with a great moaning style. But it was as much her appearance as her blues style that influenced the writing of 'Hound Dog' and the idea that we wanted her to growl it." Leiber recalled, "We saw Big Mama and she knocked me cold. She looked like the biggest, baddest, saltiest chick you would ever see."[9]

What to Listen For in the Song

Powerful Voice Big Mama Thornton was known for her strong and booming voice. Her vocal delivery was powerful and could easily fill a room.

Grit, Roughness, and Growl The grit and roughness of Thornton's voice added depth and authenticity to her performances, making her sound authentic and genuine. It also allowed her to convey a wide range of emotions, from anger and defiance to vulnerability and sadness. The roughness and grit helped her to create the growl that Leiber and Stoller desired.

Expressive Phrasing Listen to how each of her phrases are slightly different. She uses phrase weighting to tell the story she wants. Sometimes with two identical musical phrases, she will sing them slightly differently, making the song come alive to the listener. Some of the ways she changes each phrase include her use of bending and manipulating notes and adding soulful nuances to her singing. This ability helped her to connect with her audience on a visceral level.

Improvisation In the tradition of blues singers, Thornton was skilled at improvisation. She could improvise lyrics and melodies on the spot, adding a spontaneous and dynamic element to her live performances. This improvisational skill showcased her musical creativity and spontaneity. You will notice this if you listen to different recordings of her singing "Hound Dog," particularly live recordings.

Distinctive Tone Thornton's voice had a distinctive tone that made her instantly recognizable. This unique tonal quality contributed to her individuality as a singer, setting her apart from other artists of her time.

"Tutti Frutti" (1955)

Little Richard

The song "Tutti Frutti" was recorded in 1955 by Little Richard. Little Richard was born Richard Wayne Penniman in Macon, Georgia, in 1932. Like many of the rock singers we will discuss in this chapter, Penniman grew up in poverty. His father was a church deacon and brick mason and sold bootleg whiskey.[10] Because Penniman had a smaller frame, he was nicknamed "Lil' Richard" by his family. Penniman learned to sing at church and took piano lessons at an early age. To say that singing and making music in the church was a huge influence on Penniman's career would be an understatement. However, his family did not encourage him to pursue music, and at the age of thirteen, he was thrown out of his home because of his homosexuality.[11]

In 1947, when Penniman was fourteen years old, Sister Rosetta Tharpe overheard him singing her songs before her performance at the Macon

City Auditorium. She was so impressed that she invited him to open her show.[12] Two years later, he started performing with Doctor Nobilio's traveling show, and then he eventually left home to join Dr. Hudson's Medicine Show. While he was performing in these traveling shows, he began to find his own unique musical and performance style.[13] Soon he was playing in the vaudeville and minstrel circuit and eventually adopted Little Richard as his stage name.

In 1955, record executives at Specialty Records took an interest in Little Richard and were especially excited by a song he wrote while washing dishes at the Greyhound station in Macon called "Tutti Frutti." The lyrics needed to be modified in order for the song to be played over the airwaves. So Specialty Records hired Dorothy La Bostrie to help "clean up" the song lyrically.[14] The original lyrics, referring to a man's backside in a sexual manner, were as follows:

> Tutti Frutti, good booty
> If it don't fit, don't force it
> You can grease it, make it easy[15]

The lyrics were changed to these:

> Tutti Frutti, aw rooty!
> Tutti Frutti, aw rooty!

With the lyrics now more appropriate for the mainstream white audience at the time, "Tutti Frutti' was airing on the radio waves, and records were being sold. In February 1956, a white artist named Pat Boone released his cover of "Tutti Frutti," which reached number 12 in the charts, while Penniman's original reached only number 17.[16] Boone's version lacked the driving bass and the passionate falsetto "whoo's". His diction was as crisp as a choir singer, there were no screams, and his delivery of the nonsense syllables "A-wop-bop-a-loo-mop-a-lop-bam-boom" sounded foreign and uncomfortable in his crooning baritone timbre. His higher level of success was due to his race, as was often the case in the early days of popular music. Most of us today remember Little Richard's raw, passionate, lively version the most, and the impact Little Richard made to rock vocals far exceeds any impact of Pat Boone's version.

What to Listen For in the Song

Rhythmic Pattern   Little Richard's singing in "Tutti Frutti" is marked by a rapid-fire, syncopated rhythmic pattern. He uses short phrases and breaks in his vocal delivery, creating a sense of urgency and excitement.

Screams and Shouts   One of the most distinctive features of Little Richard's singing style is his use of screams and shouts. These high-pitched exclamations became a trademark of his style and influenced future generations.

Vocal Range and Dynamics   Little Richard's vocal range is impressive, allowing him to hit high notes with ease. In "Tutti Frutti," he demonstrates his versatility by effortlessly transitioning between his registers.

Melodic Improvisation   Similar to Thornton, Little Richard also was known for his ability to improvise melodies and lyrics on the spot. To experience his impressive improvisational skills, it is important to listen to live recordings of "Tutti Frutti." He embellishes the melody with spontaneous vocal runs and ornaments, showcasing his creativity and musicality. These melodic embellishments enhance the song's playful and spontaneous vibe.

Expressive Phrasing   When observing the phrasing of "Tutti Frutti," notice how highly expressive his singing is. He emphasizes certain words and syllables for dramatic effect. He uses vocal slides, bends, and nuances in pitch to convey emotions vividly. This expressive phrasing helps make the lyrics come alive.

Confidence and Charisma   Little Richard's confidence and charisma are palpable in his vocal delivery. His bold and fearless approach to singing "Tutti Frutti" exudes a sense of joy and infectious energy, captivating listeners and making the song unforgettable.

"Hard Headed Woman" (1958)

Wanda Jackson

Wanda Jackson was born in 1937 in Maude, Oklahoma, and started performing at the age of nine. By the age of thirteen, she had her own radio show and started performing country and western songs before securing a record deal with Decca in 1954. After an appearance with Elvis Presley in 1955, she began exploring rockabilly at his insistence and soon became known as the "The Queen of Rockabilly."

In 1961, Jackson recorded "Hard Headed Woman," a rock 'n' roll hit that was previously recorded by Elvis and topped the charts at number 1 in 1958. "Hard Headed Woman" is a twelve-bar blues song written by black songwriter Claude Demetrius, a well-known rockabilly songwriter of the time. By the early 1970s, Jackson had moved on to gospel when she and her husband became born-again Christians.[17]

What to Listen For in the Song

Raw Energy Jackson infused the song with raw, unbridled energy. Her vocals were robust and full of vigor, reflecting the rebellious spirit of rockabilly music. This energy added a sense of urgency and excitement to the song.

Distinctive Tone Similar to Thornton, Jackson possessed a unique and recognizable vocal tone. Her voice had a gritty and raspy quality, which added character and depth to her singing. This distinctive tone set her apart from other white female singers of her time and made her performances instantly recognizable.

Playful Attitude "Hard Headed Woman" is a playful and flirtatious song, and Jackson's vocal delivery reflected this attitude. She nuanced her singing with vocal slides, scoops, growls, rockabilly staccato stops, head voice flips, and spoken text in her singing to emphasize the song's lighthearted and mischievous tone.

Pronunciation and Diction Clear pronunciation and diction are crucial in rockabilly music, where lyrics often tell a story. Jackson enunciated her words crisply, ensuring that every word was easily understood, allowing the audience to fully grasp the narrative of the song.

"Come On, Let's Go!" (1958)

Ritchie Valens

Richard Steven Valenzuela (known as Ritchie Valens) was born on May 13, 1941, in Pacoima, California, and died on February 3, 1959. Valens was a singer/songwriter and one of the first Latin rockers from the late 1950s who not only helped set the foundation for rock music but also spearheaded the Chicano rock movement. Valens started playing guitar as a child and formed the band the Silhouettes while attending Pacoima High School.

In 1958, at the age of seventeen, Valens signed a record deal with Del-Fi Records. Later that year, his song "Come On, Let's Go" reached number 42 on the Billboard Hot 100. The following year, he hit number 2 on the chart with his double-sided single "La Bamba," based on a traditional Mexican wedding song, and "Donna," which was written for his high school sweetheart. Only eight months into his budding career, Ritchie Valens, along with Buddy Holly and the Big Bopper, died in a plane crash in Clear Lake, Iowa, which was the inspiration for the song "American Pie" by Don McLean.[18]

What to Listen For in the Song

Clear Pronunciation   Listen for how clear his pronunciation is, particularly with the title of the song "La Bamba." His clarity helped the audience connect with the song even if they didn't speak Spanish.

Emotional Expression   In "La Bamba," he expressed joy and celebration, making the song feel festive and uplifting. His emotional connection to the lyrics encouraged the listeners to also celebrate, sing along, or just have a great time.

Smooth Phrasing   Valens had a smooth and effortless phrasing style, allowing the lyrics to flow seamlessly. This contributed to the song's catchy rhythm and made it easy for listeners to sing along.

Grit   Although Valens's singing tone was on the smoother side of the rock genre, he did sometimes use grit.

Innovative   Valens made the traditional version of "La Bamba" into a rock song not only with the instrumentation but also with the way he sings it. Listen and compare this version to the traditional version.

"Johnny B. Goode" (1958)

Chuck Berry

Charles Edward Anderson (Chuck) Berry (October 18, 1926–March 18, 2017) was a singer-songwriter and guitarist. He grew up in a middle-class black family in St. Louis and learned how to play the guitar when he was a teenager. During his high school years, he was convicted of armed burglary and spent time in reform school from 1944 to 1947. After he was released, he worked on an assembly line at an auto plant, and in the evenings, he studied hairdressing and cosmetology.[19] He had a trio in 1952, and by 1955, he had met Muddy Waters, who then introduced him to Leonard Chess of Chess records.[20] In that same year, Chuck Berry had his first number 1 hit, "Maybellene," which was his rendition of the country song "Ida Red."

Chuck Berry, much like Fats Domino, was influenced by country music. In most of his early recordings, one can hear the country influence in his sound. In fact, there are reports of listeners who were surprised to find out that he was not white after hearing his songs for the first time. This did not stop Berry but instead helped him shape his songwriting and performance style. Some historians have theorized that this was a way for him to appeal to white audiences.[21]

One of the key elements of how Berry appealed to a younger audience was the subject matter of his songs. He wrote songs about the life of a teenager, focusing mainly on rebelling against parents and/or adults. For instance, "Roll Over Beethoven" is about wanting to hear rock and/or R&B, not conservative classical music parents wanted to listen to. "School Day" (originally titled "A Teenager's Day") is a story song describing the day in the life of a high school student.[22] The lyrics describe going to school and anxiously waiting until 3 p.m. to go down to the jukebox and dance with your lover. It symbolizes the growing interest of young people to get together and dance to this new style of music.

Not all of his songs were specifically about teenagers. "Johnny B. Goode" is about a "country boy" who becomes a star because he plays a guitar "like ringing a bell." Berry did admit that the song is somewhat about him and that the original lyric was "colored boy"; however, he changed it to "country boy" because he wanted it to have airplay on the radio.[23] Like much of Berry's compositions, this song is in a simple verse-chorus form, using a chord structure of the twelve-bar blues structure.

Chuck Berry's guitar solos and style had a strong influence on future rock stars. This song in particular was covered by notable artists including Jimi Hendrix, Peter Tosh, Judas Priest, and the Sex Pistols. The most memorable cover is in the film *Back to the Future*, in which Marty McFly (played by Michael J. Fox) plays the song at a high school dance and even does Berry's famous "duck walk." "Johnny B. Goode" became legendary and was even included on the Golden Record, a disc that is flying aboard the *Voyager 1* probe, which is still traveling deep into space beyond our solar system with the hope of contacting other civilizations.[24] It is possible that in the future, an alien civilization's first exposure to earthly music may be Chuck Berry.

What to Listen For in the Song

Clear Diction A staple trademark of Chuck Berry is the storytelling in his songs. His lyrics were often witty, and he had a clear and precise way of delivering his words, making it easy for listeners to understand the lyrics of his songs.

Playful Tone Berry's vocals often carried a playful and confident tone. He had a charismatic way of delivering his songs, which added to their overall appeal. This playfulness was especially evident in "Johnny B. Goode."

Rhythmic Pacing Listen closely to how aligned the vocals are with the rhythm of the guitar. Berry had a knack for syncing his vocals with the guitar riffs, creating a seamless and rhythmic flow in his songs. This synchronization between his vocals and guitar playing contributed to the energetic feel of his music.

Expressive Phrasing Berry would often stretch out words or use slight vocal embellishments to add emphasis, drawing attention to key elements of the lyrics. He also incorporated vocal inflections, such as bends and slides, into his singing.

Call-and-Response In many of his songs, including "Johnny B. Goode," Berry used call-and-response techniques, where he sang a line and then responded to it with a guitar riff. This interplay between his vocals and guitar is rooted in the blues and created an engaging musical conversation.

1960s

After rock made its appearance in the 1950s and captured public interest, there was an explosion of subgenres. As we explore the sounds being made in the 1960s, we will be examining examples of five of the most popular subgenres to emerge during the decade: surf music, garage rock, psychedelic rock, British blues rock, and progressive/art rock. You will notice that some of the artists straddle between two or even three different genres. That is because rock music has never been about conforming and always about pushing boundaries. Music historians view the 1960s rock scene as a melting pot, and therefore many subgenres spiraled out of this incredible decade of popular music. The songs that we will analyze may not have been *Billboard* top hits, but they were popular tunes that helped set roots for rock music in decades to come.

Surf Rock

Surf rock and its spin-offs of surf music, surf pop, and surf guitar was popular from 1958 to 1964. Surf culture arose out of Southern California, and much of the music was fully instrumental, focusing on reverb-heavy electric guitars.[25] Historians say that Dick Dale of the Del-Tones was the first artist to use reverb to create the "wet" sound of the guitar. Dale's uncle was Lebanese and influenced Dale to explore music beyond America's borders, including Mexican and Middle Eastern music. Those influences, such as the rapid alternate finger picking that was found in Arabic music, made their way into Dale's guitar playing.[26] These influences can be heard in Dick Dale's 1962 cover of the popular Greek folk song "Misirlou."

Surf music was almost always in 4/4 time with a medium to fast tempo. The vocal style is male dominated and features a smooth vocal quality with multitracked harmonies. Much like many of the subgenres of the early 1960s, surf music died out with the 1964 British Invasion. The birth of folk rock, blues rock, garage rock, and eventually psychedelic rock also contributed to surf rock's decline. Vocal surf groups of the time include Jan and Dean, the Rivieras, the Ventures, the Turtles, and perhaps the most well known: the Beach Boys.

"Surfin' U.S.A." (1963)

The Beach Boys

The Beach Boys were made up of three brothers (Carl Wilson, Dennis Wilson, and Brian Wilson), a cousin named Mike Love, and their high school friend Al Jardine. The Beach Boys grew up in suburban Los Angeles in the late 1950s and were influenced by the popular music around them at the time, including early rock 'n' roll, mainstream white vocal groups, and black doo-wop groups. Many of these groups used the Wall of Sound approach developed by Phil Spector, which influenced the Beach Boys' approach.[27] One of the key elements to the Beach Boys' iconic sound was band member Brian Wilson. Although the band was given a producer, Wilson eventually demanded that he should produce their records instead. Wilson's goal was to produce a huge sound like Phil Spector's projects. This can be heard in the band's recordings from 1965 and 1966, when their sound became less "surf" inspired.

"Surfin' U.S.A." (1963) is emblematic of the surf rock sound. The song is a variation of Chuck Berry's "Sweet Little Sixteen" written in 1958. In fact, Berry sued the group for copyright infringement and eventually was credited as a cowriter of the song. "Surfin' U.S.A." reached number 3 in the pop charts the same year it was recorded and released.

What to Listen For in the Song

Harmonies   The Beach Boys were renowned for their intricate vocal harmonies. In "Surfin' U.S.A.," you can hear tight harmonies that create a rich and layered sound. The blend of Brian Wilson's falsetto and the other band members' voices created a distinctive vocal texture.

Falsetto   Wilson often used falsetto vocals in the Beach Boys' songs. In "Surfin' U.S.A.," you can hear his falsetto prominently, especially in parts of the chorus. This vocal quality added a unique dimension to their sound.

Smooth Delivery   The vocal delivery is smooth and effortless. The band members had a natural ability to sing in a way that felt relaxed yet highly polished. This smoothness contributed to the song's laid-back, carefree vibe, reflecting the surf culture that the song celebrates.

Precision   Notice the precision in the vocal harmonies and instrumental arrangements. In "Surfin' U.S.A.," the vocals are precisely coordinated, showcasing the band's musical expertise and attention to detail.

Garage Rock

Garage rock, which has also been referred to as "garage punk" or "60s punk," emerged onto the rock scene in the mid-1960s in the American Northwest. Because teenagers at the time were swept up in the British Invasion and surf rock, many of them started their own bands out of their homes across the country, hence the term "garage rock." Many of the bands that were formed had hit songs on local radio stations. However, much like the doo-wop groups that preceded this era, garage bands usually were one-hit wonders, and many of them gained regional fame rather than national recognition. There was an assumption that this kind of music was being made in garages and basements on simple equipment by amateurs, but this wasn't always the case. Many of these bands were made up of professional musicians in their twenties who wanted to work outside of the mainstream labels.[28]

During the 1960s, there was not a name for this new genre, and as quickly as it became popular, it fell out of fashion. By the 1970s, critics used the term "punk rock" to describe its simple or even primitive musicianship. However, today, the term "punk rock" is associated primarily with the genre that appeared in the 1970s. Garage rock came off as rough around the edges and amateur to some critics because of the mainstream commercial music surrounding it that had sophisticated recording technology, clearer-toned voices with clean diction, and songs that utilized more than only three chords. However, teens loved garage rock and drove up the popularity of the genre because this type of music was accessible for them to make on their own with instruments and equipment they could afford.

Garage rock incorporated simple chord structures using power chords, played aggressively, on distorted electric guitars with bass, drums, and occasionally a keyboard. The singing of the lyrics was aggressive and angry, with the singers often using nasal, gritty, or shouted vocal qualities. Many times, there are screams or even shrieks during high-intensity moments of the songs.

Garage rock bands were influenced by 1950s rock 'n' roll music, which was relatively simple but hard driving with an air of independence and freedom from parental controls and societal norms. Some of the more popular garage bands of the 1960s were the Kingsmen, the Trashmen, Paul Revere and the Raiders, and Tommy James and the Shondells. The first notable national garage rock hit was "Louie Louie" by the Kingsmen.

"Louie Louie" (1963)

The Kingsmen

The recording of "Louie Louie" that we will be analyzing was made by the Kingsmen in 1963. However, the song was originally written and recorded by R&B artist Richard Berry in 1957. Take a moment to listen to the Richard Berry recording and take note of the traits we discussed in the 1950s. The song is built on the melody of "El Loco Cha Cha," which was made famous by René Touzet, a Cuban-born American bandleader, composer, and pianist. The song has a simple verse-chorus form, from the first-person perspective of a Jamaican sailor returning home to see his lover. The song utilizes the popular I-IV-V chord progression, but with a minor V instead of the usual major version of the chord. This three-chord sequence, bass line, and stop-time rhythm was inspired by the tumbao.

The tumbao is a basic rhythm played on the bass in Afro-Cuban music, which is the rhythmic pattern used in "El Loco Cha Cha," 1-2-3, 1-2, 1-2-3, 1-2. Take a moment to listen to "El Loco Cha Cha" and count along with the rhythm to get a feel for the Afro-Cuban influence.

In 1961, Rockin' Robin Roberts and the Wailers, out of Tacoma, Washington, released their recording of "Louie Louie." A few notable things in this recording are Robin Roberts's style of singing, his use of screams, and an almost southern pronunciation. Roberts was heavily influenced by R&B, as you can hear with his riffing off of phrases, and one of the most iconic rock moments in history, his scream of "right now!" If you listen to the Richard Berry version and then the Robin Roberts version, you will also notice the bending of the pronunciation Roberts uses (instead of "Louie" with a pure /i/ ending, we hear "Louie" as "Lou-aye"), and Roberts also adds in the "yea yea yea yea-ea-ea" in between phrases. More than likely, the Kingsmen, who were from Portland, Oregon, were most inspired by the Rockin' Robin Roberts and the Wailers version.

When listening to the vocals of the Kingsmen, it is difficult to understand the lyrics. It is so difficult that the 1963 recording ended up being banned from radio waves in Indiana by Governor Matthew Walsh; it was also banned in many other towns across America. Rumors stirred up among teens along with urban legends that the Kingsmen intentionally slurred the words because the lyrics were pornographic and profane. The controversy became so large that the FBI did a thirty-one-month investigation but concluded that they were "unable to interpret any of the wording in the record."[29] However, if you listen closely at 0:54 of the song, you can hear the drummer Lynn Easton yell the "f-word" after messing up a drum fill. Had this been recognized, the song surely would have been banned from the airwaves.

Unlike in the Berry and Roberts versions, in the Kingsmen version, there are no brass instruments. It is electric guitars, bass, drums, and voice. The band has said that the song was a demo that they were going to use for a cruise ship gig. The recording studio placed the microphone so high that Ely had to stand on his toes to sing, creating the signature muffled diction of the song. The recording studio purposely made the microphone higher because the recording engineer thought the vocals were too loud.[30]

"Louie Louie" is one of the most covered rock songs in the world. The Kingsmen version, however, is by far the most influential not only for covers of the song but also for future rockers in general. Alec Palao said it best in 2002 in the "Love That Louie" CD booklet:

> This is truly the quintessential garage band moment, an audio-vérité snapshot that communicates directly what red-blooded grass roots American rock 'n' roll is all about . . . the Kingsmen's "Louie Louie" spills forth with a rush of teenage hormones: raw, untutored yet seemingly ready to take on the world.[31]

What to Listen For in the Song

Gritty and Raw Voice   Ely's voice has a gritty quality, giving the song a rough and edgy feel. This rawness adds to the rebellious and energetic nature of the performance.

Mumbled and Indistinct Pronunciation   One of the most distinctive features of Ely's vocals in "Louie Louie" is the mumbled and almost indecipherable pronunciation of the lyrics. This quality ends up influencing punk, hard rock, and grunge music in the years to come.

Emphatic Shouting   The shouts are rooted in gospel and the blues and are a key feature of garage rock. Similar to the muffled diction, this trait also influenced punk and hard rock music in future decades.

Unpolished and Untamed Quality   Ely's vocals have an unpolished quality and have no connection to formal singing techniques. This raw approach contributes to the garage rock aesthetic of the performance, which was a defining feature of the mid-1960s rock 'n' roll sound.

Psychedelic Rock

Psychedelic rock came out of the hippie culture movement from San Francisco and solidified in the late 1960s. It was influenced by hallucinogens such as LSD and marijuana, and the mind-expanding use of these drugs was then reflected in the music with the use of intense volumes, electronic instruments, and feedback.[32] With the rise of psychedelic drugs, many musicians found inspiration under the influence, which shaped their creative process. Their aim was not only to make people dance, as in earlier rock music, but also to transport their listeners on a unique trip through their music.

Some of the first psychedelic rock bands were the Grateful Dead, the Doors, the Charlatans, Jefferson Airplane, the Byrds, 13th Floor Elevators, and Jimi Hendrix. Notable albums from this genre include *The Psychedelic Sounds of the 13th Floor Elevators* by the 13th Floor Elevators, *Strange Days* by the Doors, and *Surrealistic Pillow* by Jefferson Airplane.

"White Rabbit" (1966)
Jefferson Airplane

"White Rabbit" was written by Grace Slick, lead singer of Jefferson Airplane, in the winter of 1965–1966. She used imagery from Lewis Carroll's *Alice's Adventures in Wonderland* and *Through the Looking-Glass*. She said the song was a commentary on how parents read their children novels with fanciful imagery, such as taking a pill or drinking something unknown, which causes the character to change size or talk to animals, and then the parents wonder why their children later used drugs.[33] It was one of the first songs to use drug references that got past censors on the radio.

Slick was heavily influenced by Miles Davis's "Concierto de Aranjuez" and Ravel's "Bolero." You can hear the influence of "Bolero" and its continuous crescendo throughout "White Rabbit." She later stated, "Writing weird stuff about Alice backed by a dark Spanish march was in step with what was going on in San Francisco then. We were all trying to get as far away from the expected as possible."[34]

What to Listen For in the Song

Distinctive Tone Grace Slick has a unique and powerful vocal tone. Her voice is rich, deep, and slightly husky, which adds to the song's mysterious and enigmatic atmosphere.

Dramatic Pacing and Phrasing Notice the delivery of the lyrics. They are deliberate and measured, emphasizing psychedelic and surreal imagery. Slick does not rush the words, allowing the listener to absorb the meaning behind them. She also uses expressive phrasing to emphasize specific words and phrases, drawing attention to key elements of the lyrics. By using these techniques, the listener can go on a "trip" with the artist.

Articulation The articulation and clarity of the lyrics ensures that every word is heard, even amidst the psychedelic instrumentals. This clarity is essential for conveying the song's narrative effectively.

Vocal Control Slick demonstrates excellent vocal control, especially in the way she smoothly transitions between different vocal registers.

This control makes it easier for her to sing in her higher belt range with power and ease.

Playful Vocal Ornamentation and Vibrato In certain parts of the song, Slick adds playful vocal ornamentation, such as turns, ornaments, and subtle vocal slides. These embellishments contribute to the song's whimsical and dreamlike atmosphere. Also, notice the speed of her vibrato as the song intensifies, which adds some tension to the end of the song.

British Blues Rock

Between 1949 and 1960, the British government put significant restrictions on imports, including records. This made it difficult for Brits to access American music. However, wealthy collectors could find their way around the bans, as did some dealers, and only a few were caught and fined. Another source of records were sales from black American GIs who brought the albums with them while serving in England.[35] After the import ban was lifted, Britain experienced a renewed interest in the blues, especially among white audiences.[36]

The London-based blues scene in the 1960s yielded a host of influential rock musicians, including Eric Clapton, John Mayall, and Stevie Winwood, as well as the formidable songwriting duo of guitarist Keith Richards and vocalist Mick Jagger. Both Clapton and Mayall, along with Richards and Jagger, participated in the Korner and Davies sessions as teenagers, solidifying their places within the burgeoning musical movement.[37] Notable British blues bands from the 1960s are the Animals, Cream, Fleetwood Mac, the Yardbirds, and the Rolling Stones.

"(I Can't Get No) Satisfaction" (1965)

The Rolling Stones

The Rolling Stones came together as a band in 1962 in London following Mick Jagger and Keith Richards's time in a blues band known as the Blues Boys. Their interactions with members of Blues Incorporated, including Brian Jones and Ian Stewart, led to the forming of the Rolling Stones after Jones placed an ad for bandmates in *Jazz Weekly*. Brian Jones, the uncontested leader of the group at the time, named the group when a journalist from *Jazz News* asked their name. He said the first thing that came to mind was "Rollin' Stone," the name of a song on Muddy Waters's LP.[38]

The Rolling Stones were heavily influenced by Chicago-based blues and rock 'n' roll artists such as Chuck Berry and Buddy Holly. Their first single was a cover version of "Come On" by Chuck Berry. The single reached number 21 in the U.K. Singles Chart. Their third single was a cover of Buddy Holly's "Not Fade Away," which reflected Bo Diddley's style, and was released in 1964, earning it number 3 in the United Kingdom. The Rolling Stones's first international hit was "(I Can't Get No) Satisfaction," which was recorded and released in 1965.[39]

What to Listen For in the Song

Rhythmic Pacing Jagger's vocal rhythm aligns perfectly with the musical arrangement. He emphasizes certain syllables and words, syncing his delivery with the driving beat of the song.

Distinctive Phrasing Listen to how he elongates certain words and adds a distinctive drawl, giving the lyrics a bluesy quality. For example, the way he sings "no" in the line "I can't get no satisfaction" adds emphasis and character to the phrase.

Expressive Tone Jagger starts with an almost whispery, lyric tone; eventually adds more of a speechlike quality with "I tried, and I tried"; and then gets to a more aggressive, almost yelling quality at the chorus. He shifts in and out of these tones throughout the song in a way to express the meaning of the song.

Registration In the chorus, Jagger uses a chest-dominant mix belt and then flips to a heady mix for the lines "I can't get no satisfaction" at the beginning of the verses. Throughout the song, he shifts through different registrations. This change in vocal texture adds contrast to the song and makes the chorus stand out.

Ad-Libbed Phrases Throughout the song, there are ad-libbed phrases and vocalizations, adding spontaneity and a sense of improvisation to his performance. This is a trait that is rooted in the blues.

Progressive/Art Rock

Progressive/art rock's roots came from pop groups of the 1960s who used new recording techniques and a concept around a central theme to progress rock music. Albums such as the Beach Boys' *Pet Sounds* (1966) and the Beatles' *Sgt. Pepper's Lonely Hearts Club Band* (1967) were among the most influential pop-turned-progressive albums of this decade. Not only were recording techniques exploited with new technology, but there was also a blending of electric blues with a variety of other music styles, such as Asian melodies, Indian ragas, and classical music and orchestrations.[40] The progressive/art rock that was created in the late 1960s influenced the huge wave of progressive rock bands in the 1970s.

Progressive/art rock not only used more complicated rhythmic patterns than its pop counterparts but also would sometimes feature symphony orchestras or "pseudo-orchestral ensembles" to enhance the standard guitar, bass, keyboard, and drums. Reworkings of classical compositions were not out of the question either. Lyrics were often highly imaginative and generally unified, hence the term "concept album."[41] The goal of these concept albums and experimenting with new/old sounds was not necessarily to get people moving and dancing but rather for listening and meditation. Along with the Beach Boys and the Beatles, other bands of the progressive/art movement of the 1960s were the Velvet Underground, Pink Floyd, Procol Harum, Vanilla Fudge, and the Moody Blues.

"Nights in White Satin" (1967)

The Moody Blues

The Moody Blues were formed in 1964 by musicians who had been playing the blues and R&B around Birmingham, England. They started off performing mainly covers of Motown and blues and achieved their initial success with a cover of an R&B song called "Go Now," which reached number 10 on the charts in 1965 as a British beat band along with R&B influences. However, they were unable to repeat that success and started considering new directions. The group bought one of the first digital synthesizers called a Mellotron with the intent of recording a rock version of Dvorak's Symphony no. 9 but instead used the studio time to record *Days of Future Passed*. The album had psychedelic lyrics combined with complex orchestral orchestrations and was a large stepping stone for the development of the concept album, art rock, and progressive rock.[42]

What to Listen For in the Song

Smooth and Mellow Tone Justin Hayward's voice in "Nights in White Satin" is smooth and mellow, creating a calming and dreamy atmosphere that complements the song's mood.

Emotional Expression The song has a sense of longing, and the way in which Hayward has an almost sigh-like quality to his singing accentuates his desire for his love. He also uses cry-like sounds throughout the song, particularly in the lead-up to the chorus along with the chorus itself.

Vocal Range The song is sung in Hayward's mixed registration, moving seamlessly between soft, intimate passages and powerful, soaring moments. He uses a mix belt rather than a chest belt.

Phrasing and Timing Hayward lingers on the ends of the phrases and on consonants, using a dreamlike quality in his voice. The use of the phrase weighting and impeccable timing contributes to the song's overall impact.

Sustained Notes Hayward holds certain notes for extended periods, creating a sense of lingering emotion. This technique is particularly notable in the chorus, where he sustains the "You" from the line "I love you."

1970s

The 1970s was a grand time for rock music, and it is impossible to give a brief history lesson on this period because so much came out of this decade of popular music. Narrowing down genres is a feat in itself. The genres we explored in the 1960s continued to evolve and influenced what was to come, and those genres sometimes merged with other genres to create new subgenres of music. In this section, I will focus on five genres of rock that influenced the rock music that was created in the 1980s. Those genres are blues-based British rock, American southern blues and rock, glam and goth rock, arena rock, and punk rock.

Blues-Based British Rock

The British blues rock scene changed by the early 1970s due to the hippie movement, particularly Woodstock in 1969, and psychedelic music. The "hippie aesthetic," a term used by music historian John Covach, is the idea that rock artists should make music that is enlightened and that they should make that music by any means they can. Similar to progressive rock in the 1960s, this music was not necessarily made for dancing but more for listening. Some of the greatest rock groups who were the front-runners of the movement were the Yardbirds, Cream, the Rolling Stones, Led Zeppelin, and Deep Purple. The blues-based British rock genre started to dwindle out by the mid- to late 1970s, when mainstream rock, punk rock, and progressive rock started to take over the airwaves.[43] However, this genre still left a strong footprint on rock music for years to come, influencing some of the greatest rock artists in the 1980s until today.

Led Zeppelin may be the most influential of the groups of this genre throughout the 1970s. They blended blues, acoustic, and psychedelic components in their music. Some of the songs would focus more on a certain element than others, but overall, they were still a British blues band that used a lot of experimentation when producing their music.[44] One of the best examples of this is their famous recording of "Stairway to Heaven." The opening is acoustic, and then the electric guitar, bass, and drums are finally introduced. Both Robert Plant and Jimmy Page were fascinated by "mythology, Middle Earth fantasy and the occult."[45] It is no surprise the lyrics deal with spiritual enlightenment, which resonates with the hippie movement of the late 1960s. The last section then moves to heavy rock as Plant belts out high falsetto wailing, almost resembling that of the blues-based guitar solo played by Page. Another example of this genre is Deep Purple's "Highway Star," which is said to have influenced heavy metal later that decade.

"Highway Star" (1972)

Deep Purple

Deep Purple was formed in London in 1968. At one time, the band was listed as the loudest rock band by the *Guinness Book of World Records*.[46] From their beginning, they fused blues-based rock with classical music. One of their first album, *Concerto for Group and Orchestra*, featured a symphony orchestra.

"Highway Star" was written on a tour bus in 1971. Ritchie Blackmore started a riff on an acoustic guitar on a G chord and kept playing it over and over. Ian Gillan, who not only was the lead vocalist but also previously recorded Andrew Lloyd Webber's rock opera *Jesus Christ Superstar* as Jesus, improvised lyrics. That night, they refined the song live.[47] "Highway Star" is the first track on their studio album *Machine Head*, and it is the fastest-tempo song on the entire album. Continuing with their classical merger in rock music, there are two large instrumental sections in the song featuring solos, one for guitar and the other for keyboard. Both of these solos are structured more like a baroque cantata than a blues-based solo. Although the solos are classically influenced, particularly by Bach, the rhythm still has the 2-4 influence from blues rock, and the vocals are far from operatic singing.

What to Listen For in the Song

High-Pitched Screams   One of the most distinctive features of Ian Gillan's vocals in "Highway Star" is his high-pitched screams. His ability to hit and sustain extremely high notes, particularly during the song's chorus, is remarkable. His screams add a sense of urgency and excitement to the track.

Raw and Powerful   Gillan's vocal delivery in "Highway Star" is raw and powerful. His voice has a gritty edge that complements the hard-hitting instrumentation of the song. This style of singing is characteristic of classic hard rock and early heavy metal music.

Dynamic Range   Note the wide dynamic range as he moves between softer, melodic passages in the verses and the explosive, high-energy choruses and screams. This contrast in dynamics adds depth and excitement to the song.

Distinctive Timbre   Gillan's vocal timbre is unique and easily recognizable. His voice has a raspy quality that sets him apart from many other rock and metal vocalists of his era and is part of his signature sound.

Versatility   Gillan's vocal versatility is evident in "Highway Star." He seamlessly transitions between different vocal styles, including traditional singing, screams, and more aggressive, edgier tones. This versatility is a hallmark of his singing throughout his career.

American Southern Blues Rock

American southern blues rock is often referred to as American blues rock or southern rock. However, because the two genres have similar traits and the objective of this chapter is to discuss broad influences on rock, I have decided to merge the two titles.

The influence of British blues rock in the 1960s extended into the 1970s in America, particularly in the southern regions, which is why many rock history scholars spend a lot of time focusing on the southeastern part of America when discussing this genre. The Allman Brothers, Lynyrd Skynyrd, the Marshall Tucker Band, and the Charlie Daniels Band, all of whom were from the southeastern part of America, were the most popular southern rock bands of the era. However, this same music was found in other parts of the country. Creedence Clearwater Revival, the Doobie Brothers, and the Eagles all formed in California. Steely Dan formed in New York, and ZZ Top formed in Texas. Labeling this music as southern rock was a way for record companies to categorize music that wasn't quite country, folk, rock, psychedelic, or blues but all of these elements in one.[48]

All these bands have their own regional flair to their style as well. However, one band that is rarely mentioned from this same era that helped inspire the Go-Go's, the Bangles, and the Runaways was Fanny, an all-female band from California with roots in the Philippines.

"Charity Ball" (1971)

Fanny

Fanny was one of the first all-female hard rock groups to sign with a major label. The two major members of the group, June and Jean Millington, were sisters born in the Philippines. They moved to Sacramento, California, when they were eleven and nine years old, respectively, and formed their first four-piece band, the Svelts, in high school. The sisters played in a series of different bands; the last one before they became Fanny was Wild Honey, which was a Motown cover group. In 1969, at the Troubadour in Los Angeles, well-known record producer Richard Perry's secretary discovered the band while looking for an all-girl rock group.[49]

The group changed their name to Fanny when they signed with Warner Bros. because the band thought of the term as encompassing a woman's spirit that would look over the band. However, the label thought of them as a novelty act and launched a marketing campaign for the band that sexualized the group. It included ads that featured photos of the bandmates taken from the back along with bumper stickers stating "Get Behind Fanny."[50] The group struggled to gain fans, who could not see past the fact that they were an all-girl group. However, one of their biggest supporters was David Bowie, who stated in a 1999 *Rolling Stone* article,

> "They were extraordinary: they wrote everything, they played like motherfuckers, they were just colossal and wonderful, and nobody's ever mentioned them. They're as important as anybody else who's ever been, ever; it just wasn't their time."[51]

Let's explore "Charity Ball," which was their first chart single at number 40 on the Billboard Hot 100.

What to Listen For in the Song

Harmonious Vocals "Charity Ball" features tight harmonies and layered vocals. The band members, including June Millington, Jean Millington, and Nickey Barclay, provided strong vocal harmonies that were characteristic of Fanny's sound.

Rock and Blues Influences Fanny's vocal style in this song incorporates elements of rock and blues. The lead vocals, often sung by June Millington, have a bluesy quality with a strong and emotive delivery. The head voice "woos" are a direct link to blues and gospel. There are even moments of yelling and a gritty sound, reminiscent of early rock and blues.

Versatile Vocals Fanny was known for their versatility, and their vocal performances in "Charity Ball" demonstrate this. The vocalists transition between softer, more melodic passages and harder, more powerful moments, showcasing their vocal range and ability to convey different emotions within the song.

Glam and Goth Rock

Glam and goth rock are genres that rely heavily on the performance aspect of the music to create a fantasy world onstage. The genres are rooted in the tradition of concept albums like *Sgt. Pepper's Lonely Hearts Club Band*, in which the Beatles are the Lonely Hearts Club, and Jim Morrison of the Doors portraying *The Lizard King*. Both glam and goth rock were a product of psychedelia in that the music took you on a trip. Because rock concerts in the 1970s started to become bigger, many concerts were performed in arenas or stadiums as opposed to ballrooms and clubs. The venues were so large that they could accommodate stage lighting, special effects, costuming, and sets and props, along with unconventional performances of the time. This allowed rock bands to further explore the performance aspect of their music, creating a whole fantasy world onstage. These theatrical elements are why these genres are often referred to under the umbrella of rock theater. However, glam and goth rock were unique not only in their performance styles but also in their music, particularly in the subject of the songs and often the singing voice of the front man.[52]

Glam rockers generally wore showy costumes that were colorful, sparkly, and sometimes skintight with an opening from the neck down to just an inch or so below the belly button. The performers also often wore makeup, had outrageous hairstyles and/or wigs, and in the 1970s and 1980s would also wear platform shoes, creating a sense of androgyny. This is somewhat similar to Little Richard's performance style in the 1950s and then again in the 1970s. Richard was one of the first male rockers create an alter ego, wear makeup, colorful clothing, and wigs onstage. David Bowie was one of the first glam rockers, and one of his most famous alter egos was Ziggy Stardust. Other famous glam rockers were Queen, Elton John, T. Rex, and the New York Dolls.

Goth rock was similar to glam rock in that there were costumes, makeup, alter egos, and so on. However, goth rock was much darker not only with costumes, props, and sets but also in subject matter. One of the pioneers of goth rock was Alice Cooper.

"Cold Ethyl" (1975)

Alice Cooper

Alice Cooper was originally Vincent Furnier, who was born in 1948 in Detroit. He formed his band in Phoenix but then moved to Los Angeles in 1968. The band had several name changes along the way, changing from the Earwigs to the Spider and eventually to the Nazz. According to Alice Cooper, they landed on the name of "Alice Cooper" from a Ouija board that told them it was the name of a seventeenth-century witch who was reincarnated as Furnier.[53]

Alice Cooper performances often ended with mock guillotines, hangings, and beheadings of himself. Unlike Bowie, Cooper kept the same alter ego throughout his career, and the performances became more campy and over the top but still dark. His 1975 solo album *Welcome to My Nightmare*, which became one of his most represented albums on his set lists, was initially met with mixed reviews. Many considered it less hard, with no grit, and some even considered the music corny. In 1975, the production of *Alice Cooper: The Nightmare* as a prime-time TV special, coupled with his appearances on *The Hollywood Squares*, signified his acceptance as a mainstream artist.[54]

"Cold Ethyl" is an example of the darker, edgier side of Alice Cooper's writing.

What to Listen For in the Song

Sinister and Seductive Throughout the song, Alice Cooper's vocals exude a sinister and seductive quality, adding to the dark and provocative nature of the song. His delivery conveys a sense of eerie allure as he sings about his desire for "Cold Ethyl."

Range The range that Alice Cooper uses in this song is limited, sticking mainly to chest and chest-mix registration.

Playful and Lyrical Wordplay Cooper's lyrics in "Cold Ethyl" contain playful and lyrical wordplay. He personifies "Cold Ethyl" as a lifeless yet captivating companion, and his vocal delivery captures the playful and darkly humorous elements of the song's narrative.

Grit and Tightness Although the majority of Alice Cooper's singing on the album *Welcome to My Nightmare* is less gritty, in "Cold Ethyl," he adds the grit back in. There is also a sense of a high and tight laryngeal position throughout the song. Often in the chorus, he goes in and out of the grit and a "cleaner" sound.

Moans and Speech From the very beginning of the song, we hear Cooper ad-libbing little moans or words. His first sung phrase starts with a growl-like moan. Throughout the song, you can hear screams as well. Listen carefully to how he ends his phrases. The ends of the phrases often take on a speechlike quality.

Arena Rock

The 1970s saw the rise of arena rock, a genre characterized by larger-than-life performances in arenas and stadiums. Technological advancements played a pivotal role in the evolution of this genre. Recording technology advancements enabled more complex writing and arranging. Innovations in sound reinforcement technology enabled concerts to be hosted in larger venues without compromising audio quality, and sophisticated lighting setups contributed to the visual spectacle. The emergence of FM radio was also pivotal in this genre's growth.

Many bands in the 1970s started writing longer songs, following in the footsteps of the psychedelic genre. These songs did not fit into AM radio's preference for three-minute songs. AM's reduced audio quality and mono format also meant that listeners could not fully appreciate the more complex recordings these bands were making. When FM technology came into being, the Federal Communications Commission banned FM stations from rebroadcasting AM programming for more than 50 percent of the day, which meant that FM stations had to find their own way to stand out. Since these stations were new and not beholden to advertisers to the same degree as AM stations, they had the freedom to experiment with playing new music. This allowed them to push the larger-than-life music of bands like Heart that were ignored by traditional AM stations.[55]

"Crazy on You" (1976)

Heart

The band Heart was formed in Seattle, Washington, in 1973 by sisters Ann Wilson (vocals) and Nancy Wilson (guitar), alongside other members including Roger Fisher (guitar), Steve Fossen (bass), and Michael Derosier (drums). Ann was part of an all-male group formed by Fossen and Fischer named the Army, but they changed their name to White Heart and then shortened it to Heart by 1974, when Nancy joined the group.[56] They achieved significant success with their blend of rock, folk, and hard rock elements.

One of their most iconic songs, "Crazy on You," was released as the lead track on their debut album *Dreamboat Annie* in 1976. The song showcased Ann Wilson's powerful vocals and Nancy Wilson's intricate acoustic guitar work and quickly became one of their signature tunes. The song begins with a fingerpicked acoustic guitar intro and gradually builds into a powerful rock anthem. The combination of folk-inspired acoustic passages and hard-rocking electric guitar riffs made it a unique and memorable track.

What to Listen For in the Song

Singing Style Ann Wilson's vocal style in "Crazy on You" is a striking blend of rock and folk elements. She begins the song with a soft, almost ethereal folk-style singing, which is characterized by a gentle and controlled delivery. This style helps create an intimate and mysterious atmosphere at the start of the song.

Buildup As the song progresses, Ann's vocals gradually build in intensity. Her voice becomes stronger and more forceful, reflecting the song's growing emotional intensity. This buildup culminates in a powerful and raspy delivery during the song's rockier sections, showcasing her impressive vocal range.

Belting Ann Wilson is known for her impressive belting ability, and she demonstrates it in "Crazy on You." Ann uses both chest and mix belt seamlessly to convey the song's passionate and wild emotions, particularly in the chorus and toward the end of the song.

Punk Rock

Punk rock, which started in New York City in the late 1960s in the underground rock scene, was the least mainstream rock genre of the 1970s. Punk rock is more than just a genre; it's a subculture and a movement that challenges the norms of mainstream society. Similar to glam/goth rock and garage rock, the roots of punk rock can be traced back to the emergence of various countercultural and rebellious movements from the 1950s and 1960s. A contributing influence to punk was the emergence of beat generation writers such as Anna Waldman, Ted Berrigan, and Allen Ginsberg, all of whom influenced both Patti Smith and Richard Hell in their music writing.[57]

Another major influence on punk is the do-it-yourself (DIY) ethos. Major record labels, particularly in the United States, would not sign punk artists due to language, subject matter, and the aggressively loud music. To get their music heard, the bands self-produced their albums, designed their own album covers, and organized their own performance calendars. This DIY ethos helped create a network of punk artists who created their own subculture that has lasted almost fifty years.[58]

American bands like Iggy (Pop) and the Stooges, MC5, and the New York Dolls laid the foundation with their raw, high-energy music and rebellious attitudes. However, punk became more hard-core and solidified when it got to the United Kingdom in the mid-1970s. Major labels in the United States either would not sign hard-core punk because the music would not be featured on the air due to censorship laws or would tone down the music and create "new wave" music. New wave or post-punk artists include the Velvet Underground, Devo, Blondie, Elvis Costello, and Siouxsie and the Banshees along with many others. This subgenre of punk had more of a pop feel and used a lot of dance beats along with synthesizers. It gained more airplay than its more abrasive cousin and became increasingly experimental as it evolved in the 1980s.

In the United Kingdom, however, a major recession took place in the 1970s with high inflation, unemployment, and economic instability. This caused widespread frustration and disillusionment among the youth. Many young people faced limited job prospects, and the economic uncertainty fueled a sense of alienation and anger. Gone were the days of peace and love from the hippie movement. Teens were throwing away their love beads and trading them for safety pins and torn clothing. They were cutting their hair and spiking it up. The music they were making went back to the earlier form of 1950s rock 'n' roll, using fast, hard-driving drums, guitar, and bass along with screaming punctuated vocals.

The emergence of punk music and its associated culture stemmed from a desire to rebel against societal norms and the perceived failures of the establishment. The Sex Pistols, in particular, embodied this spirit of rebellion, expressing anger and frustration through their music, lyrics, and onstage antics.

"Anarchy in the U.K." (1975)

Sex Pistols

Socioeconomic frustration found a unique outlet through the rebellious spirit of punk music and culture, thanks largely to Malcolm McLaren. McLaren was the owner of the London clothing boutique Sex, which specialized in "anti-fashion." In 1975, McLaren, having previously managed the New York Dolls during their final months as a band, conceived the idea of a rock 'n' roll act that would challenge established norms and conventions.

Glen Matlock, who was a part-time employee of Sex, played in a band with Paul Cook and Steve Jones. Matlock told McLaren that they were looking for a singer, and McLaren immediately thought of nineteen-year-old John Lydon, who had been a familiar face around the jukebox at Sex and was known for his brashness. Despite having never sung before, Lydon made a lasting impression with his raw charisma and was later rechristened as Johnny Rotten. With McLaren's guidance, the group took on the name "Sex Pistols."

The Sex Pistols kicked off their gig circuit toward the end of 1975, and McLaren orchestrated a clever word-of-mouth campaign. By November 1976, they had signed a deal with EMI and released their debut single, "Anarchy in the U.K." However, due to an infamous televised interview in which they used the word "fucker," EMI dropped the band. The resulting outrage prompted local authorities to cancel most of their scheduled national tour dates and led EMI to withdraw "Anarchy in the U.K." from circulation. McLaren eventually was able to sign the band with Virgin Records in 1977, but the series of controversies and clashes with the music establishment only solidified the Sex Pistols' reputation as rebellious troublemaking punk icons.[59]

"Anarchy in the U.K." is a seminal punk rock track with a distinctive sound characterized by its raw, aggressive vocals and a straightforward musical structure. The song is considered one of the defining anthems of the punk rock movement in the late 1970s.

What to Listen For in the Song

Snarling and Aggressive Rotten's vocals are characterized by a snarling, sneering, and confrontational tone. This style of singing is a hallmark of punk rock and adds a rebellious, antiestablishment edge to the song.

Grit and Shouting The vocals used by Rotten are generally gritty. He also shouts out certain words like "Christ." His unpolished and unapologetic vocals are a reflection of the DIY ethos of punk. Rotten's delivery is not about technical perfection but about expressing attitude and discontent.

Pronunciation Rotten is using his British accent, but it is also mixed with a consistently open vowel sound, resembling a constant yell. This sound is an amped-up version of what we heard in 1960s garage rock, and we hear this morph into the vocal stylings used by grunge and pop punk bands from the 1990s to 2020s.

Rebellious Lyrics Rotten's lyrics in "Anarchy in the U.K." are provocative and rebellious. They critique the establishment and express a desire for anarchy and chaos. This lyrical content is a prime example of the punk rock ethos.

1980s

In the 1980s, most of the rock genres had already developed, and rock artists began blending them together to create unique sounds and/or subgenres while other artists remained true to the roots of the genres they performed. Several factors contributed to the proliferation of subgenres, including the birth of a twenty-four-hour cable music video network in the 1980s and the subsequent technological advancements that occurred from the late 1990s to today.

The emergence of Music Television (MTV) played a pivotal role in the development and growth of subgenres during the 1980s and 1990s. It provided a platform for artists to showcase not only their music but also their visual creativity. Rock bands in particular embraced this opportunity to create visually captivating and often highly theatrical music videos, shaping the look and style of 1980s rock. This exposure propelled lesser-known rock bands to fame and maintained the popularity of established acts.[60]

In this section, we will analyze five significant rock artists from the 1980s. These artists were chosen based on their popularity, what they were influenced by, and their influence on future generations.

New Wave

"We Got the Beat" (1980)

The Go-Go's

The Go-Go's were formed in 1978 in Los Angeles. They were one of the first all-female rock groups to earn a top *Billboard* 100 single. The original lineup consisted of Belinda Carlisle (vocals), Jane Wiedlin (guitar, vocals), Charlotte Caffey (lead guitar, keyboards), Kathy Valentine (bass), and Gina Schock (drums). They began as a punk rock band, playing in small venues around Los Angeles, where the punk scene was lighter and more melodic than the edgier punk scene in the United Kingdom and the darker punk scene in New York City at the time. They modeled their music on bands like the Buzzcocks and the Clash, who were more melodic than the Sex Pistols and other harder punk bands. Soon, they merged into the new wave genre that would take over the airwaves and MTV throughout the 1980s.[61] The use of synthesizers, along with catchy melodies and harmonies, helped create this shift and in turn made their music more commercially successful.

In 1981, the Go-Go's released their debut album, *Beauty and the Beat*, which became a massive commercial success. The album featured hits like "Our Lips Are Sealed" and "We Got the Beat." *Beauty and the Beat* was a breakthrough for the band, as it topped the charts and became one of the best-selling albums of the year.[62]

Some of the artists that influenced the Go-Go's were Fanny, the Beach Boys, the Germs, the Shangri-Las, the Shirelles, the Clash, and the Buzzcocks. Some of the artists that the Go-Go's influenced were Green Day, Avril Lavigne, No Doubt, Sleater-Kinney, and the Donnas. Other notable new wave bands and artists from the 1980s are Depeche Mode, the Cure, Blondie, Talking Heads, Duran Duran, the Smiths, and the Police.

What to Listen For in the Song

Energetic and Upbeat In "We Got the Beat," Belinda Carlisle sings with a lively and cheerful tone that complements the song's theme of having a good time and dancing to the beat. This style goes back to a garage rock feel rather than a punk feel.

Bright and Clear For the most part, Carlisle's voice has a bright and clear quality, which is well suited to the pop and new wave genre of the Go-Go's. Her diction and articulation are excellent, making the lyrics easy to understand. These qualities resemble those of Brian Wilson from the surf rock genre.

Vowels Carlisle's vowel choices resemble the same vowel choices used in 1970s punk. The vowel choices are mainly open with a rare diphthong.

Harmonious and Melodic The Go-Go's are known for their harmonious vocals, and in "We Got the Beat," Belinda Carlisle's singing is a key component of the band's tight harmonies. Her melodic lines blend seamlessly with the backing vocals of the other band members.

Heavy Metal

"Whiplash" (1983)

Metallica

Metallica was formed in Los Angeles in 1981 by drummer Lars Ulrich and guitarist/vocalist James Hetfield. Ulrich was born in Denmark, and his father wanted him to be a professional tennis player like himself. Hetfield grew up in a strict Christian Science home; his father owned a trucking company, while his mother was a light-opera singer.[63] They were later joined by lead guitarist Dave Mustaine and bassist Ron McGovney, who was replaced in 1982 by Cliff Burton.[64] In 1983, Mustaine was kicked out of the band due to his excessive drinking and aggressive behavior. He was replaced by guitarist Kirk Hammett, and this change marked a significant turning point in the band's sound. Metallica released their debut album, *Kill 'Em All*, in 1983, and it was a groundbreaking record for the thrash metal genre. The band's fast, aggressive, and intricate style set them apart. The album is a wild cry of gloom and anarchy. They originally wanted to name the album "Metal Up Your Ass," but they feared that distributors would not stock it because it would have been too explicit. Bassist Cliff Burton is credited with coming up with the name "Kill 'Em All" after stating, "Those record company fuckers . . . kill 'em all!" as a response to why they had to choose another title for the album.[65]

"Whiplash" became the album's debut single on August 8, 1983. This track is characterized by a rapid rhythm consisting of straight sixteenth notes, keeping a brisk pace of around two hundred beats per minute. Hetfield and Burton showcased their skills with precise metronomic control and the use of palm-muted techniques on the guitar. The song is about celebrating the energy of a crowd and the headbanging experience. According to rock journalist Mick Wall, "Whiplash" marked the birth of thrash metal, a defining moment in the genre's history. "If one wishes to identify the very moment thrash metal arrived spitting and snarling into the world, 'Whiplash' is indisputably it."[66]

Some of the artists that influenced Metallica were Jimi Hendrix, Deep Purple, MC5, Black Sabbath, Thin Lizzy, Led Zeppelin, Lynyrd Skynyrd, the Stooges, Judas Priest, and Merciful Fate. Some of the artists that Metallica influenced were Korn, Slipknot, Lamb of God, and Avenged Sevenfold. Other notable heavy metal bands from the 1980s include Guns N' Roses, Quiet Riot, Twisted Sister, Dio, Ozzy Osbourne, Judas Priest, Iron Maiden, and Slayer.

What to Listen For in the Song

Aggressive Tone Hetfield uses a growling and aggressive vocal tone that complements the fast-paced and heavy instrumentation of the song. This tone adds intensity to the lyrics and enhances the overall impact of the performance.

Screaming and Shouting Hetfield incorporates screaming and shouting techniques in certain parts of the song, particularly during intense moments and the chorus. These same qualities can be heard in Rob Tyner of MC5 and other punk artists from the 1970s. These techniques add a raw and visceral quality to his vocals, emphasizing the song's aggressive nature.

Rapid Phrasing In "Whiplash," Hetfield often sings with rapid phrasing, keeping up with the song's rapid tempo and contributing to its high-energy feel. He articulates the lyrics quickly and precisely, enhancing the song's intensity. This resembles the same phrasing qualities that were used in "Anarchy in the U.K." by the Sex Pistols.

Powerful Projection Hetfield projects his voice powerfully to cut through the heavy instrumentation. His strong vocal projection ensures that his lyrics are heard clearly amidst the intense guitar riffs and drumbeats. His loud, high screams resemble the same qualities Jack Ely used in "Louie Louie."

Heartland Rock

"Born in the U.S.A." (1985)

Bruce Springsteen

Bruce Springsteen was born on September 23, 1949, in Long Branch, New Jersey. He grew up in a working-class family, the son of a bus driver and a secretary.[67] At age seven, he decided that he wanted to be a musician after seeing Elvis Presley on the *Ed Sullivan Show*.[68] In 1964, he saw the Beatles perform on the *Ed Sullivan Show* several times. This, in turn, influenced thirteen-year-old Bruce to purchase his first guitar.[69] Springsteen began his musical journey in the late 1960s and early 1970s, performing in various bands around the New Jersey music scene. In 1972, he signed a record deal with Columbia Records and released his debut album, *Greetings from Asbury Park, N.J.* The album received critical acclaim but had modest commercial success.

His big breakthrough came with the release of *Born to Run* in 1975, which featured the title track and other classics like "Thunder Road" and "Jungleland." The album established Springsteen as a major rock star. The 1980s saw Springsteen release the album *Nebraska*, a stark departure from his usual sound, showcasing his acoustic storytelling abilities. He then released *Born in the U.S.A.* in 1984, which became one of the best-selling albums of all time, featuring hits like the title track, "Dancing in the Dark," and "Glory Days."[70]

The album *Born in the U.S.A.* was a look at the dark side of the American dream. Many fans thought that the song "Born in the U.S.A" was a patriotic anthem, but it actually was about the dead ends hit by a Vietnam War vet in America.[71] In fact, during a campaign rally in New Jersey, President Ronald Reagan stated, "America's future rests in a thousand dreams inside your hearts. It rests in the message of hope in the songs of a man so many young Americans admire—New Jersey's own, Bruce Springsteen." A couple of nights later, during a concert in Pittsburgh, Pennsylvania, Springsteen shared with the crowd, "Well, the president was mentioning my name in his speech the other day and I kind of got to wondering what his favorite album of mine must've been, you know? I don't think it was the *Nebraska* album. I don't think he's been listening to this one." He then launched into "Johnny 99," a song that touches on themes of factory closures and criminality.[72]

Springsteen is a pioneer of heartland rock, a genre that fuses popular rock music with lyrical depth and a socially aware message, weaving a story of the American working class's existence. He was influenced by the Animals, Elvis Presley, the Beatles, Chuck Berry, Bob Dylan, Woody Guthrie, Van Morrison, and Phil Spector. He was also influenced by the writing of John Steinbeck, the writing of Flannery O'Conner, and filmmakers John Ford and Terrence Malick.[73] Some of the artists and bands that Springsteen influenced were Bon Iver, Melissa Etheridge, Billy Ray Cyrus, Foo Fighters, the Killers, Pearl Jam, and Rage Against the Machine. Other notable heartland rock artists from the 1980s include the Eagles, Jackson Browne, Huey Lewis and the News, Tom Petty and the Heartbreakers, John Mellencamp, and Bob Seger and the Silver Bullet Band.

What to Listen For in the Song

Rawness and Grit Springsteen's voice often carries a raw, gravelly quality, especially in this song. This grittiness adds authenticity to the lyrics and reflects the working-class themes of the song. These vocal qualities resemble the same qualities of Little Richard, Wanda Jackson, and Eric Burdon of the Animals.

Range For the most part, Springsteen stays mainly in the upper part of his chest register for the majority of the song. However, there are moments when he does an aside vocal in his chest mix. He even does a yodel flip close to the end of the song. He flips into a full falsetto "woo," resembling Little Richard. As the song fades, he adds falsetto cries.

Pronunciation and Phrasing The pronunciation and phrasing that he uses are distinctive, giving his vocals a unique character. He often elongates certain syllables and uses deliberate phrasing to emphasize specific words, adding emphasis and meaning to the lyrics.

Rhythmic Precision Springsteen's vocal delivery is tightly synchronized with the song's rhythm. His sense of timing and rhythmic precision enhances the overall impact of the lyrics and complements the musical arrangement.

Passion and Conviction Throughout the song, Springsteen sings with a sense of passion and conviction, reinforcing the song's critical themes. His fervent delivery ensures that the listener feels the depth of the emotions expressed in the lyrics.

Alternative Rock

"The One I Love" (1987)

R.E.M.

R.E.M. was formed in 1980 in Athens, Georgia, by vocalist Michael Stipe, guitarist Peter Buck, bassist Mike Mills, and drummer Bill Berry. Buck and Stipe met at a record store where Buck worked. They soon realized that both shared similar tastes in music, particularly punk and proto-punk. Through a mutual friend, the two met Berry and Mills, who had played music together in high school. The quartet started rehearsing in a converted church, and within a matter of a few months, they began playing shows in and around Athens, building a local following and developing their signature sound.

In 1981, the group recorded their first demo in Winston-Salem, North Carolina. The seven-inch single was released in July of the same year by a small record label from Athens called Hib-Tone. It featured "Radio Free Europe" and "Sitting Still." Later that year, the group returned to Winston-Salem to start recording their first EP, *Chronic Town*.

R.E.M. signed with IRS Records in 1982 and released their debut album, *Murmur*, in 1983. The album received critical acclaim and established the band as a major force in the alternative rock scene. Subsequent albums like *Reckoning* (1984) and *Fables of the Reconstruction* (1985) continued to build their reputation and fan base. The band's 1987 album, *Document*, featured the hit single "The One I Love" and marked their transition to a more mainstream sound. This album helped them gain wider recognition.[74]

Even though they were influenced by punk and the DIY ethos, R.E.M. created their own sound and in turn created a new subgenre of music that became known as alternative rock. Their style had an energetic folk rock feel with Buck's Byrds-like arpeggiated style of guitar and Stipe's wailing tenor voice with cryptic lyrics and unique performance style. Their musical style was reminiscent of psychedelic rock from the late 1960s mixed with repetitive pop hooks influenced by the proto-punk movement, particularly in their earliest works, such as "Radio Free Europe" and "Gardening at Night."

Some of the artists that influenced R.E.M. were T. Rex, Mott the Hoople, Patti Smith, the Byrds, Paul McCartney, and the Velvet Underground. Some of the artists that R.E.M. influenced were Nirvana, Radiohead, Pearl Jam, Coldplay, and Alice in Chains. Other notable alternative rock artists and bands from the 1980s are the Violent Femmes, Siouxsie and the Banshees, the Pixies, and Sonic Youth.

What to Listen For in the Song

Registration For the most part, Stipe sings in a chest to chest-mix registration and occasionally goes into a mix belt. His vocal qualities are speech driven. He also uses a clear, bright tone similar to that of Ritchie Valens.

Emotional Delivery Stipe infuses the lyrics with emotion, adding depth to the song's meaning. His delivery captures the sentiment of the lyrics, making the listener feel the intensity of the words he sings.

Mysterious and Enigmatic Style In "The One I Love," Stipe sings the lyrics with a mysterious and enigmatic quality, keeping the listener intrigued. His straight tone and elongated diphthongs add to the mysterious quality of his tone, which resembles vocal sounds of the psychedelic genre of the late 1960s.

Occasional Edginess In certain parts of the song, Stipe uses a slightly edgy quality, adding a raw, authentic feel to the performance. This edginess enhances the song's intensity and complements the overall musical arrangement.

Nuanced Phrasing Stipe uses nuanced phrasing, emphasizing specific words and syllables to convey the intended meaning. He scoops into phrases and lingers on diphthongs, resembling vocal qualities of Grace Slick in "White Rabbit."

The Queen of Rock 'n' Roll

"Back Where You Started" (1987)

Tina Turner

While "Queen of Rock 'n' Roll" is not a genre, a conversation about rock would be incomplete without mentioning Tina Turner. Turner was born Anna Mae Bullock on November 26, 1939, and her musical career began in the late 1950s, when she met Ike Turner. While Ike was playing a circuit of nightclubs in St. Louis, Missouri, with his band, the Kings of Rhythm, Bullock asked if she could sing with the band. Ike said yes, yet he never let her. One night, Bullock got fed up and simply grabbed the microphone and started singing. Ike was impressed by her performance and asked her to join the group, and soon after, she changed her name to Tina. The duo's collaboration was initially successful, and they released hit songs like "A Fool in Love" in 1960. They got married in 1962 and continued to perform together.[75]

Ike created a whole show around Tina. Their successful soul act was made up of nine musicians and three scantily clad female background singers named the Ikettes. After their impressive performance on *The Big T.N.T. Show* in 1964, Phil Spector was eager to produce Turner. After a $20,000 deal was made, Turner recorded "River Deep-Mountain High," and Spector maximized Tina's energy with his Wall of Sound. The impact of the record earned Ike & Tina Turner an opening spot on the Rolling Stones' tour in the United Kingdom in the fall of 1966.[76] In November 1967, Tina Turner became the first female and first black artist to be on the cover of *Rolling Stone* magazine.[77]

After a physical altercation between Tina and Ike in 1976, Tina left Ike with only thirty-six cents and a Mobil gas card in her pocket. She filed for divorce only twenty-six days later, but the divorce was not finalized until March 1978.[78] While trying to make ends meet and sometimes surviving on food stamps, Tina pursued a solo career. She made two unsuccessful albums in the late 1970s that were composed mainly of covers. However, after touring with the Rolling Stones again in 1981 and opening some shows for Rod Stewart, she was back to touring. At the age of forty-five, Tina released her fifth solo album, *Private Dancer* (1984), which included the hit songs "What's Love Got to Do with It" and the track that won her a Grammy Award for Best Rock Vocal Performance: "Better Be Good to Me." This album sold 11 million records and catapulted her to international stardom. Her solo career continued with more successful albums like *Break Every Rule* (1986) and *Foreign Affair* (1989).[79] In 2000, Tina Turner announced her retirement from performing, but she continued to make occasional public appearances. She made a remarkable comeback in 2008 at the age of sixty-nine with her Tina!: 50th Anniversary Tour, which became one of the highest-grossing tours of all time. On May 24, 2023, Tina Turner died at her home in Switzerland at the age of eighty-three.

Tina Turner had a remarkable forty-two-year career that saw her journey from demanding the spotlight to touring with one of the world's biggest bands. She bravely walked out of an abusive marriage and started a new chapter in her career alone, middle aged, and with very little money. Her path was not an easy one, and she rose to be an even bigger star than she once was. Her electrifying stage presence, distinctive voice, dynamic performances, and unwavering grit and strength have rightfully earned her the title of "The Queen of Rock 'n' Roll."

Some of the artists that influenced Tina Turner were Big Mama Thornton, James Brown, the Rolling Stones, Etta James, Ray Charles, Ruth Brown, Sam Cooke, Mahalia Jackson, and Ann Peebles. Some of the artists that she influenced were Mick Jagger, Beyoncé, Janis Joplin, Lady Gaga, Rihanna, Jennifer Lopez, Kelly Clarkson, Gloria Gaynor, and Joan Jett. Other notable female artists from the 1980s are Ann Wilson, Lita Ford, Wendy O. Williams, Pat Benatar, Joan Jett, Stevie Nicks, Annie Lennox, and Chrissie Hynde.

The song we will be analyzing is "Back Where You Started," which was written by Bryan Adams and Jim Vallance. Turner won a Grammy Award for Best Female Rock Performance with this song in 1987.

What to Listen For in the Song

Raspy and Gritty Voice Tina Turner's voice is naturally raspy, giving her vocals a raw and gritty quality. This characteristic adds depth and emotion to her singing, making her performances incredibly powerful and soulful. These qualities are similar to those of Little Richard.

Dynamic Range Although her tone is not necessarily clear, Turner is able to move through each register seamlessly. Her vocal range is impressive, allowing her to hit both high and low notes with ease. She throws in clear head voice "woo's" similar to Big Mama Thornton. She also adds screams in her head voice, similar to those of Little Richard.

Expressive Phrasing Turner has a remarkable sense of phrasing, knowing when to hold back and when to unleash her voice for maximum impact. This control over her vocals enhances the emotional resonance of her songs.

Rock 'n' Roll Style As stated before, Turner's vocal style is deeply rooted in soul, R&B, and 1950s rock 'n' roll music. She incorporates soulful nuances, such as melismatic phrasing, and vocal embellishments, such as scooping into pitches and falling off of phrases. She also uses a variety of vocal qualities, such as grit and rawness, speechlike qualities, and clear tones, all of which contribute to the rich texture of her singing.

THE 1990s AND BEYOND

The landscape of rock music underwent a fundamental transformation in the 1990s and 2000s due to computer technology and the internet. Computer technology revolutionized the recording and production process, allowing musicians and bands to create high-quality recordings at a lower cost and with greater flexibility. This led to the rise of home recording studios and indie labels, enabling many rock bands to reach a wider audience.

The internet provided a direct platform for bands to distribute their music to fans. This democratization of music distribution allowed smaller and independent rock bands to gain a global audience without the need for major record deals. File-sharing networks such as Napster, which emerged in the late 1990s, and later peer-to-peer platforms facilitated the exchange of music files, leading to both illegal sharing and increased exposure for independent artists. The music industry responded with legal actions against file-sharing platforms, significantly impacting business models. iTunes, which came onto the scene in 2001, and later streaming services, such as Spotify and Pandora, allowed fans to purchase and download songs online or access extensive music libraries with a monthly subscription. Social media platforms such as Myspace, which launched in 2003, allowed bands to promote their music and connect directly with fans, reducing reliance on traditional marketing channels.

Rock bands started to build online communities around their music, using websites, forums, and social media platforms to interact with fans and foster stronger fan loyalty. The ease of sharing music online facilitated collaboration between artists and the rise of remix culture. Musicians from various genres could experiment with new sounds and styles. Internet radio, recommendation algorithms, and user-generated play lists made it easier for fans to discover new rock bands and music that resonated with their tastes. In the 2000s, some rock bands began live streaming their concerts, allowing fans from around the world to experience live music without being physically present. Online music publications, blogs, and forums provided a platform for music journalists, critics, and enthusiasts to discuss and analyze rock music, influencing the perception and the reception of rock bands. These advancements offered opportunities for independent artists, revolutionized recording and distribution, and empowered fans to engage with their favorite artists in new ways. However, they also presented challenges and disruptions to the traditional music industry, necessitating adaptation to new models of consumption and revenue generation.

Most readers are likely to be more familiar with the music of these eras, and since there are so many subgenres, it becomes increasingly impossible to give due credit to all of the innovations during this time. In this section, I provide you with a list of some of the most popular genres of the 1990s, 2000s, and 2010s along with their influences and major rock groups/artists associated with each genre. As you listen to this music, consider the influences we have covered so far in this chapter and start connecting the dots for yourself. Note that these genres are not strictly defined, and many bands in the 2010s incorporated a mix of influences, blurring the lines between genres. Additionally, the influence of digital technology and the internet allowed for greater experimentation and fusion of different styles within the rock music landscape. By diving deeper on your own, you will further expand your horizons and influences to help you further refine your own signature sound.

1990s

Grunge

> Influences: punk rock, garage rock, alternative rock, metal, and indie rock
> Bands: Nirvana, Pearl Jam, Soundgarden, Alice in Chains, Hole, Garbage, Breeders

Alternative Rock

Influences: post-punk, new wave, punk rock, indie rock
Bands: Radiohead, Sonic Youth, R.E.M., Beck, The Smashing Pumpkins, Red Hot Chili Peppers, Alanis Morissette, Tori Amos, and the Cranberries

Pop Punk

Influences: punk rock, power pop, pop, and alternative rock.
Bands: Green Day, Blink-182, the Offspring, NOFX, L7, PJ Harvey

Industrial Rock

Influences: industrial music, electronic music, experimental rock, goth rock
Bands: Nine Inch Nails, Ministry, Rammstein, Marilyn Manson

Nu-Metal

Influences: heavy metal, hip-hop, alternative metal, industrial rock
Bands: Korn, Limp Bizkit, Linkin Park, System of a Down

2000s

Emo

Influences: punk rock, indie rock, hard-core punk
Bands: My Chemical Romance, Dashboard Confessional, Taking Back Sunday, Paramore

Indie Rock

Influences: alternative rock, punk rock, post-punk
Bands: the Strokes, Arcade Fire, the White Stripes, Cat Power, Tegan and Sara, Death Cab for Cutie

Garage Rock Revival

Influences: 1960s garage rock, proto-punk, punk rock
Bands: the Hives, the Vines, the Strokes

Hard Rock

Influences: classic rock, blues rock, heavy metal
Bands: Disturbed, Velvet Revolver, Foo Fighters, Aerosmith, AC/DC

Nu-Metal

Influences: alternative metal, hip-hop, industrial metal
Bands: Linkin Park, Korn, Limp Bizkit, Evanescence, System of a Down

2010s

Indie Rock/Indie Pop Rock

Influences: alternative rock, post-punk, garage rock
Bands: Arctic Monkeys, Tame Impala, Vampire Weekend, the 1975

Alternative Rock

Influences: punk rock, post-punk, new wave
Bands: Radiohead, Muse, Imagine Dragons, Twenty One Pilots, Panic! At the Disco, Hozier

Garage Rock/Garage Punk

Influences: 1960s garage rock, punk rock
Bands: the Black Keys, the White Stripes, Ty Segall, Parquet Courts

Psychedelic Rock

Influences: 1960s psychedelic rock, blues rock
Bands: Tame Impala, Unknown Mortal Orchestra, King Gizzard & the Lizard Wizard, Temples

Progressive Rock/Progressive Metal

Influences: progressive rock, heavy metal
Bands: Tool, Mastodon, Dream Theater, Opeth

Folk Rock

Influences: folk music, rock 'n' roll.
Bands: Fleet Foxes, Mumford & Sons, the Lumineers, the Head and the Heart

CONCLUSION

Trying to decide which artists and songs to cover in any listening guide is challenging. The selections in this chapter represent a miniscule sample of the story of rock music, but even through this small collection, one can see and hear the evolution of rock. Today's songs have a lineage that dates back more than seventy years. Now that you have read about the history of rock music and you have listened to a variety of rock genres through the decades, you are hopefully listening to music a little different than before. A great exercise for the next step in your journey is to research your favorite artists, find out who influenced them, and listen to their music and find similarities. Then research who influenced those artists. If you write your own music, think about your influences and do the same research you did for your favorite artists. This will enrich and deepen your artistry and help you shape your signature sound.

My hope with this chapter is that anyone who reads it can hear and appreciate how much everything is connected yet also individual. Each artist sounds unique, but they are also shaped by their musical ancestors whether they know that or not. We, as listeners, want to hear authenticity in all music regardless of what genre it is. Big Mama Thornton said it best in a 1980 *New York Times* article: "When I was comin' up, listening to Bessie Smith and all, they sung from their heart and soul and expressed themselves. That's why when I do a song by Jimmy Reed or somebody, I have my own way of singing it. Because I don't want to be Jimmy Reed, I want to be me. I like to put myself into whatever I'm doin' so I can feel it."[80]

As you work through the rest of this book, I challenge you to find your own voice and fully put yourself into everything you sing.

NOTES

1. "How the 45 RPM Single Changed Music Forever," *Rolling Stone*, https://www.rollingstone.com/music/music-features/45-vinyl-singles-history-806441, accessed November 23, 2023.
2. "Rhythm and Blues," Library of Congress, https://www.loc.gov/collections/songs-of-america/articles-and-essays/musical-styles/popular-songs-of-the-day/rhythm-and-blues, accessed November 23, 2023.
3. Reebee Garofalo, *Rockin' Out Popular Music in the U.S.A.*, 3rd ed. (Upper Saddle River, NJ: Pearson, 2005), 75.
4. John Covach, *What's That Sound? An Introduction to Rock and Its History*, 2nd ed. (New York: Norton, 2009), 68.
5. Holly George-Warren and Patricia Romanowski, *The Rolling Stone Encyclopedia of Rock & Roll*, 3rd ed. (New York: Rolling Stone Press, 2001), 989.
6. George-Warren Romanowski, *The Rolling Stone Encyclopedia of Rock & Roll*, 989.
7. "Big Mama Thorton," Head Butler, https://headbutler.com/reviews/blues-singer, accessed June 3, 2023.
8. George-Warren and Romanowski, *The Rolling Stone Encyclopedia of Rock & Roll*, 989.
9. "Leiber and Stoller: Rolling Stone's 1990 Interview with the Songwriting Legends," *Rolling Stone*, https://www.rollingstone.com/music/music-news/leiber-and-stoller-rolling-stones-1990-interview-with-the-songwriting-legends-246405, accessed June 5, 2023.
10. George-Warren and Romanowski, *The Rolling Stone Encyclopedia of Rock & Roll*, 570–72.
11. George-Warren and Romanowski, *The Rolling Stone Encyclopedia of Rock & Roll*, 570–72.
12. "Sister Rosetta Tharpe: Singer Influenced Key Rock 'n' Roll Figures," *Atlanta Journal-Constitution*, https://www.ajc.com/entertainment/music/sister-rosetta-tharpe-singer-influenced-key-rock-roll-figures/UTzkpIsRNvvenWoaTGamtM, accessed June 10, 2023.
13. "From Sin to Salvation: Little Richard Tells All," *Rolling Stone*, https://www.rollingstone.com/music/music-features/little-richard-gay-preacher-biography-996737, accessed June 11, 2023.
14. George-Warren and Romanowski, *The Rolling Stone Encyclopedia of Rock & Roll*, 571.
15. "The 1950s Queer Black Performers Who Inspired Little Richard," University of Oregon, https://around.uoregon.edu/content/1950s-queer-black-performers-who-inspired-little-richard, accessed June 11, 2023.
16. "Georgia's Very Own: A-Wop Bam Boom," *Macon Journal*, accessed June 11, 2023, https://www.nytimes.com/1990/01/08/us/macon-journal-georgia-s-very-own-a-wop-bam-boom.html, accessed June 11, 2023.
17. George-Warren and Romanowski, *The Rolling Stone Encyclopedia of Rock & Roll*, 476.
18. George-Warren and Romanowski, *The Rolling Stone Encyclopedia of Rock & Roll*, 1025–26.

19. George-Warren and Romanowski, *The Rolling Stone Encyclopedia of Rock & Roll*, 69–70.
20. Covach, *What's That Sound?*, 72–75.
21. Covach, *What's That Sound?*, 72–75.
22. Covach, *What's That Sound?*, 72–75.
23. "Johnny B. Goode," *Rolling Stone*, https://web.archive.org/web/20061228112332/http:/www.rollingstone.com/news/story/6595852/johnny_b_goode, accessed June 21, 2023.
24. "Music from Earth," Jet Propulsion Laboratory, California Institute of Technology, https://voyager.jpl.nasa.gov/golden-record/whats-on-the-record/music, accessed June 22, 2023.
25. "Surf," AllMusic.com, https://www.allmusic.com/subgenre/surf-ma0000002883, accessed July 11, 2023.
26. "Guitarist Dick Dale Brought Arabic Folk Song to Surf Music: How Surf Music's Roots Stretch All the Way to Lebanon," America.gov, https://web.archive.org/web/20111020083054/http://www.america.gov/st/washfile-english/2006/September/20060914165844ndyblehs0.0821802.html, accessed July 11, 2023.
27. Covach, *What's That Sound?*, 141–45.
28. Eric James Abbey, *Garage Rock and Its Roots: Musical Rebels and the Drive for Individuality* (Jefferson, NC: McFarland, 2015), 1–14.
29. "The Lascivious Louie Louie," The Smoking Gun, https://www.thesmokinggun.com/documents/funny/lascivious-louie-louie, accessed July 24, 2023.
30. "Louie Louie Story—KISN Interview with Dick Peterson of the Kingsmen," KISN Everywhere, October 10, 2014, https://www.youtube.com/watch?v=RQdQDCC9kl0.
31. Alec Palao, *Love That Louie: The Louie Louie Files CD Liner Notes* (London: Ace Records, 2002).
32. "Psychedelic Rock," *Britannica*, https://www.britannica.com/art/psychedelic-rock, accessed August 3, 2023.
33. "Grace Slick," https://web.archive.org/web/20170507221818/http://www.jeffersonairplane.com/the-band/grace-slick, accessed August 21, 2023.
34. Marc Myers, *Anatomy of a Song* (New York: Grove Atlantic, 2016), 22.
35. Roberta Freund Schwartz, *How Britain Got the Blues: The Transmission and Reception of American Blues Style in the United Kingdom* (London: Taylor & Francis, 2016), 28.
36. Schwartz, *How Britain Got the Blues*, x–xi.
37. Covach, *What's That Sound?*, 172–84.
38. "Rolling Stones Celebrate 50 Years of Raucous Rock'n'Roll," CNN.com, https://edition.cnn.com/2012/07/12/opinion/rolling-stones-50/index.html, accessed August 23, 2023.
39. George-Warren and Romanowski, *The Rolling Stone Encyclopedia of Rock & Roll*, 831–35.
40. Covach, *What's That Sound?*, 327–38.
41. "Art Rock," *Britannica*, https://www.britannica.com/art/art-rock, accessed August 24, 2023.
42. George-Warren and Romanowski, *The Rolling Stone Encyclopedia of Rock & Roll*, 665-667.
43. Covach, *What's That Sound?*, 311–17.

44. Covach, *What's That Sound?*, 311–17.

45. George-Warren and Romanowski, *The Rolling Stone Encyclopedia of Rock & Roll*, 553–55.

46. George-Warren and Romanowski, *The Rolling Stone Encyclopedia of Rock & Roll*, 246–47.

47. "Highway Stars," SteveMorse.com, https://web.archive.org/web/20050915142246/http://www.stevemorse.com/interviews/200310guitarmagazine.html, accessed September 9, 2023.

48. Covach, *What's That Sound?*, 317–22.

49. George-Warren and Romanowski, *The Rolling Stone Encyclopedia of Rock & Roll*, 325.

50. George-Warren and Romanowski, *The Rolling Stone Encyclopedia of Rock & Roll*, 325.

51. "20 Rock Albums Rolling Stone Loved in the 1970s That You Never Heard," *Rolling Stone*, https://www.rollingstone.com/music/music-lists/20-rock-albums-rolling-stone-loved-in-the-1970s-that-you-never-heard-164876/fanny-fanny-hill-169395, accessed September 9, 2023.

52. Covach, *What's That Sound?*, 343–47.

53. George-Warren and Romanowski, *The Rolling Stone Encyclopedia of Rock & Roll*, 209–11.

54. Covach, *What's That Sound?*, 343–45.

55. "Rise and Fall of FM Rock," San Francisco Digital History Archive, https://www.foundsf.org/index.php?title=Rise_and_Fall_of_FM_Rock, accessed November 18, 2023.

56. George-Warren and Romanowski, *The Rolling Stone Encyclopedia of Rock & Roll*, 423–24.

57. "How the Irreverent Poetry of the '60s Helped Spawn Punk Music," *PBS NewsHour*, https://www.pbs.org/newshour/arts/poetry/irreverent-poetry-60s-helped-spawn-punk-music, accessed September 15, 2023.

58. Ian P. Moran, "Punk: The Do-It-Yourself Subculture," https://westcollections.wcsu.edu/server/api/core/bitstreams/10f277ba-03ad-49fc-8e3f-43712aca337d/content, accessed September 20, 2023.

59. Covach, *What's That Sound?*, 427–29.

60. Covach, *What's That Sound?*, 449–52.

61. "How the Go-Go's Perfected Pop-Punk," NPR, https://www.npr.org/2020/08/05/898998568/how-the-go-gos-perfected-pop-punk, accessed October 7, 2023.

62. George-Warren and Romanowski, *The Rolling Stone Encyclopedia of Rock & Roll*, 379–80.

63. George-Warren and Romanowski, *The Rolling Stone Encyclopedia of Rock & Roll*, 642–43.

64. George-Warren and Romanowski, *The Rolling Stone Encyclopedia of Rock & Roll*, 642–43.

65. Joel McIver, *To Live Is to Die: The Life and Death of Metallica's Cliff Burton* (London: Jawbone Press, 2009), 88–89.

66. Mick Wall, *Enter Night: A Biography of Metallica* (New York: St. Martin's Griffin, 2012), 134–35.

67. George-Warren and Romanowski, *The Rolling Stone Encyclopedia of Rock & Roll*, 930.

68. Craig Statham, *Springsteen: Saint in the City, 1949–1974* (London: Soundcheck Books, 2013), 9.

69. Statham, *Springsteen*, 12.

70. George-Warren and Romanowski, *The Rolling Stone Encyclopedia of Rock & Roll*, 930–32.

71. George-Warren and Romanowski, *The Rolling Stone Encyclopedia of Rock & Roll*, 930–32.

72. "How Ronald Reagan Changed Bruce Springsteen's Politics," *Politico*, https://web.archive.org/web/20140809012611/http://www.politico.com/magazine/story/2014/06/bruce-springsteen-ronald-reagan-107448.html#.U-V4uuzP32c, accessed October 20, 2023.

73. "The Ties That Bind: Bruce Springsteen's 25 Biggest Heroes," *Rolling Stone*, https://www.rollingstone.com/music/music-lists/the-ties-that-bind-bruce-springsteens-25-biggest-heroes-32797, accessed October 20, 2023.

74. George-Warren and Romanowski, *The Rolling Stone Encyclopedia of Rock & Roll*, 814–16.

75. George-Warren and Romanowski, *The Rolling Stone Encyclopedia of Rock & Roll*, 1009.

76. Tina Turner and Kurt Loder, *I, Tina: My Life Story*" (New York: Avon Books, 1986), 102.

77. "Tina Turner on Her Journey to Broadway," *Rolling Stone*, https://www.rollingstone.com/music/music-features/tina-turner-musical-broadway-essay-906671, accessed November 28, 2023.

78. Tina Turner, "The Shocking Story of a Battered Wife Who Escaped to Fame and Fortune," *Ebony*, November 1986, 38–41, https://books.google.com/books?id=NdkDAAAAMBAJ&pg=PA31#v=onepage&q&f=false.

79. George-Warren and Romanowski, *The Rolling Stone Encyclopedia of Rock & Roll*, 1011.

80. "Big Mama Thornton Plays Rare Club Date; The Women 'Just Sang' a Hit in 'Hound Dog,'" *New York Times*, July 4, 1980.

THE BASICS OF SINGING ROCK 'N' ROLL

In this chapter, I'll be discussing the fundamental principles of training your voice for singing rock music. The techniques and strategies presented here are aimed at helping you coordinate the movements of your instrument, providing you with options when performing a song. The exercises included in this chapter will serve as a foundation for the subsequent sections of this book, so it is important to work through these exercises before jumping ahead. The goal of this chapter is to introduce you to the range of motion of your instrument. Once you understand the range of motion and the options you have available to you, the easier it will be to hone your signature sound.

It is important to note that each reader's unique background will influence how they utilize the tools in this book. To cater to different singers, I've dedicated the next three chapters to offering tips for beginners, those who are already singing rock music, and those transitioning from classical or musical theater backgrounds. Each of these chapters will delve into maximizing the benefits of the exercises outlined here. In chapter 8, we'll explore the progression from creating sounds to making music. By amalgamating these tools, you'll be able to approach your songs from a fresh perspective and infuse them with new ideas, all while staying true to your personal identity and objectives. Before we get started with the technical work, let's cover a few introductory topics.

Overview of My Philosophy

We sing to communicate the human experience. Sometimes, the experience is a story we want to share; on other occasions, it's a medium for unburdening our emotions. And sometimes, we craft an ambiance or a vibe, and we immerse ourselves in it alongside our audience. Whatever the reason you create, you need a voice that will help you, not hinder you. If you have only one sound available to you, your ability to take others on a journey will be limited to the emotions associated with that one tonal quality.

Audiences interpret emotions from the tone, volume level, steadiness or unevenness, rhythm, and pacing of the singer's voice. To accurately share your full human experience, you must have full facility of your instrument. More than that, you need your voice to respond automatically to your intentions when you are performing. When that happens, you will not have to think about your technique, and you will be able to explore a deeper connection to the song.

When I work with singers, I use exercises that help them coordinate their instrument to make a huge variety of sounds. Then I work with them to identify what they want to say, and then we practice until the voice responds in ways that enhance the story, emotion, or vibe they are setting. In this book, I am going to introduce you to this style of working so that you can start your own journey of learning to communicate your story.

There are complexities to everything discussed in this book and singing in general. For example, in this book, I will talk about vocal fold vibrations. Technically speaking, the vocal folds generate pulsations in the airstream being released from your lungs, resulting in compression and rarefaction waves that we perceive as frequencies. We could then get into very complex discussions about what is actually happening versus what we perceive. Similarly, the resonances of the vocal tract are areas where air oscillates when stimulated. However, these intricate details are already covered in depth in other texts and are best explored after covering the basics in this book. Hence, in this book, I will concentrate on broader adjustments while encouraging readers to explore the works cited if they are interested in developing a comprehensive understanding of the complexities of vocal production.

The Role of Audio Technology Cannot Be Understated

While working through these technical exercises, it is crucial to bear in mind that the recording studio has the power to refine and enhance reality. We will delve deeper into this concept in chapter 10, but it is important to maintain this awareness throughout the book. In the realm of rock singing, it is exceedingly rare to perform without a microphone. Therefore, the microphone should be regarded as an integral part of the instrument along with audio effects that enhance the voice. Reverb and compression, for example, lend a smoother quality to the vocal line, making the voice sound more balanced than it would typically be in a live setting. Additionally, the microphone amplifies the upper frequencies, bringing clarity to the sound projected through the speakers. It is essential to recognize the limitations of acoustically projecting your voice without a microphone, so be cautious not to overexert yourself. I highly recommend that you invest in a microphone setup to practice with at home. This will allow you to hear the final result of your amplified voice when practicing, which will improve the effectiveness of your training. Another alternative is to use a microphone plugged into your digital audio workstation (DAW) while listening through headphones.

LET'S MAP YOUR INSTRUMENT

In this chapter, we will construct a map for your instrument, offering a view of your vocal capabilities that will empower you to pave your own path as a singer. This vocal map will showcase the broad range of vocal qualities that can be attained by leveraging the major structures of your instrument. By identifying the extremes and finding the middle ground within your vocal abilities, you'll gain valuable insights for making artistic choices while working on songs. This comprehensive understanding will equip you with the tools you need to express yourself effectively and authentically through your voice.

A Nonlinear System

As we explore the fundamentals of technique, it is essential to keep a significant concept in mind. While many singers traditionally view the

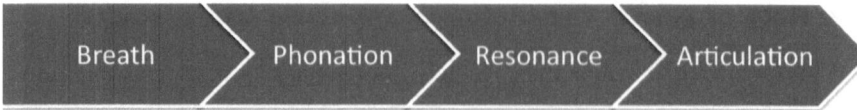

Figure 5.1. A linear system. *Courtesy of Matt Edwards*

voice as a linear system, with sound production progressing in a sequential manner from the breath to the vocal folds, resonators, and articulators (as depicted in figure 5.1), a growing body of research challenges this linear perspective, suggesting a nonlinear relationship (see figure 5.2).[1]

For example, the actions of the vocal folds have an impact on the respiratory system. When the folds are tightly pressed together, less air is released from the lungs compared to when they are lightly pressed together. Consequently, singers must adjust their breathing strategy accordingly. Resonance also influences vocal fold closure, making it important to consider resonance when encountering challenges in isolating head or chest register. Although the structure of this book may appear linear, its intention is for you to gain knowledge about all the components and eventually experiment to discover the combinations and interactions that work best for you. For a deeper understanding of how the voice's components interact with one another, I recommend exploring *Vocology: The Science and Practice of Voice Habilitation*, cited in the previous note.

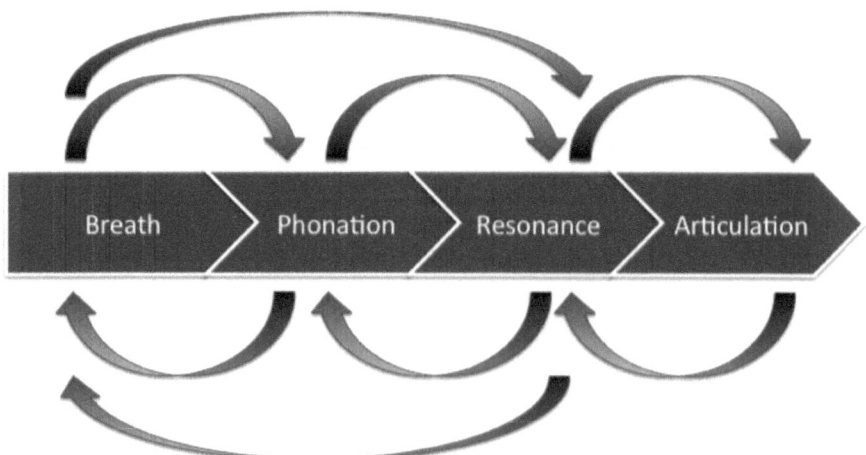

Figure 5.2. A non-linear system. *Courtesy of Matt Edwards*

POSTURE

Traditionally, a significant focus in singing has been placed on posture. Many of the ideas and principles surrounding posture have their roots in classical singing techniques, and there is a valid rationale for the importance attached to alignment in this genre. Classical singing demands a high degree of coordination among the respiratory, vibratory, and resonance systems of the voice. This intricate interplay is crucial because classical singers perform without amplification, relying solely on their vocal instrument's projection for audibility. This requires them to maintain perfect alignment of the larynx and vocal tract throughout the entire song. In contrast, rock singers almost always perform with amplification, which means they do not need the same level of precision as classical vocalists in terms of projection. A rock singer's resonance is constantly shifting to express the lyrics, and audiences expect them to move almost constantly around the stage. However, it remains essential for rock singers to manage tension effectively, which means you need to understand how your body is designed to move. One approach I have found particularly helpful in managing physical tension is addressing the six points of balance.

Six Points of Balance

The concept of six points of balance comes from the discipline of Body Mapping, which was developed by William and Barbara Conable in the 1990s. It is an outgrowth of their work with the Alexander Technique and has also been adapted for instruments other than the voice. A body map is a mental representation of how the body is structured. It helps us understand the location, size, and function of all the different parts we use to function in daily life, including singing. As we develop and refine our understanding of our body's structure, we also refine our kinesthesia, which is our body's ability to sense ourselves in motion.[2]

A full exploration of Body Mapping is beyond the scope of this text and has already been well written about in the book *What Every Singer Needs to Know about the Body*, cited in the previous note. In this section, we will review a summary of the six points of balance as described in the book, which will help you find comfort in your body when singing. The six points are the ankle joints, knee joints, hip joints, lumbar spine, arm structure, and atlanto-occipital joint (see figure 5.3).[3] All of these points are built on the structure of our feet.

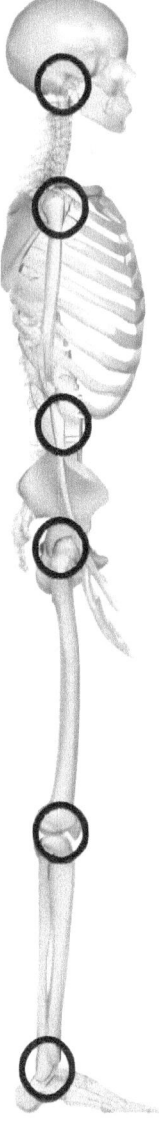

Figure 5.3. The six points of balance.
Courtesy of Matt Edwards

Feet

When we stand, we are distributing our weight across the tripod of our feet. The tripod is formed by the three arches of your foot, the transverse arch, lateral arch, and medial longitudinal arch. The transverse arch runs horizontally across the front of your foot from the ball of the big toe to the ball of the little toe. The lateral arch is located on the outer side of the foot spanning from the heel bone to the small toe. The medial longitudinal arch is perhaps the most well-known arch of the foot. It runs along the inner edge of the foot, rising from the heel to the ball of the big toe. The primary role of these arches is to provide shock absorption and distribute the body's weight across the foot during activities like standing, walking, and running. When you are standing, you want the weight of your upper body to be distributed evenly across these three arches.

The ankle joint delivers the weight of the upper body to the foot. This is where the two lower leg bones, the tibia (the outside bone) and fibula (the inside bone), connect to the talus bone of the foot. Body weight should be delivered to the foot through the tibia. However, in order for that to happen, we have to consider what is happening in the knees.

Knees

The knee joint is located behind the kneecap, which is called the patella. This joint is where the tibia and femur (thigh bone) come together. The knee can assume one of three positions: locked, bent, or balanced. A "locked" knee joint refers to a fully extended knee, where the leg is straightened and the joint is held in a stable, straight position. Locking the knee joint occurs when the tibia and femur align completely, and the knee joint's ligaments and structures provide stability without any muscular effort. This position is commonly seen when standing at attention. While the locked position provides stability, it's important not to lock the knees for prolonged periods, as it can create undue stress on the joint and hinder circulation. A "bent" knee joint refers to a flexed position where the angle between the tibia and femur is decreased. This position allows for greater mobility and absorption of shock. Flexing the knee joint is essential for actions such as crouching, sitting, squatting, and activities that require changes in elevation. A "balanced" knee joint refers to a position where the knee is neither fully extended nor significantly flexed. In this state, the knee joint maintains a neutral alignment that allows for comfortable weight distribution and optimal support. Maintaining a balanced knee position is crucial for activities such as walking, running, and most daily movements. When the knee is in balance, the joint is more adaptable to changes in direction and impact forces, reducing the risk of strain or injury. This is the ideal position for singing. To find this position, try locking your knees, then bending them, and then finding a balanced position in between those two extremes.

Pelvis

The pelvis is a central and critical component of the human body that plays a crucial role in supporting the upper body and distributing its weight to the lower limbs. It acts as a bridge between the spine and the legs, facilitating efficient weight distribution and movement coordination. The pelvis forms the foundation of the spine and supports the weight of the upper body. It is designed to withstand various forces, including gravity and impact, while maintaining stability. As the body moves and shifts its weight during activities, the pelvis adjusts its position to accommodate these changes. For example, during walking, the pelvis tilts slightly forward and backward with each step to maintain balance and facilitate fluid movement. It also acts as a shock absorber during activities that involve impact or weight bearing, such as jumping or running. The pelvis' structure and alignment help distribute the forces generated by these activities, reducing the strain on the spine and lower limbs. Proper alignment of the pelvis is essential for maintaining optimal weight distribution and preventing issues such as lower back pain. Poor pelvic alignment can lead to imbalances in muscle activation and unnecessary strain on various parts of the body. When singing, you want the weight of your upper body to be equally distributed to both hip joints, which in turn will equally distribute the weight of your upper body to both legs and feet.

Lumbar Spine

When standing in a balanced position, the position of the lumbar spine, also known as the lower back, is a critical aspect of maintaining good posture and overall spinal alignment. Proper alignment of the lumbar spine contributes to stability, comfort, and efficient weight distribution throughout the body. The lumbar spine naturally possesses a slight inward curve which helps absorb shock and maintain the spine's flexibility. When standing in a balanced position, it's important to maintain these natural curves without exaggerating or flattening them. Other parts of the spine have a curvature as well. The thoracic spine (upper back) has a slight outward curve, while the cervical spine (neck) has a slight inward curve. The lumbar curve complements these curves to maintain the spine's overall balance.

Arms

The structure of your arms consists of the clavicle (collarbone), scapula (shoulder blade), humerus (upper arm), two lower arm bones called the radius (located on the thumb side of the forearm) and the ulna (on the pinky side of the forearm), and the carpus, commonly referred to as the wrist. The hands are connected at the carpus and consist of twenty-seven additional bones. Our arms move at the shoulder joint (glenohumeral joint) where the head of the humerus (upper arm bone) articulates with the glenoid cavity of the scapula (shoulder blade). It's a ball-and-socket joint that allows for a wide range of movements. The elbow is a hinge joint that allows for flexion and extension of the forearm. Now explore the movement of these joints. Lift your shoulders toward your ears and notice what happens with the rest of your body. Pay special attention to changes in your neck and rib cage. Now relax your arms. Next, allow your arms to fall as if you were holding two heavy objects in your hands. Notice what has changed and then return your arms to neutral. Now stretch your arms out in front of you, notice what changes, and then return to neutral. Finally, stretch your arms out as if assuming the position of the letter T. Notice the changes in your body, then return to neutral. You should have noticed that your arm position affects your rib cage position, which could have an impact on the way you breathe. When singing, you want the arms to assume a position where you are free to move them for your performance. Ideally, their position and movement will have minimum impact on the rib cage and neck.

A-O Joint

Finally, let's explore the A-O joint. The A-O joint, also known as the atlanto-occipital joint, is a crucial joint located at the top of the spine between the base of the skull (occipital bone) and the first cervical vertebra (atlas). This joint plays a significant role in supporting the head, allowing nodding movements, and contributing to overall posture and balance. The primary function of the A-O joint is to facilitate the nodding movement of the head. This joint allows the head to tilt forward (flexion) and backward (extension) in a nodding motion. The head is relatively heavy compared to the rest of the body, and the A-O joint plays a key role in distributing its weight. The design of the A-O joint allows the head to balance atop the spine while maintaining minimal effort from the surrounding muscles. This helps reduce fatigue and strain on the neck muscles during activities that involve maintaining an upright posture. Find a neutral head position where the weight of your head is balanced on the cervical vertebrae and your molars are parallel to the floor. Try tilting your head forward, notice the changes you feel in your neck, and then slowly bring your head back to neutral. Now tilt your head backward, notice what changes in your neck, and then slowly bring your head back to a neutral position. You likely noticed straining and/or squeezing sensations in your neck as you shifted your head forward and backward. That's because as the neck moves, the larynx moves as well. We will discuss laryngeal positions later in this chapter, but in short, the laryngeal position has a significant impact on the timbre of your voice. When you sing, you need to make sure your neck is aligned in a way that gives you freedom to produce the vocal qualities you are seeking.

Thinking from the Top Down

In the descriptions above, we looked at alignment from the ground up. Now let us think about alignment from the top down. Find the neutral position of your head that allows the weight of your skull to balance on the top of your cervical vertebrae at the A-O joint. The optimal position is one where you can easily move your head without putting unnecessary strain on your larynx. The weight of your skull should be supported by the cervical vertebrae below. If the cervical vertebrae are locked or shifted forward, they will move your larynx into a position that is suboptimal for singing. Moving down to your arms, find a balanced position that allows them to move freely without interfering with the position of the cervical or thoracic vertebrae. The weight of the upper body should be supported by your lumbar spine, which distributes the weight to the pelvis. The pelvis divides the weight and sends it evenly down your femurs to the knees. Be sure that the knees do not lock and that they give you freedom to move. From the knees, the weight is sent down your fibula to the ankle, which will distribute the weight across your arches into the tripod of your feet. This should give you a sensation of a firm connection with the ground that gives stability to the rest of your body. By thinking of this weight distribution model, you should be able to find a comfortable balance in your body that does not include the use of unnecessary muscular tension.

Stretching

There are many different ways to tweak your alignment if you are running into issues, the easiest being stretching. The muscles that align your skeletal system work in antagonistic pairs, which means that there is always one muscle group of muscles that counterbalance movement in any given direction. For example, the bicep helps draw the hand toward the shoulder, while the tricep moves the arm away from the shoulder. If you feel like the muscles in the back of your legs are pulling your pelvis into a suboptimal position, stretch those muscles. If your abs are overly tight, lie on your back on a yoga ball and stretch your abdominal wall. In general, stretching before singing is beneficial to achieving optimal alignment.

In summary, the book *What Every Singer Needs to Know about the Body* is an excellent resource for more information about this work. If you are running into issues you cannot address on your own, a workshop or private sessions with a bodywork expert would be beneficial. Even when using mirrors or recording devices, we fail to get an accurate picture of what we are doing with our body. Working with an expert can help accelerate your progress in a much shorter time.

RESPIRATORY COORDINATION

"Respiratory coordination" is the term I like to use to describe the process of coordinating your body to release air in a way that is beneficial for singing. There will be many times when singing rock that you will not need to think about your breath at all; simply breathing like you do when talking will be enough. However, there will be other times when you need a little bit more air in your lungs, a little more pressure against the underside of your vocal folds, or a little bit more flow between them. The following section will walk you through a very simple approach to respiratory coordination that should work for most singers.

The Basics of Inhalation and Exhalation

In chapter 2, Dr. Scott McCoy covers the muscles of respiration. If you have not yet read those explanations and want to know more about the mechanics of breathing, refer to that chapter. In this section, we are going to talk about the basics of coordinating your respiratory system.

Inhalation and Exhalation

First, we are going to do a very simple breathing exercise to make sure you are breathing without tension. You are going to sit comfortably, close your eyes, and just spend a few minutes doing controlled breathing exercises. Take a deep breath through your nose over the course of five seconds. This should be a relaxed breath with minimal effort and a feeling of filling up your lungs in all directions. After you have filled your lungs, exhale through pursed lips, as if forming a narrow /u/ vowel. Try to extend your exhalation over five seconds. Take a few casual breaths, then repeat the exercise. After three to five of these breathing cycles, you are going to make a change to the exhalation phase. Instead of releasing your air on a steady stream, you are going to pulse your release on an /s/. Aim for ten pulses. As you perform this release, you will likely feel your abdominal wall pulsing as well. This is the sensation of abdominal engagement.

Abdominal Engagement

Next, we will use abdominal engagement to alter the power of the stream of air you are releasing on a hiss. Take your deep breath over five seconds, then release your air on a hiss using the /s/ we used in the previous exercises. However, this time, you are not going to pulse the hiss. Instead, you are going to maintain a steady stream. As you hold the stream, contract your abs as if doing a sit-up or plank. Do this for one to two seconds, then relax your abdominal wall. Continue sustaining the hiss and stay in the relaxed position for one to two seconds, then contract your abs again. You should have noticed that the hiss got louder and more forceful when you contracted your abs. As you will read in the following pages, we can use abdominal contraction to assist our respiratory system when singing.

Support, Control, Pressure, and Flow

You have likely heard the terms "breath support" and "breath control" before. However, many singers get confused by these terms. Breath support is usually used to describe the regulation of the muscles of respiration to regulate the amount of air pressure directed toward the larynx from the respiratory system. For example, you can choose to support a high note with more or less breath pressure. The term "breath control" is usually used to describe how we release air through the vocal folds. For example, we can release more or less air through a breathy vocal quality, giving us different shades of breathiness.[4]

Two other terms you will often come across are "breath pressure" and "transglottal airflow" or, more simply, "airflow." When we are talking about air that is resisted by the vocal folds, meaning it does not escape through them but builds up beneath the closed folds, we use the term "breath pressure." Take a deep breath, then hold your breath. What you are feeling in your throat is breath pressure, what is often called subglottic pressure because it is pressure below the glottis (closing of the vocal folds). "Breath flow," on the other hand, describes how air moves through the vocal folds. Take a deep breath and sigh. As you sighed, you had a lot of air flowing between your vocal folds. In this scenario, you had a high degree of transglottal airflow. Now take a deep breath and sustain a pitch with your full voice. In this scenario, you have less airflow because the vocal folds are resisting the release of air as they vibrate. When singing loudly, the breath pressure under the folds blows them widely apart. After they have been blown apart, they snap back together, and the cycle repeats. To sing loud, there has to be enough breath pressure to move the folds far apart. In contrast, when singing softly, the vocal folds do not move as far apart, which means you do not need as much pressure to power them.

Our respiratory system and phonatory system (the vocal folds) play vital roles in regulating both breath pressure and flow rate. As mentioned earlier, the vocal mechanism is a nonlinear system. In these examples, the action of the vocal folds has a direct impact on the respiratory system, and the respiratory system has an impact on the vocal folds. The two must be coordinated for the style of music you sing. Singing is not "all about the breath." Breathing is just one aspect of the system, and making corrections solely to the respiratory mechanism may not resolve all of your challenges at the vocal fold level. That is why you must learn how to coordinate the muscles of the respiratory system to complement what is happening in your larynx.

Coordinating Your Breath for Singing

Let's take a moment to review the key components of the respiratory system covered in chapter 2. The rib cage forms a protective enclosure around the lungs and is composed of twelve bones on each side that curve from the front to the back of the body. Muscles in between the ribs called intercostal muscles contract when we inhale. As they contract, they lift the rib cage, which expands the lungs to help fill them with air. The diaphragm, a dome-shaped muscle, also plays a crucial role in respiration. When it contracts, it pulls the lungs downward to facilitate inhalation. The combination of rib cage and diaphragmatic movement expands the lungs in all directions.

The abdominal wall encompasses several overlapping muscles encasing the internal organs. When the abdominal muscles are relaxed and the diaphragm contracts, pulling the lungs toward the pelvic floor, the abdominal organs are displaced to the lower sides of your abdomen. It is important to note that this movement is a result of the lungs' expansion, but air is not filling this part of the body. As the diaphragm slowly returns to its resting position, the abdominal contents slowly return to their resting position as well.

Elastic Recoil

When you inhale and air enters your lungs, it stretches millions of little balloon-like sacs called alveoli. When you inflate a balloon, you stretch the surface of the balloon, and if you release the valve of the balloon, the sides will collapse inward, expelling air. Just like a balloon, when the alveoli are expanded, they want to return to their resting state. At the same time the alveoli are collapsing in on themselves, the rib cage and the diaphragm, both of which have been expanded beyond their resting state, will also want to return to their origination point. The combination of these actions is what we call elastic recoil. This action is what initially powers the vocal folds when speaking or singing.

Resisting the Collapse

Many of the phrases we sing in rock music require only the natural recoil of the lungs to power the vocal folds. All you need to do is resist the collapse of the rib cage to allow the alveoli and elastic recoil to do the work. Take a full breath that expands your lungs in all directions, then release your air on an /s/. As you release your air, you may feel your body instinctually engaging your abs while also feeling the rib cage collapsing inward. This is the action we want to resist. As you release your air, relax your abs;

you do not need abdominal engagement for this approach to breath control. Turn your focus to your rib cage and imagine you are engaging the external intercostal muscles to keep your rib cage elevated, trying to maintain the position your rib cage assumed at the end of your inhalation. You are not trying to completely stop the movement of the ribcage but rather slow the return of the rib cage to its resting position.

Practice taking a full breath and releasing your air on an /s/ while resisting the collapse. See if you can sustain the /s/ for ten to fifteen seconds. Be careful to not overexert your muscles when trying to resist. This is a coordination exercise, not a strength-building exercise. It may take a while to learn this coordination; once you have figured it out, resisting the collapse should feel like a low-effort activity.

Abdominal Contraction

If you want to increase respiratory pressure beyond what is provided by elastic recoil, you can contract your abdominal wall, which will pull the rib cage down toward the pelvis. As this happens, the internal organs are compressed inside of the abdominal cavity between the pelvis and the diaphragm, which will increase the pressure of air inside the lungs, giving additional power to the voice. To contract your abdominal wall, slowly engage your abs as if performing a plank. Since we all have different levels of abdominal strength, each singer will need to find their optimal percentage of effort when engaging their abs. A singer with a six-pack or an eight-pack may need to engage their abs only at 10 to 20 percent. On the other hand, a singer who rarely exercises their abs may feel like they are engaging at 60 to 80 percent.

Practice abdominal engagement on a hiss to start. Try different percentages of engagement to find your optimal effort level. When you have coordinated a hiss, change to sustaining a vowel.

Combining Resisting the Collapse with Abdominal Engagement

After you have coordinated the ability to resist the collapse and to engage your abdominal wall, you will want to combine the two actions. Look at figure 5.4 and then read the explanation that follows.

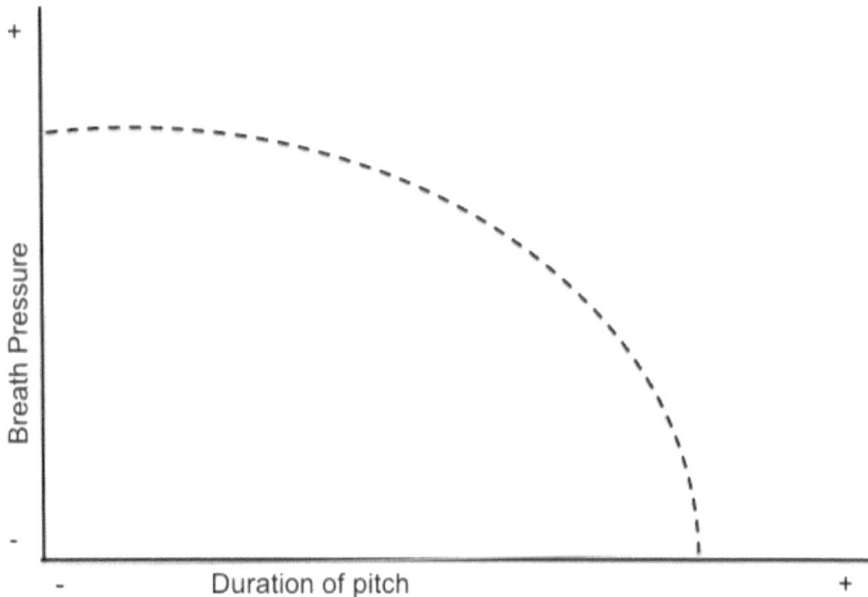

Figure 5.4. Singing without respiratory management. Courtesy of Matt Edwards

This diagram shows changes in breath pressure on a sustained note if the singer does not resist the elastic recoil of the respiratory system. On the left side of the graph, we see that on inhalation, breath pressure is at its peak. If you do nothing to control the collapse of your rib cage and abdominal wall, the air in your lungs will flow through your vocal folds, and breath pressure will decrease as you sustain the pitch. The result is a decrease in the volume of your voice and a short sustain time.

In the next illustration (figure 5.5), you will see two dotted lines, the first representing exhalation with no control (the bottom line) and the second representing controlled exhalation (the upper line). In this example, as the pitch is initiated, the singer maintains rib cage expansion while relaxing the abdominal wall (the down arrows). This active resistance slows the elastic recoil of the respiratory system. As breath pressure decreases with sustained phonation, the singer engages the abdominal muscles as if performing a plank (the upright arrows). This action helps decrease the downward slope of breath pressure, allowing the singer to maintain a steady dynamic level and vocal color throughout the duration of the note.

THE BASICS OF SINGING ROCK 'N' ROLL

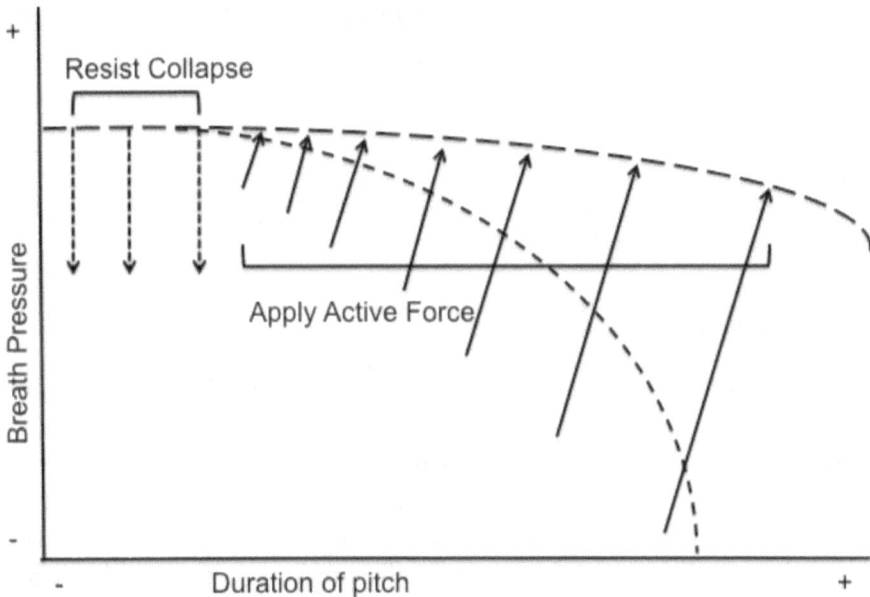

Figure 5.5. Singing with respiratory management. *Courtesy of Matt Edwards*

Try the following exercises:

- First, inhale, allowing your thorax and abdomen to expand in all directions.
- Then exhale, allowing your rib cage and diaphragm to return to their resting positions.
- Now place your hands on your bottom ribs, inhale, and feel the expansion.
- Sustain a hiss and allow the air to slowly leak between your teeth. As you release your air, attempt to keep your rib cage elevated, resisting its collapse toward its resting position.
- As the rib cage is returning to its resting position, you will reach a point where you feel like the airflow from your respiratory recoil alone is not enough to sustain your hiss. At that point, slowly contract your abdominal muscles as if performing a plank. As you slowly contract your abs, it will help pull the rib cage toward the pelvis, compressing your lungs while also compressing the abdominal contents, placing upward pressure on the diaphragm. The combination of these actions will increase the pressure inside of your lungs and return it closer to the level it was at the initiation of this exercise.

- Now try the same thing while sustaining a pitch. Pick whatever vowel is easiest for you to sing. Use all the same principles: maintain expansion by resisting the collapse and engage your abdominal muscles when you need a little boost.

For many rock singers, this straightforward approach to managing your breath is all that is needed.

The Size of Your Inhalation

It is important to note that the size of your breath directly influences your expiratory force. A larger breath generates greater expiratory force, resulting in a louder sound than a smaller breath. While a large breath can be advantageous for projecting your voice, it can pose challenges when attempting to sing a soft phrase. In order to sing a soft phrase, you need to take in less air. In general, you want to inhale only as much air as you need to sing the phrase you are singing. Excessive air beneath the vocal folds can lead to sensations of over-pressurization and tension, potentially hindering your ability to adjust your laryngeal registration.

Summary

When you take in a deep breath, you expand the alveoli. After being stretched, they will want to return to their original position, quickly expelling the air in your lungs. To counter this natural tendency, you will need to resist the return of your rib cage to its resting position. When you need a little extra help, engage your abdominal muscles. The more air you inhale, the greater the pressure in your lungs. This supports louder singing but demands more control. Conversely, when you take in less air, there's less pressure in your lungs, which often works best for softer singing. When singing softly, you can pay less attention to respiratory management than when singing loudly.

Body Type and Respiration

If you talk to different singers, you will hear a lot of opinions about where to feel expansion, how much breath to inhale before singing, and how to engage the abdominal muscles. It is important to remember that everyone's body is different and that singers will expand in different ways based on their body type. There are three main body shapes, called somatoypes, that are associated with the space between the waist and the neck. Each shape can impact the way one experiences respiratory expansion. If you are an ectomorph, someone with a torso that is rectangular in shape, you may discover that when you inhale, there is minimal abdominal expansion. You may instead find that the mid-torso area is where you feel most of your expansion when breathing. If you are a mesomorph, someone with a V-shaped torso, you may find it impossible to expand abdominally, and instead, you may feel upper chest expansion when you take a full breath. If you are an endomorph, someone with a pear-shaped torso, you may find that abdominal expansion is the most comfortable and easiest way to take a full breath. Research suggests that the outcomes from these different movement patterns as related to somatotype are statistically insignificant, meaning you can get the same results by using your body differently.[5] So be careful not to force your body into someone else's ideal movement pattern; instead, allow yourself to breathe in a way that is optimal for your body type.

It is also possible that you will benefit from feeling expansion in ways that may not align with your body type. As you experiment with respiratory coordination, try shifting your sensations of expansion to different parts of your body. Sing a phrase while feeling low expansion, then try focusing on lateral expansion, and then explore what vertical expansion feels like. Lower expansion engages something called tracheal pull, which will lower your larynx. Expansion in the upper portion of your torso will let the larynx rise and could also increase subglottic pressure. Through experimentation, you may discover that some approaches work better for some songs than others. You may also find that one approach to expansion consistently gives you the best results even though it is different than what you would expect from someone with your body type. Keep experimenting until you find what works best for you.

SING LIKE YOU SPEAK

One of the most basic concepts of singing rock 'n' roll is to build from the speaking voice. While this may come naturally to some singers, others may have deviated from speech due to specific training methods or years of suppressing their voice. If you find yourself in this category, it is essential to reestablish the connection between speaking and singing. The exercise below will help you develop that connection. If you already have a strong connection between your speaking and singing voice, you can proceed to the next section on registration.

1. Speak through the first verse of "Mary Had a Little Lamb" or another simple song without trying to add any excessive inflection to your voice.
2. Now speak the text in rhythm. Do not add pitch; just get used to speaking rhythmically.
3. Next, speak through the text as if you were a voice over artist, allowing your voice to rise and fall in pitch as you speak. We call these variations in the pitch of your speech inflection.
4. Now speak through the words again, combining inflected speech with the rhythms of the words within the song.
5. Next, you are going to repeat step 4, but this time allow the pitch of your voice to rise and fall in approximation to the pitches of the vocal line. I call this part of the process tracing.
6. In the final step, you are going to add the exact pitches. Your goal in this step is to sing the words on the notes without any attempt at being musical. Do not worry about your vocal tone; simply speak the words on pitch. ♪

After you have mastered this process with "Mary Had a Little Lamb," try the same approach with other simple songs. The goal is to break out of trying to sound a certain way and instead teach your brain to associate your speaking voice with singing. It is from this place we can build all the other qualities necessary for bringing songs to life.

Spatial Awareness

As you get comfortable with singing like you speak, experiment with changing your spatial awareness. For example, what is it like to sing like you are speaking to someone standing three or less feet away? This is what we call intimate space. What is it like to sing to someone approximately three to six feet away, what we would call personal space? Now imagine singing to someone in a social space, which is six to twelve feet away from you. Finally, sing to someone in public space, approximately twelve to thirty feet away from you. As you explore these different spatial arrangements, you will instinctually change the intensity of your voice. Intensity refers to the varying degrees of vocal effort and volume used to sing. This will be a critical factor in finding the right vocal quality for your songs.

THE BASICS OF SINGING ROCK 'N' ROLL

This May Not Come Easily to All Readers

Do not be surprised if singing like you speak and varying your spatial awareness is more difficult than you expected. Remember the learning stages, specifically the automatic stage. If you are in the automatic stage for singing that is not speech based, you will be in the cognitive stage for this exercise. That means it is not going to come automatically, and it may take a few days or weeks before you feel secure with this approach. There are additional suggestions for overcoming obstacles to speech-based singing in the section on crossing over from classical to musical theater.

REGISTERS

"Register" is a term we use to describe a series of pitches characterized by a similar vocal quality produced with similar mechanical action at the vocal fold level. By delving into the concept of registers, we can develop a deeper understanding of the intricacies of vocal production and develop a framework to categorize and understand the sounds you hear and produce. There are some texts that discuss registers from a perspective that encompasses both resonance and vocal fold activity. Resonance does indeed play a role in registration, and this unified viewpoint can be beneficial for singers in some genres. However, when it comes to rock singing, this author finds it more beneficial to discuss and train resonance and vocal fold vibration separately. Therefore, in this book, the term "register" will be used to refer to vocal qualities that share similar characteristics at the level of the vocal folds.

Why Laryngeal Registration Matters

The vocal folds create pulsations of air that we associate with vibrations that travel through the vocal tract, where various frequencies are amplified and attenuated by the cavities of the vocal tract, creating the spectrum that we perceive as vowels, consonants, and timbre. The vocal folds produce a wide range of harmonics when they vibrate; "harmonics" is a term we use to describe a numerical sequence of frequencies that are produced alongside the pitch we are singing. These frequencies give character to our sound. If you want a ringing, vibrant sound, you need the vocal folds to produce strong mid- to high-frequency harmonics. If you want a breathy sound, you need to reduce the strength of the harmonics. This is all determined by laryngeal registration. If you do not have the right closure for a belt at the vocal fold level, you will not be able to produce a ringing quality through placement, resonance, or breath adjustments. You must get the vocal folds to produce the right quality for your resonance to enhance. That is why we have to pay close attention to what is happening at the vocal fold level and the resulting laryngeal registration.

There are many opinions about how many registers we have, and there are very well-intentioned debates about categorizing this aspect of vocal production. However, it is easy to lose track of what really matters, which is the range of sounds you are able to produce. It doesn't matter what terminology you adopt; what matters most is that you can use the full spectrum of your voice. In this chapter, I am going to introduce my preferred terminology. The exercises will empower you to make a wide variety of vocal qualities that you can then define in ways that make the most sense for you.

Chest Voice

"Chest voice" or "chest register" is a term we use to describe when the vocal folds are firmly closed together to produce a sound rich in harmonics with a resulting quality that is buzzy and vibrant.[6] This quality is found primarily in the lower part of your range. Some singers relate this quality to the sound of a brass instrument; others associate the sound with the ringing of a guitar string or the vibrancy of a reed instrument like the saxophone. For vocal examples, listen to the beginning of "Mmm mmm mmm mmm" by Crash Test Dummies and "What's Up" by 4 Non Blondes; both singers are performing with a chest-dominant quality at the beginnings of these songs.

Chest register is produced when the vocal folds are closed firmly together with minimal airflow, so in the initial learning stage of this register, it is not necessary to put much emphasis on respiratory control. At first, all you need to do is breathe in as if you were getting ready to speak a long sentence. Then, as you sing, just release your air. You do not need to contract your abs, resist the collapse, or use any other strategy. Just sing.

Let's first isolate your chest register with your speaking voice. To do this, I want you to imitate the stereotypical sound of Santa Claus's laugh. We can divide the volume of your voice across a ten-point scale, with one being the softest you can use your voice and ten being the loudest you can use your voice without screaming. As you are imitating the Santa Claus laugh, I want you to experiment with volume levels somewhere between six and eight. This should feel similar to when you are speaking loudly, for example, to a group of people standing twelve to fifteen feet away from you. After you've played around with chest register in speech, it is time to put chest register on pitch.

You are going to begin by singing /ha-ha-ha-ha-ha/ with a bright /a/ vowel on a single pitch in the lower part of your range at volume eight on the scale of one to ten. You are going to be singing in staccato, meaning you will use short pulses. When you can consistently find this quality with the staccato "ha," I want you to sustain the last pitch for three seconds. Observe what you feel, hear, and/or visualize when making this sound. Some readers will feel vibrations in specific parts of their bodies, others will be more drawn to what they hear, and some may visualize colors. There is no right or wrong answer here; just take it all in and make note of what you are experiencing. ♪

When you can comfortably sustain the final note for three seconds, it's time to move on to stepwise motion. We are going to start with a simple 1-2-3-2-1 pattern at volume eight with a bright /a/. SA singers will begin at the A below middle C (A3), and TBB singers will begin on the D below middle C (D3). Most SA singers will be able to carry this quality up to the G above middle C (G4), and some will be able to carry it to A4 or higher. Most TBB singers will be able to carry this quality up to the D above middle C (D4), and some will be able to take it to G4. You will know you are carrying this quality up too high when you feel tightness in your throat, the sound gets strained, you sing flat, or you can no longer sing higher without flipping into your head voice. When practicing, pay attention to any signs of strain and do not exceed what is comfortable. When you can successfully sing in chest voice with a 1-2-3-2-1 pattern, try a 1-2-3-4-5-4-3-2-1 pattern. It is important when working on your chest register that you do not practice at the extremes. Instead, practice at about 80 percent of your range and volume. ♪

These exercises are helping you coordinate and strengthen the action of the adductors (the thyroarytenoid, lateral cricoarytenoid, and interarytenoid muscles). We call these muscles the adductors because they are responsible for bringing the vocal folds together. In order to sing with power, you need these muscles to be coordinated and have enough strength to maintain vocal fold closure while changing pitch. We will discuss these muscles again in the section on mix. However, the next step for developing your voice is to coordinate the pitch changing muscle (the cricothyroid) and the muscle responsible for reducing vocal fold closure (the posterior cricoarytenoid).

Head Voice

"Head register" or "head voice" is a term we use to describe when the vocal folds are lightly pressed together and produce weaker high-frequency harmonics than in chest register.[7] This quality is found primarily in the upper part of a singer's range and is similar to the sound of a flute. Listen to the chorus of "Heart of Glass" by Blondie and "Fields of Joy" by Lenny Kravitz; both are good examples of a headier quality in the context of a song. Remember that audio technology is at play in both recordings, so you will hear a fairly clear sound, but in person, off microphone, these voices would have more airflow than you hear in the recording.

Sing a 5-4-3-2-1 pattern in the upper part of your range on /u/, imitating a flutelike quality at volume three to four on a ten-point scale. There should be more airflow than in chest voice and a sense of freedom in the throat. All voice types can begin this pattern on the E an octave above middle C (E5). Experiment in the upper part of your range first, then carry this quality as low as you can in your range, being sure to keep the air moving. Head register should feel easy, similar to sighing. You will want to exercise this quality throughout your entire range. ♪

Head voice exercises engage the cricothyroid muscle, which is responsible for elongating the vocal folds. As the vocal folds are elongated, the pitch rises, which is why we associate this muscle with high notes. In order to have easy high notes, you need to develop the coordination of the cricothyroid muscle.

Breathy and Pressed

"Breathy" is a term we use to describe when a vocal quality has a lot of excess air escaping along with the vibrations being produced by the vocal folds. "Pressed" is a term used to describe when there is very little air released with the tone and it sounds like the vocal folds are pressed together tightly. Both chest register and head register can be breathy or pressed, as can every shade of mix. When you are first isolating these registers, try to find the middle zone between pressed and breathy. As you expand your abilities, you will want to be able to sing all registers in a breathy and buzzy quality. This will become easier as you learn how to mix. ♪

MIX

"Mix" is a term we use to describe vocal qualities that have elements of the polarities of chest and head but are neither full chest nor full head. When you are singing like you speak, you are most likely mixing. In fact, most of the singing we do is in some shade of mix. Learning how to mix can be tricky because it requires the coordination of the intrinsic muscles of the larynx introduced in chapter 2. To summarize, you have a muscle in each vocal fold (thyroarytenoid) that contracts to shorten the vocal fold while also bulking it up. The vocal folds work together, so when you are engaging the thyroarytenoid muscle, you are engaging both vocal folds in this action. You have lengthening muscles (cricothyroid) that work in opposition to the shortening muscles (thyroarytenoid), thinning the vocal folds and helping us sing high notes. We have two muscles on the sides of the larynx (lateral cricoarytenoids) and one in the back of the larynx (interarytenoid) that help bring the vocal folds together. Those muscles work in tandem with two muscles in the back of the larynx that pull the vocal folds apart (posterior cricoarytenoids) to help us regulate how breathy or pressed the tone is when we sing. If the vocal quality has more elements of chest than head, we call it chest-dominant mix or TA-dominant mix to acknowledge the bulking effect of engaging the thyroarytenoid (TA) muscle. If the quality of the mix is more like head register than chest register, we call it head-dominant mix or CT-dominant mix to recognize the thinning effects of cricothyroid (CT) engagement. Figure 5.6 shows the spectrum of registers we will use throughout this book.

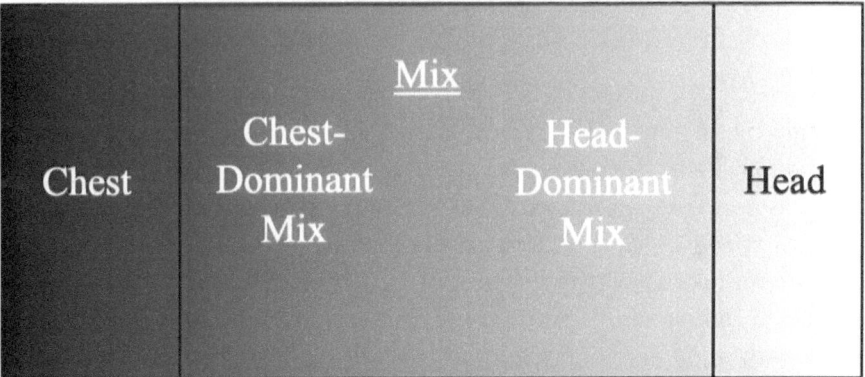

Figure 5.6. On the left side you see full chest and on the right side full head. The middle section is called mix, but that can be further broken down into chest-dominant mix and head-dominant mix. Within each zone, there are multitude of vocal qualities that can be produced. *Courtesy of Matt Edwards*

Be Patient

Sounds pretty complicated, right? It is. That's why you have to be patient with yourself when developing your mix. All of the vocal qualities in this spectrum require those five laryngeal muscles to find different ratios of engagement. They adjust with every register quality shift on every pitch you sing. The good news is that with targeted exercises, you can teach these muscles to work together. That is what the next set of exercises will help you do.

The motor learning principles we discussed earlier are especially applicable when working on your mix. When you first start this work, you will be at the beginning of the cognitive stage of learning, and your body will struggle to coordinate the action of all these muscles. It will take your body several weeks to coordinate the movement necessary to smoothly move from one register to the next and move from the cognitive stage to the motor learning stage, where you will then begin to refine your coordination. So be patient with yourself when doing this work. It is difficult, but the payoff is worth the effort.

Mixing on a Single Pitch

The first step of learning how to mix is transitioning between a breathy vocal quality and a buzzy vocal quality on a single pitch. The buzzy quality is chest register, and the breathy quality takes you to the lightest possible version of head register. The higher you go in your range, the more you will hear the head register quality we found in isolation and the less you will hear pure chest register.

Head to Chest

Begin by singing "1-2-3-4" on a single pitch with one being the breathiest and four being the buzziest. Take your time and embrace any instability that you notice in your voice. That instability comes from your laryngeal muscles trying to work out their ratios of engagement. When you can do four counts, try expanding to six or eight counts, then see if you can expand to ten counts. When you can successfully transition from head to chest, with numbers, drop the numbers and see if you can transition using a bright /a/ vowel. Some singers find it helpful to think of releasing their air at first, then decreasing airflow as they transition to the buzzier chest register quality. Others will feel shifts in placement as they transition, and some may focus on visualizations that help them make these shifts. There is no wrong way to experience this transition; just focus on getting the vocal fold closure to change. ♪

Chest to Head

After you have coordinated the movement from head to chest, try to reverse the process and work from chest to head. If the numbers helped, start with "4-3-2-1" and then incrementally increase the counts up to ten. Some singers will find it helpful to think of starting in more of a held breath position and gradually exhaling more and more until they are into their full breathy quality. As in the previous exercise, some will feel placement shifts, and others will visualize the sound shifts. Use whatever experiences resonate most with you to integrate this exercise into your instrument. ♪

Head to Chest to Head and Vice Versa

When you have coordinated the movement from chest to head and head to chest, it is time to try combining the two. Start with transitioning from head to chest and then back to head. Do this over eight beats to start. When you are able to execute that transition, try moving from chest to head and back to chest. When you are able to successfully move in both directions, you are mixing! The next step is to mix across several pitches, which will help you progress toward being able to mix in your songs.

Mixing across Your Range

Once you have learned to mix on single pitches, you will want to explore singing across multiple pitches in variations of mix. For this step, we will use glides. Glides help us coordinate the vocal folds to transition between registers as we navigate different pitch ranges.

Ascending Glides

We will start by transitioning from the bottom up using our ten-point scale. We are going to begin our glide in a chest-dominant quality, starting somewhere around volume seven to eight. You are going to sing the first pitch for one second and then glide up to the note a fifth above your starting pitch. As you glide, you will transition to a five or six on the mixing scale. Hold the top note for one second, then descend back to your starting pitch, transitioning back to the register you used to begin the exercise. TBB singers should begin on the E below middle C (E3), and SA singers should begin on the A below middle C (A3). As you get into the upper part of your range, you will need to start transitioning to a three to four on the top note. Baritones can usually take this exercise to G4 on the top. Tenors may be able to glide to B♭4. SA singers will top out somewhere between D5 and F5. When you get up that high, you are getting into belting land, which we will discuss later in the chapter. Just keep playing while working on these exercises and remember that you are not trying to get it right just yet; all you are doing is exploring. ♪

Working around the Break

When you first begin this exercise, it will be difficult, and you may notice that the break in your voice is really pronounced. That is normal in the cognitive stage of this work. With repeated practice, the laryngeal muscles will gain the coordination necessary to smooth over the break. Some singers find it easier to navigate the break by changing vowels along the glide. For example, you may want to try beginning with a bright /a/ on the bottom note and transitioning through /o/ to /u/ on the top note. Then, as you descend, transition back through /o/ and return to /a/. Other singers find it helpful to transition from /e/ on the bottom to /i/ on the top. Feel free to experiment with other vowel combinations as well. The goal in using different vowels is to find ways to elicit the response you are looking for from your larynx when glides on a single vowel are not working. Once you find your entry-point vowel, you can work on coordinating your ability to use other vowel combinations as well.

Descending 5-4-3-2-1

When you are comfortable doing ascending glides, you will want to switch to descending 5-4-3-2-1 patterns. Begin in your head register, and as you descend, transition into a chest-dominant mix. TBB singers will begin on the C an octave above middle C (C5). SA singers will begin on the E an octave above middle C (E5). When working on this exercise, you may once again discover that your break is pronounced, but as in the previous exercises, it will smooth out with continued practice. One strategy you can try in this stage is alternating between the starting point and the goal. Sing the starting pitch with the quality you want followed by the pitch you are transitioning to with the quality you want for that pitch. Alternate between the two qualities at least five times, then try singing the descending pattern again. What you are doing with this process is showing your body where you want to start and where you want to end, which gives you reference points to navigate between. Eventually, your body will connect the dots, and you will be able to transition easily between the two pitches. ♪

Explore All Variations in the Middle

As you get comfortable with the exercises above, begin focusing on establishing a speechlike mix that you can use throughout the middle of your range. Think about how your voice changes when you are talking calmly, speaking with excitement, or having an emotionally neutral conversation. You want to coordinate your laryngeal muscles to replicate those qualities. This is the baseline from which you can expand.

When your speechlike mix is consistent, you will want to start finding every variation you have available to you so that you have more options when singing songs. For example, let us say you have identified E4 to A4 as the part of your range where you would like to have multiple options. Glide from A3 to E4, transitioning from chest to some variation of mix that is not pure chest. Then immediately sing a 5-4-3-2-1 pattern beginning on B4 and ending on E4. In this pattern, transition from head register to some variation of chest mix. Then repeat the process on each half step between E4 and A4, alternating between gliding up and descending through your range. Be sure to try different vowel qualities and intensities. Along the way, you will discover lots of different ways to produce sound. Some variations will be better for upbeat songs that require belting. Other variations will be better for slow ballads. As you discover new options, think about how you can use them in your songs.

Give Yourself Time

It is important to remember that registration work can take months and for some people years to master. Take your time and maintain a growth mindset. You are not trying to find the one way to mix but rather all the possibilities of mix that are available to you throughout your range. Every day you practice, you will learn more about your voice that will help you gain a better understanding of your instrument.

BELTING

"Belting" is a term used to describe a high-energy, speechlike, chest-dominant vocal quality in the upper part of a singer's range and is usually connected to lyrics that express heightened emotional states of being. Belting is not a singular sound; rather, it is a spectrum, and it is found in many different genres. Some examples of songs that include belting are the choruses of "Alone" by Heart, "Sweet Child of Mine" by Guns N' Roses, "I Miss the Misery" by Halestorm, and "We Are the Champions" by Queen.

Chest Belt and Mix Belt

Belt can be divided into chest belt and mix belt. Chest belt is produced by carrying the chest register into the uppermost part of the range. The sound is similar in quality to a shout or a yell. SA voices can usually chest belt up to somewhere between the A above middle C (A4) and the D an octave above middle C (D5). Basses can usually carry a chest belt up to the F above middle C (F4), baritones can carry it up to G4, and tenors can carry it to A4. Mix belt is a quality that is similar to calling out to someone across a parking lot. It is chest voice dominant, but the vocal folds thin out as the singer ascends in the same way described in the ascending glides section of this chapter. SA voices can usually carry a mix belt up to somewhere between the D an octave above middle C (D5) and the F♯ above that (F♯5). Basses can usually carry a mix belt up to the G above middle C (G4), baritones can carry it up to A4, and tenors can carry it to C5.

The difference between your speechlike mix and belting is the ratio of chest register in the mix along with the intensity level. Belting is chest dominant and produced at a higher intensity level than mix. It is important to note that the intensity level does not need to reach 100 percent for it to be considered a belt. You may be able to produce a vocal quality that would pass as a belt with only 70 percent of your maximum intensity. The quality is more important than how loud it is, so find what works for you instead of trying to meet the vocal power of other singers.

Developing Your Belt

To develop your belt, you first need to add more chest into your mix. Often, singers will stumble into their belt while exploring the middle. If it does not show up on its own while using the exercises described above, you will return to the ascending fifth glides. SA singers should start on the D above middle C (D4), and TBB singers should start on the A below middle-C (A3). Begin the glide in pure chest on a bright /a/ or /ae/, and as you ascend, lighten up as little as you need to so that you reach the top note without screaming. Imagine a ten-point scale where ten is chest voice and one is head voice. When ascending, you are going to begin at ten and thin out to seven. If seven feels too heavy, try six. If seven feels too light, try eight. Keep experimenting to discover what your voice can do.

Try Calling

Some singers find it helpful to alternate between calling out to and doing the glides. Imagine you see a friend across the parking lot. Call out their name just like you would if you were outside, for example, "Hey Don!" Remember that there is a difference between yelling or shouting and calling. Find a sustainable and repeatable call. Then go back to glides and try to glide into the call quality. Keep alternating between calling out and gliding until you figure out how to match the glide quality to the calling quality.

Alternate with Your Head Voice

Throughout this work, it is a good idea to take a break from belting and vocalize in your head voice. Alternating between the two will give you better results than focusing only on your belt. If you begin to lose your voice, that is a sign you are belting with more chest register than your voice can handle. If that happens, stop and vocalize in your head voice and stop practicing your belt for the day. Once you have found your belt, you will want to use the stamina exercises in chapter 7 to work toward belting in songs.

COORDINATING THE VOCAL TRACT

As you coordinate your registers, you may notice entanglements along the way. Entanglements are involuntary muscle contractions or uncoordinated movements that interfere with your ability to produce the sounds you want to make. To address these entanglements, you will need to coordinate the vocal tract. In this chapter, we will focus on the movements of the various parts of the vocal tract. In chapters 6 to 8, I will give more details about how to apply these exercises.

Placement

Many singers I work with ask where they are supposed to place their voice. They are usually surprised to discover that I almost never talk about placement. This is because vocal placement is the outcome of the interplay between vocal fold vibrations and resonance, which together generate the sensations that you feel in your skull. Singers perceive placement in many ways. When multiple singers are producing the same vocal quality, one might sense it in their forehead, another on the bridge of their nose, another in the back of their head, and yet another might not feel any specific placement at all. Because everyone experiences vibratory sensations differently, it is impossible to give specific prescriptions for placement to all singers. So instead, I will guide you how to make a variety of vocal tract adjustments and allow you to experience any resulting sensations for yourself. You might notice that your cheekbones buzz when you sing a high G with a chest mix, open jaw, and a bright vowel. That's valuable feedback that is the result of specific technical choices you made. However, the temptation often arises to consistently place your voice in that particular spot every time you sing a G in an attempt to repeat your success, and this is where problems can emerge.

Let's say you made this discovery on a Monday. On Tuesday, you practice, but the buzzing in your cheekbones eludes you. Eager to replicate the sensation, you begin concentrating intensely on forcing the sound into that spot. What you may not realize is that the muscles around your larynx are tightening in the process. Come Wednesday, you try again, but your previous method of squeezing the sound into place no longer works, so you resort to squeezing in new ways. By Friday, your throat feels tight, and you have lost all vibratory sensations in the process of trying to find them. The real issue is that your vocal folds are not generating strong enough harmonics to experience placement or that your vocal tract is not being aligned optimally to amplify the harmonics needed to trigger the sensations. Whatever the issue may be, it needs to be addressed directly to experience real and long-lasting changes.

THE BASICS OF SINGING ROCK 'N' ROLL

While it is true that experimenting with placement might yield some improvements, you are more likely to get entangled through generalized adjustments instead of problem-specific ones. That is why I advocate for making deliberate adjustments to your vocal folds and/or vocal tract to achieve a desired outcome and then take note of any resulting sensations if you notice them at all. Those sensations can serve as a helpful gauge but avoid the temptation to force the result. It is a subtle shift in perspective, but it can significantly enhance your vocal development.

Front Room and Back Room

Kenneth Bozeman is a leading authority on vocal acoustics and has a great metaphor to help us think about how the vocal tract functions. Bozeman says we can envision the vocal tract as having two distinct sections: the "back room" and the "front room" (see figure 5.7). The back room encompasses everything from the vocal folds to the hump of the tongue, while

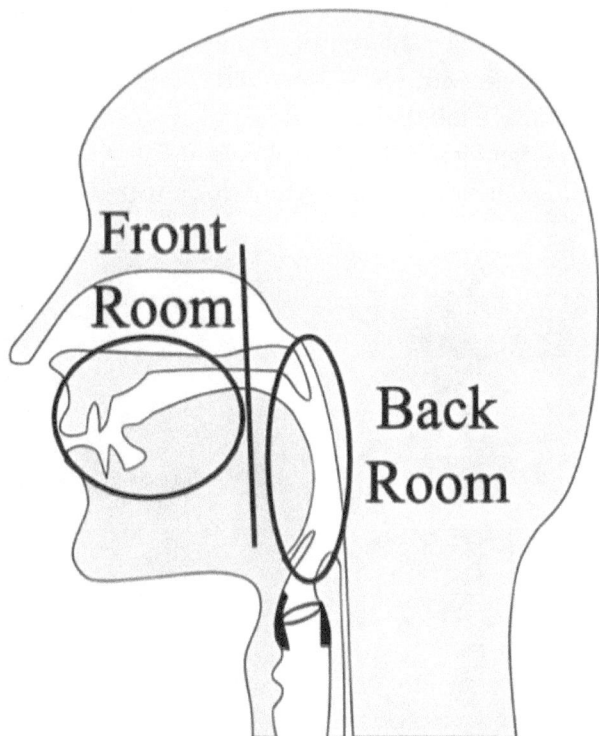

Figure 5.7. The front room back room metaphor posited by Ken Bozeman. *Courtesy of Matt Edwards*

the front room includes everything from the hump of the tongue to the opening of the lips. Changes in the back room will affect primarily timbre. "Timbre" is a term we use to describe the unique and distinctive quality of a sound that distinguishes it from other sounds of the same pitch and loudness, for example, the difference of the tone quality between two voices on the same pitch singing the same vowel. Changes in the front room will affect primarily vowel clarity, meaning how clear, spread, or rounded the vowel is when you sing.[8] There are, of course, interactions between the two, but adopting this framework can often assist singers in making more effective adjustments to achieve their desired outcomes. Now I will walk you through some exercises to explore how the different components function when using different timbre and vowel qualities.

Laryngeal Movement

We will begin with the movement of the larynx. Place your fingers on the sides of your larynx, as shown in figure 5.8, and glide from the lowest pitch to the highest pitch you can produce without manipulating the tonal quality of your voice. As you performed the glide, you should have felt the larynx ascend with pitch. Now glide from a high pitch to a low pitch; you should have felt the larynx descend as you performed this glide. This up-and-down motion is the normal movement of the larynx when we are not trying to control it; it goes up and down with the pitch. However,

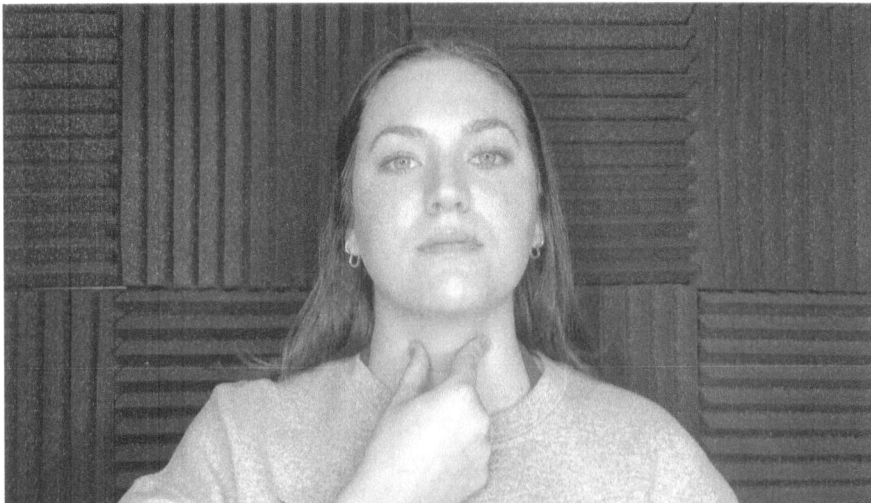

Figure 5.8.   Place your fingers gently on your larynx to monitor its movement.
Courtesy of Matt Edwards

sometimes we want the larynx to gravitate toward one of these positions to produce a specific quality.

High Larynx

Let us experiment with singing in a higher laryngeal position. You can elicit a higher laryngeal position by singing "wae wae wae wae wae" on a single pitch, imitating the cry of a baby. For most singers, the larynx will naturally rise when producing this sound. Now try singing a 1-3-5-3-1 pattern throughout your range on "wae," attempting to maintain a higher laryngeal position. Sing only as high and as low in your range as is comfortable. You should have noticed that the voice took on a brighter and perhaps harsher quality than your neutral singing voice. A higher laryngeal position shortens the length of the back room. When we decrease the size of the back room, our timbre will be brighter than when we enlarge the space. Singing with a high larynx increases the closure of the vocal folds, so we have to be cautious to not over-sing in this position. In fact, for most singers, a consistently high larynx is not ideal. The ideal is a larynx that can freely move between the extremes. ♪

Low Larynx

For the next step, we are going to focus on lowering the larynx, which will enlarge the back room and result in a warmer timbre. Place your fingers on the sides of your larynx and imagine you are sipping a string of spaghetti. You should notice your larynx dropping lower in your neck. Now try saying "ho ho ho ho ho," envisioning the deep laugh of Santa Claus and allowing your larynx to lower as it did when you sipped spaghetti. Now sing a 1-3-5-3-1 pattern on "ho," exploring the lower laryngeal position throughout your range. Sing only as high and as low in your range as is comfortable. Just as a high laryngeal position is not an ideal default, neither is a low position. However, there are only three muscles that lower your larynx, while there are seven that raise your larynx. Therefore, it is important to exercise the lowering muscles to maintain laryngeal flexibility. ♪

Neutral

After exploring these extremes, let us bring your larynx back to a neutral position. Take a few breaths in and out while keeping your fingers on the sides of your larynx. You should feel minimal movement. After a few breaths, sing an /a/ vowel in a comfortable part of your range and try to maintain the same laryngeal position as when you were inhaling and exhaling. Next, perform a slight glide upward, only as high as you can while maintaining a neutral position, and then glide back to your starting pitch. Finally, sing a 1-3-5-3-1 pattern on /a/, maintaining the neutral position. When you are singing, you can encourage your larynx to remain in a neutral position by attempting to maintain the timbre of your voice as you ascend in pitch. There are some well-known teachers and singers who advocate using a neutral position throughout the range. However, in this author's experience, maintaining a neutral position throughout the range can lead to pitch and tension problems in the upper range of the voice. ♪

Drilling All Three Positions

Perform these exercises separately until you become more familiar with the movement capabilities of your larynx. Remember to listen to your body and adjust the exercises to your own comfort and range. When you can do each one independently, try doing all three in a row on the same set of pitches. For example, you might start on A3 (A below middle C) and sing a 1-3-5-3-1 pattern. Start with "wae," allowing your larynx to rise; follow that with "ho" while maintaining a lower laryngeal position; then end with /a/ and try to keep a neutral laryngeal position. This random practice will help your brain make sense of the new movement patterns and commit the possibilities to memory. ♪

The ultimate goal is for you to think of making your voice warmer or brighter and have your larynx respond accordingly. We do not want to micromanage your laryngeal position when you sing but rather allow it to respond to your intent. By exercising its full range of motion, you are working through the stages of learning so that we can eventually reach the automatic stage where everything just comes together.

Pharyngeal Width

"Pharynx" is a term used to describe a muscular tube-shaped organ in the throat that connects the mouth and nasal passages to the esophagus and larynx, allowing air and food to pass through. Within the pharynx, there are several constrictor muscles that have the ability to narrow the space to help guide food into the esophagus. In classical and certain other singing styles, this narrowing is often considered counterproductive. However, in rock singing, it can be desirable to intentionally recruit these muscles to achieve gritty and metallic vocal qualities. The distinction between a healthy and a risky approach lies in the singer's ability to make a conscious decision to engage these muscles. It is essential for singers to have control over the recruitment of constrictor muscles in the pharynx and to exercise this control wisely. It is important to note that the degree of narrowing to add a vocal effect should be slight. If excessive constriction occurs, it can exert harmful pressure on the larynx, potentially leading to vocal problems.

To explore the sensation of pharyngeal narrowing, place your fingers on the side of your neck, as shown in figure 5.9. Take a deep breath in and out while paying attention to the width between your fingers on both hands. Now sing "ha ha ha" on a single pitch as if you are laughing. You should notice that the space between your fingers stays stable. This is a neutral configuration for your pharynx. Try singing with this quality throughout your range. Now sing "goog, goog, goog" on a 1-3-5-3-1 pattern. You should feel the distance between your hands narrow, indicating intentional pharyngeal narrowing. Practice on "goog" in the middle part of your range. Then practice alternating between a laugh position (neutral) and the slightly constricted position (goog) on a single pitch. Finally, vocalize while alternating between the two qualities throughout your range. ♪

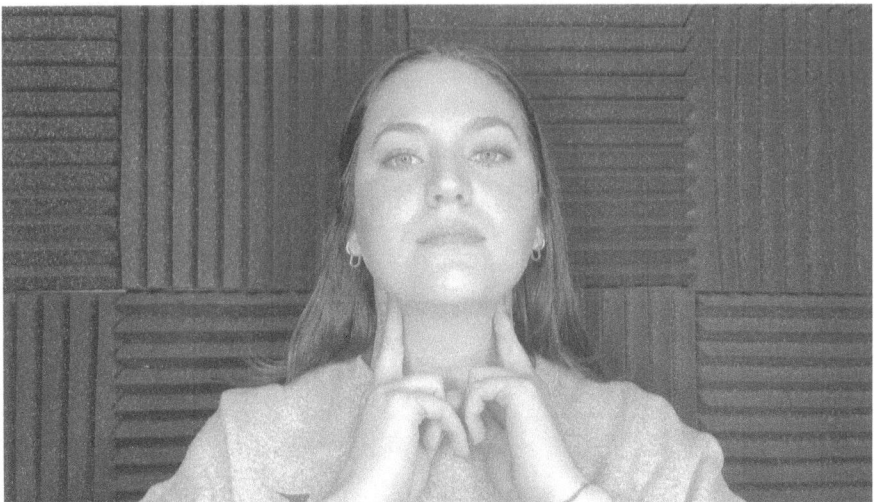

Figure 5.9. Monitoring pharyngeal narrowing. *Courtesy of Matt Edwards*

At this stage, we are simply mapping the movement potential of this aspect of your pharynx. In future chapters, we will discuss situations where intentional narrowing may be appropriate and when corrective measures may be necessary. Remember, it is crucial to approach these exercises with care and moderation, always prioritizing the health and well-being of your voice.

Soft Palate

The soft palate, also known as the velum, is a muscular structure located at the back of the oral cavity that separates the oral cavity from the nasal cavity. Shaped like a dome, the soft palate is responsible primarily for preventing food and liquids from entering the nasal cavity during swallowing, and it plays a crucial role in speech production. When it comes to singing, the soft palate can assume various positions, greatly influencing the timbre of the voice. Let's explore three different positions of the soft palate to gain a better understanding of its movement potential.

Elevated Palate

To begin, I'd like you to say "pa pa pa." In order for your body to make a /p/ sound, the soft palate must elevate. Next, start the "pa" but focus on the /p/ sound and pinch your nose shut. You should notice that air is trapped in your vocal tract with no air escaping through your nose. This sensation signifies an elevated soft palate. Now let us vocalize with an elevated soft palate. Start with a held /p/, then after one to two seconds, proceed to an /a/ vowel and sing the /a/ across a 1-2-3-2-1 or 1-2-3-4-5-4-3-2-1 pattern. You will know the palate is elevated if you pinch your nose shut and nothing changes when singing the vowel. Do this exercise until you are able to maintain an elevated soft palate. Then try vocalizing with an elevated palate on an /a/ vowel with a 1-3-5-3-1 pattern without using a /p/ to start. If your voice starts getting nasal, go back to starting with a /p/ on each pitch and then, when you are able to maintain an elevated palate, drop the /p/ and try to keep the elevation on the /a/ vowel. ♪

Low Palate

Next, let's explore a low soft palate position by singing /ng/. While singing /ng/, pinch your nose shut and observe how the sound abruptly stops.

This occurs because in the /ng/ position, sound can exit only through the nose. This is how we know the soft palate is in a lowered position. Vocalize on /ng/ with a 1-3-5-3-1 pattern in the same range as you exercised with the palate elevated. Pay attention to the differences, and once you are comfortable, advance to the next step. ♪

Half Elevated

The final of the three positions is half elevated; this is the position the soft palate assumes when speaking or singing nasalized vowels. Seal your lips gently and take slow breaths in and out through your nose. Try this for about three to five breaths. After that, exhale with a sigh while directing all the sound through your nose while keeping your lips closed. Repeat the sigh, concentrating on channeling the sound through your nasal passages. Then, while sighing, gradually begin to open your mouth toward the shape of an /o/ vowel. As your mouth opens, some of the sound will shift from your nose to your mouth's opening. Finally, begin the sigh with your mouth in the shape of an /o/ vowel; this is how you produce a nasalized /o/. Once you have coordinated the nasalized /o/, practice vocalizing in that position using a 1-3-5-3-1 pattern. The sensation should be akin to dividing the sound equally between your nose and mouth. ♪

Vocalizing All Three

Now let's vocalize all three positions back-to-back like we did when exploring the movement of the larynx. We are going to use a 1-3-5-3-1 pattern at volume five to seven. Ideally this would be produced in your mix, but if mix is still new to you, pick chest or head, whichever is easier. Sing the 1-3-5-3-1 pattern first on /ng/, followed by "pa pa pa," followed by the nasalized /o/. Explore these sounds throughout your range, never going higher or lower than is comfortable. ♪

Transitioning

Finally, we are going to explore the entire spectrum of sounds that lie between these two extremes. We will begin with a hyper-nasal /a/ sound produced with about a half inch of space between the upper and lower teeth. This sound is created by slightly elevating the soft palate from the

/ng/ position; the result will be more nasalized than the /o/ we were vocalizing with above. Once you have isolated the nasalized /a/, you will gradually morph the /a/ sound toward the "pa pa pa" place, where the soft palate is elevated. Do this on a single pitch, taking your time to explore every variation in between the nasalized /a/ and the elevated /a/. Once you've become adept at transitioning between these positions, pause at different points along the spectrum and settle into each sound. Then try singing a phrase of a song in that particular position. ♪

For rock singers, the palate is constantly moving, rarely fixed in any one of these positions. However, by coordinating them in isolation, you are training your motor system to have options. The eventual goal is for the soft palate to respond automatically to the intent of the song you are singing.

Jaw

Next, we will explore how changing the position of your mouth opening can impact your vocal quality. Before we dive into the exercises, it is important to talk about temporomandibular joint disorder (TMJD). TMJD is a condition that affects the jaw joint and surrounding muscles. This disorder can lead to a range of uncomfortable symptoms, including jaw pain, clicking or popping sounds when opening or closing the mouth, and difficulty in fully opening or closing the jaw. TMJD can be caused by various factors; the exact cause for each person is often complex and multifaceted. Those with TMJD should be careful with the exercises below. Only go as far as is comfortable and take your time. If you are unsure whether you have TMJD but experience clicking and/or popping sensations in your jaw, you should also take care not to push yourself too far. TMJD is a medical condition that needs to be diagnosed by a dentist or physician, so consult a medical professional if you are in doubt. Generally, a jaw opening up to the diameter of a wine bottle cork is comfortable for most singers and provides sufficient space for singing. Beyond this point, you are more likely to experience clicking or popping sensations.

Before we try the exercises below, let's massage one of the primary muscles responsible for closing your jaw: the masseter muscle. The masseter muscle is responsible for helping us bite when we eat. It originates from the zygomatic arch, which is a bony prominence on the side of the skull near the temple area and extends downward, attaching to the outer surface of the mandible (lower jawbone) near its angle. Because the masseter muscle is accustomed to engaging after we open our mouth, it will often try to engage when we are singing. That can cause a lot of unnecessary tension when you sing. Instead, we want to train it to relax when vocalizing.

Use your first two fingers to gently push in on the masseter muscle right below the zygomatic arch, as shown in figure 5.10. As you gently push inward, slowly open your jaw. Let your jaw hang open in this position for around fifteen seconds, then release. Rest for fifteen to thirty seconds, then repeat the exercise but this time add your voice. Once you have assumed the drop jaw position with your fingers on the masseter muscle, vocalize on an /o/ vowel. Use your fingers to encourage the masseter muscle to let go. If you still feel like your body wants to bite down when you start to sing, try massaging the temporalis muscle as well.

The temporalis muscle is situated on each side of the head in the temporal region just above the ears and behind the eyes (see figure 5.11). It spreads out like a fan across this area. Use your three middle fingers to massage this part of your head as you drop your jaw open. If you feel like you have tension in both the temporalis muscle and the masseter, you can massage both at the same time by using your middle three fingers on the temporalis muscle and your thumbs on your masseter muscle. It may take a while for these muscles to learn to let go, but it is a process worth spending time on.

Figure 5.10. Massaging the masseter muscle. *Courtesy of Matt Edwards*

Figure 5.11. Massaging the temporalis muscle. *Courtesy of Matt Edwards*

For the next exercise, you will want to wash or sanitize your hands, then place the tip of your pinky finger horizontally between your teeth. This is a narrow mouth opening. Allow your teeth to rest on your finger as you perform a 1-5-1 glide on /a/. If you feel like you need to make adjustments as you glide, you will have to make those changes in the back room of your vocal tract. Explore how changes in your laryngeal, soft palate, and tongue positions impact your singing in this position. Then try singing a phrase of a song in the same position.

Now touch the tip of your tongue to the front part of the roof of your mouth, right behind the ridge of your upper teeth. Lower your jaw until your tongue is about to pull away, then close your mouth one to two millimeters and relax into a comfortable position with your tongue resting behind your bottom teeth. This is your wide jaw opening position for singing. If you feel any tightness in your cheeks, try massaging your masseter muscles as described above. Vocalize on 1-5-1 glides on /a/ in this position and pay attention to what you experience. Try singing a phrase with a wide jaw opening. Your jaw will need to close for some vowels and consonants but, overall, try to keep a more open position than you did in the previous exercise.

Remember that these are exploratory exercises aimed at understanding the impact of jaw positioning on vocal quality. Ideally, you want your jaw to be free when you sing. However, there may be instances in rock singing where you intentionally use a more closed jaw position for a gritty verse or an open position for an epic high note. Regardless of your choice, it's crucial that it remains a conscious decision rather than the only way you can sing.

Lips

Lip positioning is a little more straightforward since you can look in a mirror and see if you are doing what you think you are when singing. In some styles of singing, performers attempt to keep their lips in a relatively stable position to produce an even resonance quality throughout their range. However, rock singers usually let the lips move without thinking too much about it. Yet it is important to remember that the lips are controlled by muscles, and like all muscles that are part of singing, it is important to make sure they are coordinated to do what you want them to do.

Stand in front of a mirror or use the selfie function on your phone and examine your resting lip position. Everyone's mouth is shaped differently; some readers will feel like their lips are wide and others narrow. What is important is they move the way you want them to move. To start, bring your lips into a narrow position as if you were about to kiss someone or something. This lip position is usually similar to what you would use to produce an /u/ vowel. In this position, try singing a song that you like to sing and notice what happens to the tone quality. Now smile, allowing your lips to spread wide open with your mouth only slightly open (think of the pinky finger space). Sing in this position and notice what happens to your tone quality. Now drop your jaw toward the wide opening we explored in the previous section and try spreading and rounding your lips. Take note of the resulting vocal qualities.

We can use these various lip positions to get different results both in tonal quality and in the communication of the song. Rounded or narrow lip positions, for example, can create a sense of restraint or internalization of emotions, which can be valuable in certain musical pieces. The narrowness of the lips attenuates higher frequencies, giving your voice a warmer vocal quality. Conversely, a spread or wide lip position with a dropped jaw can convey a powerful sense of unleashed energy. Singers often adopt this position when reaching extreme high notes or delivering intense vocal passages.

Experiment with singing phrases using different lip variations. Remember that, as I've emphasized with other concepts, it is ideal to explore and inhabit a spectrum of lip positions rather than confining yourself to a single approach. By actively engaging your lips in your practice, you are making sure your motor system is able to produce the results you are looking for in your songs.

Tongue

Finally, let's talk about your tongue. The tongue takes up a little more than half of the space in your vocal tract and extends from right above the vocal folds to the opening of your mouth. Because of its size, it is one of the most critical parts of our instrument for us to coordinate. The tongue can move in many different ways, each impacting the quality of our voice.

Retraction

The retracted tongue position usually comes from habits ingrained in our speaking voice. Many regional accents have this quality, and it can be an important part of a singer's signature sound. However, it can become problematic if the retracted tongue is pushing down on your larynx and either causing a depressed larynx when singing or creating a sense of constriction in the vocal tract. To experience a retracted tongue, dwell on the /r/ in any word starting or ending with an "r." Allow the tip of the tongue to raise toward the roof of your mouth while drawing backward in your vocal tract. The opposite of retraction is extension.

Extension

When we extend the tongue, it moves the mass of the body out of the back of the throat, which changes the timbre of the voice and can improve the clarity of your diction. Place your tongue on your bottom lip, slightly extending it from your mouth. Now vocalize in that position on the vowel /a/. You may notice that your tongue quivers. If that happens, it is a sign that the body is trying to draw the tongue back into the mouth. Try to vocalize in this position for three to five minutes to show your body that there is an alternative to pulling the tongue backward when singing. Some rock singers will use an extended tongue position on high notes to produce that extra snarl that we associate with electric guitar qualities. If you have tongue retraction that you are trying to correct, singing in an extended tongue position can help your body learn a new movement pattern, which will eventually allow you to relax into a neutral position.

Narrowing

There is a muscle inside of the tongue called the superior longitudinal lingual muscle that helps the tongue narrow its width. If this muscle engages when singing, it can contribute undesirable tone qualities. Try this exercise to see if it makes a difference for you. Look in a mirror and try to widen your tongue so that it takes up horizontal space in your mouth. It may even cover some of your bottom teeth. Vocalize on /a/ and watch your tongue. If it tries to narrow, work on coaxing it toward widening. It may help to combine tongue extension with widening as well.

Coordinating the Tongue

It is my belief that most of the issues with our tongues are related to a lack of coordination more than tension. I give variations of the following exercise routine to all of my students to help them get their tongues more agile. First, do the tongue extension and widening exercises above. One of my favorite warm-ups is to combine the tongue-out phonation with a hum. To do this, simply close your lips around your extended tongue and vocalize. Next, you are going to work on coordinating the movement of the front of your tongue. Place your hands on the sides of your face like when Kevin looks at himself in the mirror in the movie *Home Alone*. I call this "Home Alone face." Open your jaw to a comfortable position, usually between the width of a horizontal pinky finger and a vertical thumb between your front teeth. Then flick the tip of your tongue behind your upper teeth to articulate "la la la la la" on a single pitch. As you move your tongue, make sure your jaw remains still. That's what the *Home Alone* face hands are for: to help you monitor jaw movement. We want to isolate the movement of the tongue from the jaw to give you more flexibility in your singing.

After you have mastered "la la la la la," we are going to get the hump of the tongue moving with "ga ga ga ga ga." It is a little harder to keep the jaw absolutely still on "ga," but it should not be moving excessively. After you have mastered "la" and "ga" independently, you will want to pair the two together and sing "gala gala gala gala ga" on a single pitch. This is coordinating your tongue to be able to move effortlessly between forward and backward positions. As you get better with these exercises, feel free to drop the Home Alone hands. Just keep an eye on your jaw to make sure it doesn't start getting involved again. When you have mastered single pitches, extend the exercise to 1-2-3-2-1, 1-2-3-4-5-4-3-2-1, and 1-3-5-3-1 patterns. ♪

The next set of drills will activate both your lips and your tongue. We are going to use a series of syllables that are nonsense words but require constant tongue movement. The first is "diddle daeddle deedle daeddle doe." You will sing this on a single pitch as quickly as possible while making sure every syllable is clear. For the next variations, you are going to change the first consonant only. We will transition to "biddle baeddle beedle baeddle boe," then "fiddle faeddle feedle faeddle foe," and finally "tiddle taeddle teedle taeddle toe." When you have mastered each one independently, you will chain them together: "diddle daeddle deedle daeddle biddle baeddle beedle baeddle fiddle faeddle feedle faeddle tiddle taeddle teedle taeddle toe." See how fast you can get these exercises, but only go as fast as you can while maintaining clarity. ♪

As you improve the coordination of your tongue you should find it easier to sing throughout your range. If you encounter a note where the tongue engages, try singing it with an extended tongue and then with a wide tongue and then try singing it on "la" or any of the other movement patterns. By introducing these extreme movements, it should be easier to let your tongue rest back in your mouth in a neutral position and coordinate the movement necessary to get the sound you are looking for in your singing.

CONCLUSION

As you may have noticed, I have not told you how to sing but rather showed you how to explore the possibilities. This is an important distinction between the way I work with rock singers and singers of styles like musical theater, where there are standards and expectations for the final product a singer presents onstage. In the following chapters, I am going to cover some of the issues singers from different backgrounds may encounter when exploring these tools. I would suggest jumping to the chapter that seems to be most applicable to you and then reading the others as time allows. As you coordinate your instrument, you will discover sounds that you like, and after a while, what you are "supposed" to sound like should begin to reveal itself. This will hopefully make more sense as you work through the listening examples in the history and style chapters. Keep in mind this is a journey; you will be playing with your voice for as long as you sing. So enjoy the adventure and give yourself enough time to really cement these ideas into your instrument before expecting yourself to achieve mastery.

NOTES

1. Ingo R. Titze and Katherine Verdolini-Abbott, *Vocology: The Science and Practice of Voice Habilitation* (Salt Lake City, UT: National Center for Voice and Speech, 2012), 253–54.

2. Melissa Malde, MaryJean Allen, and Kurt-Alexander Zeller, *What Every Singer Needs to Know about the Body* (San Diego, CA: Plural Publishing, 2020), 1–14.

3. Malde et al., *What Every Singer Needs to Know about the Body*, 16–63.

4. Scott McCoy, *Your Voice: An Inside View* (Gahanna, OH: Inside View Press, 2004), 88–89.

5. Jennifer Griffith Cowgill, "Breathing for Singers: A Comparative Analysis of Body Types and Breathing Tendencies," *Journal of Singing* 66, no. 2 (2009): 141–47.

6. McCoy, *Your Voice*, 143–57.

7. McCoy, *Your Voice*, 143–57.

8. Kenneth W. Bozeman, *Kinesthetic Voice Pedagogy: Motivating Acoustic Efficiency* (Gahanna, OH: Inside View Press, 2021), 22.

6

TIPS FOR BEGINNERS

I know that some of the information in the previous chapters can be overwhelming for beginners. In this chapter, I am going to give you a little more insight into the terminology and help you structure a plan to start coordinating your voice. If vocal training is new to you, the best way to begin is by honing your listening skills. We are going to begin this chapter by listening to a few different singers and analyzing what they are doing, using some of the terms introduced in chapter 5. I also encourage you to read chapter 4 and listen to the examples if you have not done so yet.

Almost everything we discussed in chapter 5 can be summed up by thinking about register, intensity, and vowel quality. As we discussed earlier, "register" is a term we use to describe a series of pitches characterized by a similar vocal quality produced at the vocal fold level. "Intensity" refers to the varying degrees of vocal effort and volume used in a given register, and "vowel quality" refers to the brightness or warmth of your voice. Brightness is characterized by stronger upper frequencies in the voice, similar to turning up the treble on your stereo. Warmth is characterized by weaker upper frequencies, similar to turning down the treble and/or turning up the mid and bass frequencies. Ideally, you will reach a level of vocal coordination that enables you to focus on performing your song, and your voice will just respond. Until then, thinking in terms of register, intensity, and vowel quality can help you analyze others on your journey to finding your own signature sound.

LISTENING

"Don't Stop Me Now" by Queen

To help you gain a better understanding of how register, intensity, and vowel quality interact, let us listen to two examples. Go to your favorite streaming device and pull up "Don't Stop Me Now" by Queen. If you have access to YouTube, search for "Don't Stop Me Now Isolated Vocals," and you will find several options where the instruments have been removed from the recording. For this exercise, we are going to focus on the first verse and chorus.

Listen to the track and think about the register qualities we discussed in chapter 5. The track starts in a speechlike mix on the chest-dominant side of the spectrum. You can hear some air escaping with the tone, but it is not breathy. When he sings the word "world," he goes into a belt-like quality, and his larynx appears to rise from the more neutral position he started in. When he gets to "floating," you hear him switch to head register. Then he goes back to speechlike mix on "cause I'm. . . ." Starting at the lyric "I'm a . . . ," he stays on the chestier side of the spectrum. He does lighten the amount of chest in his mix on the highest notes; otherwise, he would get stuck. If you carry up too much chest, you end up shouting instead of singing. On "Lady Godiva," you hear a little bit of grit creep into the sound. This is the vocal fry variety of grit and is likely being produced by a higher laryngeal position with some biting tension in the jaw. He lets go of that grit on "go go," then you hear it come back on "burnin'." The higher notes of the chorus are on the lighter side of chest mix, indicating he is thinning out, the same way that we discussed reducing intensity on fifth glides in the section on learning to mix.

Now let us think about the intensity choices. At the beginning of the song, there is little perceivable effort, and the volume seems to be fairly neutral, hovering around four on a ten-point scale. When he sings "alive," it almost sounds like he is revving up his voice, much like one might rev up a motorcycle. As he does that, you hear the voice intensify toward a seven. By the time he hits "turn it inside out," we are growing toward eight. However, as soon as he sings "floating," the intensity shifts back to around a three. Then when he sings "cause I'm," he starts to intensify again, and we hear the intensity continue to hover between seven and eight. When he adds vocal distortion, it sounds like he is pushing nine to ten on the intensity level, but remember he is singing in front of a microphone, so while it sounds like he is giving a lot of intensity, we cannot be sure how loud he actually was in the room.

Now let us think about vowel quality. In the beginning of the song, his approach sounds fairly neutral. As he revs up his voice on "alive," you hear the vowels get brighter. For "and the world," we hear a return to neutral vowels, and then when he goes into his head register for "floating," the vowels get slightly warm. When he comes in on "having a . . . ," the brightness returns before going a little more neutral on "I'm a. . . ." When he gets gritty on "Lady Godiva," you can hear the vowels getting much brighter, which aids in bringing in the vocal distortion he uses in that part of the song. Then when he sings "I'm gonna . . . ," we hear him return to a warmer vocal quality. On "burnin' through . . . ," we hear the vowels go brighter again. Through the end of the chorus, he continues to alternate between neutral and bright vowel qualities. Throughout the first verse and chorus, he sings with a variety of vocal colors that bring the song to life. This is the kind of versatility I aim for with the range of motion exercises I introduced in chapter 5. The ultimate goal is for you to be able to seamlessly switch between vocal qualities just like Freddy Mercury.

"I Miss the Misery" by Halestorm

Now listen to the studio recording of "I Miss the Misery" by Halestorm. She begins with a vocal fry scream on a bright vowel with high intensity. This type of vocal production is discussed in chapter 9. The opening "Oh's" appear to have a neutral to low larynx with a chest-dominant mix and neutral vowels compared to the brighter vowel qualities we hear later in the song. When the verse kicks in with "I've been a . . . ," you hear her start in a neutral, closed vowel chest-dominant speechlike mix with a mid-level intensity around a five to six. At the lyric "Don't let me get . . . ," she intensifies her mix a bit, and the vowels start alternating between open and closed on lyrics like "don't let," "I miss," and "the fights" as the intensity builds into the chorus. As she launches into the chorus, she moves toward a chest-dominant quality on the upper end of the intensity scale. The vocals are stacked in the chorus, which makes them appear larger than life and adds additional intensity to this section of the song. She also brings some brightness into the words in a way that blends the voice with the electric guitars she's performing with in this song.

Now pull up a recording of her performing the song live. First of all, she usually starts with an extended vocal fry scream, showing her prowess in producing powerful vocal distortions. Notice how close her mouth is to the microphone and how she alternates between closed- and open-mouth positions as she sings. In the chorus, when she hits peak intensity, you will notice that she uses a wide jaw opening with spread lips. This amplifies the upper frequencies of her voice and can help produce the distortion that she uses throughout the song.

Listen on Your Own

Now do your own listening to further expand your analytical skills. Go to YouTube and search for "isolated vocal track." You'll come across a variety of options to choose from for analysis. Create or find and print a lyric sheet so that you can jot down your observations. As you listen, take notes on the singer's vocal registration. Identify whether they primarily use chest, head, or a mix of both. You can indicate chest register with the letter "C," head register with "H," and mix with "M," or you could get more specific with "CM" for chest mix and "HM" for head mix. Whenever you hear a register shift, mark the lyric where it happens. Now pay attention to what you hear in terms of intensity using a scale from one to ten, where one is the quietest and ten is the loudest. Finally, think about what you hear in terms of vowel quality. If it sounds like the artist is singing like they speak, mark it with "SL" to indicate speechlike. If the artist is using brighter vocal qualities, use "B." For warmer vocal qualities, use "W." For nasality, use "N," and if the voice is distorted, use "D."

After you have identified these elements, think about what you learned about the front room and back room of the vocal tract and take note of what you hear. Is there pharyngeal narrowing, or does the pharynx sound open? Does it sound like the singer's larynx is riding high, low, or neutral, or is it constantly moving? Is the soft palate locked high, dropped low, or in the middle to produce slight nasality, or is it constantly moving? Remember that smaller spaces in the back room produce brighter timbres than larger spaces. Clarity of the lyrics is regulated by the front of the tongue, lips, and jaw. Are the articulators agile, and is the singer producing clear, open vowels or closed, tight vowels? Does the tongue seem to move freely? Is it retracted, or is it active?

Keep repeating this exercise with several songs to solidify these concepts in your mind. When you understand how tonal goals relate to vocal function, it will make it easier for you to know which exercises you need to work on to achieve the range of motion necessary for the style of rock music you sing.

WORKING WITH A NONLINEAR SYSTEM

One of the hardest things about learning how to sing is that the voice is a nonlinear system, as we discussed in chapter 5. The nonlinearity means that one skill set might be improved by working on another skill set, but determining which one helps the other can be confusing at times. This is why a lot of beginning singers end up working with a professional teacher or coach; they need outside feedback to coordinate the systems to complement each other. In a book format, it is easiest to focus on the independent systems, which is what this author has chosen to do. If you are not able to work with someone at the moment, you can still learn a lot on your own. You just need to accept that some of the exercises may not seem beneficial in the moment, but eventually, you will combine several of the techniques to find the results you are looking for in your singing.

ENSURING GROWTH

When you are doing this work as a beginner, it is critically important to maintain a growth mindset. As mentioned earlier, a growth mindset is based on the belief that abilities and talents can be developed through dedication, hard work, and perseverance. Those with a growth mindset view challenges as opportunities for growth and see setbacks as learning experiences rather than reflections of their innate ability. In the context of singing, individuals with a growth mindset are more likely to embrace vocal challenges, seek feedback, and actively engage in practice and learning. They understand that improvement takes time and effort, and they are willing to invest that effort to develop their singing skills. In the initial stages of learning, you will need to do a lot of blocked practice in order to develop the skills necessary to take your singing to the next level. That means you will be doing the same exercise over and over again so that your motor system can create new neurological connections to execute the new movement pattern automatically. In this stage, you will benefit from external feedback from a teacher or a recording device.

Using a Recording

When using a recording device on your own, you will need to resist the temptation to judge the entirety of your vocal quality, especially if singing training is new to you. Remember that your vocal tone is produced by a combination of laryngeal vibrations, vocal tract resonances, and articulatory movements, all motivated by the intent of the song. When we are working on the vocal folds alone, it is impossible to produce a finished product because we are ignoring the vocal tract, articulatory movements, and intent of the song. Instead of focusing on the big picture, focus specifically on what you are working on. So, for example, let us say you are trying to improve your vocal fold closure through chest register work. Perform three to five repetitions of your exercise, stop the recording, and listen back. As you listen, analyze whether you are achieving your goal. Was the closure better? Did you take it too far, or do you still have a way to go until you reach your limit? Then repeat the process again. Eventually, you will reach the point where the combination of all the elements produces a product you are happy with, but you have to give yourself time to get to that point in your journey.

Honor the Process

Remember that you will work through three phases when learning any new task. The cognitive phase is the first step, and it is where you will really have to focus on the movement pattern you are trying to coordinate. After a while, you will progress to the motor learning phase, where you will start getting better results but will still need some external feedback. Eventually, you will move to the automatic phase, where you are able to execute the task without external support. When you reach the automatic stage, you will be able to add a new skill into the mix.

Honor the process and give your body the time it needs to acquire each skill. It may seem like you are working slower than you would like, but slow, deliberate practice will produce better results than rushing the process.

TIPS FOR BEGINNERS

WARMING UP YOUR BODY

Just as football players do not immediately rush onto the field and start playing their game, vocal athletes should also engage in a proper warm-up routine before practicing or performing. Try the following.

Using small circles, gently massage around your temples. You should be massaging the temporalis muscle, which is one of the muscles responsible for closing your jaw.

Next, use your pointer fingers to find the joint of your jaw that is positioned directly in front of your ears. As you open your mouth, you will feel a space open in the joint. Drop your jaw, take in a relaxed breath, and focus on releasing any tension you are holding in that joint. If you feel a clicking or popping sensation, you are opening too far. Most singers can comfortably open up to three-quarters of an inch. However, some will experience discomfort with a smaller opening. If the discomfort is consistent, talk to your dentist or physician about what you are experiencing. Hold the dropped jaw position while massaging the muscles around the joint for fifteen to thirty seconds. Then release.

Now glide your fingers forward along your cheekbone, resting them below the corner of your eye. Slowly glide your fingers along your cheek toward your lower jaw. This is the masseter muscle, another muscle responsible for closing the jaw. Drop your jaw as you massage this muscle and focus on letting go of any attempt to engage these muscles to close the mouth. Do this for fifteen to thirty seconds.

Now place both of your thumbs under your chin and gently massage the bottom of your tongue. First, try massaging this area with your tongue in your mouth and then try massaging it with your tongue extended over your bottom lip. Do this for thirty seconds.

Turn your head to look over your right shoulder. Using your right thumb, start at the base of your left ear and slowly drag your thumb toward your shoulder. Then start at the ear and drag your finger down toward your sternum and finally from your ear toward the back of your neck. Keep alternating between these three pathways for your thumb. After thirty seconds to a minute, switch your head position and work on your right side.

Some singers find additional body stretches to be helpful before singing. Here are a few worth trying.

Stretch your right arm across your chest and hold for fifteen to thirty seconds. You are targeting the muscles in your back behind your right shoulder. Now switch and do the same with your left arm. Then place both arms behind your back, grasp your hands together, and lift your arms toward the ceiling. Hold for fifteen to thirty seconds.

Next, position your feet shoulder-width apart, raise your left arm above your head, and lean to the right, elongating the muscles on the left side of your torso. Hold for fifteen to thirty seconds, then switch and do the same on your right side.

The next stretch comes from yoga and is called the sphinx pose. Lie on your stomach and then raise your torso by resting on your forearms. This will stretch your abdominal muscles, which is especially important for bodybuilders, dancers, and anyone else who has developed strength in these muscles. Hold for fifteen to thirty seconds, then release.

Come back to your feet and assume the warrior pose. This is a lunge with arms raised over your head. Now shift your upper body backward to stretch the psoas muscle, which is a deep connection between your legs and lumbar vertebrae. Hold for fifteen to thirty seconds.

Finally, slowly drop your forehead forward and allow your spine to release, vertebra by vertebra, until you reach a hanging position. Hold this position for fifteen to thirty seconds and then slowly work your way back up to a standing position.

WARMING UP YOUR VOICE

Whenever you practice or perform, you need to take a few minutes to warm up your voice as well. Vocal warm-ups are different from vocal exercises. Whereas vocal exercises are designed to accomplish specific technical goals, vocal warm-ups are meant solely to awaken your larynx and vocal tract for the coordination necessary for singing.

- Sing a sustained pitch in a comfortable part of your range on a hum. Do this three to five times, holding each repetition for at least fifteen seconds.
- Place your first finger vertically against your lips in the hum position. Open the hum to a narrow /u/ vowel and sustain a single pitch at a medium volume level, allowing your breath to flow in the same manner as it does when humming. The resulting sound will be similar to a kazoo. Do this three to five times, holding each repetition for at least ten seconds.

- Slowly glide from your lowest note to your highest note and back down on /a/ at a moderate volume. Each glide should last at least seven to ten seconds. Do this three to five times.

Sing a 1-2-3-2-1 pattern (ascending, then descending) in your chest register on /ng/.

Sing a descending 5-4-3-2-1 in your head register on /u/ at a moderate volume level, allowing your breath to flow. Work upward by half steps until you reach the top of your range and then descend into your lower range.

Now isolate the movement of your tongue from your jaw while vocalizing "ya ya ya ya ya" on a 1-3-5-3-1 pattern. Keep your jaw still; move only your tongue.

Finally, do a few transitions from buzzy to breathy and breathy to buzzy in the lower part of your range. ♪

POSTURAL WORK

When you are just getting started singing, the most important postural concern to focus on is freedom. You need to feel comfortable in your body to start; eventually, you may want to address entanglements, but there is no rush to do that work for most singers. Many of the ideas we have about posture come from western European traditions. In fact, "plumb line" posture is based on sixteenth-century military training manuals.[1] Classical singers pay a lot of attention to posture because they need to develop a very high level of coordination of their respiratory system and need their vocal tract to remain in a fairly stable position to produce a specific type of resonance required for acoustic singing. However, rock singers do not need to worry about projecting their voices since they are always singing on a microphone, and while some phrases may need you to focus on breath control, most phrases in rock music will not require a high level of attention to the respiratory system.

RESPIRATORY WORK

Let's explore the inhalation and exhalation phases of breathing a bit deeper than we did in chapter 5 to help you gain a better understanding of your respiratory system's movement potential. Lie down in a comfortable position with your spine straight and your arms by your sides. Take a moment to consciously relax your entire body. Release any tension in your muscles, starting from your feet and gradually moving upward to your head. Soften your shoulders, jaw, and facial muscles, allowing all tension to release as you relax into the ground. When your body feels relaxed, place one hand on your abdomen and the other on your chest. Close your mouth and breathe in and out through your nose. Imagine filling your lungs in all directions as you inhale. You should feel abdominal, lateral, and upward expansion of the rib cage. You will also feel expansion into the ground you are lying on. As you exhale, do so gradually and completely, allowing the breath to leave your body at a comfortable pace with your rib cage gently returning to its starting position. Keep repeating this inhalation and exhalation process to establish a steady and rhythmic pattern of breathing. Take steady, slow breaths, avoiding any sudden or jerky movements and aiming for a gentle and continuous flow of air in and out of your lungs.

When you are able to inhale and exhale from a place of relaxation, you will want to gain greater control of your inhalation and exhalation phase. This time, as you inhale, try filling your lungs over a count of four. Then hold your full breath for a moment before exhaling over a count of six. Repeat this several times and start adjusting the counts to suit your comfort level. You may have to speed them up at first, but eventually, try to slow them down or extend them through eight counts or even ten. Throughout the process, try to relax into your breathing. If you notice any tension building up, try to release it with your exhalation. As you take full, relaxed breaths, be present in the moment. Focus your attention on the breath, observing the sensation of air moving in and out of your body. If your mind wanders, gently bring your focus back to the breath. Not only can this type of breathing help you with your singing, but it can also help you manage stress and anxiety.

Once you have coordinated this type of easy breathing into your body, stand up and combine a slow inhalation with singing like you speak or your registration work. Be careful not to inhale more air than you need for the phrase you are singing. For example, if you are singing a phrase that is two seconds long, you do not need to have as much air in your lungs as you would if you were singing a phrase that is eight seconds long. Singing a breathy phrase will require a different amount of air than a phrase in chest register because more air flows between the folds when singing breathy. You will figure out what you need for each phrase and vibrational mode the more you practice and get comfortable with how your body works.

After you have figured out how to control your inhalation and sing for the length of the phrase, you can move on to the combined rib cage and abdominal wall exhalation strategy introduced in chapter 5. To start, just focus on maintaining a feeling of rib cage expansion as you release air from your lungs. Be careful not to force your ribs to stay in the exact position they assumed on inhalation. Instead, just focus on slowing down the rib cage's return to its resting position. When you can successfully slow the return of the rib cage, begin adding abdominal engagement at the end of your phrases. Some singers will find that they need abdominal engagement from the beginning of a phrase, so feel free to try that as well. At the end of the day, your respiratory management has to work well for you. You may have friends who use other breathing strategies; you should try those out as well. If they work for you, great! However, if the other strategy does not work for you, remember that everyone's body is designed differently, and most approaches to respiratory management are not universally beneficial to all singers.

SINGING LIKE YOU SPEAK

As a beginner, the best place to start is with speech-based singing exercises. These exercises will help you develop a "home base" from which you can build. Once you have established a speech-based production in a comfortable part of your range, start exploring your range through speech-based singing. Pick a simple song and just start changing keys with each repetition. Sing it low, sing it high, and sing it at various places in between. If your voice breaks as you go higher in your range, start lower in your range. As you sing, explore the spatial awareness parameters mentioned in chapter 5. For review, the four primary spaces are intimate, personal, social, and public. This will help you gain control over the intensity of your speech-based singing. The more control you have over your intensity, the easier it will be to learn how to mix.

COORDINATING YOUR REGISTERS

Registration work is of critical importance to developing your singing voice no matter what style you sing. That's because there are five intrinsic muscles that must be coordinated to produce all the possible vocal qualities you may need when singing songs. When you are doing this work, you will go through five stages of growth: coordination and stabilization, strengthening, developing stamina, improving agility, and learning how to finesse.

Coordinating and Stabilizing

The first step when working on registration exercises is to coordinate and stabilize the new movement pattern. Whenever you learn a new technique, you need to give your body time to adjust and coordinate the necessary musculature. Let's relate this to bench pressing. When you first begin bench pressing, you do not start piling weights on the bar. You begin with only the bar, and you practice coordinating your movement and stabilizing the bar before you add any additional weight. When you add additional weight, you never add more than you are capable of lifting in a coordinated and stable movement pattern. You do this not only to make sure you do not injure yourself but also because good form produces the best training outcomes.

Most people who work on improving their bench press outcomes are not trying to look good while bench pressing. Instead, they are trying to develop the strength and stamina necessary to participate in other athletic activities. Vocal exercises should be approached from the same point of view; you are doing the exercises not to sound good while doing them but rather to improve your skills so that you can sing songs without overthinking.

Your only goal during the first step of training at the vocal fold level is to coordinate the movement of the vocal mechanism and to stabilize that technique in your body. If you have never isolated your chest voice before, you will start with single pitches. Single pitches allow your body to find the right amount of engagement in the intrinsic laryngeal muscles to maintain the level of closure necessary to produce a chest register quality. When single pitches are stabilized, you will then progress to 1-2-1 glides, then 1-3-1 glides, followed by 1-4-1 glides, and eventually 1-5-1 glides. We start with glides because they train the closure muscles to maintain their position and make only small adjustments while the vocal folds are being stretched. Do this at volume five to six on a scale of one to ten (one being the softest and ten being the loudest), at a moderate tempo, and use whatever vowel works best for you. When coordinating head register, you may need to start with single pitches, especially if you have never sung in head voice before. After getting single pitches comfortable, begin gliding up a whole step, back to the starting pitch, down a whole step, and then back to the starting pitch. Do this somewhere around volume five to six on

TIPS FOR BEGINNERS 171

a ten-point scale. You will be in the cognitive stage of learning while doing this work, which means you are really going to need to think about what you are doing. Performing these exercises will take a lot of concentration and may get frustrating at times. Remember that this is just a phase; as you continue to work on these exercises, they will get easier and easier.

Building Strength

Once you have coordinated and stabilized chest and head, it is time to strengthen them. In this step, you are going to use the same vowel as in the first step, at a moderate tempo, but this time, you are going to sing at approximately volume eight on a scale of one to ten. By increasing the intensity, you are improving your intrinsic laryngeal musculature's ability to maintain the required closure for each mode. In this step, we are also going to transition to stepwise motion, which requires the muscles to develop a new level of coordination and strength.[2] In chest register, move to a 1-2-3-2-1 pattern, and then when that is comfortable, progress to a 1-2-3-4-5-4-3-2-1 pattern. Move to the next pattern only when you feel like you are singing the prior pattern successfully and consistently. In head register, you are going to use a 5-4-3-2-1 pattern, and eventually you can expand to a descending octave scale.

Developing Stamina

When it gets easy to sing these patterns in each register, you will naturally progress toward the stamina phase. This is where you improve your body's ability to repeat these exercises over an extended period of time, which will help progress you toward using these registers in songs. In this step, you are going to use the same patterns in the same order as in the second step, but you are going to slow things down and extend the pattern. So when using the 1-2-3-4-5-4-3-2-1 pattern in chest register, you will double it to sing a 1-2-3-4-5-4-3-2-1-2-3-4-5-4-3-2-1 pattern. When that gets comfortable, try three repetitions. In head register, move from a 5-4-3-2-1 pattern to a 5-4-3-2-1-2-3-4-5-4-3-2-1 pattern. You can use the same vowel as in the steps above or try other vowels if they feel comfortable. When you start finding it easier to move between vowel qualities, that means you are progressing toward the agility phase. As you make this progress, you are also transitioning into the motor learning stage. In this stage, you should be thinking less about the individual movements you are making to produce these sounds and more about the overall result. This is the phase where it gets easier to self-correct; you have an improved understanding of when you are performing the exercises correctly for the desired result, and it gets less frustrating because you have a better understanding of what you are trying to accomplish. ♪

Improving Agility

Agility in this process is about being able to make adjustments to your register, vowel, and intensity while expanding your pitch patterns to include arpeggios and larger intervals. First, use the patterns you've been using but start changing the vowels. Explore /a/, /ae/, /E/, /e/, /o/, and /u/. As you change between vowels, you may run into entanglements, usually in the tongue, jaw, and lips. It can be helpful to warm up with some of the tongue exercises if you are running into difficulties so that your tongue is awake and ready to jump between the various vowel positions. Massage your masseter muscles and move your lips around to wake them up as well. As you work through the vowels, you can begin exploring the patterns in Appendix A. You can try any other patterns you know as well since the goal of this exercise is to expand your abilities.

Finesse

Once you have developed the ability to change vowel and intensity in each register, you are ready to start mixing, which will help you gain the ability to finesse your songs. You can start the mix exercises earlier in this process if you would like; just keep in mind that you are not going to be able to finesse any of your songs until you have developed the motor skills listed above. When you are in the finesse stage, you are going to start using the tools from the styles chapter to bring your songs to life. In this phase of the process, you should be entering the automatic stage, which means you will think less and less about the mechanics of singing and should be able to just enjoy making the sounds.

MIX EXERCISES

At some point, while working through the steps above, you are going to feel like you are ready to start exploring the mix exercises. The first step, as mentioned in chapter 5, is to get comfortable with the messa di voce exercises. As a reminder, those are the fading exercises, where you transition from breathy to buzzy and buzzy to breathy. These exercises can be tricky for beginners in the cognitive phase. You never use your vocal folds in everyday life in this way, so the exercise will likely feel very challenging at first. When you begin, do not worry if it feels bumpy, if there are big breaks in the transitions, or if you cannot transition all the way from one quality to another. Just get started with what you are capable of and give it a few weeks. Week by week, as your coordination develops, you will find it easier and easier to perform these exercises. That's when you will know you are ready to move on to glides.

Ascending

The first time you do the gliding exercises, just try to make some sort of change from the bottom to the top and from the top to the bottom. You do not need to reach the uppermost part of your range; just work where it is comfortable. When you are carrying chest register into your mid-range and you hit a note that is difficult, stop and try it again. If it is still difficult the second time, go back down to the last successful note you hit. Do the exercise up to that pitch, then go down two more half steps. Then go back up by half steps until you reach the problematic note again. If it works that time, advance to the next note. If it is still difficult, bounce back down to the three notes that came before and try again. By working the notes that were successful before the difficult note, you are reinforcing success in your brain. As your body remembers what muscle coordination was necessary to reach success, you are more likely to find success on the difficult notes.

Bouncing

At some point, you will find a physiological limit, the point at which your body simply cannot produce the note you want to sing. Everyone has a limit. Sometimes, that limit will be temporary, especially when you are first beginning to sing. Other times, it will be a permanent ceiling. You have to honor your body when you hit these limits; if you fight them, you put yourself at risk for a vocal injury. When you hit a limit, focus your efforts on the three notes before that limit. For example, if C5 is hard for you, focus on A4, B♭4, and B4. As you work on those, it is possible that the C5 will get easier. If it doesn't get easier over the course of several months, that is a good indication you have reached your physiological max.

Descending

When you are descending into your mix from head voice, you may find that the transition to the lower end of your voice is a little bumpy. When this happens, sing the note you are starting on with the quality you want to use to start. Then sing the note on the bottom in the quality you want for that note. Alternate between the two qualities, then try to connect them. This process teaches your brain where you want to start and where you want to go, and then, as you sing the descending pattern, you will work out how to get from one quality to the other. Try every vowel until you find the easiest one to begin with; then, as you get more comfortable with the exercise, you will want to figure out how to execute the exercise with every vowel quality.

Managing Your Breath

As you are doing these exercises, you should be able to just breathe as you would for speaking and not need any abdominal engagement. If you are running into problems, feel free to experiment with abdominal engagement, but remember that your vocal folds are controlling the release of air from your lungs. You must get the vocal fold level vibrations coordinated before you can coordinate their interaction with your respiratory system. As you get more comfortable with the exercises, you will be in a better position to add breath management to manage longer phrases.

Vowels

As I mentioned in chapter 5, vowels can also help when navigating register isolations and transitions. When trying to isolate chest register, /o/ can be helpful in the lowest part of your range, and /a/ can be helpful when moving into the upper part of chest register. As you ascend from chest to chest mix, /ae/ can be helpful. Then, as you move toward head mix, the /e/ vowel can be helpful before shifting to /i/ and then to /u/. When isolating head register, /i/ and /u/ can be helpful. As you descend, the /i/ vowel can help with navigating head mix transitioning into chest mix, then try /e/, /ae/, /a/, and /o/.

DEALING WITH THE BREAK IN YOUR VOICE

"Break" is a term we use to describe an abrupt shift from chest-dominant singing to head-dominant singing that is common in all voice types. The break in your voice is simply a coordination issue; it has nothing to do with talent. In the lower part of your vocal range, the thyroarytenoid muscle is resisting the pull of the cricothyroid muscle as you ascend. As you sing into the upper part of your range, the resistance switches from the thyroarytenoid muscle to the vocal ligament. This transition is where the break usually occurs.[3] There are acoustic factors at play as well, but you usually overcome them by modifying your vowel quality, which is why we do the vocal tract coordination exercises.

The best way to work through breaks in your voice is through glides and doing what I call weaving through the middle. We discussed this a bit in chapter 5 under the heading "Mixing across Your Range." Before doing this work, you need to make sure you can change from full to breathy and from breathy to full on a single pitch. It will be tempting to quickly move beyond these exercises, but learning to transition on a single pitch is fundamental to mixing. When transitioning on a single pitch is easy, move on to intensifying while descending. We begin with head voice to show the body how much to thin out when ascending from chest register. In chapter 5, I said to do this with a 5-4-3-2-1 pattern, which is still the pattern we will use. However, beginners can gain some benefit by being more specific with their vowel choice. For the first step, use a really narrow and slightly nasal /i/ vowel, the half-open position we discussed in the soft palate section of chapter 5. Use the nasality to intensify your head register into a mix that is on the border of chest mix and head mix. As you work through the break and reach the point where chest mix is accessible, allow your voice to intensify into that register. Then, as you reach the point where you can transition into chest, go ahead and make that shift as well.

After you have intensified while descending, you are going to switch to ascending while lightening. For this step, you are going to use the same vowel quality as when you intensified your head register while descending, but now you are going to work upward using a 1-3-5-3-1 pattern, starting in chest and thinning out into chest mix. As you work upward through your range, you will find that the bottom will need to transition to chest mix while the top note thins out into head mix. Eventually, the lower notes will be in head mix and the highest notes in head register.

When you have reached the top of your range, change to an /e/ vowel. Allow this vowel to still have a hint of nasality but try to make it about 33 percent less nasal. Do the same process of transitioning down and then transitioning up. Then work through the process using a bright /ae/ vowel, taking the nasality down by another 33 percent. When that is comfortable, switch to a bright /a/ vowel without nasality. When a bright /a/ is comfortable, try making the /a/ vowel warmer by slightly rounding the lips and going through the process again. Finally, explore the closed vowels /o/ and /u/.

Try to make it through all of these vowels each day for the first several weeks of doing this work. At first, you will likely stumble a lot, and the break will really frustrate you. Remind yourself of what it means to maintain a growth mindset, remember that you are in the cognitive stage of learning, and allow yourself to fail. We learn by succeeding and failing; if you deny yourself the opportunity to fail, you will stunt your growth. As you struggle with the break, explore different vowel qualities. Try nasalized vowels but also try warmer versions of the vowel with no nasality; some people do better without nasality.

VOCAL TRACT

The vocal tract drills in chapter 5 are ideal for beginning singers, as they help you discover the movement potential of your voice. Explore each of the extreme positions but spend the majority of your time in between the two extremes, as this is where you will usually sing. When you are trying to gain a better understanding of your voice, it can be helpful to spend time imitating other singers. It is easiest to do with singers whose voices have a similar range as you. Find a song and think about how the parts of that artist's instrument are moving. Consider how those movements impact vowel quality and how the combination of vocal tract movement and laryngeal registration contribute to the artist's signature sound. Then try putting the sounds on your voice, experimenting with how you can mimic what you are hearing. Along the way, you will learn a lot about how your voice works, which will help you decide what you want to sound like. When you get a clearer idea of your goal, you can fine-tune your vocal tract movements to consistently produce the tones you are looking for in your singing.

CONCLUSION

For most singers, learning to sing is a journey. There are very few people for whom it comes naturally, and most of the time, the "naturals" have been singing since childhood. Because they've been developing their coordination for many more years than you, things seem to come easier for them. As you work through the exercises in this book, keep reminding yourself of the growth process and how learning works. Use that information to focus your practice on specific goals. Make those goals small, something you can achieve within a week. For example, get your chest voice strong between D3 and C4. If you can accomplish just one thing a week, in fifty-two weeks, you will have a much stronger voice than you do today.

NOTES

1. Sander L. Gilman, ""Stand Up Straight": Notes toward a History of Posture," *Journal of Medical Humanities* 35 (2014): 57–83.
2. Leda Scearce, *Manual of Singing Voice Rehabilitation* (San Diego, CA: Plural Publishing, 2016), 173–77.
3. Ingo R. Titze and Katherine Verdolini-Abbott, *Vocology: The Science and Practice of Voice Habilitation* (Salt Lake City, UT: National Center for Voice and Speech, 2012), 272.

7

TIPS FOR THOSE ALREADY SINGING ROCK 'N' ROLL

This chapter is designed for singers who are already singing rock 'n' roll. Most singers in this category will feel like they have a good handle on their voice but find some trouble spots here and there that they would like to work on. When we are thinking about the stages of learning, you are most likely in the motor learning or automaticity phase. This means you know what is working and what is not, and you are actively seeking ways to enhance your skills. Singers in this category may struggle with sustaining their performances over long sets, or they may want to expand their abilities to give them a larger vocal color palate. These are common issues that can usually be addressed through laryngeal registration work and further refining vocal tract coordination. In this chapter, we will add on to the information in chapter 5 to help you get the most out of this book.

REMEMBER THAT YOU HAVE LIMITS

Ultimately, singers want their voice to do what they want it to do when they want it to do it. While most singers can achieve a high level of vocal coordination, the body does have physiological limitations. For example, if you are a baritone, you can expand your range, but it is unlikely you will ever become a tenor because your vocal range is limited by your physiology. Vocal power also has its own limits. If your speaking voice is on the softer side and your ability to call out over long distances is limited, you may have physiological limitations to developing the power you are looking for in your singing. However, since rock music is amplified, you can still achieve a great sound with the help of a microphone. You have to work within your limitations while using the training in this book to expand your range of vocal qualities. Commit this rule to memory: never sing too high too loud for too long. The extremes are what will give you vocal fatigue. If you continue to push those extremes, you will eventually start going hoarse when practicing or performing. If you continuously push yourself to the point of hoarseness, you dramatically increase your risk for a vocal injury.

POSTURE

Most singers who are in the intermediate or advanced stage feel comfortable in their body when they sing. However, there may be imbalances that cause you to compensate in ways that are not supportive of sustainable vocal production. For example, you may have taught yourself how to sing with the microphone, but when you watch videos of your performances, you notice that your neck is always jutted forward as you lean into the mic. You may have a few high notes that are problematic at times and are seeking solutions to make things easier. The first place I would begin looking for answers is in your alignment.

When the neck juts forward, it overextends muscles that attach to your larynx. Other muscles will then have to compensate to deliver the quality you are looking for in the extended neck position, which can be problematic. Instead of addressing the constriction you feel, try rebalancing your body to see if that makes a difference. Bring your head back into balance where the A-O joint passes the weight of the head down the cervical vertebrae into the thoracic vertebrae and on down the line, as we discussed in chapter 5. Try singing the problematic phrase in this position and see what changes. You will likely feel very unstable in this position because it is new. You may also find that you actually lose some of the strength you had before. However, this process is necessary in order to release those compensatory behaviors and re-coordinate your instrument. Over time, you should be able to produce the same sound but with less extraneous muscle involvement.

Ideally, we want your practice sessions to be where you focus on getting everything lined up so that the performances can be a place where you focus solely on communicating with your audience. If you are only 60 percent successful in using the new alignment in performances, that is still progress. The goal is to eventually move toward being successful 80 to 90 percent of the time, but that will take weeks or even months of practice. As you reach the 80 to 90 percent point, it should be much easier to sing, and you should notice a significant difference in your stamina throughout your gigs.

If you run into situations where you feel like tight muscles are getting in the way, stretches can be helpful. Many singers find yoga beneficial. If you have any past physical injuries, consult a physician or physical therapist to make sure the stretches you choose will not cause further problems. The body is composed primarily of antagonistic muscle pairs. For example, your bicep curls your arm, while the tricep extends the arm. These muscles are antagonists, each doing the opposite action of the other. If one of the antagonistic muscles is tighter than the other in any part of your body, you will want to stretch the tight muscle at a 2:1 ratio with the antagonistic muscle. For example, if your hamstrings are tight, you will want to stretch your hamstring first, followed by your quad, and followed by your hamstring again. You need to hold each stretch for at least fifteen seconds for it to be effective. Beyond thirty seconds, there is no significant improvement in outcomes.

As you get to know your body, you will want to develop a stretching routine to use before practicing or singing that addresses any habitual tightness in your body. Some singers are able to practice and perform without stretching; others are constantly working on freeing their bodies. You will need to find what works best for you and develop a routine that aligns with your specific needs.

THE RESPIRATORY SYSTEM

You may have heard some singers and teachers say that singing is all about the breath. At one point in time, many thought this might be true. However, modern science has shown this is not the case. Holding on to this belief and trying to fix vocal issues with breath support alone can have many negative side effects.

Taking on the point of view that singing is all about the breath leads many singers to overbreathe or overcontract their abdominal wall, which often leads to straining in the throat. When we sing, we bring the vocal folds together; air travels up through the vocal folds, blowing them apart, and then they quickly snap back together. This action produces puffs of air that create vibrations in the atmosphere around us that our ears perceive as sound. There is no way to sing without releasing air. However, problems often arise when the singer releases too much air or uses too much breath pressure.

Overbreathing

The more air you take into your lungs, the greater the pressure will be under your vocal folds. This can lead to strong sensations of pressure in the throat. To see if too much air in the lungs might be causing problems, try taking a smaller breath than you are used to taking when singing. If you feel like you usually inhale 100 percent of what you are capable of, try only breathing to 50 percent of what you are capable of and see what happens. If you feel a reduction in tension in the throat, this is a good indication that you are taking too big of a breath when singing.

Under-breathing

Alternatively, it is possible you do not have enough air in your lungs. After experimenting with decreasing the size of your inhalation, try increasing the size. Take a slow breath and feel the air expand your lungs in all directions, filling your lower torso, upper torso, and sides of your ribs. Stop when you reach 85 to 90 percent of your capacity, then sing while maintaining your expansion, as described in chapter 5. If singing is easier with this type of inhalation, it is a good indication you are under-breathing when singing.

Immediate Abdominal Engagement

A common issue with a lot the singers I meet is they are immediately engaging the abdominal wall when singing. The abdominal muscles connect the rib cage to the pelvis, and when contracted, they pull the rib cage down, which increases the expiratory force of the respiratory system. Place your hands on the abdominal section of your body and pay attention to what happens. If you notice that your abdominal wall is contracting as soon as you begin to sing and you feel tension in your throat, the abdominal engagement may be part of the problem. Try singing while maintaining a sense of rib cage expansion and relaxation of the abdominal wall. The ribs must be allowed to return to their resting position, but try to slow down that process, letting the ribs recoil slowly as air is released from the lungs. In this approach, the abs should stay relaxed and gently return to their resting position when singing. If you find a release of throat tension when doing this work, it is an indication that your abdominal muscles are engaging more than necessary when you are singing.

Different Songs Require Different Strategies

Also, remember that different types of voice use require different respiratory strategies. If you are singing short phrases that last only a few seconds, you may not need that much air in your lungs. If you are singing long phrases, you will likely need more air in your lungs. If you are singing breathy, you will be releasing a lot of air, but if you transition to an edgier vocal quality, air will build up beneath the closed vocal folds, giving you a sensation of increased subglottic pressure. You will need to adjust your respiratory strategy accordingly. As with all the concepts I have introduced in this book, experimentation is key. Play with all the different ways you have learned to manage your breathing and find what works best for each register, intensity, and vowel quality. The more you experiment, the better the control you will have over your instrument, which will give you greater freedom in performance.

REGISTRATION

Because the vocal folds change with age, it is important to continually explore all your registers when practicing. It would be a good idea for you to work through the exercises in chapter 5, especially weaving through the middle at least once a week. It is especially important to keep working on your head voice. When I work with rock singers who are running into difficulty with their high notes, I almost always discover they are not vocalizing in their head register. Exercising only in your chest and mix is the equivalent of going to the gym and working only on your chest muscles and never your back muscles. Eventually, your chest muscles will grow stronger than the back muscles and begin pulling your shoulders forward, throwing your upper back out of alignment. Working only on chest register and mix is the equivalent for the voice.

Stamina

Keep in mind that there are five stages of development when it comes to laryngeal registration (see chapter 6). As an experienced singer, you are already past the coordinate-and-stabilize phase as well as the strengthening phase. However, you may still benefit from working on stamina and agility exercises to empower you to have full control of your artistry. There are two exercises that I recommend to intermediate and advanced singers to improve their stamina. The first uses a simple 1-3-5-3-1 or 1-3-5-8-5-3-1 pattern to improve sustained notes.

Decide what quality of mix you want to use, along with a vowel quality and intensity. Sing up the arpeggio in that mode and sustain the high note for as long as is comfortable. Use the respiratory system coordination discussed in chapter 5 as you hold the note. If you feel tightness creeping into your throat, jaw, or tongue, it is time to get off the note. If the note starts to go flat or sharp, that is also a sign to get off the note. Descend to your starting pitch, take a few seconds to rest, and then repeat. In most rock songs, you will never hold a note for more than five to ten seconds. If you regularly practice holding notes for that amount of time or longer in your practice sessions, when you encounter a sustained pitch in a song, it will feel more comfortable because you have been actively practicing that skill every week through these exercises.

The other type of stamina you need to develop is the ability to sing long phrases that never stay on any given note for more than a fraction of a second. To practice this skill, you are going to use nine-tone patterns that repeatedly turn around the top note. In figure 7.1, you will see the progression of this exercise. The first time you practice this exercise, you

Figure 7.1. 9-tone stamina drills. *Courtesy of Matt Edwards*

are only going to perform the scale as written. The second time, you will repeat the top few notes as notated on the second line of figure 7.1. You will then progress to line 3, then line 4, and then line 5. As you work through these exercises, incorporate the respiratory management strategies discussed in chapter 5. As with the sustained note variation, stop if you feel tension creeping into your instrument. ♪

Agility

As you get comfortable with the nine-tone scales, start changing vowels every time you repeat the upper notes; this will help you develop your agility, giving you a greater ability to craft your songs. As mentioned previously, vowel quality can have an impact on vocal fold vibration; working with multiple vowels will ensure that you are agile enough to navigate any song you decide to sing. As the different vowels get comfortable, experiment with changing registers throughout the exercise. Can you start in the chest, ascend into the head, do the first turnaround down into chest-dominant mix, and then carry that up to the high note and come down into a breathy chest register? Make up different variations to challenge yourself and keep your practice sessions interesting.

WORKING AROUND TROUBLE SPOTS IN THE VOCAL TRACT

As your coordination and skill level improves, you will find yourself increasingly addressing trouble spots instead of big-picture problems. If you encounter a trouble spot in your singing that is within your physiological abilities, you will want to use the coordination exercises from chapter 5 to address the issue. The general rule for troubleshooting is to introduce the opposite behavior and then explore the middle.

Laryngeal Position

For example, let's say that you struggle with your body defaulting toward a higher laryngeal position every time you sing. To address this, you will want to introduce the opposite behavior: a low laryngeal position. You would start off your practice sessions vocalizing with a lower laryngeal position by sipping spaghetti and then singing. This will show your body that it has another option that it is not utilizing. Vocalize in this position for three to five minutes. Next, you are going to alternate between your default and the opposite position you just introduced. For example, sing a 1-3-5-3-1 in your default followed immediately by the same 1-3-5-3-1 pattern with a lower laryngeal position. This is called alternate practice. You are showing your body how what you used to do is different than the new movement pattern. In this case, we don't want the larynx always traveling upward; instead, we want it to be able to come down a bit as well. After you have done the alternate practice drills, exercise in the neutral laryngeal position. Vocalize there for three to five minutes. If you feel your larynx creeping upward, do a few low larynx exercises, then try again.

Eventually, an elevated, lowered, and neutral position will be within your ability. When that is the case, you will want to start transitioning to more general ideas like tone colors. When the larynx rises, it shortens the vocal tract, which amplifies the upper frequencies of the voice. When the larynx lowers, it elongates the vocal tract, which attenuates the upper frequencies of the voice. Ideally, you should be able to choose to sing with a warmer tone, and the larynx will lower on its own. In contrast, if you want to sing with a brighter tone, the larynx should rise on its own. So begin playing with the simple intent of brighter or warmer and see if your larynx follows along accordingly. If it does, great! The coordination exercises have worked. If it does not automatically respond the way you want it to, that is an indication you need to continue to work on the coordination exercises. As you continue to develop the ability to sing with brighter and warmer timbres, explore all the options and start making connections to the stories you like to tell, the moods or emotions you convey, or the overall essence you are looking for in your singing.

Nasality

If your voice is getting nasal on high notes, sing the phrase on /pa/ with a warm timbre. If you will recall, the /p/ elevates the soft palate. After you have sung the phrase with /pa/ several times, try singing it with the words again while maintaining the feeling of soft palate elevation that accompanies the /p/. If you are still struggling, try the exercise where you morph from hyper-nasal to hooty with a single vowel on a single pitch. Work your way up to the pitches and vowels you are struggling with and repeat the exercise as needed until you find the sweet spot for each pitch/vowel combination.

Pharyngeal Constriction

If you are struggling with pharyngeal constriction, try alternating between "goog" and "ha" on a simple pattern like 1-3-5-3-1. This will remind your body of the differences between constriction and release. If your constrictors are still trying to engage on "ha," try the "sword swallowing" position. Imagine you are a circus performer about to swallow a sword. Raise your head up and back, drop your jaw, stick your tongue on top of your bottom front teeth, and vocalize on /a/, with enough space in your throat that a sword could slide down your esophagus. To be clear, do not try to swallow an actual sword. This is only a metaphor. In this position, you put your constrictor muscles in a state of stretch weakness, which means they are much less likely to engage when singing. When you find freedom in this position, lower your head halfway down. If the constrictors try to reengage, go back to looking up and then alternate between up and halfway down on the same pattern. Eventually, try to move from halfway down to a level position where your upper molars are parallel to the floor.

Enlarging versus Narrowing

In general, enlarging a space will add more mids to the timbre of your voice, and narrowing a space will add more treble to your timbre. For example, if you want to warm up your tone, explore adjustments that create more space, like finding a lower laryngeal position, elevated soft palate, and greater space in the pharynx. If you want to brighten your voice, allow your larynx to rise slightly, the soft palate to slightly drop, and the pharyngeal space to narrow.

Keep the End Goal in Mind

The eventual goal of everything in this book is to help you reach automaticity. We use voice science to inform our movement patterns, cognitive science to inform our learning process, and our human experience to deliver songs in a way that connects with an audience. Use the examples above to create your own processes for targeting trouble spots. Then vocalize daily with range-of-motion exercises to make sure your instrument stays nimble and flexible. Those traits will serve you well no matter what style of rock you sing.

RELIEVING STRAIN

A lot of established singers complain of straining for high notes. This can have a variety of causes. Below I will address a few of the most common issues for you to explore on your own. If these exercises do not produce the results you are looking for, you may want to consult a professional teacher, guide, or coach.

Alignment

Take a video of yourself performing from the front and the side. Watch the video and analyze how your body is aligning itself and how that coincides with the information introduced in chapter 5. If your head is jutting forward, that is an indication you need to work on finding a balanced position of your head, and you will likely need to do some work with stretching the muscles in the back of your neck. If you are tucking your chin, you will want to practice singing with an elevated chin as a way to show your body that it has other options. You may also notice you are locking your knees, standing with your feet too close together, or tilting your pelvis in one direction or the other. After you have identified what you are doing, consult the alignment section in chapter 5 and work on realigning your body. If you notice a reduction in straining while doing this work, it is a good indication that alignment is an area where you need to focus in your practice sessions.

Check Your Respiratory System

As mentioned previously in this chapter, you need to coordinate the action of the respiratory system to the action of the vocal folds. Too little air can be just as problematic as too much air; you have to find the right approach to breathing for your body. Try singing a problematic phrase with a smaller breath, filling your lungs to between 40 and 75 percent of capacity. Does that change your sensation of strain? If so, you are likely overbreathing. Adjust the amount of air you take for each problematic spot you encounter and see if things change. If you are currently singing with less than 90 percent capacity, give 90 percent a try and see if that helps.

TIPS FOR THOSE ALREADY SINGING ROCK 'N' ROLL

As you explore different percentages of your maximum capacity, also experiment with different amounts of abdominal engagement, including complete relaxation of the abdominal wall. Does engaging your abdominal wall help? If it does, that indicates that elastic recoil alone may not be enough for your body. If you find that abdominal relaxation releases your sensation of strain, that is a good indication that your elastic recoil is enough to power your instrument. If you make these adjustments and still feel strain, that is a clue that you need to work on your laryngeal registration.

Registration

You may recall from earlier that "registration" is a term we use to categorize the sounds the vocal folds are capable of producing. I like to think of this as a spectrum between buzzy and breathy. If you sing mainly in a buzzy place and rarely live in the breathy place, your vocal folds may get used to holding a greater amount of closure than is necessary across all of your songs. If that happens, you may find yourself straining when singing. The solution is to focus on the opposite mode of production, in this case, breathy singing. Begin by vocalizing in a breathy head voice (falsetto) in the upper part of your range and bring that light, breathy quality as low as possible. If you really struggle with breathy singing in your lower range, that's a strong indication that your body is habitually over-engaging the closure muscles. Live in the light, breathy place until you can easily sing throughout your range. Then use the register coordination exercises in chapter 5 to rebalance your registers to make your mix less chest dominant with a slight sensation of exhaling. You want to move away from the sensation of holding your breath that usually accompanies strain.

If your voice is habitually breathy and you are experiencing strain, that is an indication that your body is struggling to balance the coordination of the vocal fold closure muscles with the breath pressure being created by your respiratory system. In this situation, you will want to work on chest voice exercises. As you work on engaging your chest voice, think about how you are breathing and try the various adjustments mentioned earlier. As your chest voice strengthens, work on coordinating your head register, then proceed with the mix exercises in chapter 5. While you work on them, focus on releasing less air and allowing there to be more closure at the vocal fold level.

Vowel Quality

While we do not need to obsess about vowel quality for rock singing in the same way you may need to for other styles, there is the possibility that your vowel choices are causing the strain you experience when singing. If you are going for a warm vowel quality and it feels tight, try brightening the vowel and see if that makes a difference. If it does, then assess what changes you made. Was it something that happened in the pharynx? Was it a change in the movement of your soft palate? Did your tongue do something different? Many times, it is the tongue that is the issue. If that is the case, go through the tongue articulation exercises and see if things feel different after five to ten minutes of working on those exercises. If things are different, that is an indication you need to keep working on the tongue articulation drills. If it does not appear to be the tongue, check for jaw tension, make sure your lips are not holding tension, and then do the laryngeal and soft palate mobility exercises. Eventually, that work should lead to greater freedom in your ability to choose vowel qualities, which should lead to less strain when singing.

EXTENDING YOUR RANGE

As I mentioned earlier, your vocal range has physiological limits that were predetermined by your genetics. This does not mean that you cannot extend your range; it just means there are limits to how far you can extend it. Some singers have five octave ranges, and others feel lucky to have two octaves. No matter what internet voice teachers tell you, a five-octave range is not in the grasp of most singers. However, that does not mean that you should not try to maximize the range of your instrument.

Check for Entanglements

There are many situations where entanglements in the vocal tract or unbalanced coordination at the vocal fold level will cause singers to miss out on pitches that are otherwise within their physiological limits. If you are feeling tightness in your neck, throat, jaw, or tongue, you will want to use the exercises in chapter 5 to improve the coordination of those parts of your instrument. As you improve your vocal tract coordination, you should see at least a modest improvement in range. When you know that your vocal tract is coordinated and free from compensatory tension, you will want to work on the head or chest register to expand your range. If your goal is to expand your upper range, you need to strengthen your upper mix, which starts with strengthening your head voice. If your goal is to expand your lower range, focus on chest voice exercises.

Head Voice

If you want to expand your upper range, you need to strengthen your head register first. SA and TBB singers are going to begin on the same pitch: a D an octave above middle C (D5). Sustain this pitch on your most comfortable vowel; many singers prefer /i/ or /u/. Hold the pitch for as long as you can without tension. When your throat starts to tighten, stop. Repeat the pitch, then move up by a half step. When you reach a point where you cannot sing the next note without tension, start descending by half steps back to your starting pitch. The goal is to produce an airy flutelike quality with these exercises, similar to the flute tones you hear in meditation music.

When you can sustain pitches comfortably, you will want to introduce head-mix glides. Your head mix should have a clear flutelike tone, similar to the sound of a classical flutist. Start on the A above middle C (A4) and slowly glide up by a third and back down to the starting pitch. Begin with a strong head mix and try to maintain that quality as you ascend. Do this two or three times, then go up a half step and repeat. When you reach a point where you cannot sing the next note without tension, start descending by half steps back to your starting pitch.

Next, you should return to the mix exercises in chapter 5. Start with intensifying your head voice toward head mix using a 5-4-3-2-1 pattern. Then use ascending glides to practice carrying the strength of your head mix into your upper head register. Next, go into the middle of your range and work on fifth glides that transition from your chest-dominant mix into the lowest notes of your head-dominant mix. The chest-dominant mix you will use in this step has qualities similar to an oboe. Glide from chest mix to head mix, then try to carry slightly more chest register into your upper range with each repetition until you fall into a stronger chest-dominant mix that lies between the qualities of an oboe and a saxophone.

You will not see a change overnight; in fact, it will take several weeks or months for most singers to see significant changes. But as you strengthen your head register and work on extending your head mix, you will find it easier to find variations of chest mix, which is the quality most rock singers are looking for when trying to expand their range. All the variations you discover along the way will expand your options when working on songs.

Chest Register

If you want to expand your lower range, you are going to do so by isolating the chest register. If you are an SA singer, you will begin this work on the B♭ below middle C. If you are a TBB singer, you will start this work on the D below middle C. To start, we want to make sure your vocal folds are able to come together with firm closure. We are going to use a staccato exercise to coordinate the closure muscles. Starting with the pitches above, pulse "ha ha ha ha ha" on a single pitch. Repeat the exercise three times, then move a half step lower. Repeat the exercise, then move a half step lower. Continue working down your range until you reach the place where you are no longer able to phonate. Then go back to the note you started with and sustain the pitch on your most comfortable vowel for as long as you can without tension creeping into your voice. These are like planks for your closure muscles. Repeat each note two times, then descend by half steps until you reach your lower limit.

We also want to make sure you are releasing air in your lower range because you can push these notes just like you can push notes in your upper range. Grab a regular-size drinking straw, place it between your lips, and sing through the straw, allowing your cheeks to puff out. Start with sustained pitches as we did in the last exercise. When sustained pitches are comfortable, start using a 3-2-1 pattern. Use the upper note to coordinate your closure, then carry that closure down to the low note. When you bottom out, work your way back up.

Drill these exercises around five to ten minutes a day, and over the course of several months, you should notice a difference in the strength of your lower range. Also, go back and experiment gliding from chest to chest mix. After strengthening your chest register, you should notice you have additional options in your mix as well.

Pitch Accuracy When Doing Registration Work

It is important to note that as you release tension in your instrument, your pitch accuracy may temporarily decrease. If the exercise is new or being used in a new way, that means you are in the cognitive stage of learning. When in the cognitive stage, your body is trying to figure out how to execute the new movement pattern, and in the process, some things will be destabilized, like pitch. If you have never had pitch issues before, ignore the inaccuracies completely, and they should resolve themselves in the next few weeks. If you have had pitch issues in the past, it is understandable that you may be hesitant to ignore a reduction in pitch accuracy. However, if you try to fix it too soon, you could develop compensatory tension that will delay your progress. Instead, give yourself a few weeks with the new movement patterns and see if things improve on their own.

GENERAL PITCH ACCURACY ISSUES

Pitch issues that are not related to the learning process can be due to respiratory management, registration, and tension in the vocal tract. It is often difficult for singers to know which issue is affecting them, so explore the following if you are encountering trouble.

Going Flat

Singing flat means that you are slightly under the pitch you intend to sing. If the head register is weak, singers often lack the coordination necessary to elongate the vocal folds while reducing closure pressure, both of which are necessary ingredients for easy high notes. Take the same approach you would if addressing strain and re-coordinate the balance of your registers. Spend five to ten minutes a day isolating your head register in the upper part of your range. Ascending 1-2-3-4-5-4-3-2-1 and 1-3-5-3-1 patterns and descending 5-4-3-2-1 patterns are all useful in this work. After five to ten minutes of head register isolation, begin intensifying as you descend, which will activate the muscles responsible for bringing the vocal folds together.

Next, take a phrase from a song that is giving you difficulty and sing it in your head register. As you sing, pay attention to what is happening in your vocal tract, and if you notice any entanglements, address them according to the instructions earlier in this chapter. When you are able to sing the phrase with freedom in your head voice, start repeating it over and over again, slowly increasing the intensity with each repetition. The goal is to stumble into a mix that helps you get the sound you are looking for while remaining on pitch without any compensatory tension. Your voice will crack a lot during this process. Remember that you are trying to coordinate five muscles inside of your larynx to do things they have never done before, and developing that coordination takes time.

If that process does not give you the results you are looking for, switch over to fifth glides from the bottom up. Begin the glide on the vowel you are trying to sing and glide into the upper pitch while thinning out. Then switch back to bringing the head register down and keep weaving back and forth. Some singers will find that engaging the abdominal wall can help increase air pressure and/or flow, which will improve pitch accuracy. You may also see improvement by taking a bigger breath.

Going Sharp

When singers blow too much air pressure at the folds, they can end up singing sharp, or above the pitch they intend to sing. If you believe this might be the case, try taking a smaller breath to start. Sometimes, singers have too much air in their lungs for the phrase they are trying to sing, which pushes them above the intended pitch. You should also try relaxing the abdominal wall while singing the problematic pitch. Abdominal contraction can increase pressure beneath the vocal folds and/or airflow through them, depending on the laryngeal registration. Instead, maintain buoyancy in the rib cage and allow it to expand and slowly return to its resting place while singing. Constriction can also contribute to singing sharp, so be sure to address any entanglements in the vocal tract as well while you are doing this work. Finally, if you have not been regularly focusing on laryngeal registration exercises, go back to that work for a while to help re-coordinate the vocal folds.

AGING

As you age, you may experience changes in your voice. These are completely normal, and many of the changes are unavoidable. For example, most singers reach their total lung capacity between the ages of twenty and twenty-five and then by their forties begin to experience a gradual decline in vital capacity and forced expiratory volume (FEV1), which is the amount of air you can forcefully expel in one second. In addition, calcification of the costal cartilage reduces rib cage movement, and elastic recoil decreases. As we age, the thyroid cartilage ossifies, which changes the structural support of the vocal folds. There are also changes in the thickness and consistency of the vocal folds. Singers going through menopause or andropause will notice additional changes in the average pitch of their speaking voice and their pitch range and a loss in the strength of the upper harmonics in their voice.[1]

It is critical that singers keep singing through the changes to minimize the impact on their performance. As you work on songs, feel free to transpose them as needed to fit your voice. This rule applies to all ages but is critically important for singers in the later stages of life. For those singers going through menopause, there are hormone therapy options available, but these decisions should be made with your medical care team, as there are other factors that need to be considered beyond your voice. If you want further information about how aging throughout life impacts the singing voice, I highly recommend Karen Brunssen's book *The Evolving Singing Voice*, cited in the previous note.

VOCAL HEALTH

The better you get as a singer, the more you will be gigging. As you perform more regularly, vocal health becomes increasingly important. Many singers practice for an hour a day or less, but gigs can often run up to three hours. During breaks, audience members will likely want to talk to you, meaning you will get very little if any rest during your gig. When you combine your singing voice use with talking before and after the gig, you begin to really push your vocal limits. If you have gigs several days in a row, the fatigue factor is even greater. In order to cope with performance demands like these, you need to come up with a vocal health plan.

Build Your Stamina

The first step in your vocal health plan should be gradually extending your practice sessions so they are in line with the amount of time you will be performing during your gigs. You would never go from practicing 5Ks to running a marathon. You should also not go from practicing one hour every other day to doing two three-hour gigs in a row. Instead, start shifting your practice sessions to forty-five-minute sessions and work up to two practice sessions a day and eventually three. Give yourself as much time as you need in between sessions. During that time, use straw phonation to help reset your voice.

Straw Phonation

To perform straw phonation exercises, use a coffee stirrer or regular-size drinking straw. Experiment with both to find what works best for you. Place the straw between your lips, then slightly curl your upper and lower lips inward to assume the embouchure shown in figure 7.3. Then sustain a comfortable pitch while allowing your cheeks to puff out as you attempt to funnel your sound through the straw. The straw serves as an obstruction and reflects air backward in your vocal tract, which places downward pressure on the vocal folds, changing their vibrational pattern to one that is highly efficient. Straw phonation is backed by a plethora of scientific research, and researchers continue to identify variations that can help singers in different ways.[2]

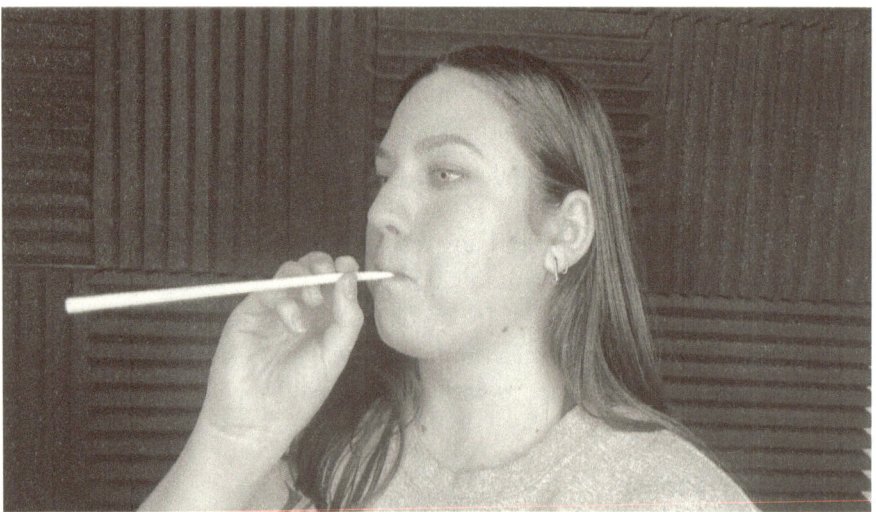

Figure 7.2. Straw phonation. *Courtesy of Matt Edwards*

Hydration

The vocal folds are covered in mucosa, and therefore hydration is critical to vocal health. When you are dehydrated, the mucosa is stickier, which can impact your sense of vocal effort and the sound of your voice. Drinking water right before and during your gig is not enough to stay hydrated. To feel the benefits of hydration, you need to be drinking plenty of water at least twenty-four hours before you plan to sing. Water intake needs vary from person to person, but a good baseline is to drink half of your body weight in ounces of water per day. So if you weigh 150 pounds, you will need to drink seventy-five ounces of water per day. In addition to drinking water, you may want to try nebulizing as well. Nebulizers create small water droplets that you inhale. As you breath in the mist, it crosses your vocal folds and directly delivers hydration to those tissues. There is some research suggesting that 0.9 percent saline solution can provide even greater hydration benefits.[3]

Alcohol

Many rock singers enjoy having an alcoholic beverage while performing. For some singers, this has no impact on their performance; for others, it can be detrimental. Alcohol has a dehydrating effect on the body, which can impact the vocal folds. Drinking while performing will not have an immediate effect on dryness, but it may impair your proprioception, leading you to take bigger vocal risks than you normally would when sober. Drinking before a gig is more likely to impact your vocal hydration, and drinking the night before is most likely to impact your singing. Every individual has different tolerance levels and must discover what their body can tolerate.

Marijuana

Marijuana is well known for its drying effects on the voice. There are multiple ways you can consume cannabis, including smoking, eating, transdermal patches, and sublingual drops. All delivery methods still put a singer at risk of marijuana's drying effects. However, smoking or vaping has the additional hazard of drawing hot air and/or unknown particles across the vocal fold tissue. Due to marijuana remaining illegal at the federal level, there is a dearth of research on intake methods. We do not know for sure if vaping is safer than smoking a bowl. We are not sure if water bongs are less irritating to the vocal folds than a joint. We do know that consuming cannabis in its edible, transdermal, or sublingual form helps users avoid subjecting the vocal folds to the potentially harmful effects of smoke. If you enjoy marijuana and it is legal in your location, make sure you know how it affects your voice before using it during or before a performance. Anecdotal evidence suggests that some singers will have no problems and that others will lose a third to a fifth of their upper range after consumption. Each singer will need to find their own personal limits until we have further research available to help us establish guidelines for singers.

CONCLUSION

Because there are hundreds of combinations of pitch, register, vowel, and intensity, there are endless ways for the interactions to fall out of alignment. The more you explore the movement potential of your voice, the more likely you will be to identify entanglements that are getting in the way when performing. By introducing the opposite movement pattern and then exploring the middle, you should be able to troubleshoot many problems on your own. When in doubt, seek out a professional coach to help.

NOTES

1. Karen Brunssen, *The Evolving Singing Voice: Changes across the Lifespan* (San Diego, CA: Plural Publishing, 2018).
2. Karin Titze Cox and Ingo R. Titze, *Voice Is FREE after SOVT* (Clearfield, UT: National Center for Voice and Speech, 2023).
3. Marci Rosenberg, "To Sing or Not to Sing? The Performer's Guide to Managing Illness and Performance Demands," *Journal of Singing* 79, no. 2 (2022): 207–11.

8

CROSSING OVER FROM CLASSICAL OR MUSICAL THEATER

There is no codified approach to classical voice training that is universally accepted as the definitive model by all voice teachers. A researcher named Richard Miller even wrote a book called *National Schools of Singing*, which covers variations of "classical technique" found throughout the world. The diversity of approaches lumped together as "classical" or "bel canto" training makes it difficult to discuss what is different between rock and classical singing. Some approaches are built on speech and register balancing, which is relatively compatible with the approaches in this book. Others train with a focus on posture, breath, and placement, which is quite different than what is described in this book.

While there are some codified techniques, such as the Estill technique, for musical theater performers, the majority of singers in that genre also come from uncodified systems of learning, and many musical theater performers have "classical training" in their background as well. Again, this makes it difficult to discuss the differences between singing musical theater and rock, as there are so many variations. There is also the issue of singing rock for a musical versus singing rock in a band. Musical theater productions require the performer to act when singing, while lead singers of bands do not usually act out their songs. The way one acts influences their vocal delivery, so most of the time, performers who are singing rock in the context of a show are actually singing a musical theater–rock hybrid.

In this chapter, I am going to make a lot of generalizations about classical and musical theater technique to make recommendations for how to get the most out of this book. These generalizations are based on my experiences working with classical and musical theater singers in lessons, masterclasses, and workshops. Through those experiences, I have noticed a lot of common roadblocks to crossing over to singing rock music. Some readers may feel like they were not taught to do any of the generalizations I describe and relate to classical and/or musical theater techniques; others will find that these explanations strongly align with their experiences. My hope is that the additional information comparing and contrasting classical and musical theater techniques with the techniques detailed in this book will make chapter 5 more approachable and applicable as you explore your rock voice.

POSTURE

Many classical singers spend a lot of time focusing on finding a physical alignment that allows their vocal tract to remain relatively stable when singing. This is necessary for achieving the type of resonance required for unamplified singing styles as well as maintaining a consistent timbre throughout the singer's range. However, in amplified styles, a stable vocal tract is not a necessity, as there is no need to maintain a specific resonance strategy to project over acoustic instruments or to maintain a specific timbre throughout the piece. In fact, too much stability in the vocal tract may lead to a uniform vocal quality that does not match the expectations of rock music. Rather than focusing on maintaining a specific alignment when working through the exercises in this book, turn your attention to physical freedom. You want the freedom to move with the music and not feel like the movement gets in the way of your singing.

Many musical theater performers have a strong dance background that has influenced the way they use their body when singing. Those performers may be used to positioning their feet a specific way, engaging their abs the way they do when dancing, and using their bodies in ways that reflect their dance training. For these performers, alignment may have a different meaning than what we discussed in chapter 5. The easiest path for many musical theater artists is to think about how the characters in musicals like *Rent* and *American Idiot* move through space in the world of their shows.

Try taking on that style of movement in your own body as you sing rock songs and see how it impacts your singing. It may also be beneficial to sit on a stool and sing instead of standing to help break your body out of a more formal stance.

"Plumb Line" Posture

Many classical and musical theater singers are taught to assume "plumb line" posture when singing. If that describes you, I want you to let that go as you work through these exercises. If you have been taught to slightly tuck your chin when singing, I want you to let go of that as well. Instead, I'd like you to focus on freedom of movement through the six points of balance discussed in chapter 5. Refocus your attention on getting your skeletal system to effortlessly carry the weight of your body instead of trying to assume a specific position.

Compensatory Tension

As you explore your alignment, you may discover that you have some compensatory tension showing up in your singing. For example, you may notice your neck muscles tightening when you sing. That could be related to laryngeal registration or pharyngeal constriction, but it could also be because you are not balancing your head on your cervical vertebrae. When you are out of balance, the muscles surrounding your larynx can be stretched into less-than-optimal positions that lead your body to compensate in counterproductive ways. If you notice this is an issue for you, try moving your head side to side and up and down while thinking about how your skull balances on the A-O joint. Then focus on how the cervical vertebrae direct the weight of your head down to the thoracic vertebrae and try singing in a balanced place that does not require compensatory muscle engagement in the neck. Take the same approach to remapping and rebalancing any other part of your body that may be leading you to make compensatory adjustments.

Get Your Body Moving

If you find that you are tensing your entire body when you sing, it may be beneficial to practice with full-body movement. Try vocalizing while doing household chores or tasks. For example, practice your songs while folding laundry. The constant motion of the folding should help you experience a different level of freedom in your body than you usually feel while singing. Practice singing your exercises while walking around your residence and try vocalizing in unusual positions. What is it like to sing when bending over from the waist? What is it like to sit and sing? What happens if you sing standing on only one leg? Each new position can illuminate tensions that you were previously unaware of in your singing. Take note of what you discover as you explore different singing positions and start integrating movement into your practice on a more regular basis. Then, as you free yourself of unnecessary tension, return to trying to find balance in your body that empowers you to produce the vocal qualities you are seeking.

RESPIRATION

If you have trained classically or are used to singing Golden Age musical theater, you are likely accustomed to singing long phrases that require a significant amount of air in your lungs and a respiratory strategy to manage that air. However, most rock songs do not have the same long extended phrases as those other styles. When performing rock music, regulate your breath according to the length of the phrase you are singing. Take in just enough air to sustain you throughout the phrase and avoid tanking up beyond that, as it can add unnecessary subglottic pressure. If the phrase you are singing is no longer than a simple sentence in everyday speech, then breathe as if you are speaking. If the phrase has epic high notes that require you to sing beyond the demands of everyday speech, then take a bigger breath than you would for speech. By breathing for the phrase, you can easily begin to eliminate overbreathing in your singing.

Changing your goals as related to projection will also influence your respiratory management. As you direct your focus toward projecting your sound into the microphone rather than projecting to the size of the performance space, you will be able to make adjustments to your breathing strategy. When singing with reduced intensity, there is no longer the need for large breaths and abdominal contraction. Instead, many singers can rely on the natural recoil of the lungs to power their instrument. When you encounter difficulty with a high note, you may need to engage your abdominal wall, but you will be engaging your abs only for specific notes instead of throughout entire phrases.

An exception to the paragraph above may be found with singers in the fourth decade of life and above. Singers in that stage of life may need to use more abdominal engagement in their singing. This is because with age, the alveoli that help power the elastic recoil of the respiratory system undergo a series of changes starting in the fourth decade of life that alter our respiratory capacity and expiratory force.[1] In that case, you may need abdominal contraction from the beginning of phrases to help power the vocal folds. As always, use this information as a baseline and find what works best for you.

If you are not sure what your body needs, try multiple approaches and experiment until you find what you like best. What happens when you keep your ribs expanded while singing? What happens when you let them collapse inward with your onset? What happens when you relax your abdominal muscles? What happens when you contract them as if performing a plank? Also, experiment with feeling expansion in different parts of your body. If you are accustomed to using lower diaphragmatic breaths, try breathing more laterally into your rib cage or into your upper back. Lower abdominal breaths engage tracheal pull, which will lower your larynx and slightly pull your vocal folds apart. This can be beneficial when singing in head-dominant mix or with warm vowels. However, when singing rock, a floating or higher laryngeal position is usually more beneficial to achieving the desired vocal quality. Therefore, a lateral rib cage breath may help your larynx float, making it easier to access your rock voice. Alternatively, if you struggle with a high laryngeal position that is causing you discomfort or cutting off your upper range, tracheal pull may help you find a more optimal configuration. The key takeaway here is that everyone is different, and exploration is the key to success.

SINGING LIKE YOU SPEAK

Musical theater singers are accustomed to singing like they speak, but while some classical techniques are based on speech, not all are grounded in that approach. We also need to make a distinction between singing from refined speech and singing with colloquial speech. Classical music is an outgrowth of the Catholic Church and the European upper class, and pronunciation of English in classical singing and some interpretations of Golden Age musical theater are rooted in refined speech. "Colloquial speech" is a term we use to describe the casual delivery that is found in everyday conversations and that is often influenced by regional dialects. This is the kind of speech-based singing we are looking for in rock music. If you are used to using refined speech, focus on building from colloquial speech when working through the sing-like-you-speak exercises in chapter 5. This will help you find the kind of speech-based approach that is the bedrock of singing rock music.

Some singers will struggle with letting go of the refinement they've worked so hard to integrate into their work. That is because refinement has become part of their automatic stage of singing. Going to colloquial speech requires you to go back to the cognitive stage of learning, which can make it feel difficult even though the concept is not complex. If you are really struggling to break out of refined speech, try working through the tongue articulation exercises in chapter 5. These will help break your tongue out of its habitual movement patterns and may make it easier to settle into colloquial speech. A microphone can also be helpful with this work, as it will make it easier to hear yourself and notice when you are falling into refined speech patterns.

REGISTERS

The idea of isolating and developing chest and head is not new. In fact, it has existed for hundreds of years. However, the chest register quality that is often used when training classical singers is usually less powerful than what is used in rock singing. Be sure to listen to the examples in chapter 5 and allow yourself to explore what full-volume chest register sounds like in your voice as you work through the chest register exercises. Musical theater singers are likely to be a little more familiar with full-volume chest register, as it is the basis of learning how to belt. However, some musical theaters may have a learned a different approach and will also benefit from dedicated work on the chest register. Regardless of your background, having a variety of chest register options available to you will make it easier to sing a wide variety of rock styles.

The head register quality we are seeking in the exercises discussed in chapter 5 is not operatic or Golden Age head voice. It is a lighter quality similar to an airy flute. To find this quality, think about being more speech-like in your vowels with less space in the back room than you would need to project acoustically. Also, let go of any forward placement or ring in your voice. If you are accustomed to keeping a lower laryngeal position, try to let the larynx float as you explore this version of head register. A floating larynx will slightly narrow the back room, giving you more brightness in your vowels. As you sing, release your air and embrace the added breathiness in your voice. This quality may not be useful in classical singing or Golden Age musical theater, but it has plenty of uses in rock music.

Notes about Mix for SA Singers

If you are a classical SA singer, it is likely that you have already established mix in the middle of your range. This is also likely the case for singers who focus on Golden Age soprano rep. However, it is a different mix than what is required for rock music. As you work through the mix exercises in chapter 5, you will want to learn how to carry more chest register into your mix than you would for classical music or Golden Age musicals. If you are a dramatic soprano or mezzo, you may find that the changes you need are more in vowel quality than in registration balance with the exception of belting, which usually requires slightly more vocal fold closure than you would use in your dramatic rep. Vowel quality, rooted in colloquial speech, will be important while you are developing your mix. If you are struggling to find speechlike vowels, work through the tongue articulation exercises, then come back to the mix exercises. Eventually, your tongue should respond more easily to your intention.

As you work on developing your chest mix and belt, be sure to vocalize with your baseline classical or Golden Age quality as well. Alternating between the two will help you improve the coordination of your instrument and help your mind make a distinction between the actions necessary to produce each sound. Also, experiment with speechlike vowels in your head mix to give yourself another option in your toolbox. You may not use that quality often in rock music, but it does not hurt to have more options available than you need.

Notes about Mix for TBB Singers

For readers who are TBB singers from a classical background or who sing musical theater with a classical influence, you will likely need to work on bringing more head register into your upper range. In acoustically projected styles of singing, the upper range is often navigated with firm vocal fold closure paired with warm vowels. When transitioning to rock, you will want to bring down the intensity, add a little more head register into the mix, and brighten the vowels so that they align more with the quality of the guitars that usually accompany rock singers in performance. As you do this, you may notice that your larynx rises more than it would in your other styles of singing. That is a normal experience and is usually harmless as long as you are not trying to sing too loud or into the uppermost part of your range. If you are concerned about the laryngeal movement you feel, use the laryngeal mobility exercises in chapter 5 to coordinate your body for freedom of movement. This will ensure that you have some control over how your larynx moves so that you can find the right option for your voice. If you are used to singing with a high soft palate, it may be beneficial to add a slight hint of nasality into your vowels when learning to mix. Explore your soft palate movement as described in chapter 5 and then spend some time transitioning between qualities until you find an option that gives you the result you are seeking.

Notes for Belters of All Genders

For musical theater performers who already belt, you likely do not need to carry more chest into your belt range. However, you should still experiment and find all of your options for mix and belt. This will increase your versatility and help you jump between multiple styles. If you are already belting, you can also explore bright and warm variations of belt. Each vowel choice can impact vocal fold vibration in different ways, and you will want to make sure you can navigate both options so that you can be as versatile as possible. A warmer quality will require your larynx to stay in a more neutral position and your soft palate to stay elevated. A brighter quality will require your larynx to slightly rise from its neutral position and your soft palate to slightly lower from its elevated position. So be sure to explore the vocal tract exercises in chapter 5 to make sure you have the coordination for your voice to respond to your intent.

Breathy Singing

For singers in both populations, breathy singing will likely need some work. Many SA classical and musical theater singers have been trained to eliminate breathiness from their voices and may find this step challenging and/or frustrating, but the payoff in flexibility in the mid-range is worth the effort. In my experience, many TBB singers really struggle with breathy singing, as they have spent hundreds if not thousands of hours singing in their full voice. Additionally, some singers feel like singing breathy should be easy, and they get frustrated when it is not. Remember that if you are in the automatic phase for one type of singing, you are going to be in the cognitive phase when re-coordinating. However, once you are re-coordinated, you will get back to the automatic phase with new options.

Go Explore

Many classical and musical theater singers have spent a lot of time trying to "get it right" when training their voices. This is especially true when it comes to registration. To find your signature sound in the world of rock music, reframe registration work as an exploration of the possibilities rather than a journey to a singular destination. As you discover new sounds, think of how you might use them for different songs. You will find qualities that are better fits for ballads and others that are better for angsty emo songs. Through exploration, you will find a wide range of possibilities that you can use in different songs to bring your set lists to life in new ways.

VOCAL TRACT

In western European classical vocal performance practice, resonance is an essential point of focus in voice training. This is because vocal tract resonance turns the small vibrations produced by your vocal folds into complex waveforms that help singers be heard over acoustic instruments without amplification. In the context of rock music, resonance shifts focus more on vocal quality than on vocal projection. While there may be instances where adjusting your resonance can help achieve a desired acoustically projected sound, in most cases, the power of the microphone will be more than sufficient to meet your goals. Therefore, as you work through these exercises, do not worry about vocal projection. Instead, focus on producing vocal qualities that fit the emotion, story, or groove of the song, knowing your voice will be amplified by a microphone that is three inches from your mouth.

Embrace Multiple Types of Resonance

In many classical singing and musical theater approaches to voice training, there is a strong emphasis on maintaining a consistent resonance quality across the vocal range. Again, this is critical for projection in acoustic singing styles but not a requirement for amplified styles. As you explore resonance adjustments when singing rock, it is important to consider how they can enhance the storytelling, mood, or groove you wish to convey rather than solely aiming to preserve a specific sound.

Develop Vocal Tract Agility

The vocal tract exploration exercises in chapter 5 are designed to develop agility in your instrument so that you can freely alter the quality of your vowels, as that is the ultimate goal for rock singers. When you sing a bright vowel, you need your vocal tract to respond accordingly, most likely allowing the back room to narrow slightly as the front room spreads open, creating a megaphone-like position in the vocal tract. If you want to warm up your vowels, your vocal tract needs to assume more of a reverse-megaphone position, narrowing in the front and opening in the back. To get your body to the place where you can automatically summon those changes through thought alone, vocalize in all vocal tract positions every day. For example, spend a few minutes alternating between "goog" and "ha" to keep your pharynx flexible. Vocalize in a hooty "ho," neutral "blah," and bright "wae" position to keep your larynx agile. Work through the soft palate exercises, being sure to cover /ng/, "pa pa," and nasalized /o/. Then pay attention to your tongue, lips, and jaw to make sure you can sing in megaphone and reverse-megaphone positions. This work will eventually make it easier to alter the quality of your voice in songs.

Tongue Retraction

Many classical and musical theater singers struggle with tongue retraction, often a result of trying to find "back space" when singing. If that sounds like an issue you struggle with, begin your practice sessions with a tongue-out hum, as discussed in chapter 5. This will help remind your body from the very beginning of your practice session that the tongue is not supposed to retract when singing. Then vocalize in your chest register with a bright /a/ or /ae/ vowel with the tongue extended on the bottom lip. After several minutes of extended tongue singing, progress to the tongue articulation drills. Before doing the "la" and "ga" exercises from chapter 5, get the middle of your tongue bouncing with the Home Alone face and "ya ya ya ya ya" on a single pitch. When single pitches are comfortable, progress to a 1-2-3-2-1 and then a 1-3-5-3-1 pattern. Then drill the other exercises from chapter 5. When doing these exercises, use brighter vocal qualities to help coax your tongue forward. Remember that these are targeted exercises for coordinating the tongue; we are not trying to produce a final vocal quality when working through these exercises.

OTHER CONSIDERATIONS

Volume

Classical singers are accustomed to filling performance spaces without amplification. Musical theater singers are often trained to also fill the space for auditions, even though they will eventually perform on a microphone. However, rock singers never sing to the space and always sing to the microphone. Since the microphone is usually held a few inches from the mouth, there is no need for operatic or musical theater volume levels when singing rock. Always prioritize the resulting quality over the resulting volume level. There will be times that you want to eliminate breathiness, and when you do, the voice will be louder, but eliminating breathiness, not the resulting volume, is the goal.

When you are learning to belt, you will be singing at high volume levels. However, belt quality, not the volume, should be the goal. A general rule that I like my clients to keep in mind is to never practice beyond 80 to 90 percent of what you are capable of producing when it comes to vocal intensity. That way, if adrenaline kicks in during a performance, you have headroom to get louder without overblowing your voice. If you constantly practice at 100 percent and adrenaline kicks in, you will likely blow your voice out and have no base level to reset to when you catch yourself oversinging. When you have cemented singing at 80 to 90 percent in your motor system, you will always have a safety zone to reset to during a performance or when you are feeling sick or vocally fatigued.

Vibrato

While most classical singers consistently incorporate vibrato into their singing, it is less common among rock singers. Vibrato is more likely to show up with higher intensity levels of singing. Therefore, if you wish to limit your vibrato, it is important to start by reducing the intensity of your singing rather than constricting and holding back. Airflow also has an impact on vibrato, so if you are used to "spinning the tone," try letting go of that approach to see if it changes your vibrato. Rather than pushing a large amount of air through your vocal cords, allow the air to leak out, mimicking the way air flows during speech. Finally, try modifying your vowels. Vowels with a lot of back-room space tend to induce vibrato, so try using brighter vowel qualities that elicit a narrower back room instead. Remember that it is crucial to avoid any harmful squeezing or straining of your vocal mechanism. You may feel a slight squeeze at the larynx level as you explore straight-tone singing, but it should be very slight and should not approach the feeling of singing the "goog" exercises. Vibrato is a personal artistic preference, so go explore until you find what you like best.

Legato

Legato is a common characteristic of classical and musical theater styles, but it is not widely used in rock music. In rock, with the exception of ballads, a rhythmic delivery usually takes precedence. If you are a classical or musical theater singer who is used to thinking about vocal lines that are horizontal, you will want to shift your mindset to thinking vertically. So instead of singing your vocal line over the top of the rhythm that is beneath, you will lock your voice into the rhythm of the song. If you are not accustomed to singing rhythmically, there are a few exercises that can assist you in developing this skill.

Start Drumming

First, try singing with a drum machine. You can utilize a drumbeat app on your smartphone for this work. Pick a beat that fits a song you are working on and sing over it without any accompanying instruments. Pay close attention to how your voice synchronizes with the drums, where it contrasts with the rhythm, and where there is interplay between your vocals and the drums. Then go back to accompanying yourself or singing with a track and lock into the rhythm in the same way you did when you were singing with the drums.

You can also try drumming a simple beat on a hand drum, tabletop, or other hard surface. Find a beat that goes along with the song you are working on and sing along as you drum, paying close attention to which words line up with your hand striking the drum and which ones anticipate or come in after you hit the drum. Then take the drumming away and allow your voice to maintain the rhythmic connection you found while drumming. You could also try singing along with karaoke tracks, focusing on how your voice interacts with other instruments, such as the guitar and bass.

Adjust Your Approach to Vowels and Consonants

Traditional legato singing emphasizes pure vowels and lightly articulated consonants for smooth, connected lines. However, for a rhythmically delivered rock style, you will need to let go of some of that control and allow the vowels and consonants to have a more speechlike delivery. When we speak, our vowels often morph as we deliver the words, which helps us communicate what we are feeling. When crossing over to rock, you will need to give your vowels the freedom to morph as you sing. For example, when singing "Caro mio ben," the singer needs to immediately get to the /a/ vowel at the beginning of "Caro" and sustain the pure form of that vowel until quickly flicking the tongue to produce the "r" before sustaining a pure /o/ for the second note. If "Caro mio ben" were a rock song, the singer could start with one quality of /a/ and let the vowel morph into another quality of /a/, slowly moving through "r" into an /o/ vowel that would also have more than one quality. Rock singers do this because they are working with colloquial speech, and in everyday life, our speech patterns adapt to what we are feeling as we express ourselves. Pure vowels are a learned trait and are necessary for acoustically projected singing but are not universally present in rock music.

Story

Classical and musical theater singers are known for their meticulous approach to acting out their songs. However, in the realm of rock singing, the delivery of lyrics often takes on a different approach. It's akin to using a pointed brush versus a broad brush when painting a picture. With a pointed brush, you can fill in all kinds of details to bring the picture vividly to life. With a broad brush, you can still represent the same idea, but it will usually be a little more abstract with less detail. Both brushes can create compelling pictures; they are just different forms of expression. In musical theater and classical music, a pointed brush is appropriate, but in rock, we usually gravitate toward a broader brush.

While classical and musical theater performers tend to employ active verbs to craft their songs, rock singers usually prioritize the mood, groove, or emotion of the piece. Instead of delivering their songs to a specific scene partner, as is common in classical and musical theater, rock singers often turn inward, drawing on their personal memories and experiences and using the text as a means of cathartic release. In contrast to the predetermined gestures often seen in classical and musical theater performances, rock singers rarely plan their movements in advance. They allow the music to guide their body's motion in the present moment. As you work on your songs, watch live performance videos to get a feel for the performance practice that is appropriate for the style. Then use your self-tape equipment to record yourself performing and make adjustments to find a delivery that is more in line with what you watched.

Getting It Right

In classical and musical theater voice training, there is often an emphasis on achieving a specific sound, adhering to established vocal standards. These standards are determined by the industry as a whole, and while you can point to plenty of examples that go against the established norm, you can usually point to more examples that fit the norm. However, in the realm of rock singing, there are no set standards. What truly matters is uniqueness. As you progress through these exercises, you may find yourself questioning whether you are doing it "right." Remember that if a particular sound feels comfortable and aligns with elements of storytelling, emotion, mood, or groove you are looking for, then it is a valuable sound to incorporate into your vocal toolbox. By experimenting with different sounds, your signature sound will gradually reveal itself. As this happens, you will gain clarity on which aspects of your voice require further coordination. Through this process, your natural rock 'n' roll style will begin to emerge. You will know you are uncovering it when things become easier, you rely less on conscious thought to produce the tone you want, and you are satisfied with the results.

SINGING IN POP/ROCK MUSICALS

Many musicals today have rock scores, and the production teams need singers who understand the style to help make the show a success. There are three different needs I consistently see in today's marketplace: imitation, emulation, and originality.

Musicals that are biographical in nature, such as *Jersey Boys*, *Million Dollar Quartet*, and *Beautiful*, need singers who can re-create the original artist's signature sound so that the audience feels like they are watching the original artist onstage. In short, they need people who are great imitators. Shows like *Tommy* and *American Idiot*, are built on songs by pop/rock artists, but instead of imitating the original singers, these shows require the performer only to emulate the original artist's style. That means the performer takes on elements of the original artist, but they also maintain their own individuality when singing. Original score musicals are those where the writing team created new material for the show; think of shows like *Waitress*, *The Outsiders*, and *Spring Awakening*. In these types of productions, the performers are expected to bring their own original pop/rock style to the show.

When learning how to imitate an artist, grab a lyric sheet or sheet music, sit down with a recording of the song, and do a deep dive into the original artist's performance. Review the tools discussed in chapter 9 and use a pen or pencil to mark every nuance you hear in the singer's voice. If possible, find an isolated vocal track recording on YouTube or make your own using one of the many available apps for this purpose. Copy every element of the vocal delivery within the limits of your voice and keep recording yourself and listening back until you get it right.

If you are emulating an artist, do the same process as above but with at least five songs by the artist you are studying. As you analyze the five songs, look for commonalities across all five selections. Does the artist consistently use the same types of onsets and releases? Do they consistently morph their vowels a certain way? How do they lock into the rhythm? By zoning in on five to ten big-picture stylistic traits that you can integrate into your singing, you can bring an element of the original artist into your work while filling in the rest of the song with your own unique attributes.

When trying to find your own pop/rock voice, you will want to start by identifying your influences (see chapter 4). What artists are you most attracted to as a singer? Make a list. Then pick two or three of your favorite songs by each artist. Sit down with a lyric sheet or sheet music and analyze everything those artists do with their voices when performing. Pick the elements you like best and start integrating those into your own voice when you sing. The end result should not sound like a singular artist but rather like you have integrated a little Bon Jovi combined with Joan Jett, flavored by Mötley Crüe and Metallica, with a side of Halestorm thrown into the mix.

Auditions

If the casting call asks for a specific era of music, follow the request. You may be tempted to use a modern song that sounds like music from that era. However, that is not what they are looking for if they have listed a desire to have music from a specific era. Begin your hunt for the perfect song by searching for the top 20 songs during the year the show takes place along with the top 20 songs of the five years before and after the show takes place. That should give you a robust list of options to begin your search. Listen to parts of each song and start thinking about which artists have voices similar to yours. When you find an artist with a similar voice, look up the other songs they have performed and see if you can find any gems among those pieces. When you find the right song, use all the tools from chapter 9 to analyze the style and create a road map for yourself.

If the casting call does not specify a specific era, you have more freedom to choose an audition song, and you should focus on showing what you do best. Try to find an artist with a voice that is similar to yours or find a song usually performed by someone of a different voice type. When you sing a song by an artist with a voice similar to yours, it helps the creative team imagine ways you could fit into their vision. By singing a song from a completely different voice type, you will have a unique take through song selection alone that can help the creative team think beyond a specific artist.

Find a lyric sheet or sheet music of the song you choose and listen to five versions of the song. Analyze what the different singers are doing and make notes of their choices. Then think about your unique point of view as it relates to the song and choose which stylistic tools you want to use to convey your authentic self through the song. The end result should be a mix of the five artists you listened to with a few of your own choices as well.

Delivering the Song in an Audition Setting

Pop/rock songs can fit into one of three categories: story songs, groove/vibe songs, and mood/emotion songs. Story songs are self-explanatory; they tell a story. In these songs, you can integrate some of the traditional musical theater acting choices you would make with your musical theater songs. Be careful not to overdo it or veer into cheesy territory unless, of course, that's the specific style the audition demands. I find that a TV/film style of acting delivery is usually the most effective for this kind of audition.

Songs that I classify as a groove or vibe song usually have lyrics that are more abstract. They may tell a story, but it is not a straightforward narrative like you find in a story song. These are songs like "Under the Bridge" by Red Hot Chili Peppers or "About a Girl" by Nirvana compared to story songs like "Livin' on a Prayer" by Bon Jovi or "Jack and Diane" by John Mellencamp. When performing songs like this, you can let the groove or mood work its way into your body. While I do not advocate choreographing the song, if you are a dancer, you can allow the desire to move to manifest itself in your performance. This will look different for every performer and each audition. The goal is to show the audition panel you feel comfortable living in the era of the show.

Finally, mood or emotion songs convey a feeling. The lyrics may be abstract or direct, but in either case, the goal is to help an audience feel something or to convey the message that the listener is not alone in what they are feeling. Practice these songs with your eyes closed and replay a scenario in your mind from a life experience that aligns with the lyrics. So, for example, if you are singing "Faithfully" by Journey, think of a time when you had to be in a long-distance relationship. Think about the situation and allow the mental video reel of you leaving your partner to creep into your mind. Think about what it felt like to walk, drive, ride, or fly away from them as you entered the unknown territory of being gone from each other for several weeks or months. Think about how the lyrics relate to what you felt and connect each part of the lyric to a conversation you had, a gift you bought your partner, or a fight you had while being apart. Keep practicing the song with your eyes closed until you have a vivid, internal music video that plays along in your mind as you sing. Then open your eyes and sing the song while allowing that video to still play in your mind. Just stand there, live in the moment, and sing.

Many songs combine elements of all these styles and require you to just show up and sing while having a good time. All you can do is show the creative team your authentic self so that they can see where you might fit into their vision. There are, of course, many other elements to delivering a successful pop/rock audition for musical theater beyond those covered here. However, making distinct choices about how you are going to deliver the song and using the tools in this book to tweak your vocal delivery will make a significant difference in your work.

CONCLUSION

While my musical journey started with rock music, I eventually found myself studying opera and musical theater. In fact, all three of my college degrees are in classical music. When I first started transitioning back to my rock 'n' roll roots, I found it very frustrating that years of classical technique had not prepared me to cross over to commercial styles. After helping hundreds of classical and musical theater singers find their rock voice, I have seen proof that it can be done, but it takes patience and a lot of time re-coordinating your instrument. Keep a growth mindset along the way, and eventually, you will be able to sing a much wider variety of music than you ever thought possible.

NOTE

1. Karen Brunssen, *The Evolving Singing Voice: Changes across the Lifespan* (San Diego, CA: Plural Publishing, 2018), 214–15.

9

DEVELOPING YOUR STYLE

In this chapter, we are going to discuss how to develop your sense of style as a singer. If you are a performer who already has your own sense of style, this chapter may cover a lot of information you already know, either intellectually or instinctually. However, if you are new to singing rock music, it is likely that you could use a little guidance on how to develop your approach to delivering songs. Style in music refers to the distinctive characteristics, elements, and conventions that define a particular genre, subgenre, or individual artist's approach to creating or interpreting music. It encompasses various aspects, including rhythm, melody, harmony, instrumentation, vocal delivery, lyrics, and production techniques. A musical style often reflects the historical, cultural, and geographical context in which it emerges and evolves, which is why it is important to know your history, as discussed in chapter 4, especially if you are performing in a cover band or auditioning for pop/rock musical theater productions.

In this chapter, we will cover the elements that make up style and talk about the tools you have at your disposal. Because this is a book, the approach will be very intellectual and theoretical. Once you have that understanding, you will need to learn by doing. You need to get out there and perform, get feedback, make adjustments, and keep refining your style until you reach the point where you feel like you are able to communicate the way you want onstage. Throughout your life, your style will evolve. You will be influenced by others, and you will continue to refine your work. So think of this as the start of your journey, not the end of it.

RHYTHM

Rock music is known for its distinctive emphasis on rhythm and beat, which gives the genre its driving sound. It typically features a strong emphasis on the backbeat, leaning into beats 2 and 4 within a four-beat measure. The bass drum often accentuates beats 1 and 3, while the snare drum hits on beats 2 and 4, creating a forceful accentuation. Sometimes, the singer locks into beats 2 and 4, as in the chorus of "The Middle" by Jimmy Eat World. Other times, the singer locks into beats 1 and 3 while the band accentuates beats 2 and 4, as in the chorus of "Complicated" by Avril Lavigne. There are also songs where the singer just moves along over the top of the driving beat without locking into specific beats, as in "Brown Eyed Girl" by Van Morrison. You will also come across syncopation, which is a term used to describe the deliberate placement of accents on unexpected beats or off-beats, creating a sense of rhythmic tension and complexity. For example, listen to the final chorus of "Tourniquet" by Breaking Benjamin.

When working on a song, pay attention to how the voice lines up with the instruments. Some singers will find themselves instinctually connecting the voice and the instrument they are performing with in a given song. Others, especially those who were taught to think about long legato lines, will have to work on this skill. Think about a song you are working on. Does the voice lock into the drums, bass, guitar, or keys? If so, where and how? If you are playing an instrument, where does the voice hit with the physical action of playing your instrument? Slow down the song if you need to figure it out, then speed it back up incrementally. When you lock your voice and instrument together, your songs will be noticeably tighter in your delivery. For singers who struggle to play and sing at the same time, I find that the process of locking the voice and instrument together often helps them overcome their limitations.

Notated Music

If music notation is helpful to you, look for the following cues in the music. Figure 9.1 shows three common rhythmic figures you will encounter. The first is a notated back phrase; this is when you come in after

Figure 9.1. Common rhythmic patterns. *Courtesy of Matt Edwards*

the beat. When you come across this figure, you will want to lean into the back-phrased notes and then lean into the next strong downbeat. "Leaning in" means you will give a slight emphasis to that note; how much emphasis should be determined by the needs of each song. The second example is a notated anticipation, meaning you come in before the beat. You treat these the same as back-phrased notes, leaning into them and then bringing the next strong downbeat to life. The third example shows syncopation; in this variation, you first sing an eighth note followed by several quarters, and then you end with an eighth note. When singing syncopated rhythms, give a little extra emphasis to the offbeats and then lean into the next strong downbeat.

Start Drumming

One of the best things you can do to improve your sense of rhythm is to start drumming. Tabletop drumming is fine to start. Start by drumming beat 1 with your dominant hand, then play beat 2 with your nondominant hand. Beat 3 goes back to the dominant and beat 4 back to the nondominant hand. Vocalize a simple 1-2-3-4-5-4-3-2-1 exercise while drumming and accentuate the notes that align with your nondominant hand. Try this simple beat with all of your vocal exercises, then try adding it to songs. When you are comfortable with a simple beat, try making it more complex, in line with the drums in the song you are working on. Then sing along and pay attention to where beats 1, 2, 3, and 4 align with the lyrics. By physicalizing the beat, you are making it a core part of your delivery instead of just an intellectual exercise.

MELODY

In our daily conversations, we employ a variety of inflections, including level, upward, downward, and circumflex, to convey our emotions and intentions in the moment. Combinations of inflection and intensity communicate different messages. For example, level inflection with moderate intensity often signals emotional stability, but if combined with high intensity, it can communicate tension. However, if you combine level inflection with low intensity, it can suggest a degree of apathy. Upward inflection with high intensity expresses varying shades of excitement, such as joy, anger, and frustration. When people ask questions, they usually combine upward inflection with moderate to light intensity. Downward inflection with moderate to high intensity can indicate finality and surety, while lower levels of intensity can suggest indecision or defeat. Circumflex inflection employs all of the above to articulate a broad spectrum of emotions and intentions with varying degrees of intensity.

When it comes to music, melodies play a crucial role in reflecting and/or altering the natural inflection of speech to enhance the meaning of the lyrics being sung. As you practice, you should be thinking about how your intensity choices align with the melodic contour. Melodies with a level inflection usually maintain a modest pitch range and are often sung with a steady level of intensity. However, how does the meaning of the lyrics change if you bring in varying degrees of intensity? Upward-inflected melodies extend into the upper vocal range of the voice, and we usually expect increasing intensity as the singer gets higher in their range. How does the meaning change if you alter the intensity level? Every variation can have a different impact on the listener's interpretation. In genres like punk and thrash, these details are not usually emphasized. However, in the context of other styles, like a folk rock ballad, inflection can significantly enhance the delivery of the lyrics.

PHRASING

In music, the term "phrase" refers to a musical idea or a musical sentence. It is a cohesive and complete musical thought that has a distinct beginning and end that can be compared to a sentence where a group of words forms a meaningful unit. A musical phrase typically consists of a melodic line or a series of chords that convey a musical idea. Phrases can vary in length and complexity. They can be short and concise, consisting of just a few notes or chords, or they can be longer and more elaborate, spanning several measures or even longer sections. Within songs, phrases are often grouped together into larger sections, such as verses, choruses, or bridges. The way one moves between pitches, bends, leans into, and meets or defies expectations within a phrase will impact and enhance the audience's interpretation of the lyrics.

Transcribing Songs

One of the best ways to improve your phrasing is to study the phrasing of others through transcription. Transcription is the process of sitting down with a lyric sheet for a song and notating every stylistic quality you notice. There is no standardized notation for this process; you get to develop your own system of lines, curves, and letters to notate what you hear.

There are some common stylistic traits you will come across. In most rock songs, there is a fair amount of scooping and sliding into and out of pitches. Slides are when you can hear the singer go through other pitches on the way up or down to a note. Scoops are when the pitches they move through are indiscriminate. I usually mark slides with a long, straight line and use a short, curved line for scoops. You may hear some singers bend notes, which is where they drag the note up and sometimes back down like you hear in electric guitar solos. I usually mark these with short lines. In early rock 'n' roll that leans toward the pop side of the spectrum, you will sometimes hear turns where the singer starts on a note and goes above the note, then below the note, and then back to the original note. You can mark these with a tilde (~). Most rock singers let the final words of phrases fall off. This means they let the final pitch fall as their voice dissipates instead of ending the phrase cleanly on a single note. I usually mark these with a small, curved line that drops down. Occasionally, you will hear licks, which are short, improvised interjections or runs that are longer interjections. I usually draw a squiggly line in the general shape of the lick or run when I come across one of these. If you are struggling to figure out what notes the artist is singing, listen to the song on YouTube and slow down the playback speed.

There will also be other stylistic elements that are not listed here. It is important to remember that most of the singers you listen to were just doing what they do; they were not overintellectualizing their choices. However, I find that many singers do not know what they can get away with, so they sing conservatively when interpreting songs. This is especially true of those who come from classical, choral, and musical theater genres, where you are expected to stick to the notes on the page. By going through this process, you will learn what is possible so that you can free yourself from any preconceived ideas you may have about the rules of singing a song.

After you have transcribed a song, practice copying all the elements you discovered in your listening by singing what you transcribed. Then repeat the process with another song. As you work on multiple songs, you will find stylistic choices that you really like. As you do, start adding those traits to your own songs. This is what it means to absorb influences, and it is how artists have been developing their artistic voice for centuries. If you want to learn more, read the book *Steal Like an Artist* by Austin Kleon.[1]

Reimagining Songs

When performing a cover, you have a lot of freedom to alter the melody to create a unique version of the tune. Many singers will change the key, rewrite the melody so that it adds higher notes, or rewrite it to fit their vocal abilities. You want to be careful not to rewrite it to the point that the song is no longer recognizable, but adding some variations throughout the song is acceptable. Postmodern Jukebox is known for their ability to transform songs; for example, look up "Black Hole Sun" by Hayley Rheinhart. Also check out "Eye of the Tiger" by Walk Off the Earth.

Using Sheet Music

If you are learning a song from sheet music, remember that the sheet music was created by a transcriber, not the songwriter. The notes on the page are a road map, and unlike in classical music and musical theater, you can go off-roading anytime you want. Listen to a live version of the song as you read the sheet music, take note of where the sheet music differs from the recording, and transcribe those differences. Then start playing around to create your own unique interpretation.

HARMONY

Chord progressions form the harmonic structure of a piece of music, contribute to its overall tonality and mood, and can help inform how you interpret the lyrics. Chords are groups of three or more notes played simultaneously. They are typically built on a root note that serves as the foundation or starting point. Additional notes are then added, usually a third and a fifth above the root. The interval relationships between these notes determine the quality and character of the chord. Common types include major, minor, diminished, augmented, and seventh chords. Chord types are frequently interpreted as having different emotional contexts.

Major chords, for example, often convey a sense of brightness and stability, while minor chords evoke a more somber or melancholic mood. Chords can also be extended by adding additional notes beyond the root, third, and fifth, such as ninth chords, eleventh chords, or thirteenth chords, which add further complexity and color to the harmony.

Understanding Chords Can Help Improve Pitch Accuracy

Rock singers do not need to know the complexities of chord structures in the same way a jazz or musical theater singer might, but if you are struggling with matching pitch, learning how you fit into the larger harmonic structure can sometimes help improve pitch accuracy. If you do not know a lot about chords and their use in songs, it would be worth investing in an online music theory course. Knowing more about how music works will help you be a smarter musician, which will make you a better singer.

Reharmonizing Songs

If you want to make a unique cover of a song, consider reharmonizing the song. You can do this by replacing existing chords with alternative chords that share similar functions or have compatible harmonic characteristics, inserting new chords within the existing chord progression to create more intricate harmonies, and/or inverting chords, which means putting a note other than the root in the bass line. For an example, search YouTube for Jacob Collier's reharmonization of "Hey Jude." In the video, he explains his thinking, which will help you further understand the process or reharmonization.

INSTRUMENTATION

The choice and combination of instruments used in a song contribute to our sense of style. Most rock bands consist of at least a singer, guitarist, bass player, and drummer. Some bands expand into multiple instruments, including two or three guitarists, keyboard players, auxiliary percussionists, backup singers, and occasionally other instruments. Guitars are capable of playing with both "clean" and "distortion" settings. Clean means that the amplification settings do not alter the tone of the guitar. Distortion is created by intentionally overdriving the signal of the guitar, resulting in a clipped waveform and harmonic saturation. This process introduces harmonics that are usually not present in an acoustic instrument playing the same note or chord. These extra harmonics create a rich, complex sound that can be produced only with the aid of technology. The level of distortion can vary, ranging from the subtle "fuzz" heard on Chuck Berry's guitar to the "distortion" in Jimi Hendrix's playing and finally to the heavily saturated "overdrive" that was part of Van Halen's signature sound. The use of distorted guitars eventually led vocalists to use more "grit" in their sound and eventually led to the extreme vocal distortions found in heavy metal.

As you are working on your songs, let the instrumentation influence the vocal qualities you choose. In a song like "Smells Like Teen Spirit" by Nirvana, you could sing with one quality in the verse when the guitar is clean and a different quality in the chorus when the guitar is distorted. If you are trying to come up with options to create a unique take on a song, it can be helpful to listen to the song on repeat and focus on different parts of the instrumentation on each listen. Pay attention to only the drums, then the bass, then the guitar and keyboard, and so on. As you listen to each layer of the song, think about the role it plays and how you might craft your vocal delivery to complement the bigger picture.

VOCALS

While rock singers are often subject to stereotypes, the reality is that the range of vocal qualities utilized by rock artists knows no bounds. Most rock voices are rooted in speech, so there's an inherent element of the artist's speaking voice embedded within their singing voice. Every artist possesses what we refer to as a "signature sound," a distinctive quality that we immediately associate with their music. It is what makes Robert Plant different than Roger Daltrey and Lzzy Hale different than Hayley Williams. That signature sound is created through the artist's choice of register, vowel, and intensity along with onsets and releases, vibrato, and the application of vocal distortion.

Registers

In chapter 5, we talked about registration and why we need to develop the polar registers and everything in between. Now we will talk about how to put that work to use to interpret a song. Consider the way that we speak when we are sad, depressed, or in an intimate setting. The vocal quality is usually lighter and often breathier than when we feel neutral about something or are in a neutral setting. Now think about what your voice does when you are excited, angry, or frustrated. It usually takes on an extra edge that involves a lot of firm closure of the vocal folds, similar to what you felt when working on the chest register exercises.

If you are singing a song that is supposed to be in a state of excitement and your voice gets breathy, the listener may be confused because the vocal quality does not meet their expectations for that emotional state of being. If you are singing a song that's supposed to be an intimate love song and your voice is overly buzzy, they are also likely to be confused. Instead, you want to adjust your vocal quality to what one would expect in that moment in relation to the lyrics. In many songs, there is a roller coaster of emotions, and your voice will need to change accordingly, including using many shades of mix. A mix that is more chesty will align more closely with anger, joy, or angst than a mix that's on the breathier side. This is why it is so important to master those registration exercises; you want your voice to just respond to your intent without overthinking things.

Next time you are listening to a song, think about how the register choices fit the lyrics. Then, as you interpret your own songs, play around with your registration choices in similar ways to bring life to the text. Harder styles like heavy metal will have less nuance than folk rock. Up-tempo songs will have less nuance than slow ballads. Yet even in the most aggressive of songs, there is usually at least some vocal variation.

You will also want to consider the intensity of your register choices. Chest register with low intensity is going to be different than chest register with high intensity. If you are singing a song where the story or emotion progressively intensifies, you will want to make sure that your registration progressively intensifies as well. Abrupt shifts in meaning may require dramatic changes in registration; this is why some artists incorporate hard breaks from chest to falsetto in their songs. For an example, listen to "Zombie" by the Cranberries.

Onsets and Releases

Onset is a term used to describe how the vocal folds come together at the beginning of a phrase. "Release" is the term we use to describe how the vocal folds end a phrase. The way we use onsets and releases colors the meaning of the lyrics.

Clean

Clean onsets and releases are achieved by synchronizing the initiation or cessation of breath with the vocal folds' vibration. This technique creates a sense of clarity that serves as a foundational starting point for most singers. Humming is the easiest way to experience a clean onset and release, as you cannot release your air before or after a hum with your lips sealed shut. Try pulsing a hum on a comfortable pitch and pay attention to how your airflow and vocal fold vibration begin at the same time. Now try alternating between a hum and an /i/. Do this on a single pitch, making sure that when you sing the /i/, your vocal folds begin to vibrate at the same moment as you release air from your lungs. When ending the /i/, make sure that your vocal folds cease to vibrate at the same time airflow stops. Next, try pulsing an /a/ five times on a single pitch with clean onsets and releases. Then try singing a simple song and start each phrase with a clean onset and end it with a clean release.

Fry

For lyrics that convey struggle, mounting frustration, or a layer of apathy, a fry onset or release can be more fitting. A fry onset or release involves a low and creaky sound, created by engaging sporadic vocal fold vibration. Sing an /a/ in the upper part of your head voice register and slowly glide down, being sure to carry your head voice to the lowest pitch you can sing. Now repeat the descending glide but with a breathy version of your head register. As you reach the bottom of the slide in your breathy head register, your vocal folds should pull apart and begin vibrating sporadically without an exact pitch. The resulting sound is a vocal fry.

Repeat the downward glide into vocal fry several times and then try to initiate your voice with vocal fry on an /a/ vowel. You should be initiating in a very light chest register. Then start with a clean /a/ vowel and let it fall into fry on your cutoff. Next, see if you can sing a 1-2-3-2-1 pattern on /a/, putting vocal fry on every pitch. When you feel comfortable with fry, sing through a few of your ballads and add fry to the beginning and ends of phrases to see how it alters your interpretation of the lyrics. Later

DEVELOPING YOUR STYLE   227

in this chapter, we will talk about how to expand your use of vocal fry into vocal distortion.

Glottal

Glottal or hard onsets are produced by closing the vocal folds and initiating vibration with a burst of air that blows the folds open before they quickly snap back together. A hard cutoff, glottal release, or compressed release occurs when the vocal folds abruptly stop vibrating, causing a buildup of air pressure beneath them. Often, a shadow vowel, such as /U/, accompanies this type of release. To create a glottal onset, take a medium size breath, hold your breath, and then initiate a pitch on /a/. This is a glottal onset. Do this several times, then try to add a hard onset to the beginning of a phrase. It is usually easiest with words that begin with a vowel. Now sing a phrase and at the end of the phrase stop singing by quickly holding your breath. This should give you a harsh stop to your vocals, what we might call a glottal stop.

Breathy

Breathy or aspirate onsets are produced by exhaling a little bit of air before bringing the vocal folds together to create a pitch. The breathiness will often extend into the delivery of the lyrics as well, which is why in chapter 5 we worked on coordinating your ability to sing with breathy qualities. Try creating a breathy onset by taking half a breath and then exhaling for one second before adding pitch on the word "I." Now start "I" and exhale through the end of it to finish with air instead of vibration. If you are a trained singer who is used to using clean onsets and releases, finding this coordination may be difficult. Keep working on initiating and ending vowels with extra air to coordinate your larynx for this approach. Then try singing through a few phrases while adding breathiness to see how it impacts the interpretation of the lyrics.

Flips

Sometimes, artists will abruptly flip from chest to head register for added effect A great example of this is Linda Perry's singing in 4 Non Blondes' "What's Up." Practice flipping on an octave interval by singing

/a/ on the bottom in chest register and /u/ on the top with head register. When you can flip from /a/ to /u/, try flipping between registers on /a/ alone. Many singers feel this shift taking place in their larynx. Not only will they feel a change in pressure caused by the abrupt change in vocal fold closure, but they may also feel their larynx leap upward on the interval. Both are normal experiences. When you can successfully flip in exercises, try singing along with "What's Up," imitating Linda Perry's flips. Then try adding flips to your songs.

Vowel Quality

Vowel quality is one of the three elements we should always be considering when crafting our vocals. The choice between bright and warm or open and closed vowels can profoundly influence the meaning and impact of the lyrics.

Open Vowels

Open, bright vowels tend to evoke a sense of energy release and are often associated with moments of high intensity, such as calling out. When opening your vowels, think of your mouth taking on the shape of a megaphone: narrow in the back and wide in the front. You may run into trouble if your masseter muscle tries to contract as you open your mouth. If that happens, go back to chapter 5 and try the masseter release exercise. Remember that if your tongue lacks coordination, there may be some involuntary contractions of the muscles surrounding your lower mandible that may get in the way of freely opening your mouth. If you struggle with TMJD, you may also struggle with using open vowels.

Closed Vowels

Closed vowels create a contrasting effect to their open counterparts, conveying a sense of drawing in energy, creating intimacy, or containing something within yourself. These vowels can give the listener a feeling of closeness, introspection, or a sense of holding back emotions. To form vowels in a closed position, imagine reversing the megaphone shape, meaning you will have narrower space in the front and more open space in the back of your mouth. Your lips will be close together, and the voice will often take on a hint of warmth compared to singing with open vowels.

Variations of Open and Closed

You can also create warm, open vowels and bright, closed vowels. For a warm, open vowel, assume the megaphone position and then round your lips. The lip rounding will dampen the upper frequencies of your voice and add warmth to your tone quality. You can add additional warmth by allowing your larynx to lower while the soft palate elevates. To produce a bright, closed vowel, assume the reverse megaphone position with a wide lip position, as if you were smiling. You can also allow the back room to decrease in size by letting the larynx rise and the soft palate fall.

Vibrato

"Vibrato" is a term we use to describe oscillations in a sustained pitch. Terms used to discuss vibrato usually include "rate," "extent," "jitter," and "shimmer." Rate measures the number of oscillations per second, extent describes variations in the frequency of the pitch the singer is sustaining, jitter measures variations in the rate of the vibrato, and shimmer refers to variations of amplitude.[2] These oscillations are likely due to the antagonistic action of the intrinsic muscles of the larynx. You can experience a vibrato-like tremor created by opposing muscular engagement by holding your hands in front of your body and attempting to pull them apart in opposite directions. As you perform this action, you will feel a tremor in your muscles. This is similar to what is happening as the thyroarytenoid muscle engages against the action of the cricothyroid muscle. The tremor affects the vibration of the vocal folds, leading to vibrato. From there, the interactions get quite complex, and readers are referred to Titze et al. for additional information.[3]

Most studies cite the desirable rate for vibrato at somewhere between five and eight oscillations per second, but it is important to note that these rates are based on western European music styles and are not necessarily representative of rock music or other non–western European styles. If you are happy with your vibrato, leave it alone. If you want to gain more control over your vibrato, the best place to start is with registration work. As you learn to alter your registration, you will likely discover that the breathier or more pressed you sing, the less vibrato you will have in your voice. When you find a balance between the extremes, vibrato will be more likely to show up.

If you are struggling to find vibrato after extensive registration work, you will want to address any constriction or compensatory behaviors in the vocal tract, as these can limit vibrato. If inconsistencies persist after vocal tract coordination work, you will want to work on the coordination of your respiratory muscles to ensure that you are in control of your subglottal pressure and transglottal airflow. If your abdominal muscles are tense or your rib cage immediately collapses as you begin phonation, it will likely increase breath pressure and impact vibrato rate. If elastic recoil alone is not enough to power your vocal folds and you are not engaging your abdominal muscles, you may not have enough breath pressure for vibrato. Try relaxing and engaging your abs to see if either choice makes a difference.

If you are looking to limit your vibrato, one of the easiest approaches is to reduce the volume level of your singing. Higher intensity levels are more likely to produce vibrato than lower intensity levels. You can also try to minimize vibrato by holding back your breath. Inhale up to about 65 percent of what you are capable of and hold your breath. Then initiate a pitch while maintaining the sensation associated with holding your breath to see if that helps minimize your vibrato. You have to be careful with this approach, as you do not want to develop tension that cannot be released. However, if you are consciously making the choice to hold your air back for select moments of songs, you should be okay. You just need to make sure that holding is not the only way you can sing.

Another option to explore when trying to straight-tone is a held jaw position. Grab a chopstick, place it horizontally between your teeth, and bite down. Then sing and see if your vibrato decreases. If it does, remove the chopstick and see if simply maintaining a narrower mouth position is sufficient to remove your vibrato. If a narrow space alone is not giving you what you are looking for, try engaging your masseter muscles as if biting down and see if that helps. Again, you are introducing tension to remove vibrato, which isn't ideal, but it's what a lot of people do instinctively to produce a straighter tone. Just make sure you are vocalizing with a released masseter muscle in your warm-ups to ensure that you are always in control of that tension and that the tension does not start to take control of you.

LYRICS

The content, themes, and storytelling style found in the lyrics of songs also influence our perception of style. Lyrics in rock music can range from personal introspection to political commentary to storytelling to abstract imagery. Sometimes, the lyrics are poetic and full of hidden meaning; other times, the words are simple, and there is not much depth put into the delivery. When singing a story-driven song, filling in the details will significantly enhance the performance. When living in the abstract, coloring in the lyrics with a nuanced delivery could further enhance the vision of the song.

Tempo

The tempo of the song is a significant factor in determining how the lyrics are delivered. Songs with faster tempos may require a more direct and straightforward approach, as there is less time to play with the lyrics. However, slower ballads allow for more time, giving you lots of possibilities for adding nuance and subtlety. Like all tools in developing one's style, the level of lyrical finesse will depend greatly on the artistic tastes of the creator.

Phrase Weighting

Phrase weighting is a powerful tool for shaping the delivery of lyrics. Phrase weighting is the process of determining which words or phrases within a lyric will receive emphasis when singing.[4] By emphasizing different words, the meaning and impact of the lyrics can be subtly or dramatically altered. For example, in the phrase "now I got the Crazy Blues," the emphasis could be placed on "now," "I," "got," "Crazy," or "Blues." Each option offers a distinct interpretation and emotional emphasis. Depending on the lyric, it can drastically alter the meaning of the phrase. Say the following sentence while emphasizing the word "eat" and leaving the rest of the words at a level inflection: "Let's go eat Grandma." Now say the same sentence and emphasize "Grandma." Those are two very different meanings from the same words. One is a friendly invitation, the other the plot of a horror movie.

Go through the lyrics of one of your ballads and explore weighting different words in each phrase. The best way to do this is to repeat the phrase over and over again, changing the emphasis from the first word, to the second, to the third, and so on. In some phrases, you may find that two or three words feel like they need the emphasis. There are no rules, so feel free to make the choices that work best for you.

Operative Words

Another way to think about phrase weighting is through operative words. These are the words that a sentence must have in order to make sense. For example, in the sentence "Let's go lie by the river and listen to the waterfall," the operative words are "go," "lie," "river," "listen," and "waterfall." These are the words you would want to emphasize. In some songs, emphasizing every operative word will be too much; in other songs, it might work. Play around with both options to find what works best for each song.

Lyric Delivery Style

Beyond phrase weighting, the delivery of the words themselves also plays a crucial role in bringing lyrics to life. Different vocal techniques can be employed to enhance the expression and emotional resonance of the lyrics. For example, a laid-back delivery may involve intentionally softening the consonants and blurring the vowels, creating a sense of ambiguity and adding intrigue to the lyrics. On the other hand, a more articulate and clear enunciation of vowels and consonants can be employed to ensure that the lyrics are easily understood and impactful. In the realm of rock music, most songs tend to fall somewhere in the middle of this spectrum, finding a balance between clarity and emotive expression.

SUMMARY

Ultimately, the art of delivering lyrics in a song involves a thoughtful combination of phrase weighting, vocal technique, and emotional expression. It requires the artist to consider the intent behind the lyrics and the musical context in which they are presented. By skillfully utilizing these tools, artists can breathe life into their lyrics, adding depth, emotion, and meaning to their music to forge a connection with their listeners. Like all the other tools in this book, your eventual goal is to instinctively make these choices

DEVELOPING YOUR STYLE

without having to overintellectualize the process. So as you dive into this work, take what resonates with you and leave the rest behind.

VOCAL DISTORTIONS

"Vocal distortion" is a term we use to describe aggressive sounds that are produced by sporadic vibrations of the vocal folds or tissues above the vocal folds. It is important to emphasize that these sounds can lead to vocal injury if done incorrectly. Many singers can sing with vocal distortion without any issues; others may find the sounds slightly or very uncomfortable. Let's think of it in terms of athletic activities. Pickleball is pretty risk free; sure, you could whack your partner on the head with a paddle, but if you are paying attention, that is unlikely to happen. Everyday conversational speaking is like pickleball when it comes to vocal injuries. Something could go wrong, but it's not that likely for most people.

Singing is more like soccer. When playing soccer, you could take a hard kick to the knee or a fast head ball and end up with an injury. The sport has some inherent risks, but most people have only minor injuries. When you do get injured, time off and physical therapy will usually get you back on the field. Singing is the same. Most people are fine, some get injured, but almost everyone who does get injured easily recovers with time off and therapy.

Singing with vocal distortions is like playing football. There are a lot of injuries in football, and they are usually a little more severe than soccer injuries. Most of the time, you can still be rehabilitated to get back on the field, but in some instances, the injuries are severe enough to require surgical intervention. Singing with vocal distortions is like playing football with your voice. Football players know their risk of injury before they start playing the game. Singers just need to be aware of the potential for injury before singing with aggressive vocal techniques. To be clear, you can learn to make these sounds in a way that is sustainable. You can absolutely minimize your risk, but it would be irresponsible not to mention that you can injure yourself if you do not learn to do it with the right coordination.

It is also important to point out that the vast majority of singers cannot learn to create these vocal qualities solely by reading about them. I'm going to show you an introductory exercise for three different qualities to introduce you to the concepts. However, if you really want to master them, you need to work with a teacher who specializes in this area.

Vocal Fry Distortions

Earlier in this chapter, we talked about using vocal fry in your onsets and releases. Fry screams are produced by extending and expanding on vocal fry to a higher intensity level that can have words layered on top of it. This vocal quality is created by sporadic activity at the vocal fold level, so it is possible you could experience some mild swelling or dryness while you are trying to figure out how to produce the sound. As long as you notice when you are getting tired and quit at that point, you should be fine. Pushing past fatigue is when troubles arise.

After you have found your vocal fry by sliding down from head voice, you will want to start consistently initiating in vocal fry. As you initiate, imagine little puffs of air being released by your vocal folds as they flutter against each other. If the puffs get too big, the fry will get sloppy. If the puffs get too small, you will end up with too much subglottic pressure to produce a fry. When you find the middle ground, start sliding the fry up and down your vocal range. Start incrementally, then begin exploring your full range. When you get comfortable moving vocal fry, we are going to try to accelerate air through the folds to produce a more intense sound.

Take a deep breath, purse your lips, and blow. You should have a small but steady stream of air exiting your lips. Now I want you to take a breath, begin releasing a stream of air, and then contract your abdominal wall as if performing a plank. Hold that position for one second, then release your abs. Keep alternating between abdominal contraction and relaxation until you run out of breath. Now add abdominal engagement to your vocal fry.

Begin with vocal fry, then contract your abs to expel more air. It is possible that when you contract your abs, your vocal folds will contract as well, limiting airflow and interrupting your vocal fry. If that happens, try again and imagine more air traveling between the vocal folds when contracting your abs. When you find the right balance of airflow and sporadic vibration, you can begin shaping your vowels to color the fry. Move your lips, jaw, and tongue in different positions to create a wide variety of screams. Then start adding lyrics. It is a good idea to practice these sounds on a microphone, as technology is a critical component of singing with this effect.

False Fold Growls

There are two folds of tissue above the true vocal folds that are called the false vocal folds. You can bring these folds together while also vibrating other supraglottic tissues to produce a growl quality. Some singers can even do this while phonating the true vocal folds to add pitch to the growl. To begin, I want you to imagine that you were just told something frustrating and you let out an audible "ugh." Now bark like a big dog, calling out "ruff" with all of the snarl that you would expect from a Rottweiler. Now put some of the park into the "ugh." Keep your vocal folds out of the sound as much as possible. As you make this sound, you may feel your throat narrowing in and your tongue pulling back. If you are not able to produce a growl and do not feel narrowing in the back, you can try again and consciously narrow the back room of your vocal tract by pulling your tongue back. As you focus on the back room, allow the tissues above the vocal folds and below the soft palate to collapse inward and vibrate with the flow of air being released from your lungs. Many singers find closed /o/ or /u/ vowels easiest to start working on this sounds. Once you can growl in those vowel shapes, try opening to an /a/.

Some singers will find that this quality is very easy to produce; others will feel like they have to constrict their throats with more effort than is comfortable. Keep experimenting until you find what works for you but do not push beyond your comfort zone into fatigue. It can take months to learn how to produce these qualities in a sustainable way. Once you can produce the sound, try adding it on the onset of phrases in your songs.

Arytenoid Rattle

The final version of distortion we will discuss is the arytenoid rattle. This has been identified by researchers at the Complete Vocal Institute in Sweden. Through stroboscopic research studies, they have identified a distortion created by rapid vibration of the arytenoids.[5] To start, produce a slow laugh on "ha" in a light chest-dominant mix. Now accelerate the laugh into triplets. We are not looking for accurate rhythms here; we just want to get the arytenoids bouncing around more quickly than in a simple laugh. Next, slowly speed up the triplets until you reach a speed that sounds like a motorcycle starting. Finally, you are going to pulse three sets of triplets and then fall into the sound of a motorcycle engine turning over. The result should sound like the vocal quality of Louis Armstrong's voice. When you can successfully get the Louis Armstrong sound, you are rattling your arytenoids. Now try to initiate vowels with that sound. Start with /a/ on a 1-2-3-2-1 scale. Then try "hey" on a 1-2-3-2-1 scale. Finally, add rattle to the beginnings of phrases in songs you are working on. Keep practicing finding and re-creating this quality until it feels easy.

Functionally Dysfunctional

Functionally dysfunctional is the academic way of saying that someone has voice damage but their voice still functions in the way they want it to function for their style of music. There are multiple pathologies that can cause some singers problems while giving others a unique vocal quality. Nodules are not always a career destroyer. In fact, some singers have nodules yet never experience any negative impact on their singing. Other singers may have a polyp or cyst that lies on a part of the fold that does not negatively impact pitch accuracy or range but instead adds a slight rattle to their voice that is part of their unique signature sound. Scar tissue on the folds can alter the way the folds vibrate, also contributing to the unique quality of a singer's voice.

No one should try to give themselves voice damage in order to enhance their signature sound, as you always run the risk of damaging your voice in a way that prevents you from singing at all. However, we must recognize that some of the vocal distortions we hear in singer's voices may be the result of voice damage, and you may not be able to replicate that sound with your voice. Even though it is tempting to replicate the vocal quality of your favorite artists, you have to work with what you have and find your own unique sound.

Summary

These are only brief introductions to producing these sounds so that you can determine if they are easy for you, difficult, or somewhere in between. We do not have a lot of research on how they are produced, and it is likely that there are many ways one can distort their voice in a sustainable way. If it feels easy to make these sounds, then have fun playing with them. Before starting your practice sessions, glide from the lowest part of your voice to the highest part of your voice as quietly as you can. Then slide from the top down. Use this as a baseline to determine if you are fatiguing as you practice your distortions. If you repeat the soft glides after several minutes of practicing vocal distortions and you notice that you can no longer perform light glides with the same ease as when you started, that is a sign that it is time to take a break. If it is difficult for you to produce vocal distortions, then limit your explorations to five minutes a day, and if you do not feel improvement, seek out a professional coach who can help you.

In general, when working on vocal distortion techniques, it is best to progressively increase the number of minutes each day you spend using these qualities. When beginning, I recommend only five to ten minutes a day of practicing these sounds. As you get accustomed to how to produce them, you will be able to increase the amount of time you sing with that quality. As you increase the amount of time, you will develop stamina so that you can use the quality in songs.

CONCLUSION

The tools in the chapter, along with the content of chapter 4, should help you expand your vocabulary and knowledge about vocal style. The best thing you can do to improve your artistry is listen at the micro-level of songs that align with way you want to sing. That means you are going to not only take in the big picture of the song but also listen repeatedly to analyze every nuance in the instruments and voices of the artists on the recording. Use lyric sheets or sheet music to make notes about what you hear and practice singing along with those songs while replicating what you heard. Through replication and experimentation, you will expand your palate of choices, which will help you take your singing to the next level.

NOTES

1. Austin Kleon, *Steal Like an Artist* (New York: Workman Publishing, 2012).
2. Julia Davids and Stephen LaTour, *Vocal Technique: A Guide to Classical and Contemporary Styles for Conductors, Teachers, and Singers*, 2nd ed. (Long Grove, IL: Waveland Press, 2020), 135.
3. Ingo R. Titze, Brad Story, Marshall Smith, and Russel Long, "A Reflex Resonance Model of Vocal Vibrato," *Journal of the Acoustical Society of America* 111, no. 5 (2002): 2272–82.
4. Donna Soto-Morettini, *Popular Singing and Style*, 2nd ed. (London: Bloomsbury Publishing, 2014) 101–2.
5. CVT Research, "Description and Sound of Rattle," https://cvtresearch.com/description-and-sound-of-rattle, accessed October 25, 2023.

10

USING AUDIO ENHANCEMENT TECHNOLOGY

Singers of popular music before 1925 performed without microphones. That meant they had to learn how to project their voices just like vaudeville singers. When microphones began appearing in recording studios in 1925, vocal performance changed forever since the loudness of a voice was no longer a factor in the singer's ability to be successful. All a singer needed was an interesting vocal quality; the microphone would take care of projecting it for others to hear.

Vocal qualities that may sound weak without a microphone can sound strong full and present with a mic. At the same time, a singer with a voice that is acoustically powerful can sound harsh and pushed if he or she lacks microphone technique. Understanding how to use audio equipment to get the sounds you want without harming the voice is crucial. The information in this chapter will help you gain a basic knowledge of terminology and equipment commonly used when amplifying or recording a vocalist as well as providing tips for singing with a microphone.

THE FUNDAMENTALS OF SOUND

In order to understand how to manipulate an audio signal, you must first understand a few basics of sound including frequency, amplitude, harmonics, and resonance.

Frequency

Sound travels in waves of compression and rarefaction within a medium, which for our purposes is air (see figure 10.1). These waves travel through the air and into our inner ears via the ear canal. There they are converted via the eardrums into nerve impulses that are transmitted to the brain and interpreted as sound. The number of waves per second is measured in Hertz (Hz), which gives us the frequency of the sound that we have learned to perceive as pitch. For example, we hear 440 Hz (440 cycles of compression and rarefaction per second) as A4, the pitch A above middle C.

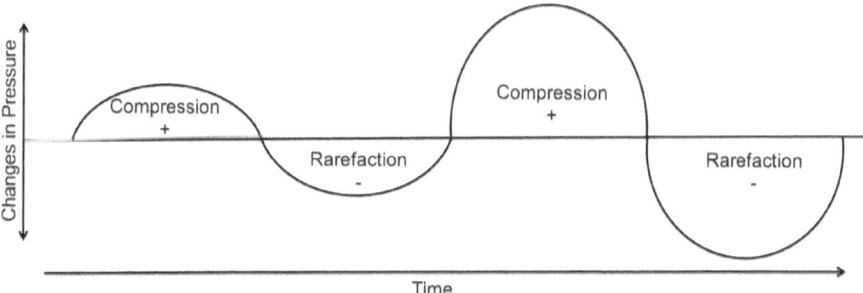

Figure 10.1. Compression and rarefaction. *Creative Commons (CC BY-SA 4.0)*

Amplitude

The magnitude of the waves of compression and rarefaction determines the amplitude of the sound, which we call its "volume." The larger the waves of compression and rarefaction, the louder we perceive the sound to be. Measured in decibels (dB), amplitude represents changes in air pressure from the baseline. Decibel measurements range from zero decibels (0 dB), the threshold of human hearing, to 130 dB, the upper edge of the threshold of pain.

Harmonics

The vibrating mechanism of an instrument produces the vibrations necessary to establish pitch (the fundamental frequency). The vibrating mechanism for a singer is the vocal folds. If an acoustic instrument, such as the voice, were to produce a note with the fundamental frequency alone, the sound would be strident and mechanical like an emergency alert signal. Pitches played on acoustic instruments consist of multiple frequencies, called overtones, which are emitted from the vibrator along with the fundamental frequency. For the purposes of this chapter, the overtones we are interested in are called harmonics. Harmonics are whole number multiples of the fundamental frequency. For example, if the fundamental is 220 Hz (A3), the harmonic overtone series would be 220 Hz, 440 Hz (fundamental frequency times two), 660 Hz (fundamental frequency times three), 880 Hz (fundamental frequency times four), and so on. Every musical note contains both the fundamental frequency and a predictable series of harmonics, each of which can be measured and identified as a specific frequency. This series of frequencies then travels through a hollow cavity (the vocal tract) where they are attenuated or amplified by the resonating frequencies of the cavity, which is how resonance occurs.

Resonance

The complex waveform created by the vocal folds travels through the vocal tract, where it is enhanced by the tract's unique resonance characteristics. Depending on the resonator's shape, some harmonics are amplified and some are attenuated. We can analyze those variations with a tool called a spectral analyzer as seen in figure 10.2. The slope from left to right is called the spectral slope. The peaks and valleys along the slope indicate

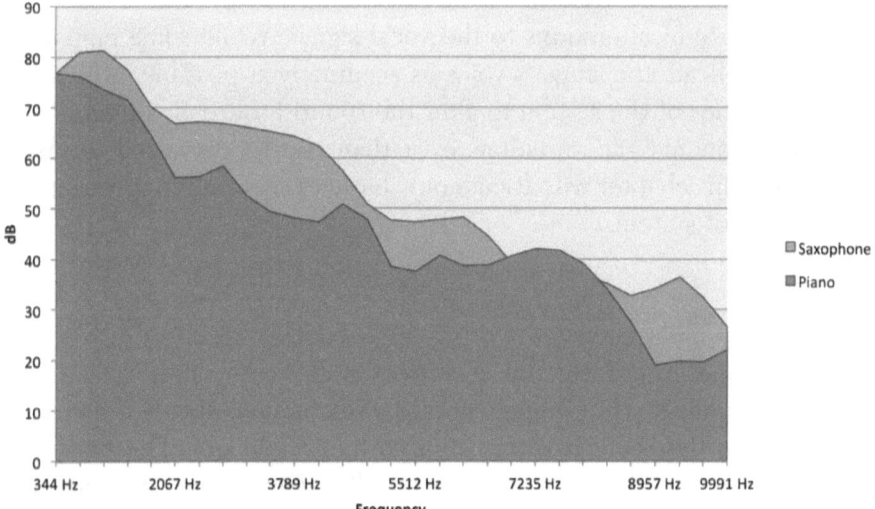

Figure 10.2. **The figure above shows two instruments playing the same pitch. The peak at the far left is the fundamental frequency, and the peaks to the right are harmonics that have been amplified and attenuated by the instrument's resonator, resulting in a specific timbre.** *Courtesy of Matt Edwards*

amplitude variations of the corresponding overtones. The difference in spectral slope between instruments (or voices) is what enables a listener to aurally distinguish the difference between two instruments playing or singing the same note.

Because the throat and mouth act as the resonating tube in acoustic singing, changing their size and shape is the only option for making adjustments to timbre for those who perform without microphones. In electronically amplified singing, the sound engineer can make adjustments to boost or attenuate specific frequency ranges, thus changing the singer's timbre. For this and many other reasons discussed in this chapter, it is vitally important for singers to know how audio technology can affect the quality of their voice.

SIGNAL CHAIN

The signal chain is the path an audio signal travels from the input to the output of a sound system. A voice enters the signal chain through a microphone, which transforms acoustic energy into electrical impulses. The electrical pulses generated by the microphone are transmitted through a series of components that modify the signal before the speakers transform it back into acoustic energy. Audio engineers and producers understand the intricacies of these systems and are able to make an infinite variety of alterations to the vocal signal. While some engineers strive to replicate the singer's voice as accurately as possible, others use the capabilities of the system to alter the sound for artistic effect. Since more components and variations exist than can be discussed in just a few pages, this chapter will discuss only basic components and variations found in most systems.

Microphones

Microphones transform the acoustic sound waves of the voice into electrical impulses. The component of the microphone that is responsible for receiving the acoustic information is the diaphragm. The two most common diaphragm types that singers will encounter are dynamic and condenser. Each offers advantages and disadvantages depending on how the microphone is to be used.

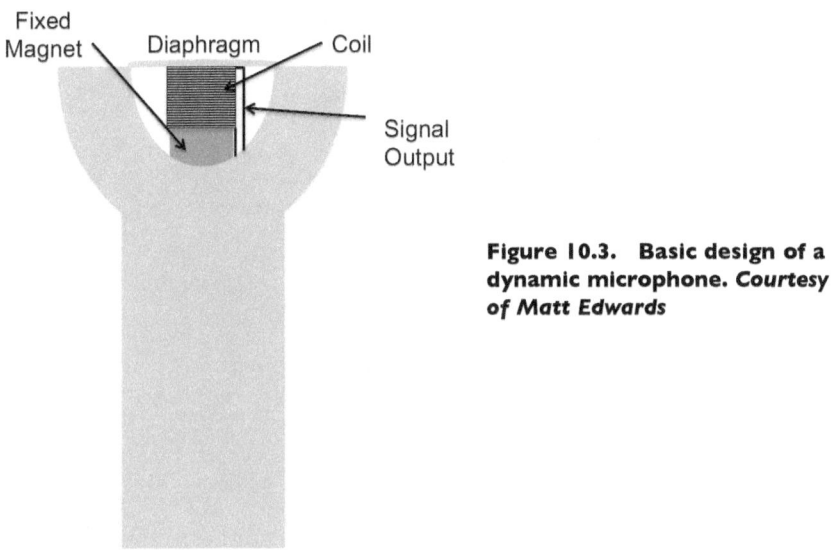

Figure 10.3. Basic design of a dynamic microphone. *Courtesy of Matt Edwards*

Dynamic Dynamic microphones are usually highly durable which makes them ideal for live performance settings. They consist of a dome-shaped Mylar diaphragm attached to a free-moving copper wire coil that is positioned between the two poles of a magnet. The Mylar diaphragm moves in response to air pressure changes caused by sound waves. When the diaphragm moves, the magnetic coil that is attached to it also moves. As the magnetic coil moves up and down between the magnetic poles, it produces an electrical current that corresponds to the sound waves produced by the singer's voice. That signal is then sent to the soundboard via the microphone cable.

The Shure SM58 dynamic microphone is the industry standard for live performance because it is affordable, nearly indestructible, and easy to use. Dynamic microphones such as the Shure SM58 have a lower sensitivity than condenser microphones, which makes them more successful at avoiding feedback. Because of their reduced tendency to feedback, dynamic microphones are the best choice for artists who use handheld microphones when performing.

Condenser Condenser microphones are known for their clarity and are ideal for use in recording studios. They are constructed with two parallel plates: a rigid posterior plate and a thin, flexible anterior plate. The anterior plate is constructed of either a thin sheet of metal or a piece of Mylar that is coated with a conductive metal. The plates are separated by air, which acts as a layer of insulation. In order to use a condenser microphone,

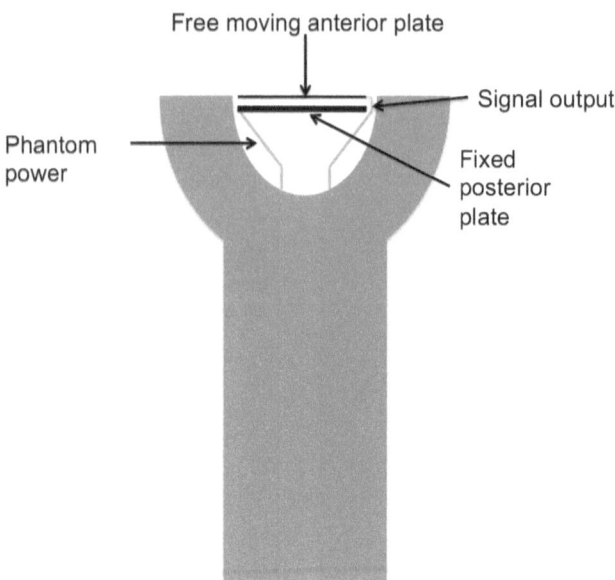

Figure 10.4. Basic design of a condenser microphone.
Courtesy of Matt Edwards

it must be connected to a soundboard that supplies "phantom power." A component of the soundboard, phantom power sends a 48-volt power supply through the microphone cable to the microphone's plates. When the plates are charged by phantom power, they form a capacitor. As acoustic vibrations send the anterior plate into motion, the distance between the two plates varies, which causes the capacitor to release a small electric current. This current, which corresponds with the acoustic signal of the voice, travels through the microphone cable to the soundboard, where it can be enhanced and amplified.

Electret condenser microphones are a type of condenser mic often used in head-mounted and lapel microphones, laptop computers, and smartphones. They have a very small diaphragm and are designed to work without phantom power, which is what sets them apart from standard condenser microphones. The anterior plate of an electret microphone is made of a plastic film coated with a conductive metal that is electrically charged before being set into place opposite the posterior plate. The charge applied to the anterior plate will last for ten or more years and therefore eliminates the need for an exterior power source.

Frequency Response Frequency response is a term used to define how accurately a microphone captures the tone quality of the signal. A

USING AUDIO ENHANCEMENT TECHNOLOGY

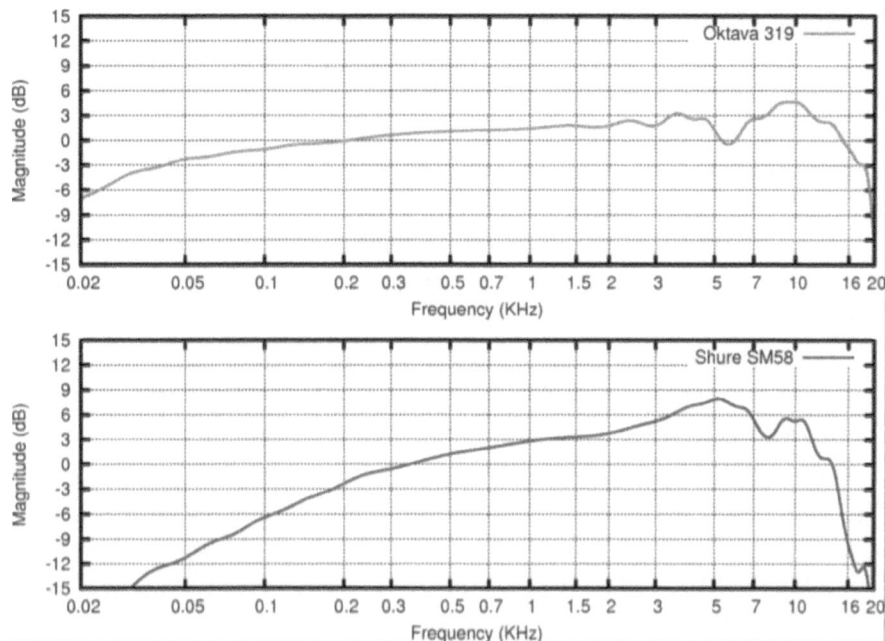

Figure 10.5. Example frequency response graphs for the Oktava 319 and the Shure SM58. *Creative Commons* (CC BY-SA 4.0)

"flat response" microphone captures the original signal with little to no signal alteration. Microphones that are not designated as "flat" have some type of amplification or attenuation of specific frequencies, also known as cut or boost, within the audio spectrum. For example, the Shure SM58 microphone drastically attenuates the signal below 300 Hz and amplifies the signal in the 3 kHz range by 6 dB, the 5 kHz range by nearly 8 dB, and the 10 kHz range by approximately 6 dB. The Oktava 319 microphone cuts the frequencies below 200 Hz while slightly boosting the frequencies above 300 Hz with approximately a 5dB boost between 7 kHz and 10K Hz (see figure 10.5). In practical terms, recording a bass singer with the Shure SM58 would reduce the amplitude of pitches below middle C compared to those above middle C, while the Oktava 319 would produce a more consistent amplitude across the singer's pitch range. Either of these options could be acceptable depending on the situation, but the frequency response must be considered before making a recording or performing live.

Sensitivity Manufacturers test microphones with a standardized 1 kHz tone at 94 dB in order to determine how sensitive the microphone's diaphragm will be to acoustic energy. Microphones with greater sensitivity can be placed farther from the sound source without adding excessive noise to the signal. Microphones with lower sensitivity will need to be placed closer to the sound source in order to keep excess noise at a minimum. When shopping for a microphone, you should audition several units plugged into the same soundboard, with the same volume level for each microphone. As you sing, you will notice that some models replicate your voice louder and clearer than others do. This change in output level is due to differences in each microphone's sensitivity. If your voice is naturally loud, you may prefer a microphone with lower sensitivity (one that requires more acoustic energy to respond). If you have a lighter voice, you may prefer a microphone with higher sensitivity (one that responds well to softer signals).

Polar Pattern A microphone polar pattern, also known as a pickup pattern or directivity pattern, describes the sensitivity of a microphone to sound from different directions. Polar pattern diagrams usually consist of six concentric circles divided into twelve equal sections. The center point of the microphone's diaphragm is labeled 0° and is referred to as "on-axis," while the opposite side of the diagram is labeled 180° and is described as "off-axis."

Although polar pattern diagrams are displayed in two dimensions, they actually represent a three-dimensional response to acoustic energy. You can use a round balloon as a physical example to help you visualize a three-dimensional polar pattern diagram. Position the tied end of the balloon away from your mouth and the inflated end directly in front of your lips. In this position, you are singing on-axis at 0° with the tied end of the balloon being 180°, or off-axis. If you were to split the balloon in half vertically and horizontally (in relationship to your lips), the point at which those lines intersect would be the center point of the balloon. That imaginary center represents the diaphragm of the microphone.

The outermost circle of the diagram indicates that the sound pressure level (SPL) of the signal is transferred without sensitivity reduction, indicated in decibels (dB). The straight lines radiating from the center are indicating angles at which you could sing towards the diaphragm. Each of the inner circle on the diagram represents a −5 dB reduction in the sensitivity of the microphone up to −25 dB. Figure 10.7 below is an example. Figures 10.8, 10.9, and 10.10 show the most commonly encountered polar patterns.

The dark black curved line that intersects the inner circles and angle lines is the polar pattern. It indicates how the sensitivity of the microphone will be reduced compared to singing at 0°. The amplitude response curve on diagram 2 in figure 10.8 is called a cardioid pattern because it looks like an upside down heart. This line shows you how the sensitivity of the microphone will change if the mic is held at a consistent distance while being turned away from the singer at an angle. For example, if you sang toward the microphone's diaphragm at 30°, there would be no difference in the sensitivity of the microphone as compared to when you are singing at 0°. However, if you tilt the microphone so that you are singing at a 60° angle toward the microphone's diaphragm, the sensitivity of the microphone from that angle is 2.5 dB less than when singing at 0°. At 90°, we see a 6 dB reduction, at 120° a 13 dB reduction, and at 180° a complete reduction.

The elimination of microphone response at 180° is great when working with an onstage floor monitor, which is why cardioid patterns are great for live performance. This pattern also helps keep other onstage instruments from bleeding into the vocal mic. The other patterns have different benefits, including picking up every sound in a room. For most entry-level users, a cardioid pattern is your best option.

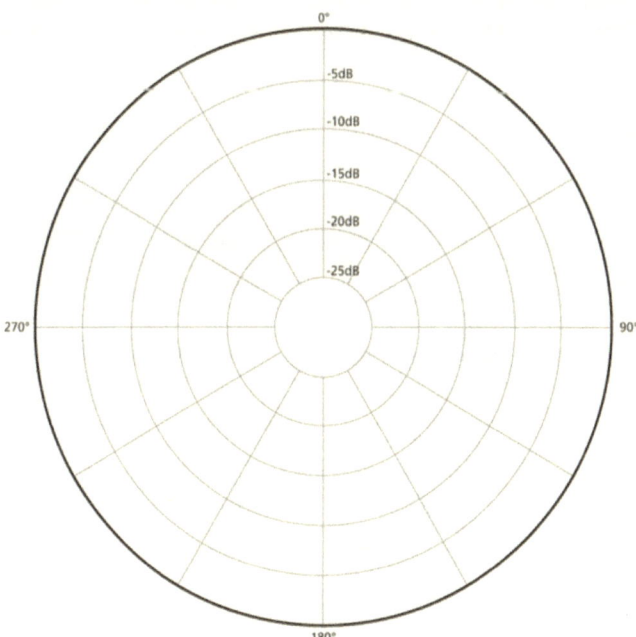

Figure 10.6. Example of a microphone polar pattern diagram. *Creative Commons* **(CC BY-SA 4.0)**

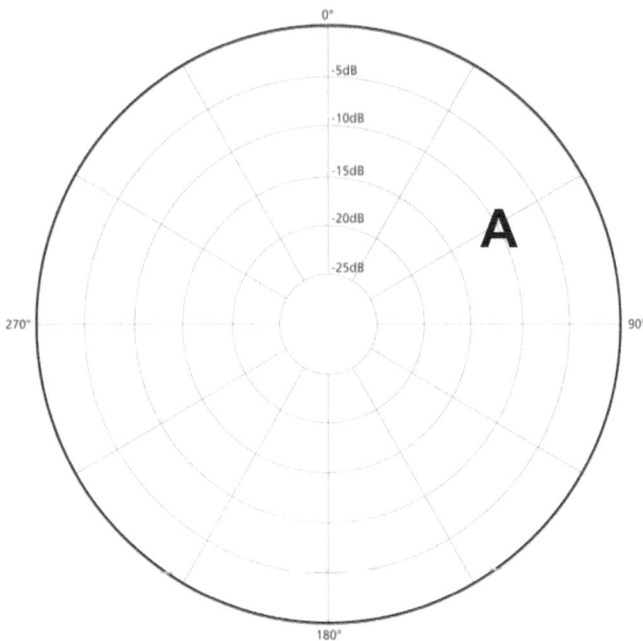

Figure 10.7. If the amplitude response curve intersected with point A, there would be a −10-dB reduction in the amplitude of frequencies received by the microphone's diaphragm at that angle. *Creative Commons* **(CC BY-SA 4.0)**

Proximity Effect It is important to note that cardioid microphones are known for their tendency to boost lower frequencies at close proximity to the sound source while attenuating those same frequencies as the distance between the sound source and the microphone increases. This is known as the "proximity effect." When you are working through the exercises at the end of this chapter, keep the proximity effect in mind and think about how the mic's distance from your mouth may be affecting the tone quality.

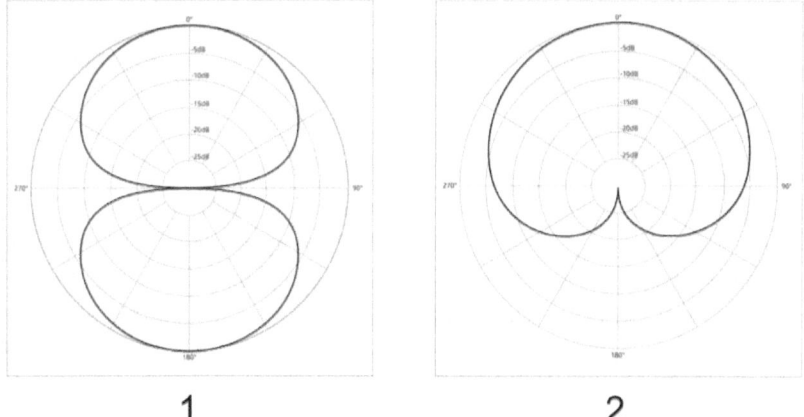

Figure 10.8. Diagram 1 represents a bidirectional pattern; diagram 2 represents a cardioid pattern. *Creative Commons* (CC BY-SA 4.0)

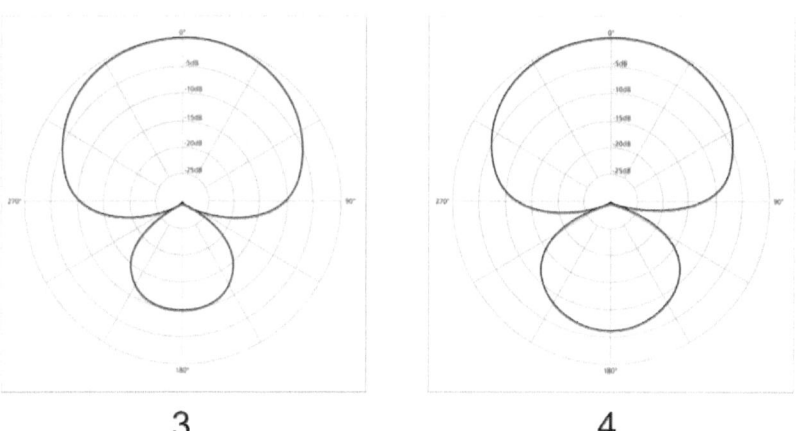

Figure 10.9. Diagram 3 represents a supercardioid pattern; diagram 4 represents a hypercardioid pattern. *Creative Commons* (CC BY-SA 4.0)

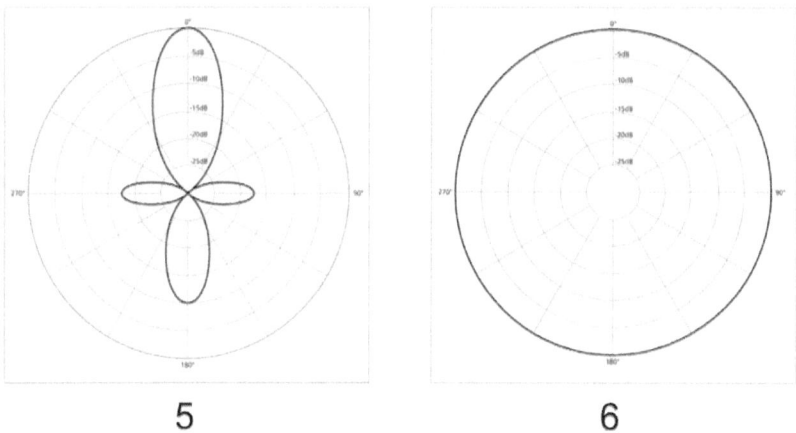

Figure 10.10. Diagram 5 represents a shotgun pattern; diagram 6 represents an omnidirectional pattern. *Creative Commons* (CC BY-SA 4.0)

Equalization (EQ)

Equalizers enable the audio engineer to alter the audio spectrum of the sound source and make tone adjustments with a simple electronic interface. Equalizers come in three main types: shelf, parametric, and graphic.

Shelf Shelf equalizers cut or boost the uppermost and lowermost frequencies of an audio signal in a straight line (see figure 10.11). While this style of equalization is not very useful for fine-tuning a singer's tone quality, it can be very effective in removing room noise. For example, if an air conditioner creates a 60-Hz hum in the recording studio, the shelf can be set at 65 Hz, with a steep slope. This setting eliminates frequencies below 65 Hz and effectively removes the hum from the microphone signal.

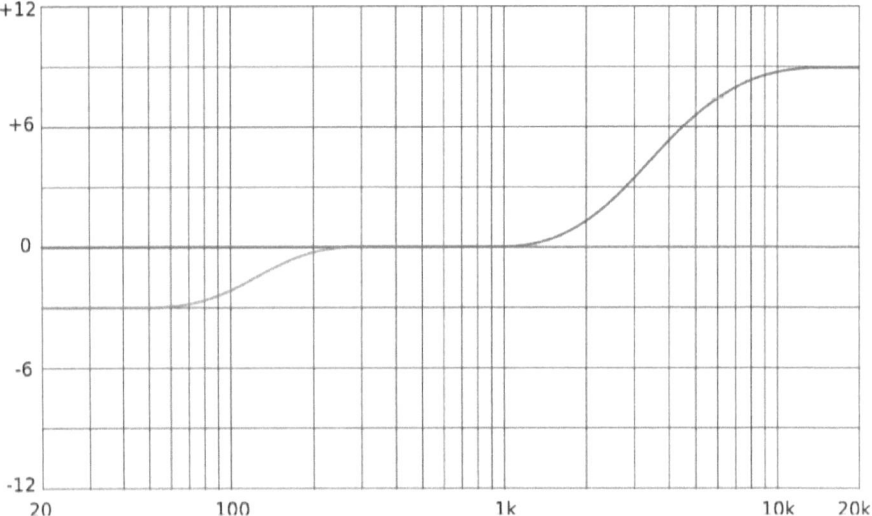

Figure 10.11. The frequency amplitude curves above show the effect of applying a shelf EQ to an audio signal. *Creative Commons* **(CC BY-SA 4.0)**

Parametric Parametric units simultaneously adjust multiple frequencies of the audio spectrum that fall within a defined parameter. The user selects a center frequency and adjusts the width of the bell curve surrounding that frequency by adjusting the "Q" (see figure 10.12). They then boost or cut the amplitude of the frequencies within the bell curve to alter the audio spectrum of the microphone signal. On some boards, the user can only adjust the amplitude of a fixed set of frequencies such as 80 Hz, 2,500 Hz, and 12,000 Hz with a fixed bell curve.

Parametric adjustments on a soundboard are made with rotary knobs similar to those in figure 10.13 below. They take up minimal space on a soundboard and offer sufficient control for many situations. Therefore,

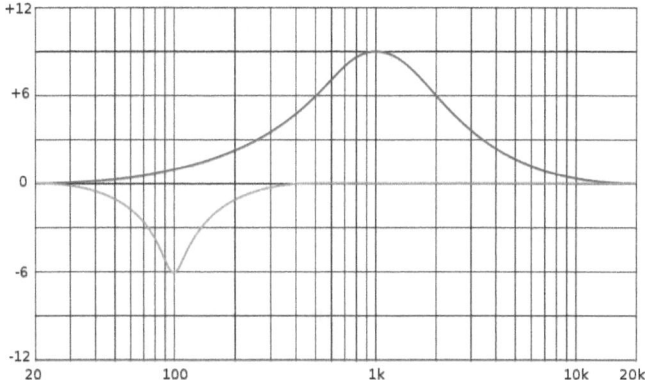

Figure 10.12. The frequency amplitude curves above display two parametric EQ settings. The top curve represents a boost of +8 dB set at 1 kHz with a relatively large bell curve—a low Q. The lower curve represents a high Q set at 100 Hz with a cut of −6 dB. *Creative Commons* (CC BY-SA 4.0)

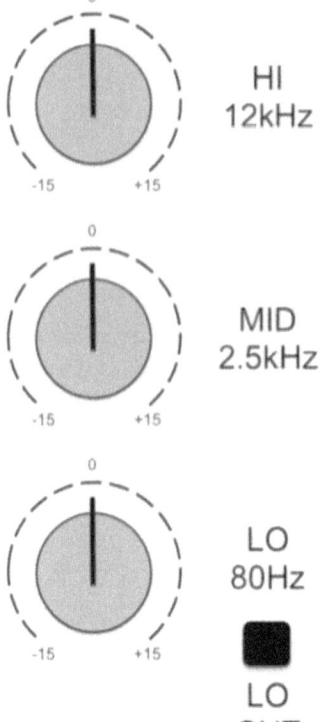

Figure 10.13. This is an example of a parametric EQ interface. The "LO CUT" button applies a shelf EQ at 80 Hz when depressed. *Courtesy of Matt Edwards*

most live performance soundboards have parametric EQs on each individual channel. Higher-end boards have electronic interfaces that give the user greater control.

Graphic Graphic equalizers enable engineers to identify a specific frequency for boost or cut with a fixed frequency bandwidth. For example, a ten-band equalizer enables the audio engineer to adjust ten specific frequencies (in Hz): 31, 63, 125, 250, 500, 1K, 2K, 4K, 8K, and 16K. Graphic equalizers are often one of the final elements of the signal chain, preceding only the amplifier and speakers. In this position, they can be used to adjust the overall tonal quality of the entire mix.

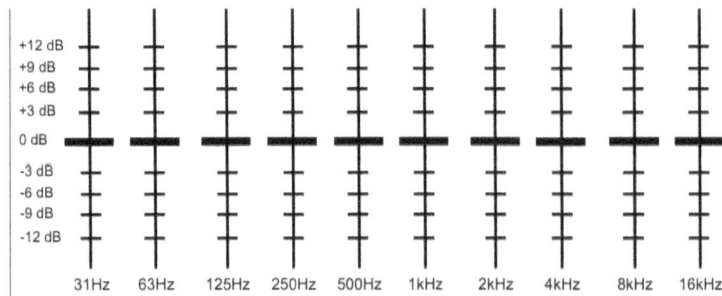

Figure 10.14. Example of a graphic equalizer interface. *Courtesy of Matt Edwards*

Utilizing Equalization Equalization can be used for many different purposes. Some users will only utilize equalization to remove or reduce frequencies that were not a part of the original sound signal. Others will only use EQ if adjusting microphone placement fails to yield acceptable results. Performers who prefer a more processed sound may use equalization liberally to intentionally change the vocal quality of their voice. For example, if the singer's voice sounds dull, the engineer could add "ring" or "presence" to the voice by boosting the equalizer in the 2- to 10-kHz range. By experimenting with these settings, you can find which approach works best for your desired result.

Compression

Many singers are capable of producing vocal extremes in both frequency and amplitude levels that can prove problematic for the sound team. To help solve this problem, engineers often use compression.

USING AUDIO ENHANCEMENT TECHNOLOGY   253

Compressors limit the output of a sound source by a specified ratio. The user sets the maximum acceptable amplitude level for the output, called the "threshold," and then sets a ratio to reduce the output once it surpasses the threshold. The typical ratio for a singer is usually between 3:1 and 5:1. A 4:1 ratio indicates that for every 4 dB beyond the threshold level, the output will only increase by 1 dB. For example, if the singer went 24 dB beyond the threshold with a 4:1 ratio, the output would only be 6 dB beyond the threshold level (see figure 10.15).

Adjusting the sound via microphone technique can provide some of the same results as compression and is preferable for the experienced artist. However, compression tends to be more consistent and also gives the singer freedom to focus on performing and telling a story. The additional artistic freedom provided by compression is especially beneficial

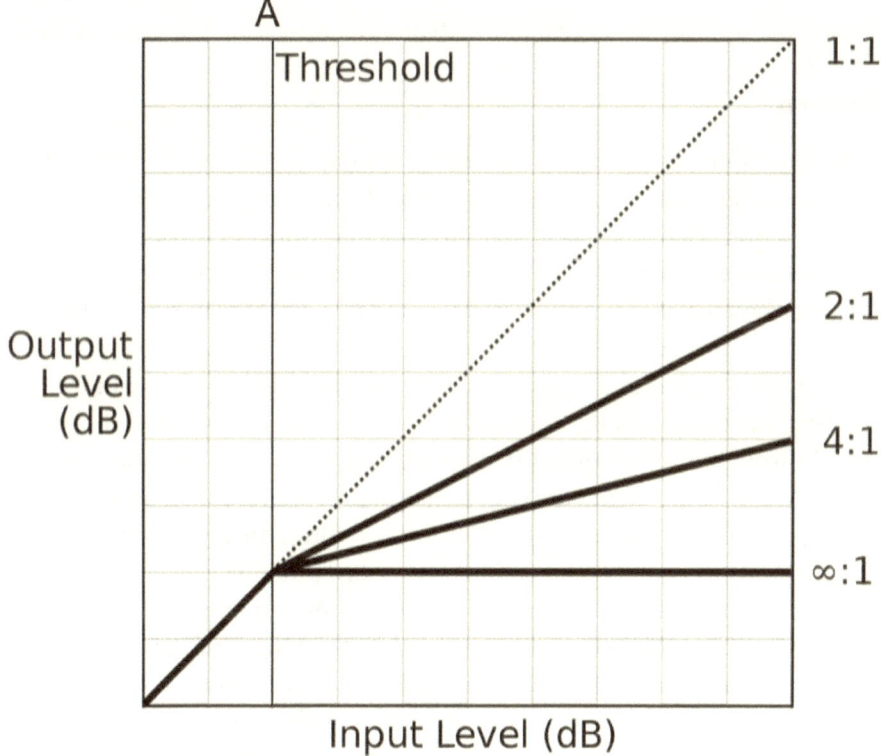

Figure 10.15. This graph represents the effects of various compression ratios applied to a signal. The 1:1 angle represents no compression. The other ratios represent the effect of compression on an input signal with the threshold set at line A. *Creative Commons* (CC BY-SA 4.0)

to singers who use head-mounted microphones, performers who switch between vocal extremes such as falsetto and chest voice, and those who are new to performing with a microphone.

If a standard compressor causes unacceptable alterations to the tone quality, engineers can turn to a multiband compressor. Rather than affecting the entire spectrum of sound, multiband compressors allow the engineer to isolate a specific frequency range within the audio signal and then set an individual compression setting for that frequency range. For example, if a singer creates a dramatic boost in the 4-kHz range every time they sing above an A4, a multiband compressor can be used to limit the amplitude of the signal in only that part of the voice. By setting a 3:1 ratio in the 4-kHz range at a threshold that corresponds to the amplitude peaks that appear when the performer sings above A4, the engineer can eliminate vocal "ring" from the sound on only the offending notes while leaving the rest of the signal untouched. These units are available for both live and studio use and can be a great alternative to compressing the entire signal.

Reverb

Reverb is one of the easier effects for singers to identify; it is the effect you experience when singing in a cathedral. An audience experiences natural reverberation when they hear the direct signal from the singer, and then, milliseconds later, they hear multiple reflections as the acoustical waves of the voice bounce off the side walls, floor, and ceiling of the performance hall.

Many performance venues and recording studios are designed to inhibit natural reverb. Without at least a little reverb added to the sound, even the best singer can sound harsh. Early reverb units transmitted the audio signal through a metal spring that added supplementary vibrations to the signal. While some engineers still use spring reverb to obtain a specific effect, most now use digital units. Common settings on digital reverb units include wet/dry, color, and options for delay time. The wet/dry control adjusts the amount of direct signal (dry) and the amount of reverberated signal (wet). The color control helps simulate the effects of various surfaces within a natural space. For example, harder surfaces such as stone reflect high frequencies and create a brighter tone quality, while softer surfaces such as wood reflect lower frequencies and create a warmer tone quality. The delay time, which is usually adjustable from milliseconds to seconds, adjusts the amount of time between when the dry signal and reflected signals reach the ear. Engineers can transform almost any room into a chamber music hall or concert stadium simply by adjusting these settings.

USING AUDIO ENHANCEMENT TECHNOLOGY

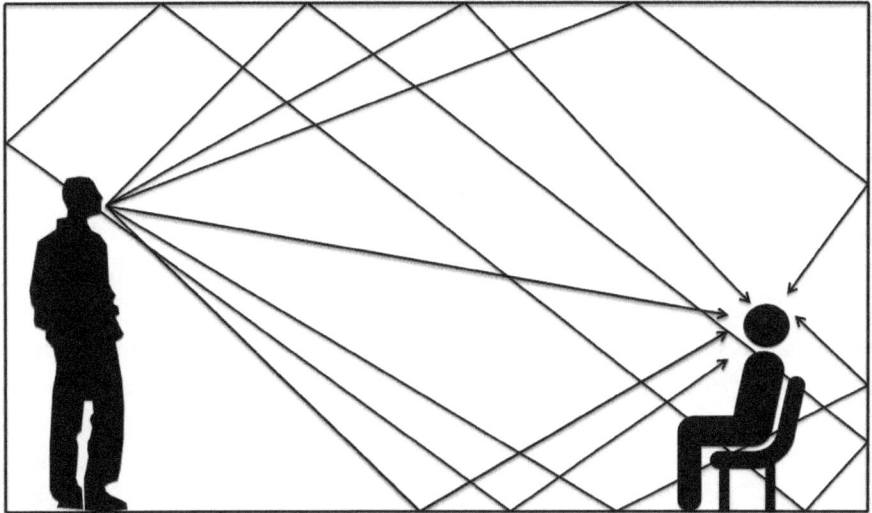

Figure 10.16. This diagram illustrates the multiple lines of reflection that create reverb. *Courtesy of Matt Edwards*

Delay

Whereas reverb blends multiple wet signals with the dry signal to replicate a natural space, delay purposefully separates a single wet signal from the dry signal to create repetitions of the voice. With delay, you will hear the original note first and then a digitally produced repeat of the note several milliseconds to seconds later. The delayed note may be heard one

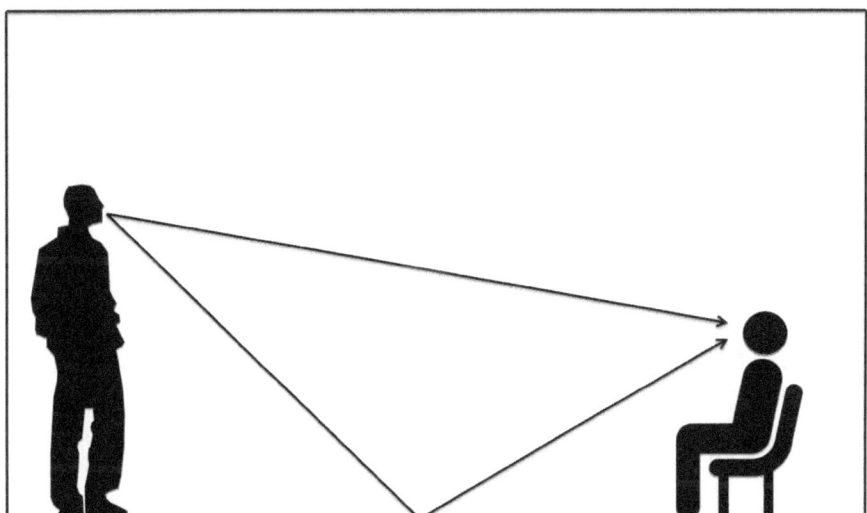

Figure 10.17. This diagram illustrates how a direct line of sound followed by a reflected line of sound creates delay. *Courtesy of Matt Edwards*

time or multiple times, and the timing of those repeats can be adjusted to match the tempo of the song.

Auto-Tune

Auto-Tune was first used in studios as a useful way to clean up minor imperfections in otherwise perfect performances. It is now an industry standard that many artists use, even if they are not willing to admit it.

Antares and Melodyne were some of the first software developers to make "auto" and "graphic" Auto-Tune available to consumers. Both developers continue to be popular with users. "Auto" Auto-Tune allows the engineer to set specific parameters for pitch correction that are then computer controlled. "Graphical" Auto-Tune tracks the pitch in the selected area of a recording and plots the fundamental frequency on a linear graph. The engineer can then select specific notes for pitch correction. They can also drag selected pitches to a different frequency, add or reduce vibrato, and change formant frequencies above the fundamental. To simplify, the "auto" function makes general corrections while the "graphic" function makes specific corrections. The "auto" setting is usually used to achieve a specific effect—for example, "Believe" (1998) by Cher (b. 1946)—while the "graphic" setting is used to correct small imperfections in a recorded performance.

Digital Voice Processors

Digital voice processors allow singers to control their own vocal effects when performing. While there are several brands of vocal effects processors available, the industry leader as of this printing is a company called TC-Helicon. TC-Helicon manufactures several different units that span from consumer to professional grade. TC-Helicon's premier performer-controlled unit is called the VoiceLive 3 Extreme. The VoiceLive gives singers access to ten vocal effects, including compression, reverb, delay, and "auto" Auto-Tune, that can be used individually or combined. The unit comes with 250 multi-effect factory presets and leaves room for 250 user-designed presets. It also offers nine guitar effects and a three-phrase looper.

One of the most impressive features of digital voice processors is the ability to add computer-generated harmonies to the lead vocal. After the user sets the musical key, the processor identifies the fundamental frequency of each sung note. The computer then adds digitized voices at designated intervals above and below the lead singer. The unit also offers the option to program each individual song, with multiple settings for every verse, chorus, and bridge.

THE BASICS OF LIVE SOUND SYSTEMS

Live sound systems come in a variety of sizes from small practice units to state-of-the-art stadium rigs. Most singers only need a basic knowledge of the components commonly found in systems that have one to eight inputs. Units beyond that size usually require an independent sound engineer and are beyond the scope of this chapter.

Following the microphone, the first element in the live signal chain is usually the mixer. Basic portable mixers provide controls for equalization, volume level, auxiliary (usually used for effects such as reverb and compression), and, on some units, controls for built-in digital effects processors. Unpowered mixers do not provide amplification, so you will need to add a separate amplifier to power the speakers. Powered mixers have been combined with an amplifier so they can directly power the speakers.

Speaker cabinets usually contain a "woofer" and a "tweeter." The woofer is a large round speaker that handles the bass frequencies, while the tweeter is a horn-shaped speaker that handles the treble frequencies. The crossover, a component built into the speaker cabinet, separates high and low frequencies and sends them to the appropriate speaker (woofer or tweeter). Speaker cabinets can be either active or passive. Passive cabinets require a powered mixer or an amplifier in order to operate. Active cabinets have an amplifier built-in and do not require an external amplifier.

Monitors are arguably the most important element in a live sound system. The monitor is a speaker that faces the performers and allows them to hear themselves and/or the other instruments on stage. Onstage volume levels can vary considerably, with drummers often producing sound levels as high as 120 dB. Those volume levels make it nearly impossible for singers to receive natural acoustic feedback while performing. Monitors can improve aural feedback and help reduce the temptation to over-sing. Powered monitors offer the same advantages as powered speaker cabinets and can be a great option for amplification when practicing. They are also good to have around as a backup plan in case you arrive at a venue and discover they do not supply monitors. In-ear monitors offer another option for performers and are especially useful for those who frequently move around the stage.

If you do not already own a microphone and amplification system, you can purchase a simple setup at relatively low cost through your local music store or online vendors such as Sweetwater.com and MusiciansFriend.com. A dynamic microphone and a powered monitor are enough to get you started. If you would like to add a digital voice processor, Digitech and TC-Helicon both sell entry-level models that will significantly improve the quality of your vocals.

MICROPHONE TECHNIQUE

The microphone is an inseparable part of the voice in contemporary styles of singing. Just as there are techniques that improve singing, there are also techniques that will improve microphone use. Understanding what a microphone does is only the first step to using it successfully. Once you understand how a microphone works, you need hands-on experience.

The best way to learn microphone technique is to experiment. Try the following exercises to gain a better understanding of how to use a microphone when singing:

1. Hold a dynamic microphone with a cardioid pattern directly in front of your mouth, at 0°, approximately one inch away from your lips. Sustain a comfortable pitch at a moderate volume and slowly move the microphone away from your lips. Listen to how the vocal quality changes. When the microphone is close to the lips, you should notice that the sound is louder and has more bass response. As you move the microphone away from your mouth, there will be a noticeable loss in volume and the tone will become brighter. The change in warmth and brightness is due to the proximity effect.
2. Next, sustain a pitch while rotating the handle down. This movement will show you how the microphone responds to your voice from different angles and will help you gain a better understanding of your microphone's polar pattern.
3. Now try singing breathy with the microphone close to your lips. How little effort can you get away with while producing a marketable

sound? This will help you gain a better understanding of the sensitivity of your microphone.
4. Experiment with adapting your diction to the microphone. Because the microphone amplifies everything, you may need to under-pronounce certain consonants when singing. You will especially want to reduce the power of the plosive consonants /b/, /d/, /g/, /k/, /p/, and /t/.
5. Finally, practice your songs with a microphone. Experiment with moving the mic closer to your mouth when singing softly and away from your mouth when singing loudly. Get used to holding it in your hand and handling the cable. Start thinking of the mic as an extension of your instrument while considering how it factors into the delivery of your songs.

FINAL THOUGHTS

This chapter is only a brief overview to get you started with audio technology. You can greatly improve your comprehension of the material by seeking other resources to deepen your knowledge. Most importantly, you must experiment. The more you play around with sound equipment on your own, the better you will understand it and the more comfortable you will feel when performing or recording with audio technology.

VOCAL HEALTH FOR SINGERS

Wendy LeBorgne

GENERAL PHYSICAL WELL-BEING

All singers, regardless of genre, should consider themselves as "vocal athletes." The physical, emotional, and performance demands necessary for optimal output require that the artist consider training and maintaining their instrument as an athlete trains for an event. With increased vocal and performance demands, it is unlikely that a vocal athlete will have an entire performing career completely injury free. This may not be the fault of the singer, as many injuries occur due to circumstances beyond the singer's control such as singing through an illness or being on a new medication seemingly unrelated to the voice.

Vocal injury has often been considered taboo to talk about in the performing world, as it has been considered to be the result of faulty technique or poor vocal habits. In actuality, the majority of vocal injuries presenting in the elite performing population tend to be overuse and/or acute injury. From a clinical perspective over the past seventeen years, younger, less experienced singers with fewer years of training (who tend to be quite talented) generally are the ones who present with issues related to technique or phonotrauma (nodules, edema, contact ulcers), while more mature singers with professional performing careers tend to present with acute injuries (hemorrhage) or overuse and misuse injuries (muscle tension dysphonia, edema, gastroesophageal reflux [GERD]) or injuries following an illness. There are no current studies documenting use and training in correlation to laryngeal pathologies. However, there are studies that document that somewhere between 35 and 100 percent of professional vocal athletes have abnormal vocal fold findings on stroboscopic evaluation. Many times, these "abnormalities" are in singers who have no vocal complaints or symptoms of vocal problems. From a performance perspective, uniqueness in vocal quality often gets hired and perhaps a slight aberration in the way a given larynx functions may become quite marketable. Regardless of what the vocal folds may look like, the most integral part of performance is that the singer must maintain agility, flexibility, stamina, power, and inherent beauty (genre appropriate) for their current level of performance taking into account physical, vocal, and emotional demands.

Unlike sports medicine and the exercise physiology literature where much is known about the types and nature of given sports injuries, there is no common parallel for the vocal athlete model. However, because the vocal athlete utilizes the body systems of alignment, respiration, phonation, and resonance with some similarities to physical athletes, a parallel protocol for vocal wellness may be implemented/considered for vocal athletes to maximize injury prevention knowledge for both the singer and the teacher. This chapter aims to provide information on vocal wellness and injury prevention for the vocal athlete.

CONSIDERATIONS FOR WHOLE-BODY WELLNESS

Nutrition

You have no doubt heard the saying "You are what you eat." Eating is a social and psychological event. For many people, food associations and eating have an emotional basis resulting in either overeating or being malnourished. Eating disorders in performers and body image issues may have major implications and consequences for the performer on both ends of the spectrum (obesity and anorexia). Singers should be encouraged to reprogram the brain and body to consider food as fuel. You want to use high-octane gas in your engine, as pouring water in your car's gas tank won't get you very far. Eating a poor diet or a diet that lacks appropriate nutritional value will have negative physical and vocal effects on the singer.

Effects of poor dietary choices for the vocal athlete may result in physical and vocal effects ranging from fatigue to life-threatening disease over the course of a lifetime. Encouraging and engaging in healthy eating habits from a young age will potentially prevent long-term negative effects from poor nutritional choices. It is beyond the scope of this chapter to provide a complete overview of all the dietary guidelines for pediatrics, adolescents, adults, and the mature adult; however, a listing of additional references to help guide your food and beverage choices for making good nutritional choices can be found online at websites such as Dietary Guidelines for Americans, Nutrition.gov Guidelines for Tweens and Teens, and Fruits and Veggies Matter. See the online companion Web page on the NATS website for links to these and other resources. ♪

Hydration

"Sing wet, pee pale." This phrase was echoed in the studio of Van Lawrence regarding how his students would know if they were well hydrated. Generally, this rule of pale urine during your waking hours is a good indicator that you are well hydrated. Medications, vitamins, and certain foods may alter urine color despite adequate hydration. Due to the varying levels of physical and vocal activity of many performers, in order to maintain adequate oral hydration, the use of a hydration calculator based on activity level may be a better choice. These hydration calculators are easily accessible online and take into account the amount and level of activity the performer engages in on a daily basis. In a recent study of the vocal habits of musical theater performers, one of the findings indicated a significantly under-hydrated group of performers.

Laryngeal and pharyngeal dryness as well as "thick, sticky mucus" are often complaints of singers. Combating these concerns and maintaining an adequate viscosity of mucus for performance has resulted in some research. As a reminder of laryngeal and swallowing anatomy, nothing that is swallowed (or gargled) goes over or touches the vocal folds directly (or one would choke). Therefore, nothing that a singer eats or drinks ever touches the vocal folds, and in order to adequately hydrate the mucous membranes of the vocal folds, one must consume enough fluids for the body to produce a thin mucus. Therefore, any "vocal" effects from swallowed products are limited to potential pharyngeal and oral changes, not the vocal folds themselves.

The effects of systemic hydration are well documented in the literature. There is evidence to suggest that adequate hydration will provide some protection of the laryngeal mucosal membranes when they are placed under increased collision forces as well as reducing the amount of effort (phonation threshold pressure) to produce voice. This is important for the singer because it means that with adequate hydration and consistency of mucus, the effort to produce voice is less and your vocal folds are better protected from injury. Imagine the friction and heat produced when two dry hands rub together and then what happens if you put lotion on your hands. The mechanisms in the larynx to provide appropriate mucus production are not fully understood, but there is enough evidence at this time to support oral hydration as a vital component of every singer's vocal health regime to maintain appropriate mucosal viscosity.

Although very rare, overhydration (hyperhidrosis) can result in dehydration and even illness or death. An overindulgence of fluids essentially makes the kidneys work "overtime" and flushes too much water out of the body. This excessive fluid loss in a rapid manner can be detrimental to the body.

In addition to drinking water to systemically monitor hydration, there are many nonregulated products on the market for performers that lay claim to improving the laryngeal environment (e.g., Entertainer's Secret, Throat Coat, Grether's Pastilles, slippery elm, etc.). Although there may be little detriment in using these products, quantitative research documenting change in laryngeal mucosa is sparse. One study suggests that the use of Throat Coat when compared to a placebo treatment for pharyngitis did show a significant difference in decreasing the perception of sore throat. Another study compared the use of Entertainer's Secret to two other nebulized agents and its effect on phonation threshold pressure (PTP). There was no positive benefit in decreasing PTP with Entertainer's Secret.

Many singers use personal steam inhalers and/or room humidification to supplement oral hydration and aid in combating laryngeal dryness. There are several considerations for singers who choose to use external means of adding moisture to the air they breathe. Personal steam inhalers are portable and can often be used backstage or in the hotel room for the traveling performer. Typically, water is placed in the steamer and the face is placed over the steam for inhalation. Because the mucus membranes of the larynx are composed of a saltwater solution, one study looked at the use of nebulized saline in comparison to plain water and its potential effects on effort or ease to sound production in classically trained sopranos. Data suggested that perceived effort to produce voice was less in the saline group than the plain water group. This indicated that the singers who used the saltwater solution reported less effort to sing after breathing in the saltwater than singers who used plain water. The researchers hypothesized that because the body's mucus is not plain water (rather it is a saltwater—think about your tears), when you use plain water for steam inhalation, it may actually draw the salt from your own saliva, resulting in a dehydrating effect.

In addition to personal steamers, other options for air humidification come in varying sizes of humidifiers from room size to whole-house humidifiers. When choosing between a warm-air or cool-mist humidifier, considerations include both personal preference and needs. One of the primary reasons warm-mist humidifiers are not recommended for young children is due to the risk of burns from the heating element. Both the warm-mist and cool-air humidifiers act similarly in adding moisture to the environmental air. External air humidification may be beneficial and provide a level of comfort for many singers. Regular cleaning of the humidifier is vital to prevent bacteria and mold buildup. Also, depending on the hardness of the water, it is important to avoid mineral buildup on the device and distilled water may be recommended for some humidifiers.

For traveling performers who often stay in hotels, fly on airplanes, or are generally exposed to other dry air environments, there are products on the market designed to help minimize drying effects. One such device is called a Humidflyer, which is a face mask designed with a filter to recycle the moisture of a person's own breath and replenish moisture on each breath cycle.

For dry nasal passages or to clear sinuses, many singers use Neti pots. Many singers use this homeopathic flushing of the nasal passages regularly. Research supports the use of a Neti pot as a part of allergy relief and chronic rhinosinusitis control when utilized properly, sometimes in combination with medical management. Conversely, long-term use of nasal irrigation (without taking intermittent breaks from daily use) may result in washing out the "good" mucus of the nasal passages, which naturally help to rid the nose of infections. A study presented at the 2009 American College of Allergy, Asthma, and Immunology annual scientific meeting reported that when a group of individuals who were using twice-daily nasal irrigation for one year discontinued using it, they had an increase in acute rhinosinusitis.

Tea, Honey, and Gargle to Keep the Throat Healthy

Regarding the use of general teas (which many singers combine with honey or lemon), there is likely no harm in the use of decaffeinated tea (caffeine may cause systemic dryness). The warmth of the tea may provide a soothing sensation to the pharynx, and the act of swallowing can be relaxing for the muscles of the throat. Honey has shown promising results as an effective cough suppressant in the pediatric population. The dose of honey given to the children in the study was two teaspoons. Gargling with salt or apple cider vinegar and water are also popular home remedies for many singers with the uses being from soothing the throat to curing reflux. Gargling plain water has been shown to be efficacious in reducing the risk of contracting upper respiratory infections. I suggest that when gargling, the singer only "bubble" the water with air and avoid engaging the vocal folds in sound production. Saltwater as a gargle has long been touted as a sore throat remedy and can be traced back to 2700 BCE in China for treating gum disease. The science behind a saltwater rinse for everything from oral hygiene to sore throat is that salt (sodium chloride) may act as a natural analgesic (painkiller) and may also kill bacteria. Similar to the effects that not enough salt in the water may have on drawing the salt out of the tissue in the steam inhalation, if you oversaturate the water solution with excess salt and gargle it, it may act to draw water out of the oral mucosa, thus reducing inflammation.

Another popular home remedy reported by singers is the use of apple cider vinegar to help with everything from acid reflux to sore throats. Dating back to 3300 BCE, apple cider vinegar was reported as a medicinal remedy, and it became popular in the 1970s as a weight loss diet cocktail. Popular media reports apple cider vinegar can improve conditions from acne and arthritis to nosebleeds and varicose veins. Specific efficacy data regarding the beneficial nature of apple cider vinegar for the purpose of sore throat, pharyngeal inflammation, and/or reflux has not been reported in the literature at this time. Of the peer-reviewed studies found in the literature, one discussed possible esophageal erosion and inconsistency of actual product in tablet form. Therefore, at this time, strong evidence supporting the use of apple cider vinegar is not published.

Medications and the Voice

Medications (over the counter, prescription, and herbal) may have resultant drying effects on the body and often the laryngeal mucosa. General classes of drugs with potential drying effects include antidepressants, antihypertensives, diuretics, ADD/ADHD medications, some oral acne medications, hormones, allergy drugs, and vitamin C in high doses. The National Center for Voice and Speech provides a listing of some common medications with potential voice side effects, including laryngeal dryness. This listing does not take into account all medications, so singers should always ask their pharmacist of the potential side effects of a given medication. Due to the significant number of drugs on the market, it is safe to say that most pharmacists will not be acutely aware of "vocal side effects," but if dryness is listed as a potential side effect of the drug, you may assume that all body systems could be affected. Under no circumstances should you stop taking a prescribed medication without consulting your physician first. As every person has a different body chemistry and reaction to medication, just because a medication lists dryness as a potential side effect does not necessarily mean you will experience that side effect. Conversely, if you begin a new medication and notice physical or vocal changes that are unexpected, you should consult with your physician. Ultimately, the goal of medical management for any condition is to achieve the most benefits with the least side effects. See the companion page on the NATS website for a list of possible resources for the singer regarding prescription drugs and herbs.

In contrast to medications that tend to dry, there are medications formulated to increase saliva production or alter the viscosity of mucus. Medically, these drugs are often used to treat patients who have had a loss of saliva production due to surgery or radiation. Mucolytic agents are used to thin secretions as needed. As a singer, if you feel that you need to use a mucolytic agent on a consistent basis, it may be worth considering getting to the root of the laryngeal dryness symptom and seeking a professional opinion from an otolaryngologist.

Reflux and the Voice

GERD and/or laryngopharyngeal reflux (LPR) can have a devastating impact on the singer if not recognized and treated appropriately. Although GERD and LPR are related, they are considered as slightly different diseases. GERD (Latin root meaning "flowing back") is the reflux of digestive enzymes, acids, and other stomach contents into the esophagus (food pipe). If this backflow is propelled through the upper esophagus and into the throat (larynx and pharynx), it is referred to as LPR. It is not uncommon to have both GERD and LPR, but they can occur independently.

More frequently, people with GERD have decreased esophageal clearing. Esophagitis, or inflammation of the esophagus, is also associated with GERD. People with GERD often feel heartburn. LPR symptoms are often "silent" and do not include heartburn. Specific symptoms of LPR may include some or all of the following: lump in the throat sensation, feeling of constant need to clear the throat/postnasal drip, longer vocal warm-up time, quicker vocal fatigue, loss of high frequency range, worse voice in the morning, sore throat, and bitter/raw/brackish taste in the mouth. If you experience these symptoms on a regular basis, it is advised that you consider a medical consultation for your symptoms. Prolonged, untreated GERD or LPR can lead to permanent changes in both the esophagus and/or larynx. Untreated LPR also provides a laryngeal environment that is conducive for vocal fold lesions to occur, as it inhibits normal healing mechanisms.

Treatments of LPR and GERD generally include both dietary and lifestyle modifications in addition to medical management. Some of the dietary recommendations include elimination of caffeinated and carbonated beverages, smoking cessation, no alcohol use, and limiting tomatoes, acidic foods and drinks, and raw onions or peppers, to name a few. Also, avoidance of high-fat foods is recommended. From a lifestyle perspective, suggested changes include not eating within three hours of lying down, eating small meals frequently (instead of large meals), elevating the head of your bed, avoiding tight clothing around the belly, and not bending over or exercising too soon after you eat.

Reflux medications fall in three general categories: antacids, H2 blockers, and proton pump inhibitors (PPIs). There are now combination drugs that include both an H2 blocker and proton pump inhibitor. Every medication has both associated risks and benefits, and singers should be aware of the possible benefits and side effects of the medications they take. In general terms, antacids (e.g., Tums, Mylanta, Gaviscon) neutralize stomach acid. H2 (histamine) blockers, such as Axid (nizatidine),Tagamet (cimetidine), Pepcid (famotidine), and Zantac (ranitidine), work to decrease acid production in the stomach by preventing histamine from triggering the H2 receptors to produce more acid. Then there are the PPIs: Nexium (esomeprazole), Prevacid (lansoprazole), Protonix (pantoprazole), AcipHex (rabeprazole), Prilosec (omeprazole), and Dexilant (dexlansoprazole). PPIs act as a last line of defense to decrease acid production by blocking the last step in gastric juice secretion. Some of the most recent drugs to combat GERD/LPR are combination drugs (e.g., Zegrid [sodium bicarbonate plus omeprazole]), which provide a short-acting response (sodium bicarbonate) and a long release (omeprazole). Because some singers prefer a holistic approach to reflux management, strict dietary and lifestyle compliance is recommended, and consultation with both your primary care physician and naturopath is warranted in that situation. Efficacy data on nonregulated herbs, vitamins, and supplements are limited, but some data do exist.

Physical Exercise

Vocal athletes, like other physical athletes, should consider how and what they do to maintain both cardiovascular fitness and muscular strength. In today's performance culture, it is rare that a performer stands still and sings, unless in a recital or choral setting. The range of physical activity can vary from light movement to high-intensity choreography with acrobatics. As performers are being required to increase their onstage physical activity level from the operatic stage to the pop-star arena, overall physical fitness is imperative to avoid compromise in the vocal system. Breathlessness will result in compensation by the larynx, which is now attempting to regulate the air. Compensatory vocal behaviors over time may result in a change in vocal performance. The health benefits of both cardiovascular training and strength training are well documented for physical athletes but relatively rare in the literature for vocal performers.

Mental Wellness

Vocal performers must maintain a mental focus during performance and a mental toughness during auditioning and training. Rarely during vocal performance training programs is this important aspect of performance addressed, and it is often left to the individual performer to develop their own strategy or coping mechanism. Yet many performers are on antianxiety or antidepressant drugs (which may be the direct result of performance-related issues). If the sports world is again used as a parallel for mental toughness, there are no elite-level athletes (and few junior-level athletes) who don't utilize the services of a performance/sports psychologist to maximize focus and performance. I recommend that performers consider the potential benefits of a performance psychologist to help maximize vocal performance. Several references that may be of interest to the singer include the audio recording *Visualization for Singers* (1992) and the classic voice pedagogy book *Power Performance for Singers: Transcending the Barriers* (1998).

Unlike instrumentalists, whose performance is dependent on accurate playing of an external musical instrument, the singer's instrument is uniquely intact and subject to the emotional confines of the brain and body in which it is housed. Musical performance anxiety (MPA) can be career threatening for all musicians, but perhaps the vocal athlete is more severely impacted. The majority of literature on MPA is dedicated to instrumentalists, but the basis of definition, performance effects, and treatment options can be considered for vocal athletes. Fear is a natural reaction to a stressful situation, and there is a fine line between emotional excitation and perceived threat (real or imagined). The job of a performer is to convey to an audience through vocal production, physical gestures, and facial expression a most heightened state of emotion. Otherwise, why would audience members pay top dollar to sit for two or three hours for a mundane experience? Not only is there the emotional conveyance of the performance but also the internal turmoil often experienced by the singers themselves in preparation for elite performance. It is well documented in the literature that even the most elite performers have experienced debilitating performance anxiety. MPA is defined on a continuum with anxiety levels ranging from low to high and has been reported to comprise four distinct components: affect, cognition, behavior, and physiology. Affect comprises feelings (e.g., doom, panic, anxiety). Affected cognition will result in altered levels of concentration, while the behavior component results in postural shifts, quivering, and trembling. Finally physiologically the body's autonomic nervous system (ANS) will activate, resulting in the "fight or flight" response.

In recent years, researchers have been able to define two distinct neurological pathways for MPA. The first pathway happens quickly and without conscious input (ANS), resulting in the same fear stimulus as if a person were put into an emergent, life-threatening situation. In those situations, the brain releases adrenaline, resulting in physical changes of increased heart rate, increased respiration, shaking, pale skin, dilated pupils, slowed digestion, bladder relaxation, dry mouth, and dry eyes, all of which severely affect vocal performance. The second pathway that has been identified results in a conscious identification of the fear/threat and a much slower physiologic response. With the second neuromotor response, the performer has a chance to recognize the fear, process how to deal with the fear, and respond accordingly.

Treatment modalities to address MPA include psycho-behavioral therapy (including biofeedback) and drug therapies. Elite physical performance athletes have been shown to benefit from visualization techniques and psychological readiness training, yet within the performing arts community, stage fright may be considered a weakness or character flaw precluding readiness for professional performance. On the contrary, vocal athletes, like physical athletes, should mentally prepare themselves for optimal competition (auditions) and performance. Learning to convey emotion without eliciting an internal emotional response by the vocal athlete may take the skill of an experienced psychologist to help change ingrained neural pathways. Ultimately, control and understanding of MPA will enhance performance and prepare the vocal athlete for the most intense performance demands without vocal compromise.

VOCAL WELLNESS: INJURY PREVENTION

In order to prevent vocal injury and understand vocal wellness in the singer, general knowledge of common causes of voice disorders is imperative. One common cause of voice disorders is vocally abusive behaviors or misuse of the voice to include phonotraumatic behaviors such as yelling, screaming, loud talking, talking over noise, throat clearing, coughing, harsh sneezing, and boisterous laughing. Chronic or less-than-optimal vocal properties such as poor breathing techniques, inappropriate phonatory habits during conversational speech (glottal fry, hard glottal attacks), inapt pitch, loudness, rate of speech, and/or hyperfunctional laryngeal-area muscle tone may also negatively impact vocal function. Medically related etiologies, which also have the potential to impact vocal function, range from untreated chronic allergies and sinusitis to endocrine dysfunction and hormonal imbalance. Direct trauma, such as a blow to the neck or the risk of vocal fold damage during intubation, can impact optimal performance in vocal athletes depending on the nature and extent of the trauma. Finally, external irritants ranging from cigarette smoke to reflux directly impact the laryngeal mucosa and ultimately can lead to laryngeal pathology.

Vocal hygiene education and compliance may be one of the primary essential components for maintaining the voice throughout a career. This section will provide the singer with information on prevention of vocal injury. However, just like a professional sports athlete, it is unlikely that a professional vocal athlete will go through an entire career without some compromise in vocal function. This may be a common upper respiratory infection that creates vocal fold swelling for a short time, or it may be a "vocal accident" that is career threatening. Regardless, the knowledge of how to take care of your voice is essential for any vocal athlete.

Train like an Athlete for Vocal Longevity

Performers seek instant gratification in performance sometimes at the cost of gradual vocal building for a lifetime of healthy singing. Historically, voice pedagogues required their students to perform vocalises exclusively for up to two years before beginning any song literature. Singers gradually built their voices by ingraining appropriate muscle memory and neuromotor patterns through development of aesthetically pleasing tones, onsets, breath management, and support. There was an intensive master–apprentice relationship and rigorous vocal guidelines to maintain a place within a given studio. Time off was taken if a vocal injury ensued or careers potentially were ended, and students were asked to leave a given singing studio if their voices were unable to withstand the rigors of training. Training vocal athletes today has evolved and appears driven to create a "product" quickly, perhaps at the expense of the longevity of the singer. Pop stars emerging well before puberty are doing international concert tours, yet many young artist programs in the classical arena do not consider singers for their programs until they are in their mid- to late twenties.

Each vocal genre presents with different standards and vocal demands. Therefore, the amount and degree of vocal training are varied. Some would argue that performing extensively without adequate vocal training and development is ill-advised, yet singers today are thrust onto the stage at very young ages. Dancers, instrumentalists, and physical athletes all spend many hours per day developing muscle strength, memory, and proper technique for their craft. The more advanced the artist or athlete, generally the more specific the training protocol becomes. Consideration of training vocal athletes in this same fashion is recommended. One would generally not begin a young, inexperienced singer on a Richard Wagner (1813–1883) aria without previous vocal training. Similarly, in nonclassical vocal music, there are easy, moderate, and difficult pieces to consider, pending the level of vocal development and training.

Basic pedagogical training of alignment, breathing, voice production, and resonance are essential building blocks for development of good voice production. Muscle memory and development of appropriate muscle patterns happen slowly over time with appropriate repetitive practice. Doing too much too soon for any athlete (physical or vocal) will result in an increased risk for injury. When the singer is being asked to do "vocal gymnastics," they must be sure to have a solid basis of strength and stamina in the appropriate muscle groups to perform consistently with minimal risk of injury.

Vocal Fitness Program

One generally does not get out of bed first thing in the morning and try to do a split. Yet many singers go directly into a practice session or audition without proper warm-up. Think of your larynx like your knee, made up of cartilages, ligaments, and muscles. Vocal health is dependent on appropriate warm-ups (to get things moving), drills for technique, and then cooldowns (at the end of your day). Consider vocal warm-ups a "gentle stretch." Depending on the needs of the singer, warm-ups should include physical stretching; postural alignment self-checks; breathing exercises to promote rib cage, abdominal, and back expansion; vocal stretches (glides up to stretch the vocal folds and glides down to contract the vocal folds); articulatory stretches (yawning, facial stretches); and mental warm-ups (to provide focus for the task at hand). Vocalises, in my opinion, are designed as exercises to go beyond warm-ups and prepare the body and voice for the technical and vocal challenges of the music they sing. They are varied and address the technical level and genre of the singer to maximize performance and vocal growth. Cooldowns are a part of most athletes' workouts. However, singers often do not use cooldowns (physical, mental, and vocal) at the end of a performance. A recent study looked specifically at the benefits of vocal cooldowns in singers and found that singers who used a vocal cooldown had decreased effort to produce voice the next day.

Systemic hydration as a means to keep the vocal folds adequately lubricated for the amount of impact and friction that they will undergo has been previously discussed in this chapter. Compliance with adequate oral hydration recommendations is important, and subsequently so is the minimization of agents that could potentially dry the membranes (e.g., caffeine, medications, dry air). The body produces approximately two quarts of mucus per day. If not adequately hydrated, the mucus tends to be thick and sticky. Poor hydration is similar to not putting enough oil in the car engine. Frankly, if the gears do not work as well, there is increased friction and heat, and the engine is not efficient.

Speak Well, Sing Well

Optimize the speaking voice utilizing ideal frequency range, breath, intensity, rate, and resonance. Singers generally are vocally enthusiastic individuals who talk a lot and often talk loudly. During typical conversation, the average fundamental speaking frequency (times per second the vocal folds are impacting) for a male varies from 100 to 150 Hz and 180 to 230 Hz for women. Because of the delicate structure of the vocal folds and the importance of the layered microstructure vibrating efficiently and effectively to produce voice, vocal behaviors or outside factors that compromise the integrity of the vibration patterns of the vocal folds may be considered phonotrauma.

Phonotraumatic behaviors can include yelling, screaming, loud talking, harsh sneezing, and harsh laughing. Elimination of phonotraumatic behaviors is essential for good vocal health. The louder one speaks, the farther apart the vocal folds move from midline, the harder they impact, and the longer they stay closed. A tangible example would be to take your hands, move them only six inches apart, and clap as hard and as loudly as you can for ten seconds. Now move your hands two feet apart and clap as hard, loudly, and quickly as possible for ten seconds. The farther apart your hands are, the more air you move and the louder the clap, and the skin on the hands becomes red and ultimately swollen (if you do it long enough and hard enough). This is what happens to the vocal folds with repeated impact at increased vocal intensities. The vocal folds are approximately 17 mm in length and vibrate at 220 times per second on A3, 440 on A4, 880 on A5, and more than 1,000 per second when singing a high C. That is a lot of impact for little muscles. Consider this fact when singing loudly or in a high tessitura for prolonged periods of time. It becomes easy to see why women are more prone than men to laryngeal impact injuries due to the frequency range of the voice alone.

In addition to the amount of cycles per second the vocal folds are impacting, singers need to be aware of their vocal intensity (volume). One should be aware of the volume of the speaking and singing voice and consider using a distance of three to five feet (about an arm's-length distance) as a gauge for how loud to be in general conversation. Using cell phones and speaking on a Bluetooth device in a car generally results in greater vocal intensity than normal, and singers are advised to minimize unnecessary use of these devices.

Singers should be encouraged to take "vocal naps" during their day. A vocal nap would be a short period of time (five minutes to an hour) of complete silence. Although the vocal folds are rarely completely still (because they move when you swallow and breathe), a vocal nap minimizes impact and vibration for a short window of time. A physical nap can also be refreshing for the singer mentally and physically.

Avoid Environmental Irritants: Alcohol, Smoking, Drugs

Arming singers with information on the actual effects of environmental irritants so that they can make informed choices on engaging in exposure to these potential toxins is essential. The glamour that continues to be associated with smoking, drinking, and drugs can be tempered with the deaths of popular stars such as Amy Winehouse (1983–2011) and Cory Monteith (1982–2013), who engaged in life-ending choices. There is extensive documentation about the long-term effects of toxic and carcinogenic substances, but here are a few key facts to consider when choosing whether to partake.

Alcohol, although it does not go over the vocal folds directly, does have a systemic drying effect. Due to the acidity in alcohol, it may increase the likelihood of reflux, resulting in hoarseness and other laryngeal pathologies. Consuming alcohol generally decreases one's inhibitions, and therefore you are more likely to sing and do things that you would not typically do under the influence of alcohol.

Beyond the carcinogens in nicotine and tobacco, the heat at which a cigarette burns is well above the boiling temperature of water (water boils at 212 degrees Fahrenheit; cigarettes burn at over 1,400 degrees Fahrenheit). No one would consider pouring a pot of boiling water on their hand, and yet the burning temperature for a cigarette results in significant heat over the oral mucosa and vocal folds. The heat alone can create a deterioration in the lining, resulting in polypoid degeneration. Obviously, cigarette smoking has been well documented as a cause for laryngeal cancer.

Marijuana and other street drugs are not only addictive but can cause permanent mucosal lining changes depending on the drug used and the method of delivery. If you or one of your singer colleagues is experiencing a drug or alcohol problem, research or provide information and support on getting appropriate counseling and help.

SMART PRACTICE STRATEGIES FOR SKILL DEVELOPMENT AND VOICE CONSERVATION

Daily practice and drills for skill acquisition are an important part of any singer's training. However, over-practicing or inefficient practicing may be detrimental to the voice. Consider practice sessions of athletes: they may practice four to eight hours per day broken into one- to two-hour training sessions with a period of rest and recovery in between sessions. Although we cannot parallel the sports model without adequate evidence in the vocal athlete, the premise of short, intense, focused practice sessions is logical for the singer. Similar to physical exercise, it is suggested that practice sessions do not have to be all "singing." Rather, structuring sessions so that one-third of the session is spent on warm-up; one-third on vocalises, text work, rhythms, character development, and so on; and one-third on repertoire will allow the singer to function in a more efficient vocal manner. Building the amount of time per practice session—increasing duration by five minutes per week, building to sixty to ninety minutes—may be effective (e.g., week 1: twenty minutes three times per day; week 2: twenty-five minutes three times per day, etc.).

Vary the "vocal workout" during your week. For example, if you do the same physical exercise in the same way day after day with the same intensity and pattern, you will likely experience repetitive strain–type injuries. However, cross-training or varying the type and level of exercise aids in injury prevention. So when planning your practice sessions for a given week (or rehearsal process for a given role), consider varying your vocal intensity, tessitura, and exercises to maximize your training sessions, building stamina, muscle memory, and skill acquisition. For example, one day you may spend more time on learning rhythms and translation, and the next day you spend thirty minutes performing coloratura exercises to prepare for a specific role. Take one day a week off from vocal training and give your voice a break. This does not mean complete vocal rest (although some singers find this beneficial) but rather a day without singing and limited talking.

Practice Your Mental Focus

Mental wellness and stress management are equally as important as vocal training for vocal athletes. Addressing any mental health issues is paramount to developing the vocal artist. This may include anything from daily mental exercises/meditation/focus to overcoming performance anxiety to more serious mental health issues/illness. Every person can benefit from improved focus and mental acuity.

ADDITIONAL VOCAL WELLNESS TIPS

When working with singers across all genres, the most common presentation in my voice clinic relates to vocal fatigue, acute vocal injury, and loss of high-frequency range. Vocal fatigue complaints are generally related to the duration of their rehearsals, recording sessions, "meet and greets," performances, vocal gymnastics, general lack of sleep, and the vocal requirements to traverse their entire range (and occasionally outside of physiological comfort range). Depending on the genre performed, singing includes a high vocal load with the associated risk of repetitive strain and increased collision force injuries. Acute vocal injuries within this population include phonotraumatic lesions (hemorrhages, vocal fold polyps, vocal fold nodules, reflux, and general vocal fold edema/erythema). Often these are not injuries related to problematic vocal technique but rather due to "vocal accidents" and/or overuse (due to required performance/contract demands). Virtually all singers are required to connect with the audience from a vocal and emotional standpoint. Physical performance demands may be extreme and at times highly cardiovascular and/or acrobatic. Both physical and vocal fitness should be foremost in the minds of any vocal performer, and these singers should be physically and vocally in shape to meet the necessary performance demands.

The advanced and professional singer must possess an flexible, agile, and dynamic instruments and have appropriate stamina. The singer must have a good command of their instrument as well as exceptional underlying intention to what they are singing as it is about relaying a message, characteristic sound, and connecting with the audience. Singers must reflect the mood and intent of the composer requiring dynamic control, vocal control/power, and an emotional connection to the text.

Commercial music singers use microphones and personal amplification to their maximal capacity. If used correctly, amplification can be used to maximize vocal health by allowing the singer to produce voice in an efficient manner, while the sound engineer is effectively able to mix, amplify, and add effects to the voice. Understanding both the utility and the limits of a given microphone and sound system is essential for the singer both for live and studio performances. Using an appropriate microphone can not only enhance the singer's performance but also reduce vocal load. Emotional extremes (intimacy and exultation) can be enhanced by appropriate microphone choice, placement, and acoustical mixing, thus saving the singer's voice.

Not everything a singer does is "vocally healthy," sometimes because the emotional expression may be so intense that it results in vocal collision forces that are extreme. Even if the singer does not have formal vocal training, the concept of "vocal cross-training"—which can mean singing in both high and low registers with varying intensities and resonance options—before and after practice sessions and services is likely a vital component to minimizing vocal injury.

FINAL THOUGHTS

Ultimately, the singer must learn to provide the most output with the least "cost" to the system. Taking care of the physical instrument through daily physical exercise, adequate nutrition and hydration, and focused attention on performance will provide a necessary basis for vocal health during performance. Small doses of high-intensity singing (or speaking) will limit impact stress on the vocal folds. Finally, attention to the mind, body, and voice will provide the singer with an awareness when something is wrong. This awareness and knowledge of when to rest or seek help will promote vocal well-being for the singer throughout his or her career.

NAVIGATING THROUGH AN EVER-EVOLVING MUSICAL LANDSCAPE

Rod Vester

The way music is created, produced, and consumed is primarily by digitalization. Whether through computer-based alternatives or through streaming services, we are in an ever-evolving digital age, and musicians who fail to respond and adapt will be left behind.

Digitization or digital transformation is the application of digital technology in all aspects of human society. Digitalization continues to impact and change society and the world. It transforms the way we work, thus altering our roles and offerings. For individuals and companies alike, digitization can bring new business opportunities and revenue, as it has the ability to turn existing services or products into digital variants of sorts. This adaptation can be complex, and some struggle to see the benefits of such a transformation. They question, How do I offer a product online? How do I "promote myself?" How do I grow an audience? How do I? How do I? Musicians and other creatives often get stuck in this cycle of questioning, which causes them to do nothing. This is problematic.

Digitization is disruptive innovation. In his formative book *The Innovator's Dilemma*, Clayton M. Christensen first proposed this theory of disruptive innovation. Focusing on "disruptive technology," he argued that even the most outstanding companies could lose their market leadership even if they do everything right by not focusing on creating new ways to innovate. Christensen's theory provides insight into looking at how innovation can influence development.[1] The ways in which individuals and organizations bring transformation through products or services define disruptive innovation.[2] Christensen and others agree that disruptive innovation occurs in a number of ways, and various versions have occurred since first introduced in 2017.[3,4] Some examples of this disruption include Uber (disrupting the taxi industry), Airbnb (disrupting the hotel industry), and the streaming of music (disrupting the music industry). As musicians and other creative entrepreneurs try to venture into their respective industries, what disruptive innovation will they bring with them?

Small businesses and creative entrepreneurs almost always enter into a market with fewer resources. When these types of businesses and individuals enter at the bottom but slowly rise to the top of the market, disruptive innovation has occurred. Additionally, when these small businesses enter a market and provide products or services that were ignored by those existing businesses, the small businesses eventually come to control the market. So why do existing businesses ignore market trends and new ways of doing things? Many existing businesses tend to focus on developing products for their current customers without thinking about innovating ways of servicing new markets and individuals. And even when new businesses enter this shared market space, those existing businesses often ignore them due to their traditional ways of thinking and doing. Because of this disregard, another progression and encroachment occur throughout this disruption; the small new business begins to attract customers of the existing business. Do you see the dilemma with this?

The music industry has been constantly within a wave of disruptive innovation. From radio being introduced in 1933 to vinyl, cassettes and compact discs, each wave of innovation disrupted the way music was produced, distributed, and consumed. In many ways, the consumers have moved away from owning music to paying for access. From iTunes to Spotify, disruptive innovation has continued to reshape the music industry, and how artists respond is critical. Understanding how disruptive innovation theory functions helps to inform the creative's present and future self.

THE CREATOR ECONOMY

Those creative individuals who engage in content creation continue to play an integral role as solopreneurs and entrepreneurs within the creative economy. This growing economy views ideas and intellectual property rather than physical materials as capital and economic value. There is a plethora of creative industries represented within the creative economy, including art, architecture, crafts, fashion, design, performing arts, film, and publishing. While music is considered the most intangible of them all, it continues to be a commanding motivator for many creatives who seek to explore a career in music and the arts. Popularized by John Howkins in his 2001 book *The Creative Economy*, the modern creative economy continues to expand and evolve. In 2019, Shapiro and Aneja claimed that an "estimated 14.8 million Americans earned income by posting their creations on Instagram, WordPress, YouTube, Tumblr, and five other platforms."[5] In 2021, the Creator Economy's economic value was estimated at $104 billion, based on revenue generation by creators and financial investment into start-ups within the Creator Economy.[6] An ecosystem involving a diverse group of individuals; writers, bloggers, podcasters, gamers, streamers, designers, illustrators, photographers, vloggers, filmmakers, artists, influencers, hobbyists, and others, the Creator Economy continues to be a central driver for online participation and economization.

In partnership with Edelman Data and Intelligence, Adobe's Future of Creativity Study gives a comprehensive view into how the creator economy is changing yet thriving throughout the United States and world. In the past three years, more than 165 million creators joined the global creator economy with more than 34 million new creators across the United States. Overall, according to this survey, there are more than 300 million creators across nine nations and a total of more than 85 million in the United States with 19 million in Japan and Germany, 18 million in South Korea, 17 million in the United Kingdom and Spain, 16 million in France, and 6 million in Australia. Thirty-nine percent of these creators seek to become business owners at some point in their careers.[7]

In a TED Talk, Adam Mosseri, CEO of Instagram, defined creator as "someone whose personality is their brand, and who uses platforms like Instagram to turn their passion into a living. . . . They generate ideas, push boundaries, and drive culture."[8] According to a 2020 survey by SignalFire, 50 million worldwide self-identified as creators with 2 million of them full-time who sell their content/products online.[9] More broadly speaking, creatives are individuals who create original content for a multitude of purposes and reasons. Whether professionals or nonprofessionals, 48 percent of creators are driven by freedom of expression with 26 percent being motivated by money. The largest generational population of creators represent millennials (42 percent) with Gen Zers coming in next (14 percent). While many lump creators and influencers into the same category and at times use these terms interchangeably, Alexander Breindel posits that there is a difference between both. Influencers are those who have leveraged social media to sell and/or promote the products of others (and sometimes their own) to become self-made celebrities.[10] Creators, on the other hand, produce, sell, and promote their own products. Creators may or not be famous. There is some overlap, but ultimately, creators create. Depending on whether creators monetize their content or not online, the data present a wide range of figures and estimations.

In the twenty-first century, creators value not only the art of creativity and talent but also individuality, transparency, and diversity. Ultimately, their mission is to either generate new or reimagine ideas that can be fostered, developed, and shared with others in hopes that these behaviors and actions will lead to paid opportunities or monetization within the digital space. Musicians and other creative entrepreneurs must learn to diversify their business and service models through creative career design. According to Ibrahimova, artists should work cooperatively and collaboratively with both governmental and nongovernmental organizations within the arts as a means of creating independence from recording contracts. Co-creation and co-innovation can help to expand opportunities and strategies.[11]

Practical Tips

1. Start with "why"
   Ask yourself, why do you want to create? Start your own business? Become an entrepreneur? The "why" explains your purpose, value, belief, and cause. It moves beyond what and how into the core and foundational premise of your creation. Identifying your why will help drive both short- and long-term goals and aspirations while keeping you true to what you have set out to accomplish.

2. Be a problem solver
   Problem solving and entrepreneurship are joined at the hip. Most entrepreneurs recognize a consumer-related problem and realize they can offer the solution. Not all solutions are disruptive and groundbreaking as those mentioned earlier, and that is okay. Problems and solutions come in all shapes and sizes. Most important is one's willingness to take a risk in entering that solution into the marketplace.

3. Find your target audience or persona
   Take time to find the specific group of people that you want to potentially sell your services or products to. If thinking about an audience feels overwhelming, think about one person (a persona). Odds are that if one person has a consumer-related problem, there are many more with the same problem. In thinking about your target audience/persona, consider location, age, education level, income, and so on. All these factors will assist in the development and marketing of your service or product. Finally, when all else fails with finding your target audience or persona, define who is *not* your target audience or persona.

4. Know your competitors
   There are two types of competitors: direct and indirect. Direct competitors are those with similar products and services, and indirect competitors are those with a different product or service as you but are solving the same problem for the same target audience/persona. Being aware of and analyzing your competitors will help you better understand their strengths, weaknesses, products, and services in comparison to your own, thus helping you fill in the necessary gaps in the industry.

5. Decide on a business structure
   There are various business structures: sole proprietorship, limited liability corporation (LLC), partnership, not for profit (501)(c)(3), and corporation. You will need to decide on a structure so that you can complete the necessary initial paperwork (for some) and the required income tax return forms each year. There are pros and cons to each business structure, so examine each closely.

6. Decide on a business model
   Deciding on a strategic way to earn profit is a crucial step in the creator economy. The business model describes how you will take your product and/or service to the market to drive sales successfully. There are many types of business models: subscription, e-commerce, bundling, retailer, manufacturer, fee-for-service, and rental or leasing, to name a few. Many businesses offer multiple models within their business; however, you must decide what you have the capacity to do in these beginning stages.

THE GLORIFICATION OF ENTREPRENEURSHIP

In today's world, entrepreneurship is glorified in an unrealistic manner in an attempt to lure people into quitting their nine-to-five to create their own business. Entrepreneurship is portrayed as an immediate fix to job dissatisfaction that presents limitless opportunities to achieve success fast. However, entrepreneurship is not for the faint of heart.

The term "entrepreneur" is elusive and contentious and can mean many different things to many different people. According to some scholars, entrepreneurship can be divided into three perspectives: people, process, and place.[12] The perspective of people focuses on character traits, personality, qualities, and skills of the entrepreneur. It is suggested that if the creative can develop and hone these basic traits, they are more likely to succeed.[13,14,15] Timmons and Spinelli maintain that "effective entrepreneurs are internally motivated, high-energy leaders with a unique tolerance for ambiguity, a keen eye towards mitigating risks, and a passion for discovery and innovation."[16] Paralleling more than fifty studies on the behaviors and attitudes of entrepreneurs, they found that these core traits and competencies can be "acquired, developed, practiced, and refined through a combination of experience and study."[17] Moving beyond a behavioral perspective, Hisrich examined entrepreneurs through a psychological lens, asserting that each entrepreneur has varied backgrounds and is not a monolith.[18] He stated that childhood, age, values, education level, work history, support systems, mentors, and motivation are all factors that should be considered when examining the desirability and potential of entrepreneurs. Hisrich believes that these physical traits are not always predictors of entrepreneurial behaviors as Timmons and Spinelli asserted. Bygrave and Zacharakis believe that such psychological and behavioral traits are based on "flimsy behavioral research into the differences between entrepreneurs and non-entrepreneurs."[19] They argue that behavioral attributes are not predictors of entrepreneurial success but that the entrepreneurs desire to control their own fate and their locus of control. Moroz and Hindle view the entrepreneurial process as "all the functions, activities and actions associated with the perception of opportunities and the creation of an organization to achieve them."[20] By examining the second perspective, process, we are better able to understand the profile of thriving entrepreneurs.

Scholars differ on the stages of the process, but the most recent research suggests that there are various stages that can be delineated and measured. According to Mamabolo and Myres, there is a five-stage progression that occurs: identifying the opportunity, assessing the opportunity, exploring the opportunity, creating a business, and establishing the business.[21] Taipale-Erävala et al. contend that there are seven phases: existence of opportunity, discovery of opportunity, decision to exploit opportunity, resource acquisition, entrepreneurial strategy, organizing process, and business performance.[22] Macães states that there are at least eight stages: having an idea, finding a business opportunity, finding the right people for the team, obtaining capital, creating a realistic business plan, implementing the business plan, controlling the execution, and the existence of management capacities.[23] While there are others, it is clear that there is some overlap in all of the presented entrepreneurial processes, which are self-explanatory. Whether in the phase of discovering ideas, applying ideas, implementing ideas, or entering into the growth phases of the business, Veciana hypothesized that certain leadership styles of entrepreneurs and characteristics of the entrepreneurial process emerge.[24] When discovering ideas, the leader's style is more transactional, as they are motivated through their own interests. During this phase, the entrepreneur welcomes all ideas (either theirs or others). When applying ideas, a transformational leadership style advances where taking risks and establishing clear objectives and goals are centralized. As one moves from applying ideas to implementing ideas, the entrepreneur allows space and time for their ideas to catch on. Finally, the growth phase is participatory and relational with those connected to the business (staff, collaborators, consumers, etc.). The entrepreneur begins to encourage and foster inclusive decision making and supports the needs of those internally and externally connected to the business. The third and final perspective is place, which highlights physicality with emphasis on external factors. For those entrepreneurs who operate outside of the digital landscape, location and proximity should be considered. Infrastructure, population, government policy, societal factors, and industrial conditions could all play an integral role in achievement and advancement. Hisrich states that being in a culture where creativity and innovation is desired and supported is an indicator of success. Additionally, place becomes important to attract and retain talent and to scale one's business.

As you can see, overall, entrepreneurship is complex, arduous, and challenging. If considering the entrepreneurial journey, approach the decision carefully, thoughtfully, and meticulously.

Formulating a Plan of Action

There are some common traits that highly effective entrepreneurs possess:

- Vision
- Passion
- Tenacity
- Drive
- Self-belief
- Resilience
- Comfort with ambiguity
- Flexibility

Some important necessary skills are as follows:

- Business management skills (leadership, strategic thinking, business acumen)
- Communication and listening skills (both written and verbal)
- Critical thinking skills
- Branding, networking, and marketing skills
- Time management and organizational skills
- Teamwork and collaborative skills

It's safe to suggest that not everyone has all the aforementioned traits and skill sets. That is okay. These traits and skills can be learned and refined. If you are uber passionate about an idea that can benefit and positively impact the lives of others, start with the traits, skills, and resources that you already possess. Seek guidance from others for areas that you are not as strong in. Remember that asking for help is a strength, and you will find that there are others eager to help you realize an idea, especially if that idea is for the greater good.

Identifying Opportunities

Entrepreneurs often talk about connecting the dots. By following and paying close attention to changes in demographics, markets, technology, policies, and other factors, they find patterns in events and trends that unearth potential opportunities that ultimately lead to new ideas and products. Opportunities are not always product driven, but they can produce new methods of doing things or the creation of an entirely new market. Once an opportunity has been identified, more exploration and research are completed to discern the need and success of such a venture. The decision to pursue an opportunity is complex, but if viable, entrepreneurs typically move through a sequence of stages: developing the opportunity, evaluating the opportunity, and assessing resources needed to design and launch the opportunity. To aid in thinking through these stages, let's discuss the creation of the entrepreneurial business plan.

THE ENTREPRENEURIAL BUSINESS PLAN

"If you fail to plan, you are planning to fail." —Benjamin Franklin

Creating a business plan helps not only to identify goals and actionable frameworks but also to solidify ideas, concepts, timeliness, and execution strategies. Individuals with business ideas often have countless ideas and thoughts floating around in their heads with little focus and direction. Extracting these ideas and placing them in written form assists in the streamlining of conceptualizations and hypotheses into possibilities. Forcing oneself to think and work through every scenario, challenge, and risk enables the entrepreneur to formulate a way forward that is informed.

Do you really need a business plan? Well, the research suggests that you do. Hechavarria et al. found that entrepreneurs who plan their venture are 152 percent more likely to launch their business and that 129 percent of those individuals are more likely to grow their business beyond the initial start-up phase.[25] Additionally, these researchers found that businesses with a plan experienced rapid sales growth in excess of 92 percent annually. Planning is only half the battle. One must execute the plan. Also, one must ask themselves some difficult questions: Do I have the skills and temperament to start a business? Am I a self-starter? Am I driven? Am I okay with taking calculated risks? Am I patient? Self-evaluation and honest reflection become an imperative part of the entrepreneurial business plan.

The entrepreneurial business plan outlines how you will achieve your business objectives while providing information about your service and/product, marketing strategies, financials, and other pertinent information. A well-written business plan also provides a way of tracking progress and scaling. However, the quality of the business plan is imperative. Let us discuss the key components of the business plan and their descriptions.

Business Description

The business description combines the key details of the business along with what it does and what makes it "unique." The information in the business description can be used for many reasons but more so for potential investors, lenders, and customers so that they can understand your concept, the benefits you provide to your customers, and your business's positioning in the market. Business descriptions can range from three to four paragraphs to a page, depending on the complexity of your business.

Mission Statement

The mission statement is what you intend to become or accomplish. It should be challenging yet achievable. This statement demonstrates that you understand your business, have defined a unique focus, and can articulate objectives concisely to your clients and others. A mission statement is not the same as a vision statement. A vision statement defines a long-term dream, and it should not be easily achievable. It becomes the business's reason for existing.

Market Analysis

A market analysis helps you understand your target audience and the conditions of the market, which will greatly help you make informed and calculated decisions. This section provides information about your customers, competitors, and industry at large. For customers, you might describe their demographics and what their needs are. For competitors, you might describe the competitor's strengths, weaknesses, and position in the marketplace as they relate to and inform how you will position yourself or business in the industry. For the industry at large, you might describe the current state of your industry and where it is headed.

Goal Setting

A goal is the aim or object of an action. It is what an individual or organization is trying to achieve. Latham found that individuals who are provided with difficult yet attainable goals that are specific outperform those who are given easy and nonspecific goals.[26] However, these individuals must also have satisfactory ability, agree with the goals, and receive feedback on performance. Goals should also be measurable and time bound.

SWOT Analysis

Strengths, Weaknesses, Opportunities, and Threats. The SWOT analysis lists not only your business's strengths, weaknesses, opportunities, and threats but also how they are going to be managed/handled. Strengths and weaknesses are internal, while opportunities and threats are external.

Financial Projections

This section shows the financial projection of expenses and revenues for the current period and business plan. These projections must be as realistic as possible, which will require some research and benchmarking. Financial projections are typically broken into either monthly, quarterly, or annual planning for effective monitoring of actual performance and timely correction of deviations.

Executive Summary

The executive summary should be the last thing drafted. After completing the other components of your business plan, you will have a clear understanding of the what, when, how, and why of your business. With that clear understanding, you can draft a good executive summary. This is a condensed but powerful synopsis of your entire business plan. It gives grantors, investors, banks, stakeholders, and others clear and concise information about what your business currently does and plans to do. While it is the last to be written, it is the first section of the business plan; therefore, it creates a first impression in the reader's mind of both you and your business.

The executive summary should do the following:

- Briefly describe the company, the product or service, and the unique opportunity your business is offering.
- Provide a brief description of key management team members (if appropriate).
- Demonstrate why the business concept will work (a clear plan for success).
- Demonstrate business objectives and a specific definable market.
- Provide a solid and believable summary of financial projections.
- Stand alone as a type of "mini" business plan within the business plan.
- Be written in a positive and confident tone.
- Be able to be read in less than five minutes.

Creating a Business Plan

1. Start with the business description
   The business description will define and summarize the what, why, and how of your business. This component serves to inform potential partners, employees, lenders, investors, and so on. The business description should give the reader a concise and crystal-clear understanding of your business and its functions.

2. Draft your mission statement
   The mission statement informs others of what the business does and how it achieves its goals. Take time to think through your mission statement, as it will drive all aspects of your business. Finally, keep the mission statement short and digestible for the average consumer (free of industry jargon where possible).

3. Conduct a market analysis
   After you gain clarity from the business description and mission statement, begin to identify and understand your intended audience, your direct and indirect competitors, and the conditions of the market in which you are wanting to enter. The market analysis provides data so that you can make informed decisions and put your plan into action.

4. Complete goal setting and the SWOT analysis

    Begin to set goals for your business that are calculated, challenging, and attainable based on the completed market analysis. Include short- and long-term goals that are measurable, and as you set goals, complete a SWOT analysis to help identify strengths, weaknesses, opportunities, and threats to design and implement a strategic plan for your business. This analysis is both internally and externally driven, identifying your business's strengths and weaknesses (internal) while exploring opportunities and being aware of industry threats (external).

5. Drafting the budget

    Now that you have a sense of your target audience and the intended market, you can begin to project revenue, expenses, and income. Create financial projections that are realistic and lean by determining your most critical financial needs. These projections will help guide short- and long-term planning for your business. As a best practice, always plan for a contingency (an additional 5 to 10 percent of the overall budget). A contingency helps to plan for a potential negative or unplanned event in the future (e.g., pandemic, economic recession, natural disaster, etc.). Finally, always consistently monitor your financial projections.

6. Draft the executive summary

    As the final piece of the business plan, draft the executive summary, which should serve as a highlight reel of sorts, encapsulating all the major parts of the business plan. As a general rule, an executive summary is usually no more than three pages. Depending on your business, it could be much shorter. Keeping this component concise by including the most pertinent parts of your business will help keep the reader engaged. The executive summary will appear first in your business plan, so you want to pique the reader's interest in the beginning so that they will be excited to continue reading the other components of your business plan.

DIGITAL CITIZENSHIP, SOCIAL MEDIA, AND YOUR ARTISTRY

There are various types of citizenship: family citizenship, citizenship by birth, citizenship by marriage, naturalization, and economic citizenship.

However, there's another type of citizenship that is not always discussed: digital citizenship.

With the technological advancements of the twenty-first century, those with whom you interact with technology have become digital citizens. Digital citizens are "those who use the Internet regularly and effectively."[27] Similar to any citizenship, there are guidelines, norms, and ways of being and behaving that exist. Ribble suggests that digital citizens must understand human, societal, and cultural issues that are related to technology.[28] These individuals should also practice safe, ethical, and legal behaviors while being responsible in their use of technology and encountered information. In addition, digital citizens should support learning and collaboration. The internet is not a platform where rules do not exist. There are guidelines for communication and behavior that serve as regulations to protect social relations and interactions online. These informal guidelines are coined "netiquette." The *Collins English Dictionary* defines netiquette as "the set of rules and customs that it is considered polite to follow when you are communicating through email or the internet." These sets of unwritten rules have been constructed over time by those responsible for the digital platforms as well as by users. Kayany believes that these guidelines are adapted from real-life etiquette rules.[29] The author of *Netiquette*, Virginia Shea urged people to "think before you post, be forgiving of other people's mistakes, respect other people's privacy, keep discussions civil and respectful even if you disagree with someone, pay attention to grammar and spelling rules, and how you appear to others."[30] Musicians and other creatives who recognize the importance of social behavior and relations within the digital space are better able to build and strengthen communities online.

"Social media has come to represent a working tool that serves the curation of a professional image and the management of social relationships for purposes of professional success and career progression."[31] In the United States, Australia, and other nations, roughly 95 percent of young people use social platforms such as Instagram, TikTok, YouTube, and WeChat on a daily basis.[32] Social media allows supporters to have direct communication with artists. This connection can have critical positive effects on the artist's reach and achievement. Because of this positive impact, artists should use social media to build relationships and encourage participation.[33] In today's music industry, creation is not controlled or beholden by record labels, executives, and others but is cultivated by the creator. Today, musicians and other creatives are better able to utilize digital platforms to meet customer demands with a greater deal of independence being achieved in music production and distribution. Entering into the music industry is now easier than before.

COVID-19 brought about major changes in all creative industries. In an effort to maintain sustainability and relevance, musicians and other creatives were forced to learn new skills while working to find alternative ways of connecting and communicating with their supporters. With live performances being canceled due to social distancing, adapting to live streaming and prerecorded materials became a new normal. These changes are here to stay and will continue to evolve.

Practical Tips for Communicating Online

1. Everything is permanent
   It is imperative to understand that everything you post online is permanent. It's permanent because someone can download or screenshot your videos and/or text even if you later delete a post. This awareness is crucial when you might want to rant about an individual, employer, bandmate, and so on. You want to protect your name (brand) as well as avoid any future problems that an outburst could pose (e.g., hiring). Take a moment to calm down and think about your actions if faced with something that is troubling you. Of course, you have complete autonomy to post what you want to post but do remember that freedom of speech does not mean freedom from accountability and consequence.

2. Avoid spamming your community of followers
   If someone were always trying to sell you something or asking for money every time you saw them, that would probably frustrate you, right? If so, avoid this along with constant self-promotion. There's a delicate balance. Of course, if you have a product or service, people should be made aware of it, but there are ways to promote your product and/or service without being intrusive.

3. Avoid fixation on the number of followers
   A large following never translates to 100 percent support or sales. Many find it difficult to separate their follower or subscriber count from their personal identity. Your self-worth should never be attached

to the number of followers or subscribers you have because this number will change all the time, either increasing, decreasing, or remaining stagnant. Of course, one should not give a blind eye to insights (i.e., ignoring massive unfollows or follows). Be aware of best practices and algorithmic changes but avoid checking the numbers too much and remember that you are worthy with zero, one hundred, or one thousand followers or subscribers.

BUILDING COMMUNITY ONLINE

How are we more connected now than ever before yet less happy and satisfied in life?[34] Most articles and books on building an audience discuss the importance of identifying and understanding your target audience, developing your brand identity, using niche hashtags, posting quality content frequently, collaborating with larger accounts, and following trends. While legit strategies, there's a deeper level of meaningful connection and intentionality that can be fostered with followers and others online by understanding the importance of interconnectedness and belonging, an essential part of human existence.[35]

In the twentieth century, psychologist Abraham Maslow arranged five human needs into a hierarchy, known as Maslow's hierarchy of needs: physiological, safety, love and belonging, esteem, and self-actualization.[36] He labeled esteem and self-actualization as basic needs and the lower three needs as deficient needs. While tiered, all of these needs are interdependent and needed to achieve one's full potential. Maslow pointed out that the essential need to belong, whether through romantic or interpersonal relationships, affiliations, or social groups, is a prerequisite for achieving a sense of self-worth. Baumeister and Leary contend that people have "a pervasive drive to form and maintain at least a minimum quantity of lasting, positive, and significant relationships."[37] People are interdependent and are in need of social connectedness, defined as "an enduring and ubiquitous experience of the self in relation to the world."[38] Baumeister and Leary argue that people have an innate need for social connections that is integral to human survival. When social connections and relationships go unfulfilled, individuals begin to experience unfavorable physical, psychological, and pathological aftereffects. Social media provides a space for social interaction, whether positive or negative. This social interaction fosters a sense of belonging for many people. Those who have a high need to belong find it vital to be accepted by others, even on social media.[39] This acceptance is reinforced with social media features that allow for interaction (e.g., commenting, liking, sharing, tagging, etc.). In their study, Büttner and Rudert found that Instagram users who were excluded reported how hurtful they felt afterward.[40] The connection between online and offline exclusion was intertwined with negative effects on the need for satisfaction. The adverse effects occur when people are unfriended, not tagged in posts, or otherwise excluded or ignored or not receiving the usual amount of likes on a post.[41] This repudiation has the same negative effects as if committed offline. With social media being a large part of many people's lives, being ignored and excluded online is just as hurtful as in real life.[42,43]

This research helps to inform musicians and other creative entrepreneurs seeking to build their business online. Create a space where people feel a sense of belonging.

Building Your Community

1. Choose a platform
   Each social media platform can serve a different purpose, as the demographics can change between some of them. Additionally, depending on the level of interaction you would like to have with members of your community, choosing the ideal platform will be important. For example, interactions are limited on LinkedIn versus Instagram, where others can send you direct messages, respond to posed questions and polls, and become subscribers to any offerings you might have. Age demographics should also be considered when choosing a platform: the largest age-groups are eighteen to twenty-four for TikTok, Snapchat, and Instagram; twenty-five to thirty-four for Facebook; thirty to thirty-nine for LinkedIn; eighteen to twenty-nine for X (formerly Twitter); and fifteen to thirty-five for YouTube.[44]

2. Build trust and credibility
   No one is perfect, so there's no need to present yourself as such. Build trust and credibility through transparency and storytelling.

Emotional connection often occurs when we share with others our mistakes and/or struggles along with how we have overcome or are overcoming them. From a business perspective, the sharing of these personal things should be relevant to the business and the problem you solve, and you can control what you are willing or ready to share. If you are offering a product, you can build trust and credibility by providing insights into how the product was made (e.g., eco-friendly, local materials, etc.). Finally, if selling a product, over-deliver and exceed expectations. Going above and beyond will help you stand out.

3. Engage with your community regularly
   Calls to action are a great way to build engagement through asking questions, requesting feedback and reviews, and more. When asking for feedback, be prepared to receive the positive and the negative. Negative feedback and criticism are never easy to see or hear, but it becomes necessary for growth. However, when receiving negative critique, always consider the source. Perhaps the critique from someone who has successfully done what you are trying to do bears more weight than the individual who hasn't. Finally, respond to those genuine messages and comments as much as possible.

4. Engage with other creators
   Oddly enough, social media is not always social and communal. However, as you build your community, you can lead by example. Engage with other creators you admire in a genuine way and avoid spam-like behavior, for example, "Go check out my page and follow me." People will find this distasteful, and it will work more against than for you.

5. Collaborate with others
   Similar to how one would collaborate with others in person, you can bring this same level of command into the digital space. If there are other creators whom you admire and whose work aligns well with yours, reach out to those individuals and collaborate. Let this interest and motive guide you, not the idea of reaching new audiences and increasing social media engagement, brand awareness, and sales. While these are wonderful, they should not drive your motive for collaborations, as this counteracts your building of trust and credibility.

FOSTERING MOTIVATION AND INTRINSIC DRIVE

Motivation and drive are not synonymous. Motivation comes and goes. It is ephemeral. Drive is a constant. It is incessant. Seeking to obtain an in-depth understanding of the determinants of motivation and drive in musicians, Johannes Lunde Hatfield studied four world-class musicians who continue to enjoy ongoing successful careers.[45] Every musician does not reach the highest level in their field, but those who do have invested thousands of hours in deliberate training and practice.[46] They also possess immense willpower and are able to cope effectively with adversity and encumbrances.[47] While the process and efforts made by world-class musicians might be viewed as extreme, their labor toward excellence cannot be denied.[48] These efforts are fueled by both internal and external factors.[49]

The participants in Hatfield's 2023 study spanned the ages of twenty-four to eighty-three, and three of the four musicians were regarded as international celebrity figures in classical music, and the other was regarded as a highly distinguished soloist and chamber musician. Through a semistructured interview style, all participants expressed being introduced to music during their childhood with no specific desire toward music prior to this introduction. One recalled being transfixed by the sound of an orchestra at the age of eight. Another shared that his parents were music connoisseurs who purchased him a violin at a young age. Some participants shared that their practice time and training were controlled and predetermined from the beginning, while others stated that they were initially able to explore music. Later, practice schedules became predetermined and enforced by parents. Similar to other studies, basic childhood psychological needs were lacking despite their early mastery of music.[50] Participants experienced a sense of loneliness in their early years of study. These promising early musicians demonstrated high performance achievements. Consistent with findings by Ericsson and Charness, the participants voiced that they followed all instructions by their teachers or other knowledgeable and experienced experts.[51] As participants moved through childhood, all recounted that they developed highly systematic practice schedules, practicing before and after school. Being systematic and deliberate helped to advance their musicianship, leading to mastery early on. Healthy and admirable relationships with their music instructors empowered their work ethic and drive. Now established and successful musicians, all participants continue to search for creativeness by exploring news of musical expressivity, including finding alternative solutions to technical problems.[52] This aligns with research by Black and Deci, who found that driven individuals seek to engage in creative processes continuously.[53] All continue to practice just as much as they did throughout their childhood. All participants aspired to be world-class musicians and believed they could achieve it. Intrinsic drive enabled them to push through adversities, and none were willing to quit and compromise or forgo all of the hard work they had invested in their craft. Practicing and training are at times completed because of pressure, external rewards, compliance, and approval from others.[54] Driven individuals continue to strive for greatness and never embrace mediocrity.

Efficient Practice Tips

Understanding that everyone is different, the following tips are general guidelines for efficiency. You are free to make modifications that will be most beneficial to you:

1. Plan beforehand and set specific goals
   There are many things one can work on in the practice session (e.g., technique, diction, fingering, speed, dexterity, etc.). While there are possibilities to scaffold these technical elements, targeted practice with specificity is often most beneficial to ensure effectiveness and efficiency. Having specific goals prevents you from trying to improve many things and instead makes one or two things great, not just better.

2. Warm up and start with the basics
   Warming up can help avoid injury for both the instrumentalist and the vocalist. Additionally, starting with the basics, whether scales, arpeggios, vocal exercises, and so on, aid in reinforcing the important foundational skills that matriculate to more advanced techniques and developments. Furthermore, technique typically comes from the repertoire you are learning.

3. Begin with the difficult sections of the music
   Normally, we are most focused and energized at the beginning of the practice session. Take advantage of this by isolating those difficult

sections of the music first. However, beware that simply working on the most difficult sections during your practice time might become discouraging at times. To combat this, play through the sections of the music that you know well or that are not as difficult.

4. Practice slowly and accurately
Practicing slowly can promote attention to detail. It can help ensure the accuracy of dynamics, color, rhythm, articulations, phrasing, pedaling, fingering, and other important musical skills. Additionally, slow practice can help you avoid mistakes that can lead to poor habits.

5. Prepare your goal(s) for the next practice session
Take some time at the end of your practice session to plan for the next. Perhaps there remains some sections that need continued attention. That's okay. However, if you find yourself consistently not completing all the goals set for the session, you might have too many goals. It's okay to scale back. The overall goal is improvement. Practice is a lifelong task—a marathon, not a sprint.

EXPANDING YOUR REPERTOIRE

The more musically diverse you are, the greater your creativity because you can bring in a multitude of soundscapes, varied scales, harmonic constructs, and interpretations into your practice regimen. While we tend to gravitate toward the music that we like, learn, and perform, we should always be open to exploring and learning other genres and styles. By doing this, we expose ourselves not just to different music but to different cultures as well. When learning music from around the world, I use a three-step process. listen to experience, listen to learn, and listen to understand.

Listen to Experience

When we listen to experience, we are not attempting to analyze the music, find the tonal center, listen for the form, and so on. We are listening simply to enjoy, embrace, and experience. It's also crucial to dismiss those musical ideals that are steeped in your specific tradition, geographic location, and so on. Not all music follows the same rules.

Listen to Learn

When we listen to learn, we begin to give notice and attention to the musical elements, form, and constructions of melody, harmony, and use of rhythmic motifs, among other fascinating factors.

During this step, we can begin to analyze the music appropriate to that location, culture, and so on.

Listen to Understand

When we listen to understand, we dive deeper into those musical elements identified in step 2. It is here that we not only understand the music but also consider cultural and societal influences brought by the composer and/or arranger. Music can never be separated from cultural and societal norms, influences, and effects.

WHAT HAPPENS NEXT?

Uncertainties, ambiguity, and fear can keep people from starting something they've never done before. For musicians specifically, it is often perfectionism that stifles the jump into the unknown with the fear of making a mistake or failing, creating mental barriers and emotional fatigue. Starting is difficult, and entrepreneurship can be messy. After all, you are taking a risk. However, all risks are not created equal. By working through the information and tips in this chapter, you will be well positioned to take a calculated risk and invest in yourself. Calculated risks are well-informed and provide you with a degree of probability based on the market data collected. While starting something new can be terrifying, it can also be wonderfully exciting. Start small. Start one step at a time. Believe in yourself and be willing to invest in yourself. You can do this, but you must start.

NOTES

1. C. O. Adekoya and A. A. Adedimeji, "Enhancing Library Performance by Exploiting the Potentials of Disruptive Innovations," *VINE Journal of Information and Knowledge Management Systems*, 2021, https://doi.org/10.1108/VJIKMS-03-2021-0032.

2. C. M. Christensen, M. E. Raynor, and R. McDonald, "What Is Disruptive Innovation?," *Harvard Business Review*, December 1, 2015, https://hbr.org/2015/12/what-is-disruptive-innovation.

3. Christensen et al., "What Is Disruptive Innovation?"

4. C. Larson, "Disruptive Innovation Theory: 4 Key Concepts," Business Insights Blog, 2016, https://online.hbs.edu/blog/post/4-keys-to-understanding-clayton-christensens-theory-of-disruptive-innovation.

5. R. Shapiro and S. Aneja, "Taking Root: The Growth of America's New Creative Economy," Recreate, 2019, https://www.recreatecoalition.org/wp-content/uploads/2019/02/ReCreate-2017-New-Creative-Economy-Study.pdf.

6. NeoReach and Influencer Marketing Hub, "Creator Earnings—Benchmark Report 2021," 2021.

7. Shapiro and Aneja, "Taking Root."

8. A. Mosseri, "A Creator-Led Internet, Built on Blockchain," TED Talk, 2022, https://www.ted.com/talks/adam_mosseri_a_creator_led_internet_built_on_blockchain.

9. Y. Yuanling and J. Constine, "What Is the Creator Economy? Influencer Tools and Trends," SignalFire, November 29, 2020, https://signalfire.com/blog/creator-economy.

10. A. Breindel, "The Difference between Content Creators and Influencers, Explained," 2018, http://resourcemagonline.com/2018/06/the-differences-between-content-creators-and-influencers-explained/90967.

11. S. G. Ibrahimova, "Features of Music Management in Azerbaijan," *Revista Inclusiones* 7 (2019): 220–34.

12. M. Minniti, A. Zacharakis, S. Spinelli, M. P. Rice, and T. G. Habbershon, eds., *Entrepreneurship: The Engine of Growth* (Westport, CT: Praeger, 2006).

13. J. A. Schumpeter, *The Theory of Economic Development* (Cambridge, MA: Harvard University Press, 1934).

14. D. McClelland, *The Achieving Society* (New York: D. Van Nostrand, 1961).

15. I. M. Kirzner, *Competition and Entrepreneurship* (Chicago: University of Chicago Press, 1973).

16. E. Timmons and S. Spinelli, "Entrepreneurship for the 21st Century," *New Venture Creation* 3 (2003): 249–56.

17. Timmons and Spinelli, "Entrepreneurship for the 21st Century."

18. R. Hisrich, "Entrepreneurship/Intrapreneurship," *American Psychologist* 45, no. 2 (1990): 209–22.

19. W. D. Bygrave and A. Zacharakis, *The Portable MBA in Entrepreneurship* (Hoboken, NJ: Wiley, 2004), 52.

20. P. W. Moroz, and K. Hindle, "Entrepreneurship as a Process: Toward Harmonizing Multiple Perspectives," *Entrepreneurship Theory and Practice* 36 (2012): 782.

21. A. Mamabolo and K. Myres, "A Systematic Literature Review of Skills Required in the Different Phases of the Entrepreneurial Process," *Small Enterprise Research* 27 (2020): 39–63; McClelland, *The Achieving Society*.

22. K. Taipale-Erävala, H. Lampela, and P. Heilmann, Survival Skills in SMEs—Continuous Competence Renewing and Opportunity Scanning. *Journal of East-West Business* 21 (2015): 1–21.

23. M. A. R. Macães, *Empreendedorismo, Inovação e Mudança Organizacional*, vol. 3 (Lisbon: Conjuntura Actual Editora, 2017).

24. J. M. Veciana, "Empresário y Proceso de Creación de Empresas," *Revista Económica de Catalunya*, no. 8 (1988).

25. D. M. Hechavarria, M. Renko, and C. H. Matthews, "The Nascent Entrepreneurship Hub: Goals, Entrepreneurial Self-Efficacy and Start-Up Outcomes," *Small Business Economics* 39, no. 3 (2011): 685–701, doi:10.1007/s11187-011-9355-2.

26. G. P. Latham, "Goal Setting: A Five-Step Approach to Behavior Change," *Organizational Dynamics* 32, no. 3 (2003): 309–18.

27. K. Mossberger, C. J. Tolbert, and R. S. McNeal, *Digital Citizenship: The Internet, Society, and Participation* (Cambridge, MA: MIT Press, 2011).

28. M. Ribble, "Passport to Digital Citizenship: Journey toward Appropriate Technology Use at School and at Home," 2008, http://www.iste.org/learn/publications/learning-leading/issues/december-january2008-2009/passport-to-digital-citizenship 05.04.2013.

29. J. M. Kayany, "Internet Etiquette (Netiquette)," *The Internet Encyclopedia*, 2004, https://doi.org/10.1002/047148296X.tie090.

30. V. Shea, *Netiquette* (San Francisco: Albion Books, 1994).

31. A. Gandini, "Digital Work: Self-Branding and Social Capital in the Freelance Knowledge Economy," *Marketing Theory* 16, no. 1 (2016): 123–41. https://doi.org/10.1177/1470593115607942.

32. H. Tankovska, "Percentage of U.S. Population Who Currently Use Any Social Media from 2008 to 2019," Statista, 2021, https://www.statista.com/statistics/273476/percentage-of-us-population-with-a-social-network-profile.

33. H. Choi and B. Burnes, "Bonding and Spreading: Co-Creative Relationships and Interaction with Consumers in South Korea's Indie Music Industry," *Management Decision* 55, no. 9 (2017): 1905–23.

34. J. M. Twenge and W. K. Campbell, "Media Use Is Linked to Lower Psychological Well-Being: Evidence from Three Datasets," *Psychiatric Quarterly* 90 (2019): 311–31, https://doi.org/10.1007/s11126-019-09630-7.

35. R. F. Baumeister and M. R. Leary, "The Need to Belong: Desire for Interpersonal Attachments as a Fundamental Human Motivation," *Psychological Bulletin* 117, no. 3 (1995): 497–529, https://doi.org/10.1037/0033-2909.117.3.497.

36. A. H. Maslow, *Toward a Psychology of Being*, 2nd ed. (New York: Van Nostrand Reinhold Company, 1968).

37. Baumeister and Leary, "The Need to Belong."

38. R. M. Lee and S. B. Robbins, "Understanding Social Connectedness in College Women and Men," *Journal of Counseling and Development* 78, no. 4 (2000): 484–91, https://doi.org/10.1002/j.1556-6676.2000.tb01932.x.

39. M. R. Leary, R. M. Kowalski, L. Smith, and S. Phillips, "Teasing, Rejection, and Violence: Case Studies of the School Shootings," *Aggressive Behavior* 29, no. 3 (2003): 202–14, https://doi.org/10.1002/ab.10061.

40. C. M. Büttner and S. C. Rudert, "Why Didn't You Tag Me?!: Social Exclusion from Instagram Posts Hurts, Especially Those \with a High Need to Belong," 2022, https://doi.org/10.1016/j.chb.2021.107062.

41. J. L. Bevan, J. Pfyl, and B. Barclay, "Negative Emotional and Cognitive Responses to Being Unfriended on Facebook: An Exploratory Study," *Computers in Human Behavior* 28, no. 4 (2012): 1458–64, https://doi.org/10.1016/j.chb.2012.03.008.

42. S. Reich, F. M. Schneider, and L. Heling, "Zero Likes—Symbolic Interactions and Need Satisfaction Online," *Computers in Human Behavior* 80 (2018): 97–102, https://doi.org/10.1016/j.chb.2017.10.043.

43. F. M. Schneider, B. Zwillich, M. J. Bindl, F. R. Hopp, S. Reich, and P. Vorderer, "Social Media Ostracism: The Effects of Being Excluded Online," *Computers in Human Behavior* 73 (2017): 385–93, https://doi.org/10.1016/j.chb.2017.03.052.

44. "Social Media Demographics to Inform Your Brand's Strategy in 2023," Sprout Social, 2023, https://sproutsocial.com/insights/new-social-media-demographics.

45. J. L. Hatfield, "Performing at the Top of One's Musical Game: The Mental Edge of Musicianship," *Frontiers in Psychology* 7 (2016): 1356.

46. K. A. Ericsson and N. Charness, "Expert Performance: Its Structure and Acquisition," *American Psychologist* 49, no. 8 (1994): 725–47.

47. Hatfield, "Performing at the Top of One's Musical Game.",

48. E. L. Deci an R. M. Ryan, "The 'What' and 'Why' of Goal Pursuits: Human Needs and the Self-Determination of Behavior," *Psychological Inquiry* 11, no. 4 (2000): 227–68.

49. P. N. Lemyre, H. K. Hall, and G. C. Roberts, "A Social Cognitive Approach to Burnout in Elite Athletes," *Scandinavian Journal of Medicine and Science in Sports* 18, no. 2 (2008): 221–34.

50. R. M. Ryan and E. L. Deci, "Intrinsic and Extrinsic Motivation from a Self-Determination Theory Perspective: Definitions, Theory, Practices, and Future Directions," *Contemporary Educational Psychology* 61 (2020): 101860.

51. Ericsson and Charness, "Expert Performance."

52. Hatfield, "Performing at the Top of One's Musical Game."

53. A. E. Black and E. L. Deci, "The Effects of Instructors' Autonomy Support and Students' Autonomous Motivation on Learning Organic Chemistry: A Self-Determination Theory Perspective," *Science Education* 84 (2000): 740–56.

54. A. Stenling, A. Ivarsson, P. Hassmén, and M. Lindwall, Longitudinal Associations between Athletes' Controlled Motivation, Ill-Being, and Perceptions of Controlling Coach Behaviors: A Bayesian Latent Growth Curve Approach," *Psychology of Sport and Exercise* 30 (2017): 205–14.

SELECT BIBLIOGRAPHY

Adekoya, C. O., and A. A. Adedimeji. "Enhancing Library Performance by Exploiting the Potentials of Disruptive Innovations." *VINE Journal of Information and Knowledge Management Systems*. 2021. https://doi.org/10.1108/VJIKMS-03-2021-0032.

Baumeister, R. F., and M. R. Leary. "The Need to Belong: Desire for Interpersonal Attachments as a Fundamental Human Motivation." *Psychological Bulletin*, 117, no. 3 (1995): 497–529. https://doi.org/10.1037/0033-2909.117.3.497.

Bevan, J. L., J. Pfyl, and B. Barclay. "Negative Emotional and Cognitive Responses to Being Unfriended on Facebook: An Exploratory Study." *Computers in Human Behavior*, 28, no. 4 (2012): 1458–64. https://doi.org/10.1016/j.chb.2012.03.008.

Black, A. E., and E. L. Deci. "The Effects of Instructors' Autonomy Support and Students' Autonomous Motivation on Learning Organic Chemistry: A Self-Determination Theory Perspective." *Science Education* 84 (2000): 740–56.

Breindel, A. "The Difference between Content Creators and Influencers, Explained." 2018. http://resourcemagonline.com/2018/06/the-differences-between-content-creators-and-influencers-explained/90967.

Büttner, C. M., and S. C. Rudert. "Why Didn't You Tag Me?!: Social Exclusion from Instagram Posts Hurts, Especially Those with a High Need to Belong." 2022. https://doi.org/10.1016/j.chb.2021.107062.

Bygrave, W., and C. Hofer. "Theorizing about Entrepreneurship." *Entrepreneurship Theory and Practice* 2, no. 16 (1991): 13–22.

Christensen, C. M. *The Innovator's Dilemma: When New Technologies Cause Great Firms to Fail*. Cambridge, MA: Harvard Business Review Press, 1997.

Christensen, C. M., M. E. Raynor, and R. McDonald. "What Is Disruptive Innovation?" *Harvard Business Review*. December 1, 2015. https://hbr.org/2015/12/what-is-disruptive-innovation.

Deci, E. L., and R. M. Ryan. "The 'What' and 'Why' of Goal Pursuits: Human Needs and the Self-Determination of Behavior." *Psychological Inquiry* 11, no. 4 (2000): 227–68.

Ericsson, K. A. "Training History, Deliberate Practice and Elite Sports Performance: An Analysis In Response to Tucker and Collins Review—What Makes Champions?" *British Journal of Sports Medicine* 47, no. 9 (2013): 533–35.

Ericsson, K. A., and N. Charness. "Expert Performance: Its Structure and Acquisition." *American Psychologist* 49, no. 8 (1994): 725–47.

Gandini, A. "Digital Work: Self-Branding and Social Capital in the Freelance Knowledge Economy." *Marketing Theory* 16, no. 1 (2016): 123–41. https://doi.org/10.1177/1470593115607942.

Hatfield, J. L. "Performing at the Top of One's Musical Game: The Mental Edge of Musicianship." *Frontiers in Psychology* 7 (2016): 1356.

Hechavarria, D. M., M. Renko, and C. H. Matthews. "The Nascent Entrepreneurship Hub: Goals, Entrepreneurial Self-Efficacy and Start-Up Outcomes." *Small Business Economics* 39, no. 3 (2011): 685–701. doi:10.1007/s11187-011-9355-2.

Henriette, E., F. Mondher, and I. Boughzala. "The Shape of Digital Transformation: A Systematic Literature Review." In *Ninth Mediterranean Conference on Information Systems (MCIS)*, Samos, Greece, 2015.

Hisrich, R. "Entrepreneurship/Intrapreneurship." *American Psychologist* 45, no. 2 (1990): 209–22.

Hisrich, R., and M. Peters. *Entrepreneurship: Starting, Developing and Managing a New Enterprise*. 4th ed. Chicago: Irwin, 1998.

Ibrahimova, S. G. "Features of Music Management in Azerbaijan." *Revista Inclusiones* 7 (2019): 220–34.

Kayany, J. M. "Internet Etiquette (Netiquette)." *The Internet Encyclopedia*. 2004. https://doi.org/10.1002/047148296X.tie090.

Kirzner, I. M. *Competition and Entrepreneurship*. Chicago: University of Chicago Press, 1973.

Larson, C. "Disruptive Innovation Theory: 4 Key Concepts." Business Insights Blog. 2016. https://online.hbs.edu/blog/post/4-keys-to-understanding-clayton-christensens-theory-of-disruptive-innovation.

Latham, G. P. "Goal Setting: A Five-Step Approach to Behavior Change." *Organizational Dynamics* 32, no. 3 (2003): 309–18.

Leary, M. R., R. M. Kowalski, L. Smith, and S. Phillips. "Teasing, Rejection, and Violence: Case Studies of the School Shootings." *Aggressive Behavior* 29, no. 3 (2003): 202–14. https://doi.org/10.1002/ab.10061.

Lee, R. M., and S. B. Robbins. "Understanding Social Connectedness in College Women and Men." *Journal of Counseling and Development* 78, no. 4 2000): 484–91. https://doi.org/10.1002/j.1556-6676.2000.tb01932.x.

Lemyre, P. N., H. K. Hall, and G. C. Roberts. "A Social Cognitive Approach to Burnout in Elite Athletes." *Scandinavian Journal of Medicine and Science in Sports* 18, no. 2 (2008): 221–34.

Lin, H. F. "Determinants of Successful Virtual Communities: Contributions from System Characteristics and Social Factors." *Information and Management* 45, no. 8 (2008): 522–27.

Macães, M. A. R. *Empreendedorismo, Inovação e Mudança Organizacional*. Vol. 3. Lisbon: Conjuntura Actual Editora, 2017.

Mamabolo, A., and K. Myres. "A Systematic Literature Review of Skills Required in the Different Phases of the Entrepreneurial Process." *Small Enterprise Research* 27 (2020): 39–63.

Maslow, A. H. *Toward a Psychology of Being*. 2nd ed. New York: Van Nostrand Reinhold Company, 1968.

McClelland, D. *The Achieving Society*. New York: D. Van Nostrand, 1961.

Minniti, M., A. Zacharakis, S. Spinelli, M. P. Rice, and T. G. Habbershon, eds. *Entrepreneurship: The Engine of Growth. Praeger Perspectives*. Westport, CT: Praeger, 2006.

Moroz, P. W., and K. Hindle. "Entrepreneurship as a Process: Toward Harmonizing Multiple Perspectives." *Entrepreneurship Theory and Practice* 36 (2012): 781–818.

Mossberger, K., C. J. Tolbert, and R. S. McNeal. *Digital Citizenship: The Internet, Society, and Participation*. Cambridge, MA: MIT Press, 2011.

Mosseri, A. "A Creator-Led Internet, Built on Blockchain." TED Talk. 2022. https://www.ted.com/talks/adam_mosseri_a_creator_led_internet_built_on_blockchain.

NeoReach and Influencer Marketing Hub. "Creator Earnings—Benchmark Report 2021." 2021. https://www.google.com/search?client=firefox-b-1-d&q=NeoReach+and+Influencer+Marketing+Hub%2C+%E2%80%9CCreator+Earnings%3A+Benchmark+Report+2021.%E2%80%9D.

Reich, S., F. M. Schneider, and L. Heling. "Zero Likes—Symbolic Interactions and Need Satisfaction Online. *Computers in Human Behavior* 80 (2018): 97–102. https://doi.org/10.1016/j.chb.2017.10.043.

Ribble, M. "Passport to Digital Citizenship: Journey toward Appropriate Technology Use at School and at Home." 2008. http://www.iste.org/learn/publications/learning-leading/issues/december-january2008-2009/passport-to-digital-citizenship 05.04.2013.

Ryan, R. M., and E. L. Deci. "Intrinsic and Extrinsic Motivation from a Self-Determination Theory Perspective: Definitions, Theory, Practices, and Future Directions." *Contemporary Educational Psychology* 61 (2020): 101860.

Schneider, F. M., B. Zwillich, M. J. Bindl, F. R. Hopp, S. Reich, and P. Vorderer. "Social Media Ostracism: The Effects of Being Excluded Online." *Computers in Human Behavior* 73 (2017): 385–93. https://doi.org/10.1016/j.chb.2017.03.052.

Schumpeter, J. A. *The Theory of Economic Development*. Cambridge, MA: Harvard University Press, 1934.

Shapiro, R., and S. Aneja. "Taking Root: The Growth of America's New Creative Economy." Recreate. 2019. https://www.recreatecoalition.org/wp-content/uploads/2019/02/ReCreate-2017-New-Creative-Economy-Study.pdf.

Shea, V. *Netiquette*. San Francisco: Albion Books, 1994.

Stenling, A., A. Ivarsson, P. Hassmén, and M. Lindwall. "Longitudinal Associations between Athletes' Controlled Motivation, Ill-Being, and Perceptions of Controlling Coach Behaviors: A Bayesian Latent Growth Curve Approach." *Psychology of Sport and Exercise* 30 (2017): 205–14.

Taipale-Erävala, K., H. Lampela, and P. Heilmann. "Surviving Skills in SMEs—Continuous Competence Renewing and Opportunity Scanning." *Journal of East-West Business* 21 (2015): 1–21.

Tankovska, H. "Percentage of U.S. Population Who Currently Use Any Social Media from 2008 to 2019." Statista. 2021. https://www.statista.com/statistics/273476/percentage-of-us-population-with-a-social-network-profile.

Twenge, J. M., and W. K. Campbell. "Media Use Is Linked to Lower Psychological Well-Being: Evidence from Three Datasets." *Psychiatric Quarterly* 90 (2019): 311–31. https://doi.org/10.1007/s11126-019-09630-7.

Veciana, J. M. "Empresário y Proceso de Creación de Empresas." *Revista Económica de Catalunya*, no. 8 (1988).

Yuanling, Y., and J. Constine. "What Is the Creator Economy? Influencer Tools and Trends." SignalFire. November 29, 2020. https://signalfire.com/blog/creator-economy.

13

IMPROVING YOUR SKILLS AFTER READING THIS BOOK

There are many ways to improve your skills as a musician, ranging from private lessons to online classes and, of course, learning by doing. This chapter will give you things to look for and consider when seeking out educational opportunities beyond this book.

PRIVATE LESSONS

While I'm thrilled that you are reading this book, I must be honest and say that reading this book alone may not be enough to make you a great rock singer. In addition to working on the exercises in this book, you might need to work one-on-one with a voice expert. When we sing without a microphone, we do not get to hear ourselves in the same way that others hear us. That is because we have two types of hearing. Sensorial-neural hearing comes from vibrations that are received through our ear canal. Conductive hearing comes from vibrations that are received through the bones in our head that surround the eardrum. When we sing, we hear ourselves with both types of hearing, but when our audience listens to us sing, they hear us only from the outside in (sensorial-neural). That means they hear something different than we do. The only way you can truly hear what others hear is by listening to a recording, which itself may not be a perfectly accurate representation (see chapter 10). However, the best time to make vocal corrections is when you are in the moment, not several minutes after the fact, which is why I personally think the best results occur when you work one-on-one with a voice teacher who has experience teaching rock singers.

Finding a Teacher

Finding a voice teacher who teaches rock singers and is capable of helping them achieve their goals can sometimes be difficult. There is no formal certification procedure for voice teachers. Other professionals, such as personal trainers, are required to take a certification test, which leads to a credential that lets clients know that the trainer is proficient in specific areas. For example, a trainer may be certified in personal training and yoga but not group fitness classes. This specificity helps clients identify the trainer best suited to their needs. However, voice teachers do not have a nationally recognized certification system. Since teacher credentials are not certified by a national organization, you must do your own homework to determine teachers' qualifications and whether they fit your needs.

The most common qualification for teaching voice is a music degree from a university music program. There are a wide variety of degrees you may encounter when researching voice teachers. You will find some with bachelor of arts degrees, which often indicates that the teacher studied all areas of music without a specific specialization. Others will hold a bachelor of science in music education, which is the standard degree for those who are or once were K–12 music teachers. Many teachers hold a bachelor of music in voice performance, which is the most common degree for classical singers. You will also encounter teachers with a bachelor of fine arts or bachelor of music in music theater, which are the most common degrees for music theater performers. There are also an increasing number of graduates from programs that offer degrees in commercial music or jazz.

Many teachers have advanced degrees, such as the master of music or a doctor of musical arts, in either voice performance or voice pedagogy. The master's degree indicates an additional two years of study after receiving an undergraduate degree. A doctorate degree indicates an additional three to four years after receiving a master's degree. Voice performance indicates a specialization in classical vocal music (opera, choral, art song, oratorio).

Voice pedagogy indicates a specialization in the science and theory behind teaching others to sing. There are also teachers who hold no degree at all and can be just as effective as those with a college degree. In fact, several of the finest teachers I have ever worked with fall into this category.

There is no perfect combination of credentials for a voice teacher, which is why it is essential that you do your homework. Technical needs can vary drastically from singer to singer. One singer may need a teacher who specializes in the basics of posture, breath, and basic vocal function. Another singer may be recovering from a vocal injury and will require a teacher called a "singing voice specialist" who is experienced in working with injured voices. Advanced performers may need detailed work on style and finesse and could benefit from working with a teacher with many years of performance experience. These professionals sometimes refer to themselves as vocal coaches. While some coaches are comfortable working on vocal technique, most prefer to focus on interpretation. What is most important is that you find someone who fits your specific needs.

In-Person and Virtual Lessons

Thanks to videoconferencing innovations spurred by the COVID-19 pandemic, you can now choose to work either with a teacher in-person or online. Videoconferencing options were available before COVID-19, but drastic improvements made during the pandemic have led to significant improvements in audio and video quality. Some platforms even enable teachers and coaches to accompany students with imperceivable delay. Teachers can get great results through both in-person and online instruction, so the best option will be the one that is aligned with your learning style. Some singers may need a lot of physical movement with yoga balls and foam rollers, in which case in person may be better. Others are constantly touring and will be better served by the flexibility of studying from varying locations.

If you are looking for an online teacher, social media platforms and YouTube can be great places to learn who is offering services that may align with your needs. There are, of course, quality control concerns when finding "experts" on the internet. Just because someone has a great social media presence does not mean that their techniques are grounded in science or are the right techniques for your needs. Hopefully, the information gained from reading this book will help you make sense of the techniques different teachers offer their clients and find the best fit for your needs.

In-person teachers can be found on the internet as well, but word-of-mouth referrals will often offer more in-depth information. Ask other musicians in your area if they have recommendations. If the same name keeps coming up in discussions, you may want to investigate that teacher on your own. Most in-person voice teachers will also have some sort of Web presence where you can find details about their background, the types of students they teach, and their teaching philosophy. However, do not judge their teaching abilities by the quality of their websites, as these teachers do not market themselves the same way as YouTube and social media personalities. In fact, some of the teachers who work with many of the celebrities you admire do not have websites at all, as word-of-mouth referrals provide more clients than they can handle.

After you've come up with a short list, contact the teachers you have been recommended and ask if you can have a trial lesson. You should expect to pay for this initial session; these are professionals, and their time is limited. Voice teacher rates vary widely depending on experience and location. In some areas, you may find respected teachers who charge $80 an hour, while in other locations, a teacher of that same caliber may charge $200 an hour. If you decide that you would like to work with a teacher on a regular basis, you will probably be asked to pay for a month or more in advance. It is very common for teachers to have cancellation policies that require you to give a twenty-four-hour notice before canceling a lesson to avoid having to pay for the missed session. Voice teachers deserve the same respect as physical therapists, counselors, or other professionals. If you miss a doctor's appointment without providing notice, you will be billed for it. Treating your teacher with the same respect will ensure that you get the most out of your lessons.

VOICE TEACHING METHODS

Many teachers associate themselves with a specific methodology or philosophy. Each of these methods and philosophies can be beneficial for some singers. However, there is no singular approach that will work for everyone; it is all about finding the right fit for you. A few of the most common methods you will come across include classical/bel canto, trademarked contemporary methods, and evidence- or science-based approaches.

Classical/Bel Canto Methods

There are many teachers who profess to teach from a classical or bel canto tradition. Unfortunately, there are no standard techniques for either, so it is difficult to compare apples to apples. What one teacher calls "bel canto" may be completely different from another teacher who also claims to teach a bel canto technique. Many classical teachers pass down traditions and techniques that were passed down to them through their teacher and that came from their teacher's teacher. Many of these techniques were developed for church musicians and classical singers in the seventeenth through early twentieth centuries. In the mid-twentieth century, dozens of modern pedagogues, voice researchers, and laryngologists changed our understanding of classical singing by publishing articles and books related to voice science. Their research revolutionized our understanding of the singing voice and led to new techniques for coordinating the voice. Today, you will find teachers from both backgrounds. Some are firmly rooted in tradition, and others have used science to enhance their understanding (more about that in the section on evidence-based teachers).

Classical teachers may be the right option for singers who enjoy learning to sing in a foreign language as they are working on their own style of singing. Others will find the diversion to classical music too confusing and will not find their fit with a classical teacher. When researching classical teachers, you will need to read their websites thoroughly and talk to current and former students to see if what they teach aligns with your needs. Ask current and former students how easy it was for them to translate the techniques to their rock music. Also ask if the teacher was supportive of singing rock and whether they were able to help with aggressive vocal production, vocal style, and vocal health. If you want to learn more about the wide spectrum of approaches that fall under the umbrella of classical voice pedagogy, read the books *National Schools of Singing* by Richard Miller, *A Spectrum of Voices* by Elizabeth Blades-Zeller, and *Great Singers on Great Singing* by Jerome Hines.[1]

Contemporary Voice Methods

There are many trademarked singing voice techniques that have been developed over the past few decades by some of the world's most respected voice pedagogues. These include methods like Estill, Complete Vocal Technique, and Lisa Popeil's Voiceworks. These techniques have their own unique terminology and specific goals that are aligned with the method. Scientific research substantiates many of the underlying principles of these techniques, with many of the creators having authored studies related to voice production.

There can be many benefits to training with a teacher of a trademarked technique. To earn their recognition, most teachers will have completed many hours in courses with other teachers from around the world. Class interactions give the teachers an extensive network and support system to turn to when they have questions about their students. The excitement of discussions in those groups often fuels the teachers to seek out additional continuing education opportunities. Their continued exposure to new techniques can end up benefiting their students and accelerating their progress.

Universities and independent organizations also offer instruction in methods provided by both individuals and groups of educators. These courses often come with various forms of recognition for teachers who complete them. Many educators choose to partake in multiple training programs, which affords them access to a diverse support network, ensuring that their students receive the most current and relevant insights. Similar training opportunities are also offered for classical teachers, but there are no trademarked methods in the classical teaching community.

Degrees in Voice Pedagogy

There are a growing number of teachers with master's and/or doctorate degrees in voice pedagogy. Voice pedagogy degrees explore the science behind singing and its practical application. Master's degree holders completed more than 450 hours of classroom instruction to earn their credentials. Those with doctorate degrees completed an additional 750 hours of classroom instruction and wrote a dissertation (usually the length of a book) to earn their credential. Most of these degrees are in classical voice, but a growing number incorporate commercial styles, and several universities now offer degrees in commercial voice pedagogy. Teachers who attended these programs also spend hundreds of hours outside of the classroom reading pedagogical texts, reading research studies, conducting research, and studying biomechanics, acoustics, and voice disorders. They are usually highly qualified instructors who have extensive knowledge about the learning process singers must go through to reach peak performance.

Vocology and Evidence-Based and Science-Informed Voice Pedagogy

Teachers in this category may hold graduate degrees in voice pedagogy, or they may have put together their own education through continuing education methods like those discussed earlier. They may focus only on classical music or contemporary styles, or they may teach all styles. Teachers who say they are science based are indicating they use our understanding of vocal function to inform their teaching. Others will use the term "evidence based" to indicate their method uses science but also personal experience and tradition.[2]

"Vocology" is a term used to describe the study of all things voice related, including the singing voice, the speaking voice, vocal health, and animal vocalization. Vocologists can earn board recognition from the Pan American Vocology Organization. Those who earn that recognition are recognized as PAVA Recognized Vocologists (PAVA-RV).

Teachers may use these labels interchangeably, as they are all very closely related. Like their colleagues listed before, these educators are actively engaged in continuing education and have extensive networks to help them stay on top of their game.

WHAT YOU SHOULD EXPECT: IN-PERSON LESSONS

Private voice lessons are usually held at a music store or school, in a private office, or in most instances at the teacher's home or apartment. Many of the country's finest voice teachers work with students in their homes or apartments in order to reduce costs for themselves and their students.

The teacher will usually tell you what to expect for your first lesson. My general advice is to arrive a few minutes early, have something available to take notes, have a recording device to record your session, and bring a bottle of water with you. First lessons usually begin either with the teacher asking you to sing for them or with them playing the piano to lead you through a series of vocal exercises. There is no reason to be nervous when singing for the teacher. Voice teachers are in business to help you reach your goals and make singing easier.

At some point, every student will work on vocal exercises like those in this book. As you've learned, exercises may seem awkward or sound strange, but they are necessary for developing your instrument. Give whatever exercises the teacher uses your best effort regardless of your initial reaction. You can evaluate whether a teacher's approach will work for you only by giving their methods 100 percent of your effort and attention. You may not notice immediate results. However, if you are intrigued by what you learn, you should try one or two months of lessons with that instructor and see what happens. If you are not seeing results in two to three months and you feel that you have been giving the teacher's advice your best efforts, then you should probably look around and see if you can find a teacher whose teaching style more closely aligns with your learning style.

WHAT YOU SHOULD EXPECT: ONLINE LESSONS

Online lessons can take place on a computer, smartphone, or tablet. While smartphones and tablets are convenient, you will usually get better results with a computer. Ideally, to get the most out of online lessons, you will want to have a pair of external speakers, a USB microphone or USB interface with a separate XLR microphone, and an Ethernet cable connection. The Ethernet cable will help reduce lag and improve the quality of your connection with the teacher. However, if those additions are cost prohibitive, know that you can still make great progress without the extra equipment. Just make sure you have the best WiFi connection possible.

Just like in-person lessons, you will either be asked to sing first or be taken through a series of vocal exercises. The main difference in the lesson experience will be how the exercises are delivered. In an in-person setting, the teacher will usually play the notes while you sing them. However, online, the teacher will often play a chord, and you will then sing a cappella. You have to do it this way due to the latency that is present in most apps. However, some teachers do use low-latency platforms that enable them to play along with you as you sing. When it comes to working on songs online, your teachers may be able to accompany you live with a low-latency system, but if they are not using a low-latency platform, you will need to accompany yourself, sing with a track, or sing a cappella. Online lessons are highly effective, and many singers find them just as valuable as in-person lessons.

INDIVIDUAL LEARNING STYLES

Whether you are online or in person, it is important to remember that not every teacher or training method will work the same way for every student. If a close friend tells you that their teacher is the best they have ever worked with yet that teacher does not connect with you, it is not necessarily because they are a bad teacher or you are a bad singer. It is possible that there are differences in teaching and learning styles between you that are getting in the way. For example, kinesthetic learners tend to respond best by focusing on physical sensations. Aural learners learn better by hearing things than by feeling them. Visual learners respond best by visualizing what they are attempting to do, for example, singing through your dolphin nose. Because of these differences, what works for one person may not work for you. Even though most teachers make an effort to convey information in a way that will make sense regardless of learning style, sometimes a student and a teacher just don't click.

TAKING CHARGE OF YOUR EDUCATION

In order to get the most out of any training, you must maintain open communication with your teacher. Many times, students will just agree with whatever they are told; they will not ask questions when something does not make sense, and they will not tell their teacher when they do not like what they are hearing. Conversely, there are students who will question everything, doubt every new idea that is presented to them, and spend the whole lesson talking instead of singing. Neither situation is ideal for either the teacher or the student.

Part of what makes teaching singing difficult for the teacher is that they can neither feel what you are feeling nor see what is happening in your throat. Yes, they can see the lips and jaw, but they cannot see the whole tongue, the movement of the soft palate, or the vibration of the vocal folds. Voice teachers listen and can usually identify which movements within the vocal mechanism produce which sounds, but a teacher's best insight often comes from the student's feedback. When I ask a student, "How was that?" or "What was that like?," their response can give me useful information. I may learn that a tone that sounds great is actually giving the student sensations of tension in their throat. From specific feedback, I can also help a student begin to differentiate between sensations that are simply awkward and uncomfortable (which is acceptable) and painful (which is not acceptable). When I know what my student is experiencing, I can proceed according to the student's individual needs. However, if the student says something vague like, "It was okay," I am left with very little information with which to help them.

How to Be a Great Student

To help your teacher give the best instruction possible, be sure to find time every day to practice and make notes of any questions or concerns you may have while practicing. Write down questions that you have about specific pitches in songs that are not working or vocal exercises that are troubling you. If the teacher asks you to try something in a lesson, give it 100 percent of your effort. If the teacher corrects you several times in a row, feel free to say, "I'm sorry, I don't think I understand what you are asking me to do." If the teacher tells you something that is especially helpful, tell them, "That explanation really helps." Your verbal feedback is essential to getting great results.

Keep in mind that what constitutes a "good sound" can be subjective. If you notice that all of a teacher's students have a certain tonal quality that you really do not like and you notice yourself taking on aspects of that tonal quality, then that teacher may not be the right match for you. Edith Victoria from Meet Me @ The Altar and Floor Jansen from Nightwish sing very differently. Both are successful, and neither's approach to singing is necessarily better or worse than the other. Preferred vocal tone is a matter of personal taste, and it is a teacher's responsibility to help you get where you want to go whether or not it is a sound they love. If the two of you have fundamental disagreements, it is completely acceptable to seek out a new instructor.

KNOWING WHEN IT IS TIME TO SWITCH TEACHERS

It is normal for the relationship between a teacher and a student to encounter difficulties. In our day-to-day lives, we all meet people whom we can connect with and others we cannot. The same is true for voice teachers. A professional teacher will understand this and should freely admit when a relationship is not working. If you encounter a teacher who will not acknowledge that their teaching style does not work for everyone, you should be cautious. If you are practicing and doing everything you are asked but it is not working, it is reasonable to expect that the teacher will try different approaches. If they are not willing to adapt their approach to fit your needs, it is probably time to move on and find a different teacher.

Abuse Is Not Okay

Unfortunately, it is not uncommon for singers to tell stories of abusive teachers they have encountered. The abuse is usually verbal or emotional, but it can also be physical or sexual. Regardless of the type, abuse is unacceptable. Here are a few examples of comments that could be considered abusive:

> "What's wrong with you? I told you what to do; why can't you get it?"
> "You are clearly not listening to me or using my technique."
> "Your voice sounds like nails on a chalkboard; it is really hard for me to sit here and listen to you sing."
> "Of course you cannot sing it like me; I am a professional; you barely know what you are doing."
> "Well your voice is just ugly, and there is no way you can sing that song."
> "You should wear tighter clothes so I can see your breathing."
> "Not everyone is meant to sing."

Believe me, there are teachers out there who make comments like these to their students. I studied with one teacher who was noticeably drunk during my lessons. Another frequently told me that I sounded terrible and would dismiss me early from my lessons but would offer no useful advice on how to make things better. Even when I knew I was not singing as poorly as I was being led to believe, it was still hard not to let those comments affect me. I left both of those teachers and never regretted it for a second. Every human being deserves respect; do not settle for anything less.

The Gray Areas

The relationship between singer and teacher is unique, and conversations about your body and emotions will likely be common. For many generations, teacher have placed their hands on singers' necks, shoulders, rib cages, stomachs, and/or backs to help draw the student's attention to those areas. Some teachers still use physical touch, while others do not. If your teacher wants to interact with you in this way, they should first ask for your permission. You do have the right to say no and expect them to honor your boundaries. If they do touch you, it should feel medical in nature, like a physical therapist helping you learn a new movement pattern or exercise. Unfortunately, there are some teachers out there who take advantage of their position and prey on younger victims. If you feel as though a teacher is trying to take advantage of you, walk out of the studio immediately and talk to someone you trust about the situation. It is also normal for singers to feel self-conscious about certain parts of their body. Teachers who specialize in trauma-informed teaching are aware that certain questions can be triggering and will work with the singer to navigate vocal technique while respecting any boundaries they may have.

Because of the interpretation component of singing, you may eventually discuss relationships and emotions in your lessons or coaching. Asking a student to talk specifically about the meaning of the text will often include connecting the text to their personal experiences. It is common for these types of discussions to include questions that explore connections to your family, life experiences, and relationships (platonic and romantic). If the conversation makes you uncomfortable, feel free to say, "I think I know what you are asking; let me try that again" or "I'm sorry, I just don't feel like talking about that right now." If you are not ready to have those conversations, you may not be ready to sing that song, and that is okay. Songs are conversations between the artist and the audience about the human experience. Getting comfortable with telling your story in a safe environment is the first step to being comfortable telling it to a room full of strangers.

If It Hurts, It Is Probably Wrong

When you are learning to sing, your teacher will likely try many new techniques that may feel or sound strange to you. An experienced instructor knows the difference between sensations that occur when strengthening the voice and sensations that indicate something may not be functioning correctly. You must communicate with your teacher to protect your vocal health. Sometimes, a great sound will not feel good for the first few weeks. As long as the sound is not making you hoarse, it is worth exploring. However, if you start losing your voice as you practice, tell your teacher. If the teacher does not know what to do to relieve the pain or voice loss, you may need to find someone else to work with. In general, if a new technique makes you feel a little tired or uncomfortable, it is probably okay. Those sensations are usually due to performing the exercises incorrectly while trying to figure out how to perform them correctly. The discomfort should go away as you perfect the exercise. If an exercise causes pain (beyond simple discomfort) and leads you to lose your voice, it is probably wrong.

You can keep yourself safe by remembering three cues that your voice is fatiguing: loss of volume, loss of range, and loss of vibrancy. If you have been practicing with 80 percent of your effort and getting a volume nine on a ten-point scale but forty-five minutes later it takes 100 percent effort to get the same volume, that is a sign your voice is getting fatigued. If you were able to sing a high C at the beginning of your practice session but thirty minutes later you can only sing a B, that is a sign your voice is getting tired. If the vibrancy of your voice begins to disappear, that is also a sign you are getting tired. When you encounter any of these signs, do some cooldown exercises, take a ten- to fifteen-minute break, then try again. If the signs of fatigue are still there, it is time to cool down and call it quits for the day.

ONLINE LEARNING

The internet has brought the entire world of knowledge into the home. It has completely revolutionized the way we learn, which has both positive and negative consequences. There are no regulatory agencies that control what can be published on the internet. There are many articles concerning the singing voice on blogs and websites that have no grounding in voice science or commonly accepted vocal techniques. In fact, some of these resources offer advice that could be harmful. For example, if you look up "how to sing death metal" online, you will find several videos of people sitting in their bedroom offering advice. Some of these "experts" demonstrate sounds that might sound quite good, but some of the techniques they advocate could easily lead to vocal damage. Others are spot on with their advice. When engaged in self-guided learning, it is very important to remember that if it hurts, it is probably wrong. Just as with many other goods and services, let the buyer beware. Take what you learn from online resources, compare it to what you know to be true, and decide what is worth keeping and what you should ignore.

YouTube

YouTube is an incredible resource for singers, with many great instructional videos available from some of the leading voice experts in the world. Live performance videos of your favorite artists can be highly educational as well. As mentioned previously, searching for "isolated" or "a cappella" vocal tracks will deliver hundreds of results that enable you to hear what artists sound like without the backing tracks. You can also use YouTube to learn how to play instruments, write songs, learn to use audio equipment, and record yourself at home. If you want to know about it, you can probably find a video on YouTube to help you learn.

Social Media

Social media has become an important resource for many singers. There are hundreds of teachers offering daily free tips to help you enhance your singing. Many will also respond to questions and offer advice for singers who are struggling with technical or artistic issues. Many of these teachers offer online courses, webinars, and other learning opportunities to dive further into their work. Many of the options are low cost and can really help enhance your education without breaking the bank.

Online Courses

Online courses are a great way to improve your skills from the comfort of your home. Online courses are offered by universities, for-profit academies like Udemy, and more recently by independent teachers who offer their courses through their own platforms. Courses come in three types: synchronous, which means you are taking the class with other learners in real time with the teacher; asynchronous, which means you are studying the material on your own time; and hybrid learning, which combines synchronous and asynchronous content. Asynchronous courses can be great, but you have to be a self-motivated learner, as there are no accountability systems in place for many of these courses. Some courses offer certificates for purchase after completion, which can be helpful if you also teach and want a way to share your credentials with others. For those interested only in performing, the certificates are usually not as valuable and are not worth the extra cost. When researching courses, you will usually find plenty of online reviews and testimonials. As you read them, think about your own learning style and evaluate the feedback from that lens.

MAJORING IN ROCK 'N' ROLL

I wish I could provide you a long list of well-known universities that offer degrees in rock music, but unfortunately, I cannot. There are only a few universities that offer degrees in commercial voice, although the list expands year by year. Because there are so many new programs coming into existence, the best resource for finding these programs is the Singing in Popular Musics blog at https://singinginpopularmusics.wordpress.com/commercial-voice-programs-us.

Commercial Voice Degrees

Degree programs in commercial voice are designed to offer a comprehensive, four-year education to prepare students for the music industry. This specialized course of study delves into various aspects of singing, performance, and music business, equipping students with the skills, knowledge, and versatility necessary for success in contemporary music genres.

One of the core components of a commercial voice degree program is an in-depth exploration of vocal techniques and artistry. Students receive training in developing their vocal range, control, and stamina. They work on mastering various vocal styles, cultivating a distinctive sound, developing their expressive abilities, and learning to adapt to different musical genres and performance contexts. Students will also learn the art of stagecraft, which goes beyond just singing. Performance training covers stage presence, body language, connecting with audiences, and conveying emotion while performing. Students in commercial voice programs often engage in ensemble work, group performances, and collaborative projects. This not only hones their ability to work with other musicians but also helps them establish valuable connections within the industry.

Most college degree programs also give students a strong foundation in music theory and ear training. This usually includes learning to read music, understanding chord progressions, and developing your ear for harmony, melody, and rhythm. This knowledge enhances students' musicality, enabling them to collaborate effectively with other musicians and adapt to various musical arrangements. Since the music industry encompasses recording and production, students often receive training in recording studio techniques. They learn how to work with producers, engineers, and studio equipment and gain an understanding of the technical aspects of recording vocals and creating high-quality recordings.

Beyond vocal, musical, and production skills, a commercial voice degree program also typically includes coursework in music business and marketing. Students learn about contracts, copyright, music distribution, promotion, and the broader industry landscape. This knowledge equips them to navigate the intricacies of the music business and promote their own careers effectively.

Music Industry Degrees

A degree in music industry offers a comprehensive education designed to equip students with the knowledge and skills required to navigate the multifaceted and ever-evolving landscape of the music business. These programs delve into various aspects of music production, distribution, marketing, management, and entrepreneurship, preparing students for a range of roles within the industry.

A fundamental component of a music industry degree is a comprehensive understanding of the basic principles of the music business. Students learn about copyright law, music licensing, contracts, intellectual property, and legal considerations that pertain to the creation, distribution, and consumption of music. A strong grasp of music production techniques and technology is also essential in today's digital music landscape. Therefore, students learn about recording, mixing, and mastering processes as well as the use of digital audio workstations and other production tools.

Effective marketing and promotion are crucial for success in the music industry. Most music industry degree programs include courses where students study various marketing strategies, including social media campaigns, branding, public relations, and digital distribution platforms. They also explore ways to reach and engage target audiences in an increasingly competitive market. Understanding artist management and development is also vital for those interested in working with musicians and performers. In these courses, students learn how to nurture artists' careers, manage bookings, negotiate contracts, and handle the day-to-day operations that contribute to an artist's success. In addition, there are usually courses that explore the economics of the music industry and emerging trends. Students learn to analyze revenue streams, streaming platforms, touring economics, and the impact of technology on music consumption.

Many music industry degree programs emphasize entrepreneurship, empowering students to create their own opportunities within the industry. This includes learning how to start and run music-related businesses, whether as independent artists, record label owners, event organizers, or music tech innovators. Since the realm of live music events is a critical part of the industry, students also gain insights into event planning, production logistics, stage management, sound engineering, and concert promotion. Many music industry degree programs offer opportunities for students to build connections within the industry. Internships, guest speakers, and collaborations with industry professionals provide students with real-world exposure and valuable networking opportunities.

Alternative Paths

If you find yourself drawn to the idea of obtaining a college degree but are uncertain about committing to a music-focused path, there are several alternative avenues to explore. Pursuing a degrees in a field such as business, marketing, or communications at a university with a vibrant live music scene can be a viable option. These degree programs equip you with skills in strategic thinking, effective communication, project management, and understanding market dynamics. These are all skills that can be valuable when promoting yourself, connecting with audiences, and managing your artistic endeavors. You can then create your own music education opportunities in the community and/or by taking advantage of online opportunities. By gigging around town, you will hone your craft while actively engaging with your target audience, building a dedicated fan base, and refining your stage presence. Shared experiences with fellow musicians will foster camaraderie, collaborative opportunities, and provide a network that can prove invaluable throughout your career. You may even be able to take music-related courses as electives or by minoring in music.

CONCLUSION

There are many different ways to improve your skills as a musician. Private lessons, online classes, college degree programs, and experiential learning are all viable options. If music is your hobby, online courses and in-person or online courses will give you more than enough new ideas to keep you busy for years to come. For those interested in pursuing a career as a professional musician, the college degree options listed above along with online courses and music industry conferences will help jump-start your career. Regardless of which path you choose, don't forget to maintain a growth mindset. Along the way, you will encounter information that may not immediately appeal to you. Do not immediately reject it; instead, take time to evaluate, see things from different viewpoints, and expand your perspectives. As Benjamin Franklin once said, "An investment in knowledge pays the best interest."

NOTES

1. Richard Miller, *National Schools of Singing: English, French, German, and Italian Techniques of Singing Revisited*, 2nd ed. (Lanham, MD: Scarecrow Press, 1997); Elizabeth Blades-Zeller, *A Spectrum of Voices: Prominent American Voice Teachers Discuss the Teaching of Singing* (Lanham, MD: Scarecrow Press, 2002); Jerome Hines, *Great Singers on Great Singing: A Famous Opera Star Interviews 40 Famous Opera Singers on the Technique of Singing* (Lanham, MD: Limelight, 2004).

2. Kari Ragan, "Defining Evidence-Based Voice Pedagogy: A New Framework," *Journal of Singing* 75, no. 2 (2018): 157.

14

FINAL THOUGHTS

We have covered a lot of information in this book, and it is likely you will need to reread some of the sections multiple times to fully grasp the content. No book is perfect, and I have no doubt questions will remain after reading this one. However, my hope is that I have inspired you to learn more about your voice and to structure your training in a way that optimizes your practice time. If you want to learn more about the topics in this book, be sure to review the sources in the chapter endnotes and in the bibliography in chapter 12. Also, be sure to check out the online resources if you have not done so already.

What is most important is that you do not lose sight of why you started singing in the first place. It is easy to get so caught up in the technique that you forget the "why." For some singers, the why is simple: "I love to sing." Others will have a more complex why: "I sing to make people think deeply about social issues that affect my community." No matter why you sing, do not forget that you are sharing the human experience with others. Even if you are thrashing onstage in a heavy metal band, there is an experience you want to create or share. It may not reach the deep complexities of tackling the world's social issues, but it is no less important to the audience member who needs the cathartic release that a mosh pit provides.

I want to thank you for including this book as part of your journey. I have thoroughly enjoyed the connections I have made since the first edition was released, and I look forward to connecting with new singers and teachers in the coming years. Thank you for reading!

—Matt

Appendix A

VOCAL EXERCISE PATTERNS

These basic exercise patterns can be used for all of the exercises in this book.

Figure A.1. 1-2-3-2-1 pattern. *Courtesy of Matt Edwards*

Figure A.2. 1-2-3-4-5-4-3-2-1 pattern. *Courtesy of Matt Edwards*

Figure A.3. 5-4-3-2-1 pattern. *Courtesy of Matt Edwards*

Figure A.4. 1-3-5-3-1 pattern. *Courtesy of Matt Edwards*

Figure A.5. 1-3-5-8-5-3-1 pattern. *Courtesy of Matt Edwards*

Figure A.6. Octave scale. *Courtesy of Matt Edwards*

Figure A.7. 9-tone pattern. *Courtesy of Matt Edwards*

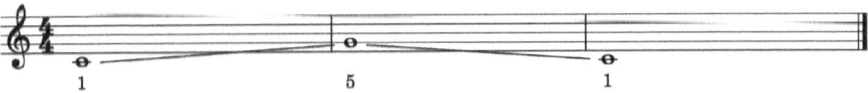

Figure A.8. 1-5-1 glide. *Courtesy of Matt Edwards*

Figure A.9. 1-8-1 glide. *Courtesy of Matt Edwards*

Appendix B

PHONETIC SYMBOLS

These symbols are used to notate vowels and consonants throughout the text. Examples are provided for each symbol.

Symbol	Examples
/æ/	mama, nana
/ɑ/	father, ponder
/i/	see, me
/I/	it, sit
/ɛ/	Fred, Ed
/o/	so, go
/ɔ/	sought, ought
/u/	sue, shoe
/ʊ/	put, foot
/ng/	sung, flung
/m/	hum, murmur

GLOSSARY

Abductors. Muscles responsible for opening the vocal folds for inhalation and reducing vocal fold closure during phonation.
Adductors. Muscles responsible for bringing the vocal folds together during phonation.
Alexander technique. A method for improving posture and movement, often used by singers to enhance body awareness, coordination, and efficiency in vocal production.
Alternate practice. Alternating between two different vocal exercises back-to-back when vocalizing.
Attenuate. To reduce or lessen the intensity of sound.
Automatic stage. A phase in skill acquisition where a singer can perform a task without conscious effort.
Automaticity. Another term for the automatic stage of skill acquisition.
Back room. The resonant space behind the hump of the tongue.
Beat. The pulse that creates the rhythmic foundation that underlies a piece of music.
Belt. A vocal quality similar to calling out across a long distance that is associated with the upper range of a singer's voice. The belt voice is produced by firm closure at the vocal fold level combined with vocal tract resonance that amplifies the upper frequencies of the voice.

Body mapping. Developed by William Conable, body mapping is rooted in the principles of kinesthetic awareness and experiential learning to enhance the individual's bodily self-awareness and coordination.
Break. A sudden shift or transition between vocal registers.
Breath control. The ability to regulate and manage airflow and/or pressure during singing.
Breath pressure. The force exerted by the airflow from the lungs.
Breath support. The coordination of the muscles of respiration used to regulate the amount of air pressure directed toward the larynx from the respiratory system.
Breathy. A vocal quality characterized by the audibility of breath in the sound.
Bright. A vocal quality with strong amplitude of the higher frequencies of the sound spectrum.
Buzzy. A vocal quality that is rich in harmonics. Its qualities are similar to a vibrating acoustic guitar string or the tone of a brass instrument.
Chest mix. A register of the singing voice that combines elements of chest and head but leans toward the chest side of the spectrum.
Chest register. A register of the singing voice that is characterized by firm vocal fold closure and contraction of the thyroarytenoid muscle. This mode of production produces a buzzy quality that has similarities to a brass instrument.
Chest voice. Another name for chest register.
Cognitive stage. The initial phase of skill acquisition where the learner consciously processes the task.
Compensatory. Actions or adjustments made to overcome vocal challenges or deficiencies in coordination.
Constriction. Unwanted tension or tightness in the throat that hinders optimal vocal production.
Cover song. A performance or recording of a song previously recorded by another artist.
Cricothyroid. A muscle involved in pitch adjustment by lengthening and tensing the vocal folds. It originates from the cricoid cartilage, inserts into the thyroid cartilage, and pulls the front of the thyroid cartilage down toward the front of the cricoid cartilage.
Downbeat. The first beat of a musical measure.
Elastic recoil. The ability of lung tissue to return to its original shape after inhalation, aiding in efficient exhalation during singing.

Entanglements. A term used to describe compensatory behaviors of the extrinsic muscles of the larynx and/or muscles within and/or around the vocal tract.

Forced expiratory volume. The amount of air forcefully exhaled from the lungs in a specific time frame, usually one to three seconds.

Front room. The resonant space in front of the hump of the tongue.

Glides. Smooth transitions between pitches, often used for vocal warm-ups and technical exercises.

Glottis. The opening between the vocal folds.

Harmonics. Overtones or additional frequencies produced along with the fundamental frequency that contribute to the richness of the vocal tone.

Head mix. A register of the singing voice that combines elements of chest and head but leans toward the head side of the spectrum.

Head register. A register of the singing voice that is characterized by light vocal fold closure and relaxation of the thyroarytenoid muscle. This mode of production produces a quality that is similar to a flute.

Head voice. Another term for head register.

Inflection. Variations in pitch, tone, or the rhythm of lyrics that are used to convey emotion or emphasis in singing.

Intensity. The strength or power of the vibrations produced by the vocal folds. Resonance can further amplify the vibrations, leading to additional increases in intensity.

Interarytenoid. Muscles that connect the arytenoids to each other and are responsible for adducting the vocal folds, contributing to vocal fold closure during phonation.

Kinesthesia. The awareness of one's own body movements and position.

Lateral cricoarytenoid. Muscles involved in adducting the vocal folds that originate from the sides of the cricoid cartilage and insert into the arytenoids. When engaged, these muscles assist in adducting the vocal folds.

Mix. A vocal production that combines elements of chest and head register, allowing for a seamless transition between chest and head.

Motor learning stage. A phase of skill acquisition when a singer is progressing from cognitive understanding to automatic execution.

Ossification. The process in which cartilages harden into bone.

Pelvic floor. A group of muscles that form a supportive hammock-like structure in the pelvis.

Phonate. The act of sending air between the vocal folds, setting them into vibration to produce sound.

Phonatory system. A term used to describe the components of the larynx that are involved in phonation.

Posterior cricoarytenoid. Muscles responsible for abducting the vocal folds, allowing the singer to inhale. They originate at the cricoid cartilage and insert into the arytenoids. These muscles also assist in reducing vocal fold closure during phonation.

Power chords. A chord structure commonly used in rock music, consisting of the root note and the fifth. The lack of a third adds ambiguity to the chord.

Random practice. Randomly alternating between exercises to help the body remember the differences between tasks.

Signal chain. The sequence of audio devices (such as microphones, effects, and amplifiers) used in the transmission of the vocal signal during a performance.

Signature sound. The unique vocal quality and/or style that sets a singer apart from other singers.

Skill acquisition. The process of learning and mastering a motor skill, including the cognitive, motor learning, and automatic phases of learning.

Staccato. A style of singing characterized by short and detached notes, often used for stylistic emphasis and precision.

Stacked vocals. Layering multiple vocal tracks or harmonies to create a fuller sound.

Stepwise motion. Progressing through a set of notes within a scale in sequential order.

Straw phonation. A vocal exercise involving singing or humming through a straw.

Subglottic pressure. The air pressure below the vocal folds.

Thyroarytenoid. One of the intrinsic muscles of the larynx. It originates at the thyroid cartilage and inserts into the arytenoids. When it contracts, it shortens and thickens the vocal folds, affecting pitch and register.

Timbre. The unique tonal quality or color of a voice or instrument, determined by the combination of harmonics and resonance.

Total lung capacity. The maximum volume of air the lungs can hold, influencing breath support and endurance in singing.

Tracheal pull. A downward movement of the trachea during inhalation that lowers the larynx while slightly abducting the vocal folds

Transglottal airflow. The flow of air through the glottis (the space between the vocal folds), essential for sound production during singing.

Triplets. A rhythmic pattern involving three evenly spaced notes, commonly used in various musical genres to create a distinct rhythmic feel.
Vital capacity. The maximum amount of air that can be expelled from the lungs after a maximum inhalation.
Warmth. A quality of vocal tone that is created when the vocal tract amplifies the lower and middle frequencies of the spectrum.
Whole step. An interval in music representing two half steps.

INDEX

Active cabinet, 257
Adductors, 133
Agility, 170, 171, 185, 208
Aging, 194
Airflow, 17
A-O joint, 119
Alcohol, 197, 275
Alternative Rock, 97
Alto, 11
Alveoli, 14, 124, 203
American Southern Blues Rock, 83
Amplitude, 240
Antagonistic, 17, 121, 181
Arena Rock, 87
Arms, 119
Art Rock, 79
Articulators, 27–29
Arytenoids, 21, 235
Attention, 37
Automatic stage, 6, 164
Automaticity, 6, 36, 54
Autonomic nervous system, 270
Auto-tune, 256

Back room, 143, 162
Baritone, 11

Bass, 11
Beach Boys, The, 72
Bel Canto, 199, 311
Belting, 89, 140–41, 205, 206
Berry, Chuck, 69
Black American Music, 61, 63
Blocked practice, 5, 50, 163–64
Blues-Based British Rock, 81
Body mapping, 115
Boyle's Law, 14
Break, 138, 175
Breath, 15, 123, 128, 166–68, 174, 181, 202
Breath control, 17, 122
Breath Pressure, 17, 123, 126
Breath support, 17, 122
Breathy, 134, 227
British Blues Rock, 78
Business plan, 287–91

Catastrophizing, 7
Chest, 129, 168;
    belt, 81, 89, 140–41
    coordinating, 170–74
    dominant mix belt, 79
    mix, 87, 138, 160, 161, 162, 176, 185
    mode, 22

muscles, 19
register, 87, 96, 98, 114, 132–37, 141, 160, 162, 169–75, 183, 185, 189, 191–92, 204, 225
voice, *See* register
Classical:
  singers 3
  singing, 33
  training, 199, 311
Cognitive distortions, 6–9
Cognitive stage, 5, 136, 164, 170–71, 193
Community, 294
Compression, 252
Constant practice, 49
Constriction, 187
Cooper, Alice, 86
Coordinating:
  breath, 121–23
  vocal tract, 141
  tongue, 155
  registers, 169
Creator economy, 280
Cricoid Cartilage, 21
Cricothyroid, 22

Declarative Learning, 32
Degrees:
  commercial voice, 321
  music industry, 322
  voice pedagogy, 312
Delay, 254
Deliberate Practice, 33
Deep Purple, 82
Degrees, 312
Diaphragm:
  muscle, 15, 35, 124
  breaths, 203
  microphone, 242
Digital citizenship, 291
Digital voice processors, 256
Digitization, 279
Distributed practice, 49
Dryness, 263

Elastic recoil, 16, 124, 195, 203
Entrepreneurship, 284

Epiglottis, 21
Equalization, 250;
  shelf, 250
  parametric, 250
  graphic, 252
Exhalation, 17, 121, 126
Exercise, 269
External Intercostal muscles, 16–18, 125
External feedback, 5

Falsetto, 11, 22
Fanny, 84
Fatigue, 49, 180, 277
Feet, 116
Finding a teacher, 308
Fixed mindset, 9
Flat:
  pitch, 184, 193
  response, 245
Forced Resonance, 24
Formant, 25
Free Resonance, 24
Frequency, 240
Front room, 143, 162
Functionally dysfunctional, 236

Garage Rock, 73
Gargle, 266
GERD, 267
Glam Rock, 85
Glottis, 19, 22, 123
Go-Go's, The, 92
Goth Rock, 85
Growth mindset, 9, 163

Harmonics, 23. 26, 131, 142, 240
Head, 119–20, 165–66, 180, 187–88, 201;
  elevating, 268
  mix, 79, 203, 205
  register, 4–7, 11, 85, 101, 114, 134–139, 141,160, 161, 162, 168, 169–72, 174–76, 183, 189, 191, 193–94, 204
  voice, *See* register
Hearing, 307
Heart, 88
Heartland Rock, 95

INDEX

Heavy Metal, 93
Higher order skills, 33
Honey, 266
Hydration, 197, 263
Hyoid bone, 21

Inhalation, 121–24, 128, 167–69, 182,
Injury prevention, 271
In-person lessons, 309
Intensity, 24, 130
Internal Intercostal muscles, 17
Intrinsic feedback, 6

Jackson, Wanda, 67
Jaw, 150, 165, 230
Jefferson Airplane, 77

Kingsmen, The, 74
Knees, 117

Laryngeal movement, 144–46, 206
Laryngopharyngeal reflux (LPR), 267
Larynx, 19–24
Learning, 34
Linear system, 114
Lips, 27, 144, 153, 156
Live sound system, 257
Longevity, 272
Long-term memory, 44
Lumbar spine, 118

Magnifying, 7
Marijuana, 197, 276
Massed practice, 49
Masseter muscle, 150, 228, 230
Medications, 266
Melody, 219
Menopause, 195
Mental Wellness, 269
Messa di voce, 173
Metallica, 93
Microphone:
    condenser, 243
    dynamic, 243
    extension of the voice, 113
    frequency response, 244

polar pattern, 246
proximity effect, 248
sensitivity, 246
technique, 258–59
vocal distortions, 234
Mind reading, 8
Mix:
    belt, 140
    register, 135–39, 172, 184, 189, 205, 225
Mixer, 257
Moody Blues, The, 80
Motivation, 297
Motor learning, 5, 31, 32, 45–46, 57, 136, 164
Multitasking, 41
Musical performance anxiety, 270

Napster, 1
Negative focus, 8
New Wave, 92
Non–linear system, 114
Nutrition, 262

Online:
    Courses, 320
    learning, 319
Onsets:
    description, 225
    fry, 226
    glottal, 227
    breathy, 227
    flips, 227
Operative words, 232
Overtones, 23, 241

Passive Cabinet, 257
Pelvis, 118
Pharynx, 24, 146–48, 266
Phrasing, 220
Phrase weighting, 231
Physiological max, 174
Phonotraumatic behaviors, 274
Plosives, 259
Polarized thinking, 8
Practicing, 49, 113, 195, 276, 297, 298, 316
Pressed, 114, 134
Procedural learning, 32

Progressive Rock, 79
Proprioception, 35
Psychedelic Rock, 76
Posture, 115, 167, 180, 200, 201
Punk Rock, 89
Pure vowels, 211

Random practice, 5, 50
Reflux, 267
Register(s), 131, 135, 159, 183, 189, 204, 224
Registration. *See* Register(s)
Releases, 225
R.E.M., 97
Resisting the collapse, 124–25
Resonance, 24–27, 207, 241
Respiratory System, 14–19, 114, 121–29, 167–69, 181–83, 202–03
Reverb, 254
Rhythm, 210, 218
Richard, Little, 65
Rolling Stones, The, 78

SA, 11
Sex Pistols, 90
Six points of balance, 115
Skill acquisition, 3–6, 51, 276
Self-taught, 4
Sharp, 194
Signal chain, 242
Smoking, 275
Social media, 291
Soft palate, 148–50, 175, 186
Somatype, 128–29
Soprano, 10
Spatial awareness, 130
Spatial orientation, 35
Speaking voice, 224, 274–75
Speech-like singing, 129–30
Springsteen, Bruce, 95

Stabilizing, 170–71
Stamina, 171–72, 181, 183–85, 195
Straw phonation, 196
Strength: abdominal, 125; harmonics, 132; registers, 171
Stretching, 121, 181, 273
Surf Rock, 72

TBB, 11
Tea, 266
Teaching methods, 310
Tenors, 11
Temporomandibular joint disorder (TMJD), 150
Thorton, Big Mama, 63
Thyroarytenoid, 22, 135, 175
Thyroid Cartilage, 21
Timbre, 22–23, 25, 120, 131, 144–46, 162, 186–87, 241
Tongue, 27–28, 143, 154–56, 208
Trachea, 21
Tracheal pull, 129, 203
Turner, Tina, 99
Tweeter, 257

Valens, Ritchie, 68
Varied practice, 49–51
Vibrato, 210, 229–30, 256
Virtual lessons, 209
Vocal distortion, 233
Vocal folds, 19–24, 114, 123, 131–35, 183, 189, 197, 225–28, 263, 274
Vocal injury, 173, 180, 261, 271
Vocal Tract, 24–27, 141–56, 176, 185, 207–09, 241

Warming up, 165–67, 298
Woofer, 257

YouTube, 319

ABOUT THE AUTHORS

Matt Edwards is an associate professor of voice and the artistic director of the CCM Vocal Pedagogy Institute at Shenandoah Conservatory, a Van L. Lawrence Fellowship recipient, and National Association of Teachers of Singing (NATS) internship master teacher. Former and current students can be found gigging around the world in a wide range of vocal styles. Some have been seen on *American Idol*, and others have performed on-Broadway, off-Broadway, on national and international tours, and in regional theaters. He has written numerous articles for the *Journal of Singing*, the *Journal of Voice*, *VoicePrints*, *American Music Teacher*, *The Voice*, *Southern Theatre*, and *Voice Council* magazine. He has contributed chapters to *A Dictionary for the Modern Singer*, *Vocal Athlete*, *Manual of Singing Voice Rehabilitation*, *Get the Callback*, *The Voice Teacher's Cookbook*, and the CCM, Musical Theatre, Folk Music, Blues, Sacred Music, Gospel, A Cappella, and Country editions of the So You Want to Sing book series. He has given presentations, master classes, and workshops for groups including the NATS National Conference, Voice Foundation Annual Symposium, Israeli Voice Association, Acoustical Society of America, Southeastern Theatre Conference, Musical Theatre Educators Alliance, Pan-American Vocology Association, Poland Mix Singers Association, U.S. Air Force Singing Sergeants, U.S. Navy Sea Chanters, and Summer Vocology Institute as well as at numerous universities, including Penn State,

Florida State, the University of Toronto, Memorial University of Newfoundland, Brigham Young, Wright State, Otterbein, Illinois Wesleyan, Missouri State, the University of Northern Colorado, and Bårdar Academy (Oslo, Norway), and at NATS chapters in Toronto, New York, Minnesota, Texas, Virginia, Georgia, North Carolina, Wisconsin, Pennsylvania, Missouri, Arizona, and elsewhere. More can be found online at EdwardsVoice.com and CCMInstitute.com.

* * *

Lynn Helding is professor of practice in voice and voice pedagogy at the University of Southern California Thornton School of Music and creator of its vocology curriculum. She is an associate editor of the *Journal of Singing* and founding author of its "Mindful Voice" column. Her forthcoming book *The Musician's Mind: Teaching, Learning, and Performance in the Age of Brain Science* illuminates current research in the cognitive, neurological, and social sciences. Her honors include the 2005 Van L. Lawrence Fellowship, awarded jointly by the Voice Foundation and the National Association of Teachers of Singing (NATS), and election by her peers to head the founding of the first nonprofit voice science association, the Pan-American Vocology Association (PAVA). She currently serves on the PAVA advisory board and the NATS voice science advisory committee. Her stage credits include leading roles with the Harrisburg Opera, Nashville Opera, Tennessee Opera Theatre, and Ohio Light Opera as well as numerous solo recitals throughout the United States, Italy, France, England, Germany, Spain, Australia, and Iceland.

Wendy LeBorgne is a voice pathologist, speaker, author, and master class clinician. She actively presents nationally and internationally on the professional voice and is the clinical director of two successful private practice voice centers: the ProVoice Center in Cincinnati and BBIVAR in Dayton. She holds an adjunct professorship at the University of Cincinnati College–Conservatory of Music as a voice consultant, where she also teaches voice pedagogy and wellness courses. She completed a BFA in musical theater from Shenandoah Conservatory and her graduate and doctoral degrees from the University of Cincinnati. Her original peer-reviewed research has been published in multiple journals, and she is a contributing author to several voice textbooks. Most recently, she coauthored *The Vocal*

Athlete textbook and workbook with Marci Rosenberg. Her patients and private students currently can be found on radio, on television, in film, on cruise ships, on-Broadway, off-Broadway, on national tours, on commercial music tours, and on opera stages around the world.

Scott McCoy is a noted author, singer, conductor, and pianist with extensive performance experience in concert and opera. He is professor of voice and pedagogy, director of the Swank Voice Laboratory, and director of the interdisciplinary program in singing health at Ohio State University. His voice science and pedagogy textbook *Your Voice: An Inside View* is used extensively by colleges and universities throughout the United States and abroad. He is the associate editor of the *Journal of Singing* for voice pedagogy and is a past president of the National Association of Teachers of Singing (NATS). He also served NATS as vice president for workshops, program chair for the 2006 and 2008 national conferences, chair of the voice science advisory committee, and a master teacher for the intern program. Deeply committed to teacher education, he is a founding faculty member in the New York Singing Teachers' Association Professional Development Program, teaching classes in voice anatomy, physiology, acoustics, and voice analysis. He is a member of the distinguished American Academy of Teachers of Singing.

Rod Vester is an educator, researcher, entrepreneur, pianist, organist, composer, and producer who excels in gospel, jazz, classical, and contemporary music. He has performed with numerous artists across genres, including Grammy Award winners CeCe Winans, Kirk Franklin, and the late Aretha Franklin. He is director and assistant professor of contemporary music at Shenandoah Conservatory. He is also the creator and director of the Contemporary Musicianship and Entrepreneur Development undergraduate program and the CONTEMPO Ensemble, a contemporary student music ensemble composed of vocalists and instrumentalists from all musical backgrounds at Shenandoah Conservatory. He holds a bachelor's degree in psychology, a master's degree in counseling, a master's degree in musicology, and a PhD in music education.

Jacqlyn Zito-Edwards is an auxiliary adjunct assistant professor of voice at Shenandoah Conservatory. Her degrees are from the Cleveland Institute of Music/Case Western Reserve University and Louisiana State

University. She has performed with Wayside Theatre, KNOW Theatre, Tri-Cities Opera, Bay View Music Festival, Hudson Symphony, Case Western Symphony, Findlay Light Opera, Atlantic Coast Opera Festival, and many others. Current and former students gig regularly in a wide variety of venues; some have appeared on *American Idol*, on- and off-Broadway, on television and in film, in regional theaters, and on national tours and cruise ships. She has presented at the Virginia Theatre Association, published "The Emerging Future of Collegiate Voice Instruction: Updated SWOT Analysis of Current Practice and Implications for the Next Generation" with Dr. David Meyer and Matt Edwards in the *Journal of Singing*, and appeared on the *A Voice Beyond* podcast to talk about the historical bias against popular music education.

www.ingramcontent.com/pod-product-compliance
Lightning Source LLC
Chambersburg PA
CBHW021846300426
44115CB00005B/33